GOD HAS PRESERVED HIS TEXT!

The Divine Preservation of the New Testament

Fourth Edition

Wilbur N. Pickering, ThM PhD

ISBN: 978-0-9974686-9-4

Foreword

Wilbur N. Pickering is a Christian missionary living in Brasília, Brazil. He has a ThM and a PhD in Linguistics. Of those actively involved in NT textual criticism, no one holds a more radical view in defense of the inerrancy and objective authority of the Sacred Text. This includes the position that the precise original wording has been preserved to our day and that we can know what it is. This book offers a scientific defense of that conviction.

Dr. Pickering joined Wycliffe Bible Translators in 1958. After three years of preparation for the field, he arrived in Brazil in 1961, where he and his wife began the translation work with the Apurinã people. In 1996 he resigned from Wycliffe to pursue other interests.

For some time Dr. Pickering has felt that among the many hundreds of Greek manuscripts of the NT known to exist today, surely God would have preserved the original wording. After years of searching and comparing such manuscripts, he has concluded that God used a certain line of transmission to preserve that wording. That line is by far the largest and most cohesive of all manuscript groups, or families. It is distinguished from all other groups by the high level of care with which it was copied (Dr. Pickering holds copies of perfect manuscripts, of that family's archetype, for 22 of the 27 books). It is both ancient and independent, and is the only one that has a demonstrable archetypal form in all 27 books. That archetypal form has been empirically, objectively identified by a wide comparison of family representatives, and it is indeed error free. As he expected, that error-free text is not seriously different from some of the other "good" Greek texts. Nevertheless he has done an English translation based on it: *The Sovereign Creator Has Spoken: Objective Authority for Living*, Second Edition; available from his site: www.prunch.org, and from Amazon.com.

Acknowledgment

I wish to acknowledge my debt to Dr. William Penning (PhD in Astronomy) for formatting this book. He is a computer specialist working to support Bible translation, mainly in Brazil.

I also wish to thank Daniel Jore for contributing the cover picture.

Contents

PART I: The Historical Evidence

Preamble

In any discussion involving the interpretation of evidence, three things need to be clearly distinguished: evidence, interpretation and presupposition. True evidence, objective reality, should be the same for everyone. However, the interpretation that different people give to that evidence can vary considerably. The different interpretations derive from differing sets of presuppositions. Since it is impossible to work without presuppositions, no one should be criticized for having them. That said, however, since presupposition controls, or at least heavily influences, interpretation, any honest participant in a discussion of evidence should understand his own presuppositions and state them openly and plainly. A failure to state one's presuppositions is dishonest and reprehensible. For someone who does not state his presuppositions to criticize someone else who does, is simply perverse; it is a despicable proceeding. Any and all discussions involving the interpretation of evidence should begin with a declaration of presuppositions. At this point a question presents itself: can presuppositions be evaluated, and if so, how? I offer the following opening attempt.

The fundamental question that governs human existence on our planet is the question of authority: who has it, if he has it, and under what conditions. The competition between worldviews (ideologies, religions, philosophies-of-life), in the marketplace of the world, goes back to that question. I am aware that few people concern themselves with ultimate cause, being content to live out their lives as their culture dictates—perhaps 'content' is not the best word here; they do not have time and opportunity to dream up alternatives. But what happens when an agent of change shows up? The agent of change is promoting an alternative worldview; he is challenging the culture. Even if the question of authority is not overtly stated, it lurks in the background. I submit for due consideration that the most basic factor is the existence (or not) of a Sovereign Creator. If such a Creator exists, then He will have absolute authority over what He created. Where more than one candidate is presented, the correct choice should depend upon the evidences. In today's world, it is common to deny the existence of any Creator, the existence of the universe that surrounds us being attributed to evolutionary processes.

All genuine science is based on the principle of cause and effect—we observe an effect and try to isolate the cause; and it is logically impossible for a cause to produce an effect larger or more complex than itself. Any human being who is both honest and intelligent, when confronted with the observable universe with its incredible organization and complexity, is obliged to conclude that there must be a CAUSE, a Cause with intelligence and power beyond our understanding—to refuse to do so is to be perverse. Since we have personality, He must also.

The only alternative to a Cause would be chance working with nothing. But it is stupidly, ridiculously impossible that chance, working with nothing, could produce anything. 10 x 0 = 0, 1,000 x 0 = 0, 1,000,000 x 0 = 0, and so on; no matter how many times you multiply zero, the result is always zero. If you multiply zero by something every day during five billion (or trillion) years, the result will always be zero. That chance plus nothing produced the universe is stupidly, ridiculously impossible. Even if one starts with the superstition of a 'big bang' of inorganic (without life) material, where did life come from. [I bypass the question of where all that inorganic material came from.]

The science of physics tells us that the inorganic [no life] known universe can be described with up to 350 information 'bits'; but it takes 1,500 information 'bits' to describe the smallest protein—it is so small that it cannot live by itself, but it is part of a living system. So how could evolution produce life? Where could chance find 1,150 'bits' of new information, if in the whole universe there were only 350? Not only that, the 'e-coli' bacteria takes about seven million 'bits', and one human cell takes around twenty billion 'bits'! The theory of evolution, to explain the origin of life, is stupidly, ridiculously impossible!!

The science of genetics, with its genome projects, has discovered that a random change of only three nucleotides is fatal to the organism. Consider the chimpanzee, presumably man's 'nearest relative': the genetic difference is said to be about 1.6%. That may not sound like much, but it is around 48 million nucleotide differences, and a random change of only three nucleotides is fatal to the animal—it follows that it is simply impossible for a chimp to evolve until it becomes a man (some 15 million chimps would perish in the attempt, never getting beyond the first three nucleotides!). Each different type of animal had to be created separately, just as Genesis affirms. Any evolutionary hypothesis, to explain the different types of animals (not to mention birds, insects, fish, plants, etc.) is scientifically impossible, stupidly, ridiculously impossible.

The so-called 'geologic column' is a fiction. In Australia there are fossilized tree trunks, upright, passing through various layers of sedimentary rock, that according to the 'geologic column' represent many millions of years-- stupidly, ridiculously impossible! In the U.S. there is a high plateau (mesa) with a layer of older rock on top of a layer of newer rock (according to the 'column'), but the area involved is so extensive that no known force would be able to overcome the friction caused by an attempt to have one layer slide over the other layer (the argument that is used)—this also is impossible for the 'geologic column'.

Some 60 miles southwest of Dallas, Texas, there is a town called Glen Rose, that is close to the Paluxy River. The Dinosaur Valley State Park is located there, because the river bed has tracks of two types of dinosaur: three-toed and four-toed. Upriver from the park a paleontologist named Dr. Carl Baugh bought a significant amount of land on both sides of the river, so he could do his own excavations. On his property he has a museum that I myself have visited. In the **same layer** of sedimentary rock he encountered the following: two trilobite fossils, that evolutionists say existed 550 million years ago; a fossilized moss called 'lapidodendron', that evolutionists say existed 250 million years ago; a complete fossil of a dinosaur called 'acrocanthasaurus' (40 feet long), that evolutionists say existed 100 million years ago; seven tracks of a huge 'cat', that evolutionists say existed 6 million years ago; 57 human footprints (some being inside a dinosaur track); the fourth finger of a woman's left hand, fossilized; and even a pre-deluvian iron hammer (its iron does not rust, being 96.6% iron and 2.7% chlorine)—**all of that in the very same layer of sedimentary rock**!

It follows that a geologic column does not exist; it is a perverse invention perpetrated by dishonest and perverse persons. All those fossils were produced by Noah's Flood, about 4,365 years ago; otherwise, how can you explain that all those things are in the very same layer of rock? (We may note in passing that it is common for defenders of the 'geologic column' to argue in a circle: the age of a rock layer is determined by the fossils it contains, while the age of a fossil is determined by the rock layer where it is found!)

Furthermore, the earth is young. In the royal observatory in England they have been measuring the force of the magnetic field that surrounds the earth each year since 1839. They have found that the magnetic force is diminishing at a constant rate, or geometric progression: plotting the yearly values on a graph, they form a cline. This means that it is possible to project the line in both directions. If we project the line to a point 10,000 years ago, the magnetic force would be so strong that it would crush all life on the planet. It follows that any theory that requires millions, or billions of years is stupidly, ridiculously impossible.

The Mississippi river dumps 80,000 tons of sediment into the gulf of Mexico every hour! All you have to do is measure the delta to see that the earth is young. Evolutionists say that granite took 300 million years to crystalize, but within granite there are polonium 'haloes' with half-lives of minutes, or even seconds. Granite had to be created instantaneously. Symbiotic plants and insects had to be created at the same time, and require 24-hour days. And so on.

In short, the evolutionary hypothesis of origins is scientifically impossible; stupidly, ridiculously impossible. A number of decades ago the scholar Sir Frederick Hoyle was contracted to evaluate the scientific probability that life could have appeared on the planet by chance (he had unlimited funding and free access to libraries). He arrived at the following conclusion: it would be easier for a whirlwind to pass through a junk yard and a perfect Boeing 747 come flying out of the other side than for life to have appeared on our planet by chance. Well, well, well, that life could have originated by an evolutionary process is obviously, stupidly, ridiculously impossible. [By the way, any questions about the morality of the Creator have nothing to do with science.]

So a Cause must exist, and that Cause must be incredibly intelligent and powerful. That Cause must also have personality, since He created beings with personality. The customary term used for that Cause is 'God', but I will use Sovereign Creator. In the marketplace of the world, there is no lack of differing ideas about 'God'. Genesis 1:27 informs us that "God created man in His own image", and ever since, man has been trying to return the favor! I wonder if people understand that any god that they create will be smaller than they are.

Since a Sovereign Creator exists, He holds absolute authority over what He has created. But in what ways can authority be exercised? It can be exercised by fiat, by sovereign intervention, but doing that to beings created in God's own image would turn them into robots, which would be contradictory to the purpose in creating such beings. As the Sovereign said to the Samaritan woman, while He walked this earth: "the true worshippers will worship the Father in spirit and truth; for the Father is seeking such to worship Him. God is Spirit, and those who worship Him must worship in spirit and truth" (John 4:23-24). If the Father is seeking spontaneous, or at least voluntary, worship, then it cannot be coerced, or forced. But how can man know what the Sovereign Creator wants? There must be communication. But what form could such communication take? To communicate concepts, He would have to use human language.[1]

---

[1] Since human language is governed by rules—phonological, grammatical, semantic—the

If the Creator was only concerned to transmit information to a given individual, or group, at a given point in time, for a specific purpose, it could be done orally, either speaking directly, or through a representative. But if the Creator's purpose was to furnish orientation that would be valid for subsequent generations as well, then the appropriate form would be in writing. Consider 1 Chronicles 16:15, "the word which He commanded for a thousand generations". Well now, there have scarcely been 300 generations since Adam, so the Creator's written revelation will be in effect until the end of the world. However, to be in effect until the end, it must be kept available until the end, but I am getting ahead of myself.

If the Sovereign Creator exists, and if He has addressed a written Revelation to our race, then nothing is more important for us than to know what He said (with a view to obeying it, if we are smart). This because such a revelation will have objective authority over us (although the Creator gives us the option of rejecting that authority [but due regard should be given to the consequences]).[1] Objective authority depends on verifiable meaning; if a reader/hearer can give any meaning he chooses to a message, any authority it ends up having for him will be relative and subjective (the 'neo-orthodox' approach).

As a linguist (PhD) I affirm that the fundamental principle of communication is this: both the speaker/writer and the hearer/reader must respect the norms of language, in particular those of the specific code being used. If the encoder violates the rules, he will be deceiving the decoder (deliberately, if he knows what he is doing). If the decoder violates the rules, he will misrepresent the encoder (deliberately, if he knows what he is doing). In either event, communication is damaged; the extent of the damage will depend on the circumstances.

Several times the Lord Jesus referred to the Holy Spirit as "the Spirit of the Truth", and Titus 1:2 affirms that God cannot lie—it is one thing He cannot do, being contrary to His essence; "He cannot deny Himself" (2 Timothy 2:13). It should be obvious to one and all that the Sovereign will not take kindly to being called a liar. To interpret the Sacred Text in a way that is not faithful to the rules of Hebrew and Greek, respectively, is to ascribe to the Author the intention of deceiving us, is to call Him a liar—not smart. But to interpret the Text, we must have it, and I will take up the subject of preservation below.

Creator would have to limit Himself to the repertoire of possibilities offered by the language of choice.

1 The enemy has always understood this better than most of us, and began his attacks early on—"Yea, hath God said,...?" (Genesis 3:1).

But first, how can we know whether or not the Creator did in fact address a written revelation to us; and if He did, how can we identify it? Taking the point of view that the Sovereign Creator decided to furnish orientation to our race, He would know that He would have to make it recognizable for what it was, and the evidences would need to remain available to succeeding generations. But how can we know what means He would use to make His revelation recognizable? We can know by looking at what He has done, and working back, as it were. At this point, I must jump ahead to what I have concluded, based on the evidence, and then work back to see if my conclusion holds. I here state the presuppositions that I bring to my task: the Sovereign Creator exists, He has addressed a written Revelation to our race, and He has preserved it intact to this day to the extent that we can know what it is, based on objective criteria.

Introduction

Inspiration

When I write a book,[1] I identify myself as the author, and usually give some indication as to my purpose in writing it. As a Christian, I was taught that our Bible (containing 66 'books') is a written Revelation given by the Sovereign Creator. So I ask: does the Bible identify itself, does it claim to be divinely inspired? I begin with the claim, and then attempt to verify it.

The claim

Genesis 1:1, "In the beginning God created the heavens and the earth". The only One who could pass this information on to Adam (as I assume) was the Creator Himself; the Author is identifying Himself. Adam certainly developed a written form for the language God gave him, and he would have made a written record of all that the Creator told him about the beginning of this planet. Hundreds, if not thousands, of times throughout the Bible we encounter "God said", or "the Lord said". The prophetic books expressly claim to be messages given by God. Here is just one example: "The word of the LORD that came to Micah of Moresheth in the days of Jotham, Ahaz and Hezekiah, kings of Judah" (Micah 1:1).

Psalm 138:2, "You have magnified Your word above all Your name". Since a person's name represents that person, the point of that statement would appear to be that God's word represents His person even better than does His name. "Forever, O LORD, Your word is settled in heaven" (Psalm

---

1 I have published eight, so far, plus a Greek Text.

119:89). If the word is in heaven, then it must be God's, and only an eternal Being could produce an eternal word. 1 Peter 1:25 quotes Isaiah 40:8, "the word of the LORD endures forever", and there are a number of further passages that say essentially the same thing. Again, only an eternal Being could produce an eternal word.[1]

Matthew 5:18, "assuredly I say to you, until heaven and earth pass away, not one iota nor one tittle shall pass away from the Law until everything happens". Sovereign Jesus is making a statement about the preservation through time of the precise form of the Sacred Text. Only a maximum Authority could guarantee something like that. "All Scripture is God-breathed" (2 Timothy 3:16). Paul coins an expression to describe the intimate connection between God and His written Revelation; it is like His very breath.

Romans 14:24, "Now to Him who has power to establish you according to my Gospel and the proclamation of Jesus Christ, according to the revelation of the mystery kept secret through long ages, 25 but now revealed and made known through the prophetic Scriptures, according to the command of the eternal God, with a view to obedience of faith among all ethnic nations."[2] Since it is being revealed only 'now', these 'prophetic Scriptures' must be New Testament writings, given by God!

2 Peter 1:20-21, "knowing this first, that no Prophecy of Scripture comes to be from private release;[3] for no Prophecy ever came by the will of man, rather holy men of God spoke as they were carried along by the Holy Spirit." Here we have an impressive description of the process of Inspiration. I like the definition of the Scriptures that we find in Romans 2:20—"having in the Law the embodiment of knowledge and truth". Who but the Sovereign Creator could produce a written Revelation that embodies knowledge and truth?[4]

---

[1] I have already referred to 1 Chronicles 16:15.

[2] 5.2% of the Greek manuscripts place verses 24-26 at the end of the book, rather than here. Paul habitually places doxologies throughout his letters—they do not occur only at the end.

[3] The word rendered "release" occurs only here in the New Testament, but the basic meaning of the root is 'to loose' or 'release'. With reference to a prophetic word, it could refer either to its enunciation/origination or to its interpretation. Verse 21 makes clear that here it is the origination. False or fake prophecies derive from the will of the 'prophet' (or demonic influence), but true prophecy never does.

[4] I take it that the declarations I have cited affirm the existence of a written Revelation, but they do not give us the identity of the inspired writings that make up that revelation, the composition of the Canon. I will take up that question in its turn.

The evidence

I consider that I have dealt adequately with the claim, so I now move on to the evidences, or the verification. A literature that claims supernatural origin should be intrinsically supernatural and should produce supernatural results. I will begin with the supernatural results, which will also tell us something about the Creator's purpose in giving the Revelation.

Paul wrote to Timothy: "from infancy you have known the Sacred Scriptures which are able to make you wise into salvation through the faith that is in Christ Jesus. All Scripture is God-breathed and is valuable for teaching, for reproving, for correcting, for training in righteousness, so that the man of God may be fully competent, thoroughly equipped for every good work"[1] (2 Timothy 3:15-17). Certainly one of the most important purposes is to show how to obtain eternal salvation. Paul goes on to say that Scripture is valuable for four things. Notice the sequence: 1) the Scripture provides objectively true information; 2) then the Holy Spirit uses His Sword to convict of sin; 3) this leads to repentance and conversion; 4) then the Word is our food and water for spiritual growth. As we grow, we can help others move through the sequence. A very great many Christians, from around the world, have found the above to be true in their personal experience.

Hebrews 4:12-13, "the Word of God is living and efficient, and sharper than any two-edged sword, actually penetrating to the point of separating soul and spirit,[2] joints and marrow; in fact, it is able to evaluate a heart's reflections and intentions. Nothing in all creation is hidden from His sight; rather all things are naked and open to the eyes of Him to whom we must give account." Meditating on God's Word can be rather uncomfortable; it is a 'mirror' that tells us the truth about ourselves (James 1:25). Ephesians 6:17 calls it "the sword of the Spirit". A word that can separate soul from spirit must be supernatural. A very great many Christians, from around the world, have found the above to be true in their personal experience. Returning to Hebrews 4:13, we must give an account to a Judge who knows ALL the facts. This knowledge really ought to turn us into serious people, diligent seekers of God, but . . . .

"This Book of the law shall not depart from your mouth, but you shall meditate in it day and night, that you may observe to do according to all that is written in it. For then you will make your way prosperous, and then

---

[1] Access to Scripture is necessary for spiritual growth and work.

[2] If soul and spirit can be separated, they obviously cannot be the same thing, just as joints and marrow are not the same thing.

you will have good success" (Joshua 1:8). James 1:25 says something very similar. Moses said to the Israelites: "Set your hearts on all the words which I testify among you today, which you shall command your children to be careful to observe—all the words of this law. For it is not a futile thing for you, because it is your life" (Deuteronomy 32:46-47). A very great many Christians, from around the world, have found the above to be true in their personal experience.

Romans 1:16-17, "I am not ashamed[1] of the Gospel of Christ,[2] because it is the power of God for the salvation of each one who believes (for the Jew first, then the Greek); because in it God's righteousness is revealed, from faith to faith; just as it is written: 'The righteous one will live by faith'."[3] The Gospel is the power for the salvation. As Sovereign Jesus said in John 14:6—"I am the way, the truth, and the life. No one comes to the Father except through me." There are not many ways, only one. Millions of lives have been transformed by the power of God's Word; so where did that power come from?

The inspiration of the Sacred Text is an intrinsic quality; it is because it is. However, we can perceive the inherent quality, comparing inspired material with material that is not inspired. Consider the nature of the Bible's content, or message: it is not the sort of thing that the human being would wish to write, even if he could; nor is it the sort of thing that he could write, even if he wished to. And then there is the unity of the Bible: even though the 66 books were written by at least thirty different human authors, during some 2,000 years, and in two very different languages (Hebrew and Greek),[4] the whole is coherent, it does not contradict itself. There are also specific and detailed prophecies, even including a person's name, given centuries before the fact, that were precisely fulfilled.

For those who believe Jesus Christ to be God, His attitude toward the Old Testament will be relevant. He ascribed absolute authority to the OT; in John 5:45-47 He placed the writings of Moses on a par with His own word, that He declared to have eternal validity (Luke 21:33). As reported in the four Gospels, He cited at least Genesis, Exodus, Numbers, Deuteronomy, Psalms, Isaiah, Jeremiah, Daniel, Hosea, Jonah, Zechariah and Malachi. In Luke 24:44 He explicitly recognized the three divisions of the

---

1 Where did Paul get the idea of 'shame'? A world controlled by Satan does all it can to cow any who dare to proclaim the Truth.

2 Perhaps 3% of the Greek manuscripts omit "of Christ", to be followed by NIV, NASB, TEV, etc.—an inferior proceeding.

3 See Habakkuk 2:4. To 'live by faith' you must move from one exercise of faith to another.

4 A very few chapters were written in Aramaic.

Hebrew Canon: Law, Prophets and Writings (Psalms). And then there is Matthew 23:35—"so that upon you may come all the righteous blood shed on the earth, from the blood of righteous Abel up to the blood of Zechariah son of Berechiah, whom you murdered between the temple and the altar". Jesus is here concluding His denunciation of the scribes and Pharisees. The murder of Abel is the first one recorded in the Bible (Genesis 4:8). Please note that Jesus affirms the historicity of Abel, and since Abel had parents, of necessity, Jesus is also affirming the historicity of Abel's parents, Adam and Eve! Zechariah was a contemporary of Ezra and Haggai at the time of the construction of the second temple. So "all the righteous blood shed" between those two men covers the whole OT, some 3,500 years!

Having said all of the above, however, I recognize that to affirm the divine inspiration of the Bible is a declaration of faith—an intelligent faith that is based on evidences, but still faith, since the evidences are not absolute;[1] and they are not absolute for a very good reason. The Sovereign Creator deliberately does not allow the evidences to be absolute, because then there would be no true test. The Creator requires that men choose between good and evil, and the choice may not be coerced. That last night, in the upper room, Sovereign Jesus referred to the Holy Spirit as "the Spirit of the Truth" and declared that "He will guide you into all the truth" (John 16:13). It is the Holy Spirit's prerogative to convict and convince.

Its nature

We use the term 'inspiration' to refer to the process that the Sovereign Creator used to produce his written Revelation. The Creator chose to use human authors, with the exception of the stone tablets containing the Decalog, that the Creator Himself engraved (Exodus 31:18, 32:16). By comparing the style of books written by different people, it is evident that the personality of the author was not squelched, or blocked: Paul writes in one way, John writes in a different way, and so on. And the same author will change style, depending on the intended audience, or recipient. So when Peter writes that the authors were "carried along by the Holy Spirit" (2 Peter 1:21), we may understand that the 'carrying' guaranteed that the words that were written expressed correctly the meaning that the Holy Spirit wished to convey. Both the living Word and the written Word involve a hypostatic union: how Jesus Christ can be 100% God and 100% man at the same time is a mystery; how the written Word can be 100% divine and 100% human at the same time is also a mystery.

---

[1] So we are not dealing with science, in an objective sense.

But there is more to the story. The way inspiration works varies with the type of literature.

1) Strictly speaking, 'revelation' signifies information given directly to someone by the Creator (sometimes using an angel). True prophecy is a prophet repeating verbatim what the Creator said to him: "the word of the LORD came to me saying" (Jeremiah 1:4). Of necessity, the information contained in the first chapter of Genesis was given directly to Adam by the Creator. Similarly, the information contained in Job 1:6-12 and 2:1-7 had to be given directly to the author of the book (perhaps Elihu, the son of Barachel—Job 32:2). Acts 1:16 says that the Holy Spirit spoke by the mouth of David. With reference to the 'Lord's Supper', Paul wrote: "I received from the Lord that which I also transmitted to you" (1 Corinthians 11:23). I could add further references, but I have given enough to illustrate 'revelation'; such revelation is usually normative, it serves to orient our behavior.

2) Historical information is somewhat different; inspiration guarantees the veracity of what is described—things happened in just that way. It should be obvious that descriptions of sin, lying, crime, or perversity are not normative, although they serve as negative examples to warn us. Genesis 3:4 registers a lie; "Then the serpent said to the woman: You will not surely die". Obviously inspiration is not agreeing with the lie, it merely guarantees that the serpent said precisely that. Historical information, or record, may include normative orientation. It is always necessary to pay close attention to the context, that may appropriately be called the 'king of interpretation'.

3) Poetic material is more difficult. It is a genre of communication that has its own rules, and the context is most important. The Song of Solomon is made up of thirteen 'canticles'; they are not presented as being normative. Since the relationship between man and woman is fundamental to human existence, it is natural that the subject finds a place in the written Revelation. That the Creator chose the poetic genre, was His prerogative, and it goes with the subject matter; emotion often finds expression in poetic form.

In contrast, the Proverbs are generally normative. In Ecclesiastes 12:9-11, Solomon declares the inspiration of the proverbs: they were "given by one Shepherd".

On the other hand, Solomon himself does not make the same claim for Ecclesiastes, another book that he wrote. The second verse, "Vanity of vanities, says the preacher, Vanity of vanities, all is vanity", obviously does not agree with the rest of the Bible. To serve God is not vanity, salvation in Christ is not vanity, and so on. Indeed, Solomon declares openly how the book came to be: "I set my heart to seek and search out by wisdom" (1:13), "I communed with my heart" (1:16), "I set my heart to know wisdom and to know madness and folly" (1:17), "I searched in my heart how to gratify my flesh" (2:3). The book is clearly an attempt to understand life and the world using a purely humanistic analysis, leaving the Sovereign Creator out of the picture. That analysis was undertaken by a man who was very intelligent. I take it that the book was included in the Canon precisely to show to what conclusion a purely humanistic analysis of life must arrive—to emptiness and despair. However, the author concluded the book by stating the true truth, so no one would be deceived: "Let us hear the conclusion of the whole matter: Fear God and keep His commandments, for this is man's all. For God will bring every work into judgment, including every secret thing, whether good or evil."

Illumination

I submit that it is important that we distinguish between inspiration and illumination, with reference to Scripture. Inspiration refers to the writing of biblical material; illumination refers to the interpretation of biblical material. Both of them, inspiration and illumination, are the work of the Holy Spirit. Illumination is usually reserved for those who have been regenerated. "Now a soulish man does not receive the things of the Spirit of God, for they are foolishness to him; indeed, he cannot understand them, because they are spiritually discerned" (1 Corinthians 2:14). That is what the Text says. A 'soulish' person cannot understand spiritual things, which sounds rather like a congenital defect. The concrete facts contained in an historical record can be understood by anyone. That David killed Goliath is a fact that anyone can understand. But to understand the Holy Spirit's purpose behind an inspired statement depends on illumination, and to receive it one must be spiritual (1 Corinthians 2:15).

The Canon

I now come to the question of the canonicity of the Sacred Text: why does our Bible have the exact assortment of books that it has—no more, no less, and no others? Inspiration refers to divine activity in the act of writing the material, guaranteeing the result. In contrast, the canonizing of the Text refers to human activity, recognizing the divine quality of that material. The process of that recognition took place within the community of the Faith—the Hebrew community, for the OT, and the Christian community, for the NT. I have already referred to the attitude that the Lord Jesus Christ demonstrated with regard to the OT, which was all of the

Bible that existed at that point. He evidently recognized the Canon of 39 books that had been defined by His time. He cited a number of books—taken from the Law, history, prophecy and poetry—and He did so as being God's Word, something true, holy and authoritative. The human authors of the NT demonstrated the same respect for the OT, which was their Bible as well.

I have said that the OT contains 39 books, and so it was until the sixteenth century of the Christian era. The Council of Trent was a reaction of the Roman Catholic Church against the Protestant Reformation. It started in 1545 and concluded its work in 1563. It added fourteen 'books' to the OT, although the fourteen had never been recognized by the Hebrew community. In Protestant circles, those books are generally referred to as the 'Apocrypha', while in Roman Catholic circles they are referred to as being 'Deutero-canonical'. The Canon of the NT was formally closed by the Council of Carthage in 397 AD, the Canon of the OT having been closed centuries earlier. Surely 1563 was altogether too late to be adding books to the Sacred Text.[1]

Now then, canonization has everything to do with the preservation of the Text. Surely, because the community of the Faith would only concern itself to transmit and protect the 'canonical' books, those that were held to be inspired.[2] When I take up the question of preservation, below, I will argue that it is precisely the preservation of the Text that proves its

---

[1] 1 Maccabees (c. 175-135 BC) makes no claim to be Scripture and indeed claims to be written after the age of the prophets (see 9:27; 4:46; 14:41). 1 Macc. 9:27 acknowledges that the succession of Old Testament prophets had already ceased. 1 Macc. 4:46 says that Israel was waiting till the Messiah when a prophet might arise to tell them what to do with the heap of stones. Apparently no prophet was in existence at the time of the writing. The absence of prophets can be seen in 1 Macc. 14:41; 2 Esdras 14:45; etc. Thus, in the Prologue to Sirach, the grandson makes clear that ben Sirach was simply a wise man and he was simply translating. See the apology of the author in 2 Macc. 15:38—"And if I have done well, and as is fitting the story, it is that which I desired: but if slenderly and meanly, it is that which I could attain unto." A prophet would speak with authority, not apologize for how poorly he wrote. [I owe this information to Dr. Phillip Kayser.]

[2] For example, there are those who argue that the Autograph of Matthew was written in Hebrew. But there is a small difficulty with that thesis: there is not even one known copy of that Gospel in Hebrew. Since it was only the Greek Matthew that the Church protected and transmitted, then the autograph was written in Greek, obviously. However, it seems to me to be equally obvious that Matthew, and anyone else who could write, filled 'notebooks' with his annotations of what Jesus said and did. Yes, because Luke 1:1 states that "many have undertaken to set in order a narrative concerning those things". All notes taken on the spot would have to be in Hebrew, because that was the language Jesus used. As Matthew wrote his Gospel in Greek, he certainly consulted his notes written in Hebrew. The lack of even one Greek copy of such things as the gospel of Thomas, or Judas, or whatever, indicates that they were not inspired and were not recognized by the Church.

canonicity. The human part in the transmission of the Text is obvious, but was there also divine activity, protecting the Text (including its exact wording)? And how might one 'measure' such divine activity? I see two relevant 'tools' to do the measuring: logic and history. I begin with the argument from logic.

Inspiration is a result or quality of Revelation—with that statement we are affirming that the Sovereign Creator decided to transmit some objective information to the human race. If the Creator was only concerned to transmit information to a given individual, or group, at a given point in time, for a specific purpose, it could be done orally. But if His purpose was to reach a sequence of generations (up to a thousand of them, 1 Chronicles 16:15), then the appropriate form would be in writing. Now then, if the Creator intended that His Revelation should arrive intact, or at least entire and in reliable condition, to the XXI century, He would absolutely have to watch over the process of transmission down through the centuries. He would have to forbid the irrecoverable loss of any genuine material, as well as forbid any unrecognizable insertion of spurious material. The original wording should be available, in whatever generation, to persons who were sufficiently interested in having that wording that they would pay the necessary price (time, travel, money) to obtain it. (In general, people would be satisfied with the wording they had, so long as they regarded it to be reliable.) So then, a person who believes in the divine inspiration of the NT, for example, should also believe in the divine preservation of the NT—it is a question of logic. But what about the historical evidences; do they agree with our logic, or do they not? To that question I now turn.

The Historical Evidence for Preservation

To begin, I submit that the following references may reasonably be understood as a statement by the Sovereign Creator that He intended to preserve His Text, but He gave no indication as to just how He proposed to do it. We must work back from what He did. But first, the references:

1 Chronicles 16:14-15 is part of a psalm of praise to God that was sung when the Ark was brought to Jerusalem. "He is the LORD our God; His judgments are in all the earth. Remember His command forever, the word which He commanded for a thousand generations." For the Word to be binding until the thousandth generation, it would have to be preserved until that generation, and it would need to be available to each generation along the way. I take it that "a thousand generations" is parallel to "forever". "Forever, O LORD, Your word is settled in heaven. Your faithfulness is to all generations" (Psalm 119:89-90). "Forever" is parallel to "all generations". "The grass withers, the flower fades, but the word of our

God stands forever" (Isaiah 40:8). To 'stand' forever, it must be preserved forever. {Psalm 102:18 and 1 Corinthians 10:11}

Matthew 5:17-18 are part of the so-called 'Sermon on the Mount', delivered by Sovereign Jesus while He walked this earth. "Do not suppose that I came to destroy the Law or the Prophets; I did not come to destroy but to fulfill. For assuredly I say to you, until heaven and earth pass away, not one iota nor one tittle shall pass away from the Law until everything happens." The Lord here makes an impressively strong statement about the preservation through time of the precise form of the Sacred Text. Since our only access to the meaning is through the form, any alteration in the form will alter the meaning. (One of the most effective ways of annulling a commandment is to corrupt the Text—something Satan understands quite well.) "It is easier for heaven and earth to pass away, than for one tittle of the Law to fail" (Luke 16:17). "Heaven and earth will pass away, but my words will by no means pass away" (Luke 21:33). Sovereign Jesus declares that His words have eternal validity, and are therefore on a par with God's written Revelation (see Psalm 119:89).

In Matthew 4:4 Sovereign Jesus rebuts Satan, quoting Deuteronomy 8:3. "It is written: 'Man shall not live by bread alone, but by every word coming out of God's mouth'." If we are to live by 'every word', then every word must be kept available.[1] Notice also Deuteronomy 29:29, "the secret things belong to the LORD our God, but those which are revealed belong to us and to our children forever, that we may do all the words of this law". "All the words" includes each individual word that contributes to the whole; and for the three hundredth generation to obey them all, they all must still be available. Consider also Isaiah 59:21—"As for Me", says the LORD, "this is My covenant with them: My Spirit who is upon you, and My words which I have put in your mouths, shall not depart from your mouth, nor from the mouth of your descendants, nor from the mouth of your descendants' descendants", says the LORD, "from this time and forevermore". "My words" includes each individual word that contributes to the whole, and they are to be available "from this time and forevermore", which includes all intervening generations. Revelation 22:18-19 also emphasizes the individual words.

I submit that the references presented above may reasonably be understood to constitute a declaration that the Sovereign Creator intends that His written Revelation be available to all generations until the end of the

---

[1] Luke 4:4 is precisely parallel, where less than half a percent of the extant Greek manuscripts, of objectively inferior quality, omit "but by every word of God" (lamentably followed by NIV, NASB, LB, TEV, etc.).

world—His concern extends to the individual words, and even the letters (Matthew 5:18)! However, since He gave no indication as to just how He proposed to do it, we must deduce the answer by analyzing what He did. I will begin with the New Testament. I proceed to marshal the evidences.

The Autographs

When I speak of the divine preservation of the New Testament Text, I am referring to the precise wording of the original documents, the Autographs. When I speak of preservation, I am presuming divine inspiration; they are logically interdependent. Why would God inspire a written revelation if He was not going to preserve it? Why would God preserve writings that He had not inspired? I consider that the preservation of the NT Text is perhaps the strongest argument in favor of its inspired nature. The same holds true for the precise selection of books that make up the NT Canon. Since I consider that Matthew's Gospel was the first NT book to be released to the public ('published'), I will begin with it.

By the time that Matthew 'published' his Gospel in AD 38,[1] the production of books in the Roman Empire was widespread, but there was no 'copyright'. As soon as a book was turned loose it became 'public domain'; anyone could use it and change it. Now then, if the Holy Spirit gave thought to protecting the works that He was inspiring, protecting against free editing, what could He do? I suggest that the most obvious way would be to have those works 'published' in the form of multiple copies. Today the first run of a book will usually be thousands of copies, but in those days each copy had to be handwritten (manuscript).

A book the size of Matthew's Gospel would represent a considerable investment of time and effort, as well as papyrus and ink. I believe the NT writings were prepared in book form from the first (not scroll), and the material used was probably papyrus.[2] However, papyrus cannot stand a lot of handling, and by the year 38 there were many Christian congregations just in the Jewish territory, not to mention elsewhere. If the Holy Spirit intended that the NT writings should have a wide circulation, which would seem to be obvious, it would be necessary to start out with multiple copies.

---

[1] The colophones in 50% of the MSS, including Family 35, say that Matthew was 'published' eight years after the ascension of the Christ. Since Jesus ascended in 30 AD, Matthew was released in 38. The colophones say that Mark was published two years later (40), and Luke another five years later (45), and John in 62.

[2] "Bring the books, especially the parchments" (2 timothy 4:13). We may gather from this that parchment was already in use, but the 'books' were presumably on papyrus; otherwise, why the contrast?

A single copy of Matthew would be falling apart before it got to the twentieth congregation (if on papyrus).

But why do I insist on papyrus instead of parchment? Well, a single copy of Matthew would represent around fifteen sheep or goats; on that basis, who could afford multiple copies? That said, however, the master copy may indeed have been done on parchment, for two reasons: if a master copy was to be kept, for quality control, it should be on durable material; if multiple copies of the master copy were to be made before turning it loose to the public, a master copy on papyrus could not last.

The idea of publishing a book in the form of multiple copies may be inferred from the Epistles. 2 Corinthians was written to "the church of God which is at Corinth, with all the saints who are in all Achaia" (verse 1). How many congregations would there have been "in all Achaia"? Was Paul thinking of multiple copies? 1 Corinthians was addressed to "all those everywhere who call on the name of our Lord Jesus Christ" (verse 2). Now how many copies would **that** take? Galatians was written to "the churches of Galatia" (verse 2). Could a single copy get to all of them?

Consider the case of Peter's first letter: it is addressed to believers in "Pontus, Galatia, Cappadocia, Asia and Bithynia" (verse 1). Well now, what basis could Peter (apostle to the circumcised, Galatians 2:8) have for writing to people in those places? Probably a good number of the older leaders had been with Peter at Pentecost, and had sat under his ministry until the persecution under Saul sent them packing back home, presumably (Acts 8:4). Notice that the list of places in Acts 2:9-11 includes the following places in Asia Minor: Asia, Cappadocia, Pamphylia, Phrygia and Pontus. Three of the five are in Peter's list, and we need not assume that his list was exhaustive; for that matter, the list in Acts 2:9-11 is probably not exhaustive.

Have you ever looked at a map to see the location of Peter's five provinces? They basically represent the whole of Asia Minor (today's Turkey)! 'Asia' seems to have been used in different ways. Acts 27:2 has Asia including Cilicia and Pamphylia (verse 5). The glorified Christ put the seven churches in Asia (Revelation 1:4). In Acts 16:6 the term seems to refer to a more limited area, which, however, presumably included Ephesus, to which Paul returned later. Proconsular Asia included Mysia and Phrygia. Now how many congregations would there have been in all of Asia Minor? And how could a single copy get around to all of them? If the letter was written on papyrus (as seems likely—cheaper, more abundant) it would be falling apart by the time it got to the twentieth congregation, if not before (papyrus cannot stand all that much handling).

Now let us just suppose, for the sake of the argument, that Peter sent five copies of his letter, one to each province. What would the implications be for the transmission of its Text? It means that you multiply the process and progress of transmission by five! It means that you have the beginnings of a 'majority text' very early on. It means that the basic integrity of the text would be guaranteed (the more so if God was superintending the process). If Peter sent out more than five copies, so much the more. And what about James; how many copies would it take to reach "the twelve tribes that are in the dispersion" (verse 1)? (Does not the very term 'dispersion' suggest that they were widely scattered? And what if the 'twelve tribes' is literal?) Peter's second letter does not list the five provinces, but 3:1 would appear to indicate that he was targeting the same area.

To see that I did not pull the idea of multiple copies out of thin air, let us consider 2 Peter 1:12-15. Verses 12 & 13 refer to repeated reminders while he is still in his 'tent', which would be his own ongoing activity; so why the 'moreover' in verse 15? In the NKJV verse 15 reads: "Moreover, I will be careful to ensure that you always have a reminder of these things after my decease". Well, how can you 'ensure' that someone will 'always have a reminder' of something? It seems clear to me that the something has to be written down; a reminder has to be in writing, to be guaranteed. So what is Peter's intention? He specifies "a reminder of these things", so what are the 'these things'? They are evidently the things he will discuss in this letter. But he must be referring to something more than the initial draft of the letter (or the verse becomes meaningless)—hence, multiple copies.[1]

---

[1] It was Dr. Mike Loehrer, a pastor in California, who called 2 Peter 1:12-15 to my attention and got me started thinking about it. With reference to verse 15 he wrote me the following: "Could choosing to use *mneme* with *poieo* in the middle voice mean to ensure a way of always being able to validate a memory? In those days most people could not afford their own copy of a writing, and the church would no doubt become the repository of an autograph anyway. The usual way of getting the Scripture back then was by committing it to memory when hearing it during the public reading. Having multiple autographs in multiple locations would definitely ensure a way of validating a memory. Even if the leaders of a church or synagogue were imprisoned and their autograph was seized or destroyed, they could rest assured that they could locate another autograph to validate their memory of the way a verse or passage was actually written."

The idea of validating a memory is as interesting as it is suggestive. Peter's use of *μνημη*, basically reflexive, with *ποιεω* in the middle voice, makes Mike's suggestion a reasonable one, as it seems to me. It goes along with the multiple copies. Irenaeus puzzled over verse 15 and came up with the suggestion that Peter intended to get copies of Mark's Gospel to those regions. Evidently the idea of multiple copies was not strange to him. And how about other books?

If Peter wrote his second letter under divine inspiration, then 1:15 is inspired, and in that event the idea of multiple copies came from God. It would be an efficient means of preserving the Text and guaranteeing its integrity down through the years of transmission. The churches in Asia Minor could always cross check with one another whenever a doubt arose or need required. If it was God's idea that a small letter be 'published' in the form of multiple copies, then how much more the larger books. Obviously God knew what He was doing, so the practice would have begun with the very first NT book, Matthew.[1]

If not the first book, how about the last book? Consider Revelation 1:10-11. "I was in spirit on the Lord's day and I heard a voice behind me, loud as a trumpet, saying, 'Write what you see in a book and send it to the seven churches: to Ephesus, to Smyrna, to Pergamos, to Thyatira, to Sardis, to Philadelphia and to Laodicea'." Note that he is to write what he sees, not what he merely hears (the seven letters were dictated to him, he didn't 'see' them). He is to send what he writes to the seven churches; the obvious way to do that would be to send a separate copy to each church. In that event Revelation was 'published' in at least seven copies (he may have kept a copy for himself).

The idea is so good that it became the norm, the more so if it was a divine order. I believe all the NT books were released in the form of multiple copies, with the exception of the letters addressed to individuals. (Since Luke and Acts are addressed to an individual, they also may have started out as a single copy, unless Theophilus was a 'benefactor' who was financing the multiple copies. Luke and Acts are the two longest books of the NT, and multiple copies of them would represent a significant financial investment.) Again I say, the idea is so good, I would not be surprised if once they got it the churches would set about making multiple copies of other writings they considered to be inspired, such as letters to individuals. A 'majority text' would be well established throughout the Aegean area (Greece and Asia Minor) already in the first century. The 'heartland of the Church' (to use K. Aland's phrase) simply kept on using and copying that form of text—hence the mass of Byzantine MSS that have come down to us.

---

[1] Quite apart from the idea of 'publishing' via multiple copies, consider what would happen when a congregation received a copy of 1 Peter, James, or any of Paul's Epistles, accompanied by the instruction that they had to pass it on. If you were one of the leaders of that congregation, what would you do? I would most certainly make a copy for us to keep. Wouldn't you? The point is, as soon as an inspired book began to circulate, the proliferation of copies began at once. And that means that a 'majority text' also began at once!

Early Recognition[1]

Naturalistic critics like to assume that the New Testament writings were not recognized as Scripture when they first appeared and thus, through the consequent carelessness in transcription, the text was confused and the original wording 'lost' (in the sense that no one knew for sure what it was) at the very start. Thus Colwell said: "Most of the manuals and handbooks now in print (including mine!) will tell you that these variations were the fruit of careless treatment which was possible because the books of the New Testament had not yet attained a strong position as 'Bible'."[2] And Hort had said:

> Textual purity, as far as can be judged from the extant literature, attracted hardly any interest. There is no evidence to show that care was generally taken to choose out for transcription the exemplars having the highest claims to be regarded as authentic, if indeed the requisite knowledge and skill were forthcoming.[3]

Rather than take Hort's word for it, prudence calls for a review of the premises. The place to start is at the beginning, when the apostles were still penning the Autographs.

The apostolic period

It is clear that the apostle Paul, at least, considered his writings to have divine authority; we may begin with Romans 16:24-25. "Now to Him who has power to establish you according to my Gospel and the proclamation of Jesus Christ, according to the revelation of the mystery kept secret through long ages, but now revealed and made known through the prophetic Scriptures, according to the command of the eternal God, with a view to obedience of faith among all ethnic nations."[4] Paul declares that **now**, in his day, revelation was happening "through the prophetic Scriptures, according to the command of the eternal God", and those Scriptures included the Gospel that he, Paul, was preaching, and "the proclamation

---

[1] From this point on, this Part I is basically a reproduction (with a few embellishments) of most of Chapter 5 in my book, *The Identity of the New Testament Text IV*, available from Amazon.com, as well as from my site, www.prunch.org.

[2] Colwell, *What is the Best New Testament?*, p. 53. [He subsequently changed his mind.]

[3] B.F. Westcott and F.J.A. Hort, *The New Testament in the Original Greek* (2 vols.; London: Macmillan and Co., 1881), II, "Introduction", p. 9. Cf. p. 7. It is clear that Hort regarded the "extant literature" as representative of the textual picture in the early centuries. This gratuitous and misleading idea continues to be an important factor in the thinking of some scholars today.

[4] According to 95% of the Greek manuscripts, the correct position for 16:24-26 is 14:24-26, while the wording remains exactly the same.

of Jesus Christ" (a reference to the four Gospels, presumably). The objective was conversions in all ethnic nations; only the Word of God could achieve that. To reach all nations, that Word would have to be translated into their languages; "the command of the eternal God" includes a worldwide distribution!

Now consider 1 Corinthians 2:13, "which things we also expound, not in words taught by human wisdom, but in those taught by the Holy Spirit". Paul plainly declares that he received instruction from the Holy Spirit. And now 1 Corinthians 14:37, "If anyone thinks that he is a prophet or spiritual, let him acknowledge that the things I write to you are the Lord's commands". Was Paul on an ego trip, or was he aware that he was writing under inspiration? Since he says something similar in a number of his letters, it is clear that he believed he was writing Scripture. Like in Galatians 1:11-12. "Now I want you to know, brothers, that the Gospel preached by me is not according to man; because I did not receive it from any man, nor was I taught it; rather it came through a revelation from Christ." The plain meaning of these verses is that Paul is claiming revelation, and that he received it directly from the glorified Christ!

Ephesians 3:5, "which in different generations was not made known to the sons of men, as it has <u>now</u> been revealed by the Spirit to His holy apostles and prophets." Paul declares that the Holy Spirit gave Revelation to various people. An apostle, upon receiving a revelation, would also function as a prophet, but people like Mark and Luke were prophets without being apostles. Colossians 1:25-26, "the Church, of which I became a servant according to the stewardship from God that was given to me towards you, to **complete** the Word of God, the secret that has been hidden from past ages and generations, but <u>now</u> has been revealed to His saints." The normal and central meaning of the Greek verb here, πληροω, is precisely 'to complete', not 'to fulfill', or something similar. Why reject the normal meaning? Paul declares that God commissioned him to write Scripture! In fact, God caused fourteen of his epistles to be included in the NT Canon.

1 Thessalonians 2:13, "when you received from us the spoken Word of God, you welcomed it not as the word of men but, as it actually is, the Word of God". Paul refers to the speaking or applying of the Word, emphasizing its divine origin. 2 Thessalonians 2:15 also deals with the authority of God's Word, whether spoken or written.

It is clear that Paul expected his writings to have a wider audience than just the particular church addressed. In fact, in Galatians 1:2 he addresses "the church**es** of Galatia"; not to mention 2 Corinthians 1:1, "all the saints in Achaia", and 1 Corinthians 1:2, "all who in every place"! In fact, as I have already suggested, it is probable that Paul sent out multiple copies of his letters.

John also is plain enough—Revelation 1:1-2. "Jesus Christ's revelation, which God gave Him to show to His slaves—things that must occur shortly. And He communicated it, sending it by His angel to His slave John, who gave witness to the word of God, even the testimony of Jesus Christ—the things that He [Jesus] saw, both things that are and those that must happen after these." That is how the book begins; and here is how it ends, 22:20: "He who testifies to these things says, 'Yes, I am coming swiftly!' Oh yes!! Come, Sovereign Jesus!" In other words, the whole book is what the glorified Christ is testifying, is revealing—as an eyewitness!! So then, the entire book is inspired.

And so is Peter plain. In 1 Peter 1:12,, he says with reference to the OT prophets, "It was revealed to them that they were not ministering these things to themselves, but to you; which things have now been announced to you by those who proclaimed the gospel to you, with the Holy Spirit sent from heaven." Peter declares that various people, certainly including himself, proclaimed the Gospel, accompanied by the Holy Spirit. 1 Peter 1:23-25: "having been begotten again, not from a corruptible seed but an incorruptible, through the living Word of God that remains *valid* forever. For: "All flesh is as grass, and all man's glory as flower of grass. The grass withers and its flower falls off, but the Lord's word endures forever." Now this is the good word that was proclaimed to you." [He quoted Isaiah 40:6-8] They were regenerated by means of the Gospel of Jesus Christ, and that is found in the NT. Peter places NT material on the same level as the OT—it is the Word of God that endures forever. When Peter wrote, at least Mathcw and Mark were already in circulation, and maybe Luke as well. 2 Peter 3:2 is to the same effect. Both Paul and Peter declare that a number of people were writing Scripture in their day.

I take it that in 1:3 Luke also claims divine inspiration; here are the first four verses:

> Given that many have undertaken to set in order a narrative concerning those things that really did take place among us,[1] just as

[1] Upon reflection it seems obvious that anyone who knew how to write would likely jot down salient points about Jesus, but Luke affirms that there were 'many' who attempted a serious account. Such records may well have furnished material, presumably factual, for spurious 'improvements' added to the four inspired accounts in the early decades of copying.

those who became eyewitnesses, from the beginning, and ministers of the Word delivered them to us,[1] it seemed good to me also, most excellent Theophilus, having taken careful note of everything from **Above**, to write to you with precision and in sequence,[2] so that you may <u>know</u> the certainty of the things in which you were instructed.[3]

It will be noticed that I rendered "everything from Above", rather than 'everything from the beginning'. The normal meaning of the Greek word here, *ανωθεν*, is precisely 'from above', and I see no reason to reject that meaning. The more so since in the prior verse he already used the normal phrase, *απ αρχης*, that means 'from the beginning'. I take it that Luke is claiming divine inspiration, up front.

Now I will consider a few verses where one apostle recognizes that another is writing Scripture. I begin with 1 Timothy 5:18. "For the Scripture says: 'You shall not muzzle an ox while it treads out grain', and 'The worker is worthy of his wages'". The part about the ox is a quote from Deuteronomy 25:4, definitely Scripture, but the part about the worker is a quote from Luke 10:7! Now this is very instructive. Paul, a former Pharisee, presumably ascribed the highest level of inspiration to the five books of the Law, so we expect him to call Deuteronomy Scripture. But for him to place Luke on a par with Moses is little short of incredible. Although there may have been close to fifteen years between the 'publishing' of Luke and the writing of 1 Timothy, Luke was recognized and declared by apostolic authority to be Scripture not long after it came off the press, so to speak. For a man who was once a strict Pharisee to put Luke (still alive) on a level with Moses is astounding; it would have required the direction of the Holy Spirit. Indeed, if Paul wrote this letter under the inspiration of the Holy Spirit, as I believe, then God Himself is declaring Luke to be Scripture!

In 2 Peter 3:15-16, Peter puts the Epistles of Paul on the same level as "the other Scriptures". Although some had been out for perhaps fifteen years, the ink was scarcely dry on others, and perhaps 2 Timothy had not yet been penned when Peter wrote. Paul's writings were recognized and declared by apostolic authority to be Scripture as soon as they appeared.

---

[1] Luke insists that his information comes from responsible eyewitnesses, who were there all the time.

[2] In fact, with a few exceptions, Luke's narrative is in chronological sequence, and as a physician he doubtless valued precision.

[3] Given Luke's stated purpose in writing, his account needs to be historically accurate. Note that Theophilus had already received some instruction.

1 Corinthians 15:4 reads like this: “and that He was buried, and that He was raised on the third day according to the Scriptures”. “The Scriptures” here presumably refers to the Gospels, because “on the third day” is not to be found in the OT. Did you get that? Since “on the third day” is not in the OT, the reference is to the Gospels, presumably.

In John 2:22 I would translate, “so they believed the Scripture, even the word that Jesus had spoken”—what Jesus said in John 2:19 was already circulating as ‘Scripture’ in Matthew 26:61 and 27:40 (when John wrote, in 62 AD).

Clement of Rome, whose first letter to the Corinthians is usually dated about AD 96, made liberal use of Scripture, appealing to its authority, and used New Testament material right alongside Old Testament material. Clement quoted Psalm 118:18 and Hebrews 12:6 side by side as “the holy word” (56:3-4).[1] He ascribes 1 Corinthians to “the blessed Paul the apostle” and says of it, “with true inspiration he wrote to you” (47:1-3). He clearly quotes from Hebrews, 1 Corinthians and Romans and possibly from Matthew, Acts, Titus, James and 1 Peter. Here is the bishop of Rome, before the close of the first century, writing an official letter to the church at Corinth wherein a selection of New Testament books are recognized and declared by episcopal authority to be Scripture, including Hebrews (and involving at least five different authors).

The Epistle of Barnabas, variously dated from AD 70 to 135, says in 4:14, “let us be careful lest, as it is written, it should be found with us that ‘many are called but few chosen’.” The reference seems to be to Matthew 22:14 (or 20:16) and the phrase “as it is written” may fairly be taken as a technical expression referring to Scripture. In 5:9 there is a quote from Matthew 9:13 (or Mark 2:17 or Luke 5:32). In 13:7 there is a loose quote from Romans 4:11-12, which words are put in God’s mouth. Similarly, in 15:4 we find: “Note, children, what ‘he ended in six days’ means. It means this: that the Lord will make an end of everything in six thousand years,

[1] I am aware that it could be Proverbs 3:12 (LXX) rather than Hebrews 12:6. Clement quotes from both books repeatedly throughout the letter, so they are equal candidates on that score. But, Clement agrees verbatim with Hebrews while Proverbs (LXX) differs in one important word. Further, the main point of Clement's chapter 56 is that correction is to be received graciously and as from the Lord, which is also the point of Hebrews 12:3-11. Since Clement evidently had both books in front of him (in the next chapter he quotes nine consecutive verses, Proverbs 1:23-31) the verbatim agreement with Hebrews is significant. If he deliberately chose the wording of Hebrews over that of Proverbs, what might that imply about their rank?

for a day with Him means a thousand years. And He Himself is my witness, saying: 'Behold, the day of the Lord shall be as a thousand years'."[1]

The author, whoever he was, is clearly claiming divine authorship for this quote which appears to be from 2 Peter 3:8.[2] In other words, 2 Peter is here regarded to be Scripture, as well as Matthew and Romans. Barnabas also has possible allusions to 1 and 2 Corinthians, Ephesians, Colossians, 1 and 2 Timothy, Titus, Hebrews, and 1 Peter.

The second century

The seven letters of Ignatius (c. AD 110) contain probable allusions to Matthew, John, Romans, 1 Corinthians and Ephesians (in his own letter to the Ephesians Ignatius says they are mentioned in "all the epistles of Paul"—a bit of hyperbole, but he was clearly aware of a Pauline corpus), and possible allusions to Luke, Acts, Galatians, Philippians, Colossians, 1 Thessalonians, 1 and 2 Timothy, and Titus, but very few are clear quotations and even they are not identified as such.

On the other hand, Polycarp, writing to the Philippian church (c. 115 AD?), weaves an almost continuous string of clear quotations and allusions to New Testament writings. His heavy use of Scripture is reminiscent of Clement of Rome; however, Clement used mostly the Old Testament while Polycarp mainly used the New. There are perhaps fifty clear quotations taken from Matthew, Luke, Acts, Romans, 1 and 2 Corinthians, Galatians, Ephesians, Philippians, Colossians, 1 and 2 Thessalonians, 1 and 2 Timothy, 1 and 2 Peter, and 1 John, and many allusions including to Mark, Hebrews, James, and 2 and 3 John. (The only NT writer not included is Jude! But remember that the above refers to only one letter—if Polycarp wrote other letters he may well have quoted Jude.) **Please note that the idea of a NT 'canon' evidently already existed in 115 AD, and Polycarp's 'canon' was quite similar to ours**.

His attitude toward the New Testament writings is clear from 12:1: "I am sure that you are well trained in the sacred Scriptures,... Now, as it is said in these Scriptures: 'Be angry and sin not,' and 'Let not the sun go down upon your wrath.' Blessed is he who remembers this."[3] Both parts

---

[1] I have used the translation done by Francis Glimm in *The Apostolic Fathers* (New York: Cima Publishing Co., Inc., 1947), belonging to the set, *The Fathers of the Church*, ed. Ludwig Schopp.

[2] J.V. Bartlet says of the formulae of citation used in Barnabas to introduce quotations from Scripture, "the general result is an absolute doctrine of inspiration", but he is unwilling to consider that 2 Peter is being used. Oxford Society of Historical Research, *The New Testament in the Apostolic Fathers* (Oxford: Clarendon Press, 1905), pp. 2, 15.

[3] Francis Glimm, again.

of the quotation could come from Ephesians 4:26 but since Polycarp split it up he may have been referring to Psalm 4:5 (LXX) in the first half. In either case he is declaring Ephesians to be "sacred Scripture". A further insight into his attitude is found in 3:1-2.

> Brethren, I write you this concerning righteousness, not on my own initiative, but because you first invited me. For neither I, nor anyone like me, is able to rival the wisdom of the blessed and glorious Paul, who, when living among you, carefully and steadfastly taught the word of truth face to face with his contemporaries and, when he was absent, wrote you letters. By the careful perusal of his letters you will be able to strengthen yourselves in the faith given to you, "which is the mother of us all",...[1]

(This from one who was perhaps the most respected bishop in Asia Minor, in his day. He was martyred in AD 156.)

The so-called second letter of Clement of Rome is usually dated before AD 150 and seems clearly to quote from Matthew, Mark, Luke, Acts, 1 Corinthians, Ephesians, 1 Timothy, Hebrews, James, and 1 Peter, with possible allusions to 2 Peter, Jude, and Revelation. After quoting and discussing a passage from the Old Testament, the author goes on to say in 2:4, "Another Scripture says: 'I came not to call the just, but sinners'" (Matthew 9:13; Mark 2:17; Luke 5:32). Here is another author who recognized the New Testament writings to be Scripture.

Two other early works, the *Didache* and the letter to Diognetus, employ New Testament writings as being authoritative but without expressly calling them Scripture. The *Didache* apparently quotes from Matthew, Luke, 1 Corinthians, Hebrews, and 1 Peter and has possible allusions to Acts, Romans, Ephesians, 1 and 2 Thessalonians and Revelation. The letter to Diognetus quotes from Acts, 1 and 2 Corinthians while alluding to Mark, John, Romans, Ephesians, Philippians, 1 Timothy, Titus, 1 Peter and 1 John.

Another early work—the Shepherd of Hermas—widely used in the second and third centuries, has fairly clear allusions to Matthew, Mark, 1 Corinthians, Ephesians, Hebrews, and especially James.

From around the middle of the second century fairly extensive works by Justin Martyr (martyred in 165) have come down to us. His "Dialogue with Trypho" shows a masterful knowledge of the Old Testament to which he assigns the highest possible authority, evidently holding to a dictation view of inspiration—in *Trypho* 34 he says, "to persuade you that you have

---

[1] *Ibid.*

not understood anything of the Scriptures, I will remind you of another psalm, dictated to David by the Holy Spirit."[1] The whole point of *Trypho* is to prove that Jesus is Christ and God and therefore what He said and commanded was of highest authority.

In *Apol.* i.66 Justin says, "For the apostles in the memoirs composed by them, which are called Gospels, thus handed down what was commanded them..."[2] And in *Trypho* 119 he says that just as Abraham believed the voice of God, "in like manner we, having believed God's voice spoken by the apostles of Christ..."

It also seems clear from *Trypho* 120 that Justin considered New Testament writings to be Scripture. Of considerable interest is an unequivocal reference to the book of Revelation in *Trypho* 81. "And further, there was a certain man with us whose name was John, one of the apostles of Christ, who prophesied, by a revelation that was made to him, that those who believe in our Christ would dwell a thousand years in Jerusalem."[3]

Justin goes right on to say, "Just as our Lord also said", and quotes Luke 20:35, so evidently he considered Revelation to be authoritative. (While on the subject of Revelation, in 165 Melito, Bishop of Sardis, wrote a commentary on the book.)

A most instructive passage occurs in *Apol.* i.67.

> And on the day called Sunday there is a meeting in one place of those who live in cities or the country, and the memoirs of the apostles or the writings of the prophets are read as long as time permits. When the reader has finished, the president in a discourse urges and invites us to the imitation of these noble things.[4]

Whether or not the order suggests that the Gospels were preferred to the Prophets, it is clear that they both were considered to be authoritative and equally enjoined upon the hearers. Notice further that each assembly

---

[1] I have used the translation in Vol. I of *The Ante-Nicene Fathers*, ed., A. Roberts and J. Donaldson (Grand Rapids: Wm. B. Eerdmans Publishing Co., 1956).

[2] I have used the translation by E.R. Hardy in *Early Christian Fathers*, ed., C.C. Richardson (Philadelphia: The Westminster Press, 1953).

[3] Roberts and Donaldson, again.

[4] E.R. Hardy, again. His careful study of the early Christian literary papyri has led C.H. Roberts to conclude: "This points to the careful and regular use of the scriptures by the local communities" (*Manuscript, Society and Belief in Early Christian Egypt* [London: Oxford Univ. Press, 1979], p. 25). He also infers from P. Oxy. iii. 405 that a copy of Irenaeus' *Adversus Haereses*, written in Lyons, was brought to Oxyrhynchus within a very few years after it was written (*Ibid.*, pp. 23, 53), eloquent testimony to the extent of the traffic among the early churches.

must have had its own copy of the apostles' writings to read from, and that such reading took place every week.

Athenagorus, in his "Plea", written in early 177, quotes Matthew 5:28 as Scripture: "...we are not even allowed to indulge in a lustful glance. For, says the Scripture, 'He who looks at a woman lustfully, has already committed adultery in his heart'" (32).[1] He similarly treats Matthew 19:9, or Mark 10:11, in 33.

Theophilus, bishop of Antioch, in his treatise to Autolycus, quotes 1 Timothy 2:1 and Romans 13:7 as "the Divine Word" (iii.14); quotes from the fourth Gospel, saying that John was "inspired by the Spirit" (ii.22); Isaiah and "the Gospel" are mentioned in one paragraph as Scripture (iii.14), and he insists in several passages that the writers never contradicted each other: "The statements of the Prophets and of the Gospels are found to be consistent, because all were inspired by the one Spirit of God" (ii.9; ii.35; iii.17).[2]

The surviving writings of Irenaeus (died in 202), his major work *Against Heretics* being written about 185, are about equal in volume to those of all the preceding Fathers put together.

> His testimony to the authority and inspiration of Holy Scripture is clear and unequivocal. It pervades the whole of his writings; and this testimony is more than ordinarily valuable because it must be regarded as directly representing three churches at least, those of Lyons, Asia Minor, and Rome. The authoritative use of both Testaments is clearly laid down.[3]

Irenaeus stated that the apostles taught that God is the Author of both Testaments (*Against Heretics* IV. 32.2) and evidently considered the New Testament writings to form a second Canon. He quoted from every chapter of Matthew, 1 Corinthians, Galatians, Ephesians, Colossians and Philippians, from all but one or two chapters of Luke, John, Romans, 2 Thessalonians, 1 and 2 Timothy, and Titus, from most chapters of Mark (including the last twelve verses), Acts, 2 Corinthians, and Revelation, and from every other book except Philemon and 3 John. These two books are so short that Irenaeus may not have had occasion to refer to them in his extant works—it does not necessarily follow that he was ignorant of them

---

[1] I have used the translation by C.C. Richardson in *Early Christian Fathers*.

[2] Taken from G.D. Barry, *The Inspiration and Authority of Holy Scripture* (New York: The McMillan Company, 1919), p. 52.

[3] *Ibid*., p. 53.

or rejected them. **Evidently the dimensions of the New Testament Canon recognized by Irenaeus are very close to what we hold today**.

From the time of Irenaeus on there can be no doubt concerning the attitude of the Church toward the New Testament writings—they are Scripture. Tertullian (in 208) said of the church at Rome, "the law and the prophets she unites in one volume with the writings of evangelists and apostles" (*Prescription against Heretics*, 36).

Attention please! The contribution of the evidence so far presented to our discussion is this: the implications of their attitude towards the Text. Whether or not someone today agrees with them is beside the point. The early Christians believed that the NT 'books' were divinely inspired, constituting a second Canon. As a consequence of their belief, they would treat those writings with care and respect.

Were Early Christians Careful?

It has been widely affirmed that the early Christians were either unconcerned or unable to watch over the purity of the text. (Recall Hort's words given above.) Again a review of the premises is called for. Many of the first believers had been devout Jews who had an ingrained reverence and care for the Old Testament Scriptures which extended to the very jots and tittles. This reverence and care would naturally be extended to the New Testament Scriptures.

Why should modern critics assume that the early Christians, in particular the spiritual leaders among them, were inferior in integrity or intelligence? A Father's quoting from memory, or tailoring a passage to suit his purpose in sermon or letter, by no means implies that he would take similar liberties when transcribing a book or corpus. Ordinary honesty would require him to produce a faithful copy. Are we to assume that everyone who made copies of New Testament books in those early years was a knave, or a fool? Paul was certainly as intelligent a man as any of us. If Hebrews was written by someone else, here was another man of high spiritual insight and intellectual power. There was Barnabas and Apollos and Clement and Polycarp, etc., etc. The Church has had men of reason and intelligence all down through the years. Starting out with what they **knew** to be the pure text, the earliest Fathers did not need to be textual critics. They had only to be reasonably honest and careful. But is there not good reason to believe they would be **especially** watchful and careful?

The apostles

Not only did the apostles themselves declare the New Testament writings to be Scripture, which would elicit reverence and care in their treatment, they expressly warned the believers to be on their guard against false teachers. Consider Acts 20:28-31. "So take heed to yourselves and to all the flock, in which the Holy Spirit has placed you as overseers, to shepherd the congregation of the Lord and God[1] which He purchased with His own blood. Because I know this, that after my departure savage wolves will come in among you, not sparing the flock. Yes, men will rise up from among you yourselves, speaking distorted things, to draw away the disciples after them. Therefore be alert." Could Paul be any clearer?

Now consider Galatians 1:6-9. "I am sadly surprised that you are turning away so quickly from the one who called you by the grace of Christ, to a different gospel—it is not a mere variation, but certain people are unsettling you and wanting to distort the Gospel of the Christ. Now even if we, or an angel out of heaven, should preach any other gospel to you than what we have preached to you, let him be accursed! As we have just said, I here emphatically repeat: If anyone preaches any other gospel to you than what you have received, let him be accursed!!"[2] Could Paul be any more emphatic? Note that Paul is claiming to be competent to define the only true Gospel of Christ, and he could only do so genuinely by divine inspiration.

Now consider 2 Peter 2:1-2. "However, there were also false prophets among the people, just as, indeed, there will be false teachers among you, who will introduce destructive heresies, even denying the Owner who bought them (bringing on themselves swift destruction). And many will follow their licentious ways, because of which the way of the Truth will be defamed." Peter warned the believers to be on their guard against false teachers.

And then there is 2 John 7 and 9-11. "Now many deceivers have come into the world,[3] who do not acknowledge Jesus Christ as coming in

---

[1] The sheep belong to the Lord, not to the elders. Some 7% of the Greek manuscripts omit 'the Lord and', as in most versions. "The Lord and God" refers to Jesus.

[2] 'Other gospels' would seem to be in plentiful supply; those who promote them are under a curse.

[3] Some 82% of the Greek manuscripts have "come into" rather than 'go out into' (as in most versions). The 18% presumably have the deceivers going out from the church into the world, but that is not John's point. The deceivers have been introduced into the world by Satan, the original and boss deceiver.

flesh[1]—this is the deceiver, even the Antichrist!" "Anyone who turns aside and does not continue in the teaching of Christ does not have God; but whoever continues in Christ's teaching does have both the Father and the Son. If anyone comes to you and does not bring this teaching, do not receive him into your house; do not even tell him, "I wish you well", because whoever tells him, "I wish you well", participates in his malignant works."[2] Some might feel that John's language is a little strong, but he was definitely warning them. Going back to verse 7, The Text has "coming", not 'having come', so evidently John is referring to Christ's second coming, which will certainly be "in flesh". Recall the word of the angels in Acts 1:11.

Peter's statement concerning the "twisting" that Paul's words were receiving (2 Peter 3:16) suggests that there was awareness and concern as to the text and the way it was being handled. I recognize that the Apostles were focusing on the interpretation rather than the copying of the text, and yet, since any alteration of the text may result in a different interpretation we may reasonably infer that their concern for the truth would include the faithful transmission of the text.

Indeed, we could scarcely ask for a clearer expression of this concern than that given in Revelation 22:18-19. "I myself testify to everyone who hears the words of the prophecy of this book: If any one adds to them, may God add to him the seven plagues written in this book! And if anyone takes away from the word**s**[3] of the book of this prophecy, may God remove his share from the tree of life and out of the Holy City, that stand written in this book!" Since it is the glorified Christ who is speaking, would not any true follower of His pay careful attention?

---

[1] Recall the word of the angels in Acts 1:11, "This very Jesus who is being taken up from you into the sky, He will come again in the precise manner that you observed Him going into the sky." The angels are emphatic; the return is going to be just like the departure. I take it that the Lord will return with the same glorified human body, visibly, come out of a cloud, and His feet will touch down at the same spot where they left (see Matthew 24:30, "coming on the clouds", and Zechariah 14:4, "His feet will stand on the Mount of Olives").

[2] People who do not believe and teach what Christ taught are on the other side. To be malignant is to be aggressively evil. Obviously, we should avoid anything that might be interpreted as identification with such people.

[3] "Words", plural, includes the individual words that make up the whole. Those textual critics who have wantonly removed words from the Text, on the basis of satanically inspired presuppositions, are out. Those who interpret the Text in such a way as to avoid its plain meaning, likewise. Jehovah the Son affirms that the words are "true and **faithful**", and He expects us to interpret them that way.

Sovereign Jesus clearly expressed this protective concern early in His earthly ministry. In Matthew 5:19 we read: "whoever annuls one of the least of these commandments, and teaches men so…" Note, "one of the least"; the Lord's concern extends down to "the least".

The early leaders

The early leaders furnish a few helpful clues as to the state of affairs in their day. The letters of Ignatius contain several references to a considerable traffic between the churches (of Asia Minor, Greece and Rome) by way of messengers (often official), which seems to indicate a deep sense of solidarity binding them together, and a wide circulation of news and attitudes—a problem with a heretic in one place would soon be known all over, etc. That there was strong feeling about the integrity of the Scriptures is made clear by Polycarp (7:1), "Whoever perverts the sayings of the Lord… that one is the firstborn of Satan". Present-day critics may not like Polycarp's terminology, but for him to use such strong language makes clear that he was not merely aware and concerned; he was exercised.

Similarly, Justin Martyr says (*Apol.* i.58), "the wicked demons have also put forward Marcion of Pontus". Again, such strong language makes clear that he was aware and concerned. And in *Trypho* xxxv he says of heretics teaching doctrines of the spirits of error, that fact "causes us who are disciples of the true and pure doctrine of Jesus Christ to be more faithful and steadfast in the hope announced by Him."

It seems obvious that heretical activity would have precisely the effect of putting the faithful on their guard and forcing them to define in their own minds what they were going to defend. Thus Marcion's truncated canon evidently stirred the faithful to define the true canon. But Marcion also altered the wording of Luke and Paul's Epistles, and by their bitter complaints it is clear that the faithful were both aware and concerned. We may note in passing that the heretical activity also furnishes backhanded evidence that the New Testament writings were regarded as Scripture—why bother falsifying them if they had no authority?

Dionysius, Bishop of Corinth (168-176), complained that his own letters had been tampered with, and worse yet the Holy Scriptures also.

And they insisted that they had received a pure tradition. Thus Irenaeus said that the doctrine of the apostles had been handed down by the succession of bishops, being guarded and preserved, without any forging of the Scriptures, allowing neither addition nor curtailment, involving public reading without falsification (*Against Heretics* IV. 32:8).

Tertullian, also, says of his right to the New Testament Scriptures, "I hold sure title-deeds from the original owners themselves... I am the heir of the apostles. Just as they carefully prepared their will and testament, and committed it to a trust... even so I hold it."[1]

Irenaeus

> In order to ensure accuracy in transcription, authors would sometimes add at the close of their literary works an adjuration directed to future copyists. So, for example, Irenaeus attached to the close of his treatise *On the Ogdoad* the following note: "I adjure you who shall copy out this book, by our Lord Jesus Christ and by his glorious advent when he comes to judge the living and the dead, that you compare what you transcribe, and correct it carefully against this manuscript from which you copy; and also that you transcribe this adjuration and insert it in the copy."[2]

If Irenaeus took such extreme precautions for the accurate transmission of his own work, how much more would he be concerned for the accurate copying of the Word of God? In fact, he demonstrates his concern for the accuracy of the text by defending the traditional reading of a **single letter**. The question is whether John the Apostle wrote *χξς'* (666) or *χις'* (616) in Revelation 13:18. Irenaeus asserts that 666 is found "in all the most approved and ancient copies" and that "those men who saw John face to face" bear witness to it. And he warns those who made the change (of a single letter) that "there shall be no light punishment upon him who either adds or subtracts anything from the Scripture" (xxx.1). Presumably Irenaeus is applying Revelation 22:18-19.

Considering Polycarp's intimacy with John, his personal copy of Revelation would most probably have been taken from the Autograph. And considering Irenaeus' veneration for Polycarp his personal copy of Revelation was probably taken from Polycarp's. Although Irenaeus evidently was no longer able to refer to the Autograph (not ninety years after it was written!) he was clearly in a position to identify a faithful copy and to declare with certainty the original reading—this in 186 AD. Which brings us to Tertullian.

---

1 *Prescription against Heretics*, 37. I have used the translation done by Peter Holmes in Vol. III of *The Ante-Nicene Fathers*.

2 B.M. Metzger, *The Text of the New Testament* (London: Oxford University Press, 1964), p. 21.

Tertullian

Around the year 208 he urged the heretics to

> run over the apostolic churches, in which the very thrones of the apostles are still pre-eminent in their places, in which their own authentic writings (*authenticae*) are read, uttering the voice and representing the face of each of them severally. Achaia is very near you, (in which) you find Corinth. Since you are not far from Macedonia, you have Philippi; (and there too) you have the Thessalonians. Since you are able to cross to Asia, you get Ephesus. Since, moreover, you are close upon Italy, you have Rome, from which there comes even into our own hands the very authority (of the apostles themselves).[1]

Some have thought that Tertullian was claiming that Paul's Autographs were still being read in his day (208), but at the very least he must mean they were using faithful copies. Was anything else to be expected? For example, when the Ephesian Christians saw the Autograph of Paul's letter to them getting tattered, would they not carefully execute an identical copy for their continued use, and which would have a declaration that it had been authenticated? Would they let the Autograph perish without making such a copy? (There must have been a constant stream of people coming either to make copies of their letter or to verify the correct reading.) I believe we are obliged to conclude that in the year 200 the Ephesian Church was still in a position to attest the original wording of her letter (and so for the others)—but this is coeval with P^{46}, P^{66} and P^{75}!

Both Justin Martyr and Irenaeus claimed that the Church was spread throughout the whole earth, in their day—remember that Irenaeus, in 177, became bishop of Lyons, in **Gaul**, and he was not the first bishop in that area. Coupling this information with Justin's statement that the memoirs of the apostles were read each Sunday in the assemblies, it becomes clear that there must have been thousands of copies of the New Testament writings in use by 200 AD Each assembly would need at least one copy to read from, and there must have been private copies among those who could afford them.

We have objective historical evidence in support of the following propositions:

- The true text was never 'lost'.

[1] *Prescription against Heretics*, 36, using Holmes' translation.

- In AD 200 the exact original wording of the several books could still be verified and attested.
- There was therefore no need to practice textual criticism and any such effort would be spurious.

The discipline of textual criticism (of whatever text) is predicated on the assumption/allegation/declaration that there is a legitimate doubt about the precise original wording of a text. No one does textual criticism on the 1611 King James Bible, for example, since copies of the original printing still exist. With reference to New Testament textual criticism, the crucial point at issue is the preservation of its Text. **For any text to have objective authority, we have to know what it is.**

But to continue, presumably some areas would be in a better position to protect and transmit the true text than others.

Who Was Best Qualified?

What factors would be important for guaranteeing, or at least facilitating, a faithful transmission of the text of the N.T. writings? I submit that there are four controlling factors: access to the Autographs, proficiency in the source language, the strength of the Church and an appropriate attitude toward the Text.

Access to the Autographs

This criterion probably applied for well less than a hundred years (the Autographs were presumably worn to a frazzle in that space of time) but it is highly significant to a proper understanding of the history of the transmission of the Text. Already by the year 100 there must have been many copies of the various books (some more than others) while it was certainly still possible to check a copy against the original, or a guaranteed copy, should a question arise.[1] The point is that there was a swelling stream of faithfully executed copies emanating from the holders of the Autographs to the rest of the Christian world. In those early years the producers of copies would know that the true wording could be verified, which would discourage them from taking liberties with the text.

However, distance would presumably be a factor—for someone in north Africa to consult the Autograph of Ephesians would be an expensive proposition, in both time and money. I believe we may reasonably conclude that in general the quality of copies would be highest in the area

[1] But see the section above, where I suggest the possibility that the Autographs started out as multiple copies.

surrounding the Autograph and would gradually deteriorate as the distance increased. Important geographical barriers would accentuate the tendency.

So who held the Autographs? Speaking in terms of regions, Asia Minor may be safely said to have had twelve (John, Galatians, Ephesians, Colossians, 1 and 2 Timothy, Philemon, 1 Peter, 1 and 2 and 3 John, and Revelation), Greece may be safely said to have had six (1 and 2 Corinthians, Philippians, 1 and 2 Thessalonians, and Titus in Crete), Rome may be safely said to have had two (Mark and Romans)—as to the rest, Luke, Acts, and 2 Peter were probably held by either Asia Minor or Rome; Matthew and James by either Asia Minor or Palestine; Hebrews by Rome or Palestine; while it is hard to state even a probability for Jude it was quite possibly held by Asia Minor. Taking Asia Minor and Greece together, the Aegean area held the Autographs of at least eighteen (two-thirds of the total) and possibly as many as twenty-four of the twenty-seven New Testament books; Rome held at least two and possibly up to seven; Palestine may have held up to three (but in AD 70 they would have been sent away for safe keeping, quite possibly to Antioch); Alexandria (Egypt) held **none**.

The Aegean region clearly had the best start, and Alexandria the worst—the text in Egypt could only be second hand, at best. On the face of it, we may reasonably assume that in the earliest period of the transmission of the NT Text the most reliable copies would be circulating in the region that held the Autographs. Recalling the discussion of Tertullian above, I believe we may reasonably extend this conclusion to AD 200 and beyond. So, in the year 200 someone looking for the best text of the NT would presumably go to the Aegean area; certainly not to Egypt.[1]

Proficiency in the source language

As a linguist (PhD) and one who has dabbled in the Bible translation process for some years, I affirm that a 'perfect' translation is impossible. (Indeed, a tolerably reasonable approximation is often difficult enough to achieve—the semantic areas of the words simply do not match, or only in part.) It follows that any divine solicitude for the precise form of the NT

---

[1] Aland states: "Egypt was distinguished from other provinces of the Church, so far as we can judge, by the early dominance of Gnosticism". He further informs us that "at the close of the 2nd century" the Egyptian church was "dominantly gnostic" and then goes on to say: "The copies existing in the gnostic communities could not be used, because they were under suspicion of being corrupt". Now this is all very instructive—what Aland is telling us, in other words, is that up to AD 200 the textual tradition in Egypt **could not be trusted**. (K. and B. Aland, p. 59 and K. Aland, "The Text of the Church?", *Trinity Journal*, 1987, 8NS:138.)

Text would have to be mediated through the language of the Autographs—Koine Greek. Evidently ancient Versions (Syriac, Latin, Coptic) may cast a clear vote with reference to major variants, but precision is possible only in Greek (in the case of the NT). That by way of background, but our main concern here is with the copyists.

To copy a text by hand in a language you do not understand is a tedious exercise—it is almost impossible to produce a perfect copy (try it and see!). You virtually have to copy letter by letter and constantly check your place. (It is even more difficult if there is no space between words and no punctuation, as was the case with the NT Text in the early centuries.) But if you cannot understand the text it is very difficult to remain alert. Consider the case of P^{66}. This papyrus manuscript is perhaps the oldest (c. 200) extant NT manuscript of any size (it contains most of John). It is one of the worst copies we have. It has an average of roughly two mistakes per verse—many being obvious mistakes, stupid mistakes, nonsensical mistakes. From the pattern of mistakes it is clear that the scribe copied syllable by syllable. I have no qualms in affirming that the person who produced P^{66} did not know Greek. Had he understood the text he would not have made the number and sort of mistakes that he did.

Now consider the problem from God's point of view. To whom should He entrust the primary responsibility for the faithful transmission of the NT Text (recall 1 Chronicles 16:15)? If the Holy Spirit was going to take an active part in the process, where should He concentrate His efforts? Presumably fluent speakers of Greek would have the inside track, and areas where Greek would continue in active use would be preferred. For a faithful transmission to occur the copyists had to be proficient in Greek, and over the long haul. So where was Greek predominant? Evidently in Greece and Asia Minor; Greek is the mother tongue of Greece to this day (having changed considerably during the intervening centuries, as any living language must). The dominance of Greek in the Aegean area was guaranteed by the Byzantine Empire for many centuries; in fact, until the invention of printing. Constantinople fell to the Ottoman Turks in 1453; the Gutenberg Bible (Latin) was printed just three years later, while the first printed Greek New Testament appeared in 1516. (For those who believe in Providence, I would suggest that here we have a powerful case in point.)

How about Egypt? The use of Greek in Egypt was already declining by the beginning of the Christian era. Bruce Metzger observes that the Hellenized section of the population in Egypt "was only a fraction in comparison with the number of native inhabitants who used only the Egyptian languages".[1] By the third century the decline was evidently well advanced. I have already argued that the copyist who did P^{66} (c. 200) did not know Greek. Now consider the case of P^{75} (c. 220). E.C. Colwell analyzed P^{75} and found about 145 itacisms plus 257 other singular readings, 25% of which are nonsensical. From the pattern of mistakes it is clear that the copyist who did P^{75} copied letter by letter![2] This means that he did not know Greek—when transcribing in a language you know you copy phrase by phrase, or at least word by word. K. Aland argues that before 200 the tide had begun to turn against the use of Greek in the areas that spoke Latin, Syriac or Coptic, and fifty years later the changeover to the local languages was well advanced.[3]

Again the Aegean Area is far and away the best qualified to transmit the Text with confidence and integrity. Note that even if Egypt had started out with a good text, already by the end of the 2nd century its competence to transmit the text was steadily deteriorating. In fact the early papyri (they come from Egypt) are demonstrably inferior in quality, taken individually, as well as exhibiting rather different types of text (they disagree among themselves).

The strength of the Church

This question is relevant to our discussion for two reasons. First, the law of supply and demand operates in the Church as well as elsewhere. Where there are many congregations and believers there will be an increased demand for copies of the Scriptures. Second, a strong, well established church will normally have a confident, experienced leadership—just the sort that would take an interest in the quality of their Scriptures and also be able to do something about it. So in what areas was the early Church strongest?

Although the Church evidently began in Jerusalem, the early persecutions and apostolic activity caused it to spread. The main line of advance seems to have been north into Asia Minor and west into Europe. If the selection of churches to receive the glorified Christ's "letters" (Revelation 2 and 3) is any guide, the center of gravity of the Church seems to have shifted from Palestine to Asia Minor by the end of the first century. (The

---

1 B.M. Metzger, *The Early Versions of the New Testament* (Oxford: Clarendon Press, 1977), p. 104.

2 E.C. Colwell, "Scribal Habits in Early Papyri: A Study in the Corruption of the text", *The Bible in Modern Scholarship*, ed. J.P. Hyatt (New York: Abingdon Press, 1955), pp. 374-76, 380.

3 K. and B. Aland, *The Text of the New Testament* (Grand Rapids: Eerdmans, 1981), pp. 52-53.

destruction of Jerusalem by Rome's armies in AD 70 would presumably have been a contributing factor.) Kurt Aland agrees with Adolf Harnack that "about 180 the greatest concentration of churches was in Asia Minor and along the Aegean coast of Greece". He continues: "The overall impression is that the concentration of Christianity was in the East... Even around AD 325 the scene was still largely unchanged. Asia Minor continued to be the heartland of the Church."[1] "The heartland of the Church"—so who else would be in a better position to certify the correct text of the New Testament?

What about Egypt? C.H. Roberts, in a scholarly treatment of the Christian literary papyri of the first three centuries, seems to favor the conclusion that the Alexandrian church was weak and insignificant to the Greek Christian world in the second century.[2] Aland states: "Egypt was distinguished from other provinces of the Church, so far as we can judge, by the early dominance of Gnosticism."[3] He further informs us that "at the close of the 2nd century" the Egyptian church was "dominantly gnostic" and then goes on to say: "The copies existing in the gnostic communities could not be used, because they were under suspicion of being corrupt".[4] Now this is all very instructive—what Aland is telling us, in other words, is that up to AD 200 the textual tradition in Egypt **could not be trusted**. Aland's assessment here is most probably correct. Notice what Bruce Metzger says about the early church in Egypt:

> Among the Christian documents which during the second century either originated in Egypt or circulated there among both the orthodox and the Gnostics are numerous apocryphal gospels, acts, epistles, and apocalypses... There are also fragments of exegetical and dogmatic works composed by Alexandrian Christians, chiefly Gnostics, during the second century... In fact, to judge by the comments made by Clement of Alexandria, almost every deviant Christian sect was represented in Egypt during the second century; Clement mentions the Valentinians, the Basilidians, the Marcionites, the Peratae, the Encratites, the Docetists, the Haimetites, the Cainites, the Ophites, the Simonians, and the Eutychites. What proportion of Christians in Egypt during the second century were orthodox is not known.[5]

---

[1] *Ibid.*, p. 53.

[2] C.H. Roberts, *Manuscript, Society and Belief in Early Christian Egypt* (London: Oxford University Press, 1979), pp. 42-43, 54-58.

[3] K. and B. Aland, p. 59.

[4] K. Aland, "The Text of the Church?", *Trinity Journal*, 1987, 8NS:138.

[5] Metzger, *Early Versions*, p. 101.

But we need to pause to reflect on the implications of Aland's statements. He was a champion of the Egyptian ('Alexandrian') text-type, and yet he himself informs us that up to AD 200 the textual tradition in Egypt could not be trusted and that by 200 the use of Greek had virtually died out there. So on what basis can he argue that the Egyptian text subsequently became the best? Aland also states that in the 2nd century, 3rd century, and into the 4th century Asia Minor continued to be "the heartland of the Church". This means that the superior qualifications of the Aegean area to protect, transmit and attest the N.T. Text carry over into the **4th century**! It happens that Hort, Metzger and Aland (along with many others) have linked the "Byzantine" text-type to Lucian of Antioch, who died in 311. Now really, wouldn't a text produced by a leader in "the heartland of the Church" be better than whatever evolved in Egypt? Of course I ask the above question only to point out their inconsistency. The 'Byzantine' text-type existed long before Lucian.

Attitude toward the Text

Where careful work is required, the attitude of those to whom the task is entrusted is of the essence. Are they aware? Do they agree? If they do not understand the nature of the task, the quality will probably do down. If they understand but do not agree, they might even resort to sabotage—a damaging eventuality. In the case of the NT books we may begin with the question: Why would copies be made?

We have seen that the faithful recognized the authority of the NT writings from the start, so the making of copies would have begun at once. The authors clearly intended their writings to be circulated, and the quality of the writings was so obvious that the word would get around and each assembly would want a copy. That Clement and Barnabas quote and allude to a variety of NT books by the turn of the 1st century makes clear that copies were in circulation. A Pauline corpus was known to Peter before AD 70. Polycarp (XIII) c. 115, in answer to a request from the Philippian church, sent a collection of Ignatius' letters to them, possibly within five years after Ignatius wrote them. Evidently it was normal procedure to make copies and collections (of worthy writings) so each assembly could have a set. Ignatius referred to the free travel and exchange between the churches and Justin to the weekly practice of reading the Scriptures in the assemblies (they had to have copies).

A second question would be: What was the attitude of the copyists toward their work? We already have the essence of the answer. Being followers of Christ, and believing that they were dealing with Scripture, to a basic honesty would be added reverence in their handling of the Text, from the start. And to these would be added vigilance, since the Apostles had repeatedly and emphatically warned them against false teachers. As the years went by, assuming that the faithful were persons of at least average integrity and intelligence, they would produce careful copies of the manuscripts they had received from the previous generation, persons whom they trusted, being assured that they were transmitting the true text. There would be accidental copying mistakes in their work, but no deliberate changes.

It is important to note that the earliest Christians did not need to be textual critics. Starting out with what they knew to be the pure text, they had only to be reasonably honest and careful. I submit that we have good reason for understanding that they were especially watchful and careful—this especially in the early decades. And in one line of transmission this continued to be the case. Having myself collated at least one book in over 120 MSS belonging to the line of transmission that I call Family 35, I hold a perfect copy of at least 22 of the 27 NT books, copies made in the 11th, 12th, 13th, 14th and 15th centuries. For a copy to be perfect in the 14th century, all of its 'ancestors' had to be perfect, all the way back to the family archetype. I believe that the archetype of Family 35 is the Autograph, but if not, it must date back to the 3rd century, at least.

As time went on regional attitudes developed, not to mention regional politics. The rise of the so-called 'school of Antioch' is a relevant consideration. Beginning with Theophilus, a bishop of Antioch who died around 185, the Antiochians began insisting upon the literal interpretation of Scripture. The point is that a literalist is obliged to be concerned about the precise wording of the text since his interpretation or exegesis hinges upon it.

It is reasonable to assume that this 'literalist' mentality would have influenced the churches of Asia Minor and Greece and encouraged them in the careful and faithful transmission of the pure text that they had received. For example, the extant MSS of the Syriac Peshitta are unparalleled for their consistency. (By way of contrast, the 8,000+ MSS of the Latin Vulgate are remarkable for their extensive discrepancies, and in this they follow the example of the Old Latin MSS.) It is not unreasonable to suppose that the Antiochian antipathy toward the Alexandrian allegorical interpretation of Scripture would rather indispose them to view with favor any competing forms of the text coming out of Egypt. Similarly the Quarto-deciman controversy with Rome would scarcely enhance the appeal of any innovations coming from the West.

To the extent that the roots of the allegorical approach that flourished in Alexandria during the third century were already present, they would also be a negative factor. Since Philo of Alexandria was at the height of his influence when the first Christians arrived there, it may be that his allegorical interpretation of the O.T. began to rub off on the young church already in the first century. Since an allegorist is going to impose his own ideas on the text anyway, he would presumably have fewer inhibitions about altering it—precise wording would not be a high priority.

The school of literary criticism that existed at Alexandria would also be a negative factor, if it influenced the Church at all, and W.R. Farmer argues that it did. "But there is ample evidence that by the time of Eusebius the Alexandrian text-critical practices were being followed in at least some of the scriptoria where New Testament manuscripts were being produced. Exactly when Alexandrian text-critical principles were first used... is not known."[1] He goes on to suggest that the Christian school founded in Alexandria by Pantaenus, around 180, was bound to be influenced by the scholars of the great library of that city. The point is, the principles used in attempting to 'restore' the works of Homer would not be appropriate for the NT writings when appeal to the Autographs, or exact copies made from them, was still possible.

Conclusion

What answer do the "four controlling factors" give to our question? The four speak with united voice: "The Aegean area was the best qualified to protect, transmit and attest the true text of the NT writings." This was true in the 2nd century; it was true in the 3rd century; it continued to be true in the 4th century. So in AD 350, the middle of the 4th century, where should we go to find the most correct copies of the NT? To the Aegean area; Egypt would be the last place to go. If the transmission of the NT Text was reasonably normal, the Aegean area would continue to have the best Text down through the succeeding centuries. But there are those who have argued that the transmission was not normal, so to that question I now turn.

Was the Transmission Normal?

Beginning with Saul of Tarsus, Christians were persecuted here and there throughout the Roman Empire until Constantine started relief in AD 312. The persecutions included the sporadic destruction of copies of the

---

1 W.R. Farmer, *The Last Twelve Verses of Mark* (Cambridge: University Press, 1974), pp. 14-15. He cites B.H. Streeter, *The Four Gospels: A Study of Origins* (London: Macmillan and Co., 1924), pp. 111, 122-23.

NT, in whole or in part, here and there. But in AD 303 Diocletian decreed the most severe persecution that Christianity had experienced, up to that point. It included the burning of the sacred books; they were to be destroyed, wherever found. Although the persecution was Empire-wide, it was especially severe in Asia Minor, where Christianity was the strongest, and it continued for at least ten years.

Many MSS were found, or betrayed, and burned, but others must have escaped. That many Christians would have spared no effort to hide and preserve their copies of the Scriptures is demonstrated by their attitude towards those who gave up their MSS—the Donatist schism that immediately followed Diocletian's campaign partly hinged on the question of punishment for those who had given up MSS. The Christians whose entire devotion to the Scriptures was thus demonstrated would also be just the ones that would be the most careful about the pedigree of their own MSS; just as they took pains to protect their MSS they presumably would have taken pains to ensure that their MSS preserved the true wording.

In fact, the campaign of Diocletian may even have had a purifying effect upon the transmission of the text. If the laxity of attitude toward the text reflected in the willingness of some to give up their MSS also extended to the quality of text they were prepared to use, then it may have been the more contaminated MSS that were destroyed, in the main, leaving the purer MSS to replenish the earth.[1] But these surviving pure MSS would have been in unusually heavy demand for copying (to replace those that had been destroyed) and been worn out faster than normal.

But to return to our question: Was the transmission normal? Yes and no. Assuming the faithful were persons of at least average integrity and intelligence they would produce reasonable copies of the manuscripts they had received from the previous generation, persons whom they trusted, being assured that they were transmitting the true text. There would be accidental copying mistakes in their work, but no deliberate changes. But there were others who expressed an interest in the New Testament writings, persons lacking in integrity, who made their own copies with malicious intent. There would be accidental mistakes in their work too, but also deliberate alteration of the text. I will trace first the normal transmission.

---

[1] Here was an excellent opportunity for the "Alexandrian" and "Western" texts to forge ahead and take 'space' away from the "Byzantine", but it did not happen. The Church rejected those types of text. How can modern critics possibly be in a better position to identify the true text than was the Church universal in the early 4th century?

The normal transmission

We have seen that the faithful recognized the authority of the New Testament writings from the start—had they not they would have been rejecting the authority of the Apostles, and hence not been among the faithful. To a basic honesty would be added reverence in their handling of the text, from the start. And to these would be added vigilance, since the Apostles had repeatedly and emphatically warned them against false teachers.

With an ever-increasing demand and consequent proliferation of copies throughout the Graeco-Roman world and with the potential for veryfying copies by having recourse to the centers still possessing the Autographs, the early textual situation was presumably highly favorable to the wide dissemination of MSS in close agreement with the original text. By the early years of the second century the dissemination of such copies can reasonably be expected to have been very widespread, with the logical consequence that the form of text they embodied would early become entrenched throughout the area of their influence.

The considerations just cited are crucial to an adequate understanding of the history of the transmission of the text because they indicate that a basic trend was established at the very beginning—a trend that would continue inexorably until the advent of a printed N.T. text. I say "inexorably" because, given a normal process of transmission, the science of statistical probability demonstrates that a text form in such circumstances could scarcely be dislodged from its dominant position—the probabilities against a competing text form ever achieving a majority attestation would be prohibitive no matter how many generations of MSS there might be.[1] It would take an extraordinary upheaval in the transmissional history to give currency to an aberrant text form. We know of no place in history that will accommodate such an upheaval.

The argument from probability would apply to secular writings as well as the New Testament and does not take into account any unusual concern for purity of text. I have argued, however, that the early Christians did have a special concern for their Scriptures and that this concern accompanied the spread of Christianity. Thus Irenaeus clearly took his concern for textual purity (which extended to a single letter) to Gaul and undoubtedly influenced the Christians in that area. The point is that the text form of the NT Autographs had a big advantage over that of any secular

---

[1] The demonstration vindicating my assertion is in Appendix C of my book, *The Identity of the New Testament Text IV*, available from Amazon.com as well as from my site, www.prunch.org.

literature, so that its commanding position would become even greater than the argument from probability would suggest, and all the more so if the Autographs were 'published' as multiple copies. The rapid multiplication and spread of good copies would raise to absolutely prohibitive levels the chances against an opportunity for aberrant text forms to gain any kind of widespread acceptance or use.[1]

It follows that within a relatively few years after the writing of the NT books there came rapidly into existence a 'Majority' text whose form was essentially that of the Autographs themselves. This text form would, in the natural course of things, continue to multiply itself and in each succeeding generation of copying would continue to be exhibited in the mass of extant manuscripts. In short, it would have a 'normal' transmission. The law of supply and demand operates within the Church, as well as elsewhere. True believers would be far more interested in obtaining copies of the NT writings than people who were not. Opponents of Christianity, who might attempt to confuse the issue by producing altered copies, would have a much smaller 'market' for their work.

The use of such designations as "Syrian", "Antiochian", and "Byzantine" for the Majority Text reflects its general association with that region. I know of no reason to doubt that the "Byzantine" text is in fact the form of the text that was known and transmitted in the Aegean area from the beginning.

In sum, I believe that the evidence clearly favors that interpretation of the history of the text which sees the normal transmission of the text as centered in the Aegean region, the area that was best qualified, from every point of view, to transmit the text, from the very first. The result of that

---

[1] I have avoided introducing any argument based on the providence of God, up to this point, because not all accept such argumentation and because the superiority of the Byzantine Text can be demonstrated without recourse to it. Thus, I believe the argument from statistical probability given above is valid as it stands. However, while I have not argued on the basis of Providence, I wish the reader to understand that I personally do not think that the preservation of the true text was so mechanistic as the discussion above might suggest. From the evidence previously adduced, it seems clear that a great many variant readings (perhaps most of the malicious ones) that existed in the second century simply have not survived—we have no extant witness to them. We may reasonably conclude that the early Christians were concerned and able watchdogs of the true text. I would like to believe that they were aided and abetted by the Holy Spirit. In that event, the security of the text is considerably greater than that suggested by probability alone, including the proposition that none of the original wording has been lost.

normal transmission is the "Byzantine" text-type. In every age, including the second and third centuries, it has been the traditional text.[1]

So then, I claim that the NT text had a normal transmission, namely the fully predictable spread and reproduction of reliable copies of the Autographs from the earliest period down through the history of transmission until the availability of printed texts brought copying by hand to an end.

The abnormal transmission[2]

Turning now to the abnormal transmission, it no doubt commenced right along with the normal. The apostolic writings themselves contain strong complaints and warning against heretical and malicious activity. As Christianity spread and began to make an impact on the world, not everyone accepted it as 'good news'. Opposition of various sorts arose. Also, there came to be divisions within the larger Christian community—in the NT itself notice is taken of the beginnings of some of these tangents. In some cases faithfulness to an ideological (theological) position evidently became more important than faithfulness to the NT Text. Certain it is that Church Fathers who wrote during the second century complained bitterly about the deliberate alterations to the Text perpetrated by 'heretics'. Large sections of the extant writings of the early Fathers are precisely and exclusively concerned with combating the heretics. It is clear that during the second century, and possibly already in the first, such persons produced many copies of NT writings incorporating their alterations.[3] Some apparently were quite widely circulated, for a time. The result was a welter of variant readings, to confuse the uninformed and mislead the unwary. Such a scenario was totally predictable. If the NT is in fact God's Word

---

[1] Within the broad Byzantine stream there are dozens of rivulets (recall that F. Wisse isolated 36 groups, which included 70 subgroups), but the largest distinct line of transmission is Family 35, the main stream, and it was specifically this family that God used to preserve the precise original wording. For more on this please see Part II.

[2] I have been accused of inconsistency in that I criticize W-H for treating the NT like any other book and yet myself claim a "normal transmission" for the Majority Text. Not at all; I am referring to a normal transmission of an inspired Text, which W-H denied. I refer to believers copying a text that **they** believed to be inspired. Further, I also recognize an 'abnormal transmission', whereas W-H did not. Fee seriously distorts my position by ignoring my discussion of the abnormal transmission (G.D. Fee, "A Critique of W.N. Pickering's *The Identity of the New testament Text*: A Review Article", *The Westminster Theological Journal*, XLI [Spring, 1979], pp. 404-08) and misstating my view of the normal transmission (*Ibid*., p. 399). I hold that 95% of the variants, the obvious transcriptional errors, belong (for the most part) to the normal transmission, whereas most of the remaining 5%, the 'significant' variants, belong to the abnormal transmission.

[3] J.W. Burgon, *The Revision Revised* (London: John Murray, 1883), pp. 323-24.

then both God and Satan must have a lively interest in its fortunes. To approach the textual criticism of the NT without taking due account of that interest is to act irresponsibly.

Most damage done by 200 AD

It is generally agreed that most significant variants existed by the end of the second century. "The overwhelming majority of readings were created before the year 200", affirmed Colwell.[1] "It is no less true to fact than paradoxical in sound that the worst corruptions to which the New Testament has ever been subjected, originated within a hundred years after it was composed", said Scrivener decades before.[2] Kilpatrick commented on the evidence of the earliest Papyri.

> Let us take our two manuscripts of about this date [AD 200] which contain parts of John, the Chester Beatty Papyrus and the Bodmer Papyrus. They are together extant for about seventy verses. Over these seventy verses they differ some seventy-three times apart from mistakes.
>
> Further in the Bodmer Papyrus the original scribe has frequently corrected what he first wrote. At some places he is correcting his own mistakes but at others he substitutes one form of phrasing for another. At about seventy-five of these substitutions both alternatives are known from other manuscripts independently. The scribe is in fact replacing one variant reading by another at some seventy places so that we may conclude that already in his day there was variation at these points.[3]

The Bodmer papyrus is P^{66}, and what Kilpatrick does not tell you is that in those 75 places the scribe was alternating between Byzantine and Alexandrian readings: sometimes he started with a Byzantine reading and then changed it to an Alexandrian and sometimes he did the opposite. He obviously had such exemplars before him, which means that the Byzantine Text was already in existence in the year 200!

---

[1] E.C. Colwell, "The Origin of Texttypes of New Testament Manuscripts", *Early Christian Origins*, ed. Allen Wikgren (Chicago: Quadrangle Books, 1961), p. 138.

[2] F.H.A. Scrivener, *A Plain Introduction to the Criticism of the New Testament*, fourth edition edited by E. Miller (2 Vols.; London: George Bell and Sons, 1894), II, 264.

[3] G.D. Kilpatrick, "The Transmission of the New Testament and its Reliability", *The Bible Translator*, IX (July, 1958), 128-29.

G. Zuntz also recognized all of this. "Modern criticism stops before the barrier of the second century; the age, so it seems, of unbounded liberties with the text".[1]

Kilpatrick goes on to argue that the creation of new variants ceased by about 200 AD because it became impossible to 'sell' them. He discusses some of Origen's attempts at introducing a change into the text, and proceeds:

> Origen's treatment of Matthew 19:19 is significant in two other ways. First he was probably the most influential commentator of the Ancient Church and yet his conjecture at this point seems to have influenced only one manuscript of a local version of the New Testament. The Greek tradition is apparently quite unaffected by it. From the third century onward even an Origen could not effectively alter the text.
>
> This brings us to the second significant point—his date. From the early third century onward the freedom to alter the text which had obtained earlier can no longer be practiced. Tatian is the last author to make deliberate changes in the text of whom we have explicit information. Between Tatian and Origen Christian opinion had so changed that it was no longer possible to make changes in the text whether they were harmless or not.[2]

He feels this attitude was a reaction against the re-handling of the text by the second-century heretics. Certainly there had been a great hue and cry, and whatever the reason it does appear that little further damage was done after AD 200.[3] However, I certainly disagree with Kilpatrick's "freedom to alter the text which had obtained earlier"; there was no such 'freedom', it was the perversity of enemies of the Truth.

The aberrant text forms

The extent of the textual difficulties of the 2nd century can easily be exaggerated. Nevertheless, the evidence cited does prove that aberrant forms of the NT text were produced. Naturally, some of those text forms may have acquired a local and temporary currency, but they could scarcely become more than eddies along the edge of the 'majority' river. Recall that

---

[1] G. Zuntz, *The Text of the* Epistles (London: Oxford University Press, 1953), p. 11.

[2] Kilpatrick, "Atticism and the Text of the Greek New Testament", *Neutestamentliche Aufsatze* (Regensburg: Verlag Friedrich Pustet, 1963), pp. 129-30.

[3] I believe we may reasonably understand that significant variants that first appear at a later date, within extant MSS, had actually been created much earlier.

the possibility of checking against the Autographs, or guaranteed copies, must have served to inhibit the spread of such text forms.

For example, Gaius, an orthodox Father who wrote near the end of the second century, named four heretics who not only altered the text but had disciples who multiplied copies of their efforts. Of special interest here is his charge that they could not deny their guilt because they could not produce the originals from which they made their copies.[1] This would be a hollow accusation from Gaius if he could not produce the Originals either. I have already argued that the churches in Asia Minor, for instance, did still have either the Autographs or exact copies that they themselves had made—thus they **knew**, absolutely, what the true wording was and could repel the aberrant forms with confidence. A man like Polycarp would still be able to affirm in 150 AD, letter by letter if need be, the original wording of the text for most of the New Testament books. And presumably his MSS were not burned when he was.

Not only would there have been pressure from the Autographs, but also the pressure exerted by the already-established momentum of transmission enjoyed by the majority text form. As already discussed, the statistical probabilities militating against any aberrant text forms would be overwhelming. In short, although a bewildering array of variants came into existence, judging from extant witnesses, and they were indeed a perturbing influence in the stream of transmission, they would not succeed in thwarting the progress of the normal transmission.

The Stream of Transmission

Now then, what sort of a picture may we expect to find in the surviving witnesses on the assumption that the history of the transmission of the New Testament Text was predominantly normal? We may expect a broad spectrum of copies, showing minor differences due to copying mistakes but all reflecting one common tradition. The simultaneous existence of abnormal transmission in the earliest centuries would result in a sprinkling of copies, helter-skelter, outside of that main stream. The picture would look something like *Figure A*.

The MSS within the cones represent the "normal" transmission. To the left I have plotted some possible representatives of what we might style the "irresponsible" transmission of the text—the copyists produced poor copies through incompetence or carelessness but did not make deliberate changes. To the right I have plotted some possible representatives of what

---

[1] Cf. Burgon, *The Revision Revised*, p. 323.

we might style the "fabricated" transmission of the text—the scribes made deliberate changes in the text (for whatever reasons), producing fabricated copies, not true copies. I am well aware that the MSS plotted on the figure below contain both careless and deliberate errors, in different proportions (7Q5, 4, 8 and $P^{52,64,67}$ are too fragmentary to permit the classification of their errors as deliberate rather than careless), so that any classification such as I attempt here must be relative and gives a distorted picture. Still, I venture to insist that ignorance, carelessness, officiousness and malice all left their mark upon the transmission of the New Testament text, and we must take account of them in any attempt to reconstruct the history of that transmission.

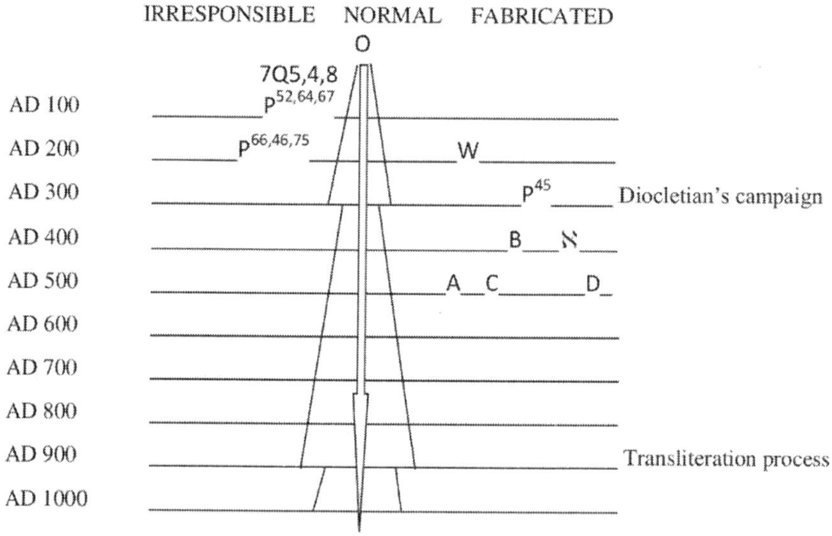

Figure A[1]

As the figure suggests, I argue that Diocletian's campaign had a purifying effect upon the stream of transmission. In order to withstand torture rather than give up your MS(S), you would have to be a truly committed believer, the sort of person who would want good copies of the Scriptures. Thus it was probably the more contaminated MSS that were destroyed, in the main, leaving the purer MSS to replenish the earth.[2] The arrow within the cones represents Family 35 (see Part II below).

---

[1] The history of the place where Codex W was found suggests that it must have been copied before AD 200: it was found in the ruins of a town that was abandoned in 200 AD when its water dried up. That town is in an isolated area surrounded by desert. Since W shows Byzantine influence, that text-type already existed in the second century,.

[2] For a fuller discussion of this point please see the section "Imperial repression of the

Another consideration suggests itself—if, as reported, the Diocletian campaign was most fierce and effective in the Byzantine area, the numerical advantage of the 'Byzantine' text-type over the 'Western' and 'Alexandrian' would have been reduced, giving the latter a chance to forge ahead. But it did not happen. The Church, in the main, refused to propagate those forms of the Greek text.

What we find upon consulting the witnesses is just such a picture. We have the Majority Text (Aland), or the Traditional Text (Burgon), dominating the stream of transmission with a few individual witnesses going their idiosyncratic ways. In Chapter 4 of my *Identity IV* I demonstrate that the notion of 'text-types' and recensions, as defined and used by Hort and his followers, is gratuitous. Epp's notion of 'streams' fares no better. There is just one stream (actually a river), with a number of small eddies along the edges.[1] When I say the Majority Text dominates the stream, I mean it is represented in about 95% of the MSS.[2]

Actually, such a statement is not altogether satisfactory because it does not allow for the mixture or shifting affinities encountered within individual MSS. A better, though more cumbersome, way to describe the situation would be something like this: 100% of the MSS agree as to, say, 50% of the Text; 99% agree as to another 40%; over 95% agree as to another 4%; over 90% agree as to another 2%; over 80% agree as to another 2%; only for 2% or so of the Text do less than 80% of the MSS agree, and a disproportionate number of those cases occur in Revelation.[3]

N.T." in Chapter 6 of my book, *The Identity of the New Testament Text IV.*, available from Amazon.com as well as from my site, www.prunch.org.

[1] One might speak of a P^{45}, W eddy or a P^{75}, B eddy, for example.

[2] Although I used, of necessity, the term 'text-type' in some of my writings, I view the Majority Text as being much broader. It is a textual tradition which might be said to include a number of related 'text-types', such as von Soden's K^a, K^i, and K^l. I wish to emphasize again that it is only agreement in error that determines genealogical relationships. It follows that the concepts of 'genealogy' and 'text-type' are irrelevant with reference to original readings—they are only useful (when employed properly) for identifying spurious readings. Well, if there is a family that very nearly reflects the original its 'profile' or mosaic of readings will distinguish it from all other families, but most of those readings will not be errors (the competing variants distinctive of other families will be errors).

[3] I am not prepared to defend the precise figures used, they are **guesses**, but I believe they represent a reasonable approximation to reality. I heartily agree with Colwell when he insists that we must "rigorously eliminate the singular reading" ("External Evidence and New Testament Criticism", *Studies in the History of the Text of the New Testament*, ed. B.L. Daniels and M.J. Suggs [Salt Lake City: University of Utah Press, 1967], p. 8) on the altogether reasonable assumption (it seems to me) that a solitary witness against the world cannot possibly be right.

And the membership of the dissenting group varies from reading to reading.[1] Still, with the above reservation, one may reasonably speak of up to 95% of the extant MSS belonging to the Majority textual tradition.

I see no way of accounting for a 95% (or 90%) domination unless that text goes back to the Autographs. Hort saw the problem and invented a revision. Sturz seems not to have seen the problem. He demonstrates that the "Byzantine text-type" is early and independent of the "Western" and "Alexandrian text-types", and like von Soden, wishes to treat them as three equal witnesses.[2] But if the three "text-types" were equal, how could the so-called "Byzantine" ever gain a 90-95% preponderance?

The argument from statistical probability enters here with a vengeance. Not only do the extant MSS present us with one text form enjoying a 95% majority, but the remaining 5% do not represent a single competing text form. The minority MSS disagree as much (or more) among themselves as they do with the majority. For any two of them to agree so closely as do P^{75} and B is an oddity. We are not judging, therefore, between two text forms, one representing 95% of the MSS and the other 5%. Rather, we have to judge between 95% and a fraction of 1% (comparing the Majority Text with the P^{75},B text form for example). Or to take a specific case, in 1 Timothy 3:16 some 600 Greek MSS (besides the Lectionaries) read "God" while only nine read something else. Of those nine, three have private readings and six agree in reading "who".[3] So we have to judge

---

[1] I will of course be reminded that witnesses are to be weighed, not counted; for my discussion of that point please see the section "Should not witnesses be weighed, rather than counted?" in Chapter 6 of my *Identity IV*.

[2] Sturz, *Op. Cit.* A text produced by taking two 'text-types' against one would move the UBS text about 80% of the distance toward the Majority text.

[3] The readings, with their supporting MSS, are as follows:

ο – D

ω – 061

ος Θεος – one cursive, 256 (and one Lectionary)

ος – ℵ, 33, 365, 442, 1175, 2127 (plus three Lectionaries)

Θεος – A,C^{vid},F/G^{vid}, K, L, P, Ψ, some 600 cursives (besides Lectionaries) (including four cursives that read *ο Θεος* and one Lectionary that reads *Θεου*).

It will be observed that my statement differs from that of the UBS text, for example. I offer the following explanation.

Young, Huish, Pearson, Fell, and Mill in the seventeenth century, Creyk, Bentley, Wotton, Wetstein, Bengel, Berriman, and Woide in the eighteenth, and Scrivener as late as 1881 all affirmed, upon careful inspection, that Codex A reads "God". For a thorough discussion please see Burgon, who says concerning Woide, "The learned and conscientious editor of the Codex declares that so late as 1765 he had seen traces of the *Θ* which twenty years later (viz. in 1785) were visible to him no longer" (*The Revision Revised*, p.

434. Cf. pp. 431-36). It was only after 1765 that scholars started to question the reading of A (through fading and wear the middle line of the *theta* is no longer discernible).

H.C. Hoskier devotes Appendix J of *A Full Account and Collation of the Greek Codex Evangelium 604* (London: David Nutt, 1890) (the appendix being a reprint of part of an article that appeared in the *Clergyman's Magazine* for February 1887) to a careful discussion of the reading of Codex C. He spent three hours examining the passage in question in this MS (the MS itself) and adduces evidence that shows clearly, I believe, that the original reading of C is "God". He examined the surrounding context and observes, "The **contracting-bar** has often vanished completely (I believe, from a cursory examination, more often than not), but at other times it is plain and imposed in the same way as at 1 Timothy iii.16" (Appendix J, p. 2). See also Burgon, *Ibid.*, pp. 437-38.

Codices F/G read *OC* wherein the contracting-bar is a slanting stroke. It has been argued that the stroke represents the aspirate of *ος*, but Burgon demonstrates that the stroke in question never represents breathing but is invariably the sign of contraction and affirms that "*ος* is **nowhere** else written *OC* [with a cross-bar] in either codex" (*Ibid.*, p. 442. Cf. pp. 438-42). Presumably the cross-line in the common parent had become too faint to see. As for cursive 365, Burgon conducted an exhaustive search for it. He not only failed to find it but could find no evidence that it had ever existed (*Ibid.*, pp. 444-45) [I have recently been informed that it was later rediscovered by Gregory].

(I took up the case of 1 Timothy 3:16, in the first edition of my book, *Identity*, solely to illustrate the argument from probability, not as an example of "how to do textual criticism" [cf. Fee, "A Critique", p. 423]. Since the question has been raised, I will add a few words on that subject.)

The three significant variants involved are represented in the ancient uncial MSS as follows: O, OC, and *Θ*C (with a contracting-bar above the two letters), meaning "which", "who", and "God" respectively. In writing "God" a scribe's omitting of the two lines (through haste or momentary distraction) would result in "who". Codices A, C, F, and G have numerous instances where either the cross-line or the contracting-bar is no longer discernible (either the original line has faded to the point of being invisible or the scribe may have failed to write it in the first place). For both lines to fade away, as in Codex A here, is presumably an infrequent event. For a scribe to inadvertently omit both lines would presumably also be an infrequent event, but it must have happened at least once, probably early in the second century and in circumstances that produced a wide ranging effect.

The collocation "the mystery… who" is even more pathologic in Greek than it is in English. It was thus inevitable, once such a reading came into existence and became known, that remedial action would be attempted. Accordingly, the first reading above, "the mystery… which", is generally regarded as an attempt to make the difficult reading intelligible. But it must have been an early development, for it completely dominates the Latin tradition, both version and Fathers, as well as being the probable reading of the Syr^{p} and Coptic versions. It is found in only one Greek MS, Codex D, and in no Greek Father before the fifth century.

Most modern scholars regard "God" as a separate therapeutic response to the difficult reading. Although it dominates the Greek MSS (over 98 percent), it is certainly attested by only two versions, the Georgian and Slavonic (both late). But it also dominates the Greek Fathers. Around AD 100 there are possible allusions in Barnabas, "*Ιησους ... ο υιος του Θεου τυπω και εν σαρκι φανερωθεις*" (Cap. xii), and in Ignatius, "*Θεου ανθρωπινως φανερουμενου*" (*Ad Ephes.* c. 19) and "*εν σαρκι γενομενος Θεος*" (*Ibid.*, c. 7). In the between 98.5% and 1%, "God" versus "who". It is hard to imagine any possible set of circumstances in the transmissional history sufficient to produce the cataclysmic overthrow in statistical probability required by the claim that "who" is the original reading.

It really does seem that those scholars who reject the Majority Text are faced with a serious problem. How is it to be explained if it does not reflect the Original? Hort's notion of a Lucianic revision has been abandoned by most scholars because of the total lack of historical evidence. The eclecticists are not even trying. The "process" view has not been articulated in sufficient detail to permit refutation, but on the face of it that view is flatly contradicted by the argument from statistical probability.[1] How could any amount of 'process' bridge the gap between B or Aleph and the TR?

---

third century there seem to be clear references in Hippolytus, "*Θεος εν σωματι εφανερωθη*" (*Contra Haeresim Noeti*, c. xvii), Dionysius, "*Θεος γαρ εφανερωθη εν σαρκι*" (*Concilia*, i. 853a) and Gregory Thaumaturgus, "*και εστιν Θεος αληθινος ο ασαρκος εν σαρκι φανερωθεις*" (quoted by Photius). In the 4th century there are clear quotes or references in Gregory of Nyssa (22 times), Gregory of Nazianzus, Didymus of Alexandria, Diodorus, the Apostolic Constitutions, and Chrysostom, followed by Cyril of Alexandria, Theodoret, and Euthalius in the fifth century, and so on (Burgon, *Ibid*, pp. 456-76, 486-90).

As for the grammatically aberrant reading, "who", aside from the MSS already cited, the earliest version that clearly supports it is the gothic (fourth century). To get a clear Greek Patristic witness to this reading pretty well requires the sequence *μυστηριον ος εφανερωθη*, since after any reference to Christ, Savior, Son of God, etc. in the prior context the use of a relative clause is predictable. Burgon affirmed that he was aware of no such testimony (and his knowledge of the subject has probably never been equaled) (*Ibid.*, p. 483).

It thus appears that the "Western" and "Byzantine" readings have earlier attestation than does the "Alexandrian". Yet if "which" was caused by "who", then the latter must be older. The reading "who" is admittedly the most difficult, so much so that to apply the "harder reading" canon in the face of an easy transcriptional explanation [the accidental omission of the two strokes of the pen] for the difficult reading seems unreasonable. As Burgon so well put it:

> I trust we are at least agreed that the maxim "*proclivi lectioni praestat ardua*," does not enunciate so foolish a proposition as that in choosing between two or more conflicting readings, we are to prefer **that** one which has the feeblest external attestation,—provided it be but in itself almost unintelligible? (*Ibid.*, p. 497).

Whatever the intention of those editors who choose 'who', their text emasculates this strong statement of the deity of Jesus Christ, besides being a stupidity—what is a 'mystery' about any human male being manifested in flesh? All human beings have bodies. In the Greek Text the relative pronoun has no antecedent, so it is a grammatical 'impossibility'.

[1] For further discussion see the final pages of Appendix C in my *Identity IV*.

But there is a more basic problem with the process view. Hort saw clearly, and correctly, that the Majority Text must have a common archetype. Recall that Hort's genealogical method was based on community of **error**. On the hypothesis that the Majority Text is a late and inferior text form, the large mass of common readings which distinguish it from the so-called 'Western' or 'Alexandrian text-types' must be **errors** (which was precisely Hort's contention) and such an agreement in error would have to have a common source. The process view fails completely to account for such an agreement in error (on that hypothesis).

Hort saw the need for a common source and posited a Lucianic revision. Scholars now generally recognize that the 'Byzantine text-type' must date back at least into the second century. But what chance would the original 'Byzantine' document, the archetype, have of gaining currency when appeal to the Autographs was still possible (if it was a separate invention)?

Candidly, there is only one reasonable explanation for the Majority Text that has so far been advanced—it is the result of an essentially normal process of transmission and the common source for its consensus is the Autographs. Down through the centuries of copying, the original text has always been reflected with a high degree of accuracy in the manuscript tradition as a whole. The history of the text presented above not only accounts nicely for the Majority Text, it also accounts for the inconsistent minority of MSS. They are remnants of the abnormal transmission of the text, reflecting ancient aberrant forms. It is a dependence upon such aberrant forms that distinguishes contemporary critical/eclectic editions of the Greek New Testament, and the modern translations based upon them.

What Is the Actual Evidence?

What is the actual evidence that needs to be evaluated? The continuous text MSS are the primary witnesses. The Lectionaries are secondary witnesses. The ancient Versions and patristic citations are tertiary witnesses. Any historical evidence, to the extent that it can be verified, is ancillary. The relevance of the secondary and tertiary types of evidence depends upon the presuppositions that the original wording was lost, and that the transmission of the text was not normal. Since both those presuppositions are false, I will confine my attention to the primary witnesses, the more so since there are so many of them.

The primary witnesses are customarily treated as being of three types: the papyri, the uncials and the cursives. The papyri and the uncials are both written with upper case letters (often without spacing between words), the difference being in the material used, papyrus or parchment (leather). The cursives are written with lower case letters, often run together, and usually with spacing between words; the material used was parchment or paper. The uncial script was exclusively used until the ninth century, when the first cursive MSS appear. By the eleventh century the cursive script had taken over.

The international list of extant (known) NT MSS is maintained by the Institute for New Testament Textual Research (INTF) in Münster, Germany. It is called the *Kurzgefasste Liste*.[1] As of February, 2018, that list contained 133 papyri, 282 uncials (majuscules) and about 2,850 numbered cursives (minuscules).

The dating of MSS is a slippery business, vulnerable to presupposition, bias and 'party line'. The reader should understand that the dates that have been assigned to the individual MSS may be little more than rough guesses; so much so that they are usually given as a century. When a MS has a specific date, the copyist wrote the date when he finished.

I made a rough tabulation of the papyri by century (taking the later date when there was an option);[2] they range from the II to the VIII: II—4, III—49, IV—31, V—14, VI—16, VII—16, VIII—3. Of those 133 papyri, 35 have less than five verses (they are mere fragments);[3] 76 have between six and twenty verses (still fragments); 13 more have less than two chapters; only 9 of them are of significant size. For some 40 chapters throughout the NT there is no papyrus witness. Only Luke, John, Acts, Hebrews, 1 & 2 Peter and Jude have a papyrus witness for a full chapter. Only one papyrus has a complete book: P^{72} contains 1 & 2 Peter and Jude. The importance attached to the papyri will depend on one's presuppositions.

I made a rough tabulation of the uncials by century (taking the later date when there was an option); they range from the III to the XI: III—2, IV—18, V—50, VI—65, VII—36, VIII—27, IX—62, X—20, XI—2. Of these 282 uncials, 182 have less than one chapter (most of them have only a few verses; some even less); another 37 have less than a whole book; only 63 have a complete book or more. The importance attached to the uncials will depend on one's presuppositions.

---

[1] Kurt Aland, ed., *Kurzgefasste Liste der Grieshischen Handschriften des Neuen Testaments* (Berlin: Walter de Gruyter, 1994).

[2] This paragraph, and the next, are simply based on the *Liste* (whether I agree, or not).

[3] In my opinion, the only contribution of a fragment is to establish that any variant it contains existed when it was written, if it was not created by the copyist. A fragment earlier than AD 100 establishes that the book existed at that time.

The cursives range in date from the IX to the XVII centuries. The heavy majority of them, some 2,130, are bunched in four centuries: XI – XIV. Around 90 of them are rather fragmentary, and many more are not complete. Around 25 of them have a number, but so little is known about them that they evidently are not available; and as many more have disappeared from sight. Even so, there are enough left to keep us busy for a long, long time.

Until the invention of paper, the materials used for making copies were papyrus and parchment (leather), both of which are thicker than paper. A complete NT bound in one volume would be rather bulky, and quite expensive. So early on, the books started to be bound in smaller groups: the four Gospels, the letters of Paul (including Hebrews), Acts and the General Epistles, with Revelation added on here and there. The Gospels were by far the most popular, followed by Paul's letters. At this writing, we know of around 2,350 MSS (including fragments) that contain some part of the Gospels, around 800 that contain some part of Paul's letters, over 650 that contain some part of Acts, over 600 that contain some part of the Generals, and about 300 that contain some part of Revelation. We know of around 60 complete New Testaments, another 150 that contain all but Revelation, and around 270 that contain Acts through Jude.

Not all of the above will be available for an interested person to work with. Consider the Gospels: of the 2,350 MSS mentioned above, for any single Gospel (like John) the number will be around 2,000. But because of fragments, damage and lacunae, for any given verse the number will be around 1,700. The INTF in Münster, Germany, holds microfilms of almost all of them. **However**, such an interested person needs to understand that he is not dealing with 1,700 independent witnesses—those MSS represent a variety of lines of transmission, or 'families'; such families would be the witnesses.[1] But there will be inter-relationship between families, and to be sure about such relationships we need a scientifically elaborated reconstruction of the history of the transmission of the NT Text. Lamentably, no such reconstruction exists. Worse, due to the soporific effect of the Hortian theory, the families have yet to be defined. I have scientifically defined Family 35 for the whole NT, but so far as I know, no other family

---

[1] Frederik Wisse collated and compared 1,386 MSS in Luke 1, 10 and 20 (three chapters); he reduced those MSS to 37 groups (families) (plus 89 "mavericks"). *The Profile Method for the Classification and Evaluation of Manuscript Evidence* (Grand Rapids: Eerdmans, 1982). It happens that 36 of the 37 fall within the broad Byzantine river of transmission. He found 70 subgroups within the 36, so felt able to define those relationships, based on the profiles. I submit that this is a step in the right direction.

has been similarly defined. It may be that no other family exists throughout the entire NT, but that has yet to be determined.

Those who catalog NT MSS inform us that the 12th and 13th centuries lead the pack, in terms of extant MSS, followed by the 14th, 11th, 15th, 16th and 10th, in that order. There are over four times as many MSS from the 13th as from the 10th, but obviously Koiné Greek would have been more of a living language in the 10th than the 13th, and so there would have been more demand and therefore more supply. In other words, many hundreds of really pure MSS from the 10th perished. A higher percentage of the really good MSS produced in the 14th century survived than those produced in the 11th; and so on. That is why there is a progressive level of agreement among the Byzantine MSS, there being a higher percentage of agreement in the 14th than in the 10th. But had we lived in the 10th, and done a wide survey of the MSS, we would have found very nearly the same level of agreement (perhaps 98%). The same obtains if we had lived in the 8th, 6th, 4th or 2nd century. In other words, THE SURVIVING MSS FROM THE FIRST TEN CENTURIES ARE NOT REPRESENTATIVE OF THE TRUE STATE OF AFFAIRS AT THE TIME.[1]

---

[1] Consider what Maurice Robinson concluded as a result of doing a complete collation of 1,389 MSS that contain the Pericope, John 7:53 – 8:11:

> However, contrary to this writer's earlier speculations, the extensive collation of the PA MSS has conclusively demonstrated that cross-comparison and correction of MSS occurred only *rarely* and *sporadically*, with little or no perpetuation of the corrective changes across the diversity of types represented [italics his, also below].
>
> If cross-correction did not occur frequently or extensively in that portion of text which has more variation than any other location in the NT, and if such corrections as were made did not tend to perpetuate, it is not likely that such a process occurred in those portions of the NT which had less textual variety... the lack of systematic and thorough correction within the PA as well as the lack of perpetuation of correction patterns appears to demonstrate this clearly. Cross-comparison and correction *should* have been rampant and extensive with this portion of text due to the wide variety of textual patterns and readings existing therein; instead, correction occurred sporadically, and rarely in a thoroughgoing manner.
>
> Since this is the case, the phenomenon of the relatively unified Byzantine Textform *cannot* be explained by a "process" methodology, whether "modified" or not...
>
> Based upon the collated data, the present writer is forced to reverse his previous assumptions regarding the development and restoration/preservation of the Byzantine Textform in this sense: although textual transmission itself is a process, it appears that, for the most part, the lines of transmission remained separate, with relatively little mixture occurring or becoming perpetuated...
>
> Certainly, all the types of PA text are distinct, and reflect a long line of transmission and preservation in their separate integrities... ... ...
> ... ...

Aland seems to grant that down through the centuries of church history the Byzantine text was regarded as "the text of the church", and he traces the beginning of this state of affairs to Lucian.[1] He makes repeated mention of a "school of/at Antioch" and of Asia Minor. All of this is very interesting, because in his book he agrees with Adolf Harnack that "about 180 the greatest concentration of churches was in Asia Minor and along the Aegean coast of Greece".[2] This is the area where Greek was the mother tongue and where Greek continued to be used. It is also the area that started out with most of the Autographs. But Aland continues: "Even around A.D. 325 the scene was still largely unchanged. Asia Minor continued to be the heartland of the Church". "The heartland of the Church"—so who else would be in a better position to identify the correct text of the New Testament? Who could 'sell' a fabricated text in Asia Minor in the early fourth century? I submit that the Byzantine text dominated the transmissional history because the churches in Asia Minor vouched for it. And they did so, from the very beginning, because they knew it was the true text, having received it from the Apostles. The Majority Text is what it is just because it has always been the **Text of the Church**.

Concluding Remarks

Up to this point I have dealt with the broad river of the normal transmission of the NT Text. This broad river is commonly referred to as the

---

It thus appears that the Byzantine minuscule MSS preserve lines of transmission which are not only independent but which of necessity had their origin at a time well before the 9th century. The extant uncial MSS do not and cannot account for the diversity and stability of PA textual forms found among even the earliest minuscules of the 9th century, let alone the diversity and stability of forms which appear throughout all centuries of the minuscule-era. The lack of extensive cross-comparison and correction demonstrated in the extant MSS containing the PA precludes the easy development of any existing form of the PA text from any other form of the PA text during at least the vellum era. The early uncials which contain the PA demonstrate widely-differing lines of transmission, but not all of the known lines. Nor do the uncials or minuscules show any indication of any known line deriving from a parallel known line. The 10 or so "texttype" lines of transmission remain independent and must necessarily extend back to a point long before their separate stabilizations occurred—a point which seems buried (as Colwell and Scrivener suggested) deep within the second century. ("Preliminary Observations regarding the *Pericope Adulterae* based upon Fresh Collations of nearly all Continuous-Text Manuscripts and over One Hundred Lectionaries", presented to the Evangelical Theological Society, Nov. 1998, pp. 11-13.)

[1] K. Aland, "The Text of the Church?", *Trinity Journal*, 1987, 8NS:131-144 [actually published in 1989], pp. 142-43.

[2] *The Text of the New Testament*, p. 53.

'Byzantine' text or text-type. But this broad river is made up of many distinct lines of transmission within it—recall that F. Wisse posited 36 such lines, based on his study of Luke, chapters 1, 10 and 20. Among those 36 lines, one is by far the largest, in terms of the number of representative MSS, and I will argue that it is also clearly the best. I call that line of transmission 'Family 35', and my discussion of that 'family' occupies Part II.[1] There I will argue that Family 35 constitutes the ultimate proof that God has preserved the NT Text.

Given my presuppositions, I consider that I have good reason for declaring the divine preservation of the precise original wording of the complete New Testament Text, to this day. That wording is reproduced in my edition of the Greek NT, *The Greek New Testament According to Family 35*. The book may be ordered from Amazon.com, and it may be downloaded from my site, www.prunch.org. I here list my conclusions, promising the reader that I will then give the evidence that leads to those conclusions (besides that already given above).

On the basis of the evidence so far available I affirm the following:

1. The original wording was never 'lost', and its transmission down through the years was basically normal, being recognized as inspired material from the beginning.
2. That normal process resulted in lines of transmission.
3. To delineate such lines, MSS must be grouped empirically on the basis of a shared mosaic of readings.
4. Such groups or families must be evaluated for independence and credibility.
5. The largest clearly defined group is Family 35.
6. Family 35 is demonstrably independent of all other lines of transmission throughout the NT.
7. Family 35 is demonstrably ancient, dating to the 3rd century, at least.
8. Family 35 representatives come from all over the Mediterranean

---

[1] This Part I is basically a reproduction (with a few embellishments) of Chapter 5 in my book, *The Identity of the New Testament Text IV*, available from Amazon.com, as well as from my site, www.prunch.org. My refutation of eclecticism, whether 'reasoned' or 'rigorous', occupies Chapter 2 of that book. My refutation of the Westcott-Hort critical theory occupies Chapters 3 & 4. Chapter 6 takes up four "possible objections": 1) Are not the oldest MSS the best?; 2) Why are there no early "Byzantine" MSS?; 3) "But there is no evidence of the Byzantine Text in the early centuries"; 4) Should not witnesses be weighed rather than counted? I direct the interested reader to those discussions.

area; the geographical distribution is all but total.

9. Family 35 is not a recension, was not created at some point subsequent to the Autographs.
10. Family 35 is an objectively/empirically defined entity throughout the NT; it has a demonstrable, diagnostic profile from Matthew 1:1 to Revelation 22:21. (That profile is given in Part II.)
11. The archetypal form of Family 35 is demonstrable—it has been demonstrated.
12. The Original Text is the ultimate archetype; any candidate must also be an archetype—a real, honest to goodness, objectively verifiable archetype; there is only one—Family 35.
13. God's concern for the preservation of the Biblical Text is evident: I take it that passages such as 1 Chronicles 16:15, Psalm 119:89, Isaiah 40:8, Matthew 5:18, Luke 16:17 and 21:33, John 10:35 and 16:12-13, 1 Peter 1:23-25 and Luke 4:4 may reasonably be taken to imply a promise that the Scriptures (to the tittle) will be preserved for man's use (we are to live "by *every* word of God"), and to the end of the world ("for a thousand generations"), but no intimation is given as to just how God proposed to do it. We must deduce the answer from what He has indeed done—we discover that He **did**!
14. This concern is reflected in Family 35; it is characterized by incredibly careful transmission (in contrast to other lines). [I have a perfect copy of the Family 35 archetypal text for most NT books (22); I have copies made from a perfect exemplar (presumed) for another four (4); as I continue to collate MSS I hope to add the last one (Acts), but even for it the archetypal form is demonstrable.]
15. If God was preserving the original wording in some line of transmission other than Family 35, would that line be any less careful? I think not. So any line of transmission characterized by internal confusion is disqualified—this includes **all** the other lines of transmission that I have seen so far.
16. I affirm that God used Family 35 to preserve the precise original wording of the New Testament Text; it is reproduced in my edition of the Greek Text.[1]

---

[1] And God used mainly the Eastern Orthodox Churches to preserve the NT Text down through the centuries—they have always used a Text that was an adequate representation of the Original, for all practical purposes. Also, among the families of Lectionary MSS, in terms of the number of representatives, Family 35 is the second largest, and it was used

I claim to have demonstrated the superiority of Family 35 based on size (number of representatives), **independence** (it is demonstrably independent of all other lines of transmission), **age** (it dates to the 3rd century, at least), **geographical distribution** (all over the Mediterranean area), **profile** (empirically determined), **care** (by the copyists) and **range** (all 27 books). **I challenge any and all to do the same for any other line of transmission!**

The Original Text is the ultimate archetype; any candidate must also be an archetype—a real, honest to goodness, objectively verifiable archetype; there is only one that has been identified so far—Family 35. I now move on to Part II, where I provide further evidence, the evidence that gives rise to my conclusions.

---

in the very first printed edition, the da Sabbio edition of 1539.

PART II: The Best Line of Transmission

Just what is Family 35?

I can well imagine that many of my readers are hearing about Family 35 for the first time. It refers to a line of transmission within the broad 'Byzantine' river of MSS, and I gave it that name. So far as I know, the academic world is severely ignoring my work, as they must, to be sure, since I expose the falsehoods they have been purveying for generations. I will begin with a bit of recent history.

When Thomas Nelson Inc. published my first book in 1977, *The Identity of the New Testament Text*, the best printed Greek New testament that was readily available was the *Textus Receptus*, the Received Text—it was the Greek Text of the Protestant Reformation. John William Burgon, Dean of Chichester, called it the 'Traditional Text'. Although Zane C. Hodges and Arthur L. Farstad had started working on a Majority Text, based on the work of Hermann von Soden,[1] it was not published until 1982. In 1977 I demonstrated that the Westcott-Hort critical theory was false at every point, and that demonstration has never been refuted since, that I know of. But when it came to offering an alternative, I was limited to generalities and Burgon's seven "Notes of Truth".[2] Thomas Nelson put my book through at least three further printings, including some revision, the last one appearing in 1990. Even then, I had nothing better to offer.

However, in 1988 I helped to start the Majority Text Society, along with Zane Hodges, Art Farstad and Frank Carmichal, and was its first president. At that time I began to seriously work on Majority Text theory, and during the next decade developed what I was pleased to call Original Text theory. I used it as a steppingstone to my present approach to NT textual criticism (that we may call Family 35 Priority Theory). Here it is:

1. First, OTT is concerned to identify the precise original wording of the NT writings.[3]

---

[1] *Die Schriften des Neuen Testaments in ihrer ältesten erreichbaren Textgestalt* (Teil 1, Berlin: Verlag von Alexander Duncker, 1902-1910; Teil 2 Göttingen: Vandenhoeck und Ruprecht, 1913).

[2] They are: 1. Antiquity, or Primitiveness; 2. Consent of Witnesses, or Number; 3. Variety of Evidence, or Catholicity; 4. Respectability of Witnesses, or Weight; 5. Continuity, or Unbroken Tradition; 6. Evidence of the Entire Passage, or Context; 7. Internal Considerations, or Reasonableness. Burgon, *The Traditional Text*, p. 29.

[3] Here I reject the allegation that the original wording is lost and gone.

2. Second, the criteria must be biblical, objective and reasonable.[1]
3. Third, a 90% attestation will be considered unassailable, and 80% virtually so.[2]
4. Fourth, Burgon's "notes of truth" will come into play, especially where the attestation falls below 80%.[3]
5. Fifth, where collations exist, making possible an empirical grouping of the MSS on the basis of shared mosaics of readings, this must be done. Such groups must be evaluated on the basis of their performance and be assigned a credibility quotient. A putative history of the transmission of the Text needs to be developed on the basis of the interrelationships of such groups. **Demonstrated groupings and relationships supersede the counting of MSS.**[4]
6. Sixth, it presupposes that the Creator exists and that He has spoken to our race. It accepts the implied divine purpose to preserve His revelation for the use of subsequent generations, including ours. It understands that both God and Satan have an ongoing active interest in the fate of the NT Text—to approach NT textual criticism without taking due account of that interest is to act irresponsibly.[5]
7. Seventh, it insists that presuppositions and motives must always be addressed and evaluated.[6]

I use the term 'steppingstone' because I was still thinking in terms of a large majority, and that was because Family 35 had not yet come to my attention (I was still limited to generalities). However, the fifth point above

---

[1] Here I reject the dependence on subjective criteria and a purely rationalistic approach.

[2] This is now superseded by advances in point 5, although a 90% attestation remains difficult to assail.

[3] This is now superseded by advances in point 5, although his 'notes' remain valid, in general.

[4] Please note that I am not referring to any attempt at reconstructing a genealogy of MSS—I agree with those scholars who have declared such an enterprise to be virtually impossible (there are altogether too many missing links). I am indeed referring to the reconstruction of a genealogy of readings, and thus of the history of the transmission of the Text. The last sentence has always been emphasized. Once all MSS have been collated and empirically grouped, we can dispense with counting them.

[5] Those who exclude the supernatural from their model are condemning themselves to never arrive at the Truth—God and Satan exist, and both have been involved in the transmission of the NT Text.

[6] In any scientific inquiry a rigorous distinction must be made between evidence, presupposition and interpretation. Since one's presuppositions heavily influence, even control, his interpretation of the evidence (that should be the same for everyone), any honest scholar needs to state his presuppositions openly. It is doubtless too much to expect sinners to expose their motives to the light of day (John 3:20).

shows the direction in which I was heading; note especially the last sentence, which has always been in bold type, and most especially the term 'demonstrated'.[1] For example, my critical apparatus for Revelation gives the evidence in terms of Hoskier's nine groups, rather than percentages of MSS.

Nonetheless, in 2003, Wipf and Stock Publishers published *The Identity of the New Testament Text II*, as an academic reprint. It contained further revision, but it still used Burgon's 'Notes of Truth', although I introduced a Family 18, that I soon changed to Family 35. By 2002 I had become aware of Family 35, but my development of a theory surrounding it was still tentative and incomplete. By the time Wipf and Stock published *The Identity of the New Testament Text III* in 2012, I had done sufficient work on that theory to replace Burgon's 'Notes of Truth' with it.

It was the Hodges-Farstad Majority Text's representation of the evidence for the *Pericope Adulterae* that caught my attention, being based on von Soden's supposed collation of over 900 MSS.[2] As stated in their apparatus, there were three main streams: $\mathbf{M}^{5}$, $\mathbf{M}^{6}$ and $\mathbf{M}^{7}$. **7** was always in the majority [except for one five-way split where there is no majority] because it was always accompanied by either **5** or **6** [5 + 6 never go against 7]. This looked to me like three independent streams, where seldom would more than one go astray at any given point. Being the common denominator, **7** was clearly the best of the three, and presumably also the oldest.

Then I went to Revelation (in H-F) and noticed three main streams again: $\mathbf{M}^{a\text{-}b}$, $\mathbf{M}^{c}$ and $\mathbf{M}^{d\text{-}e}$. The picture was analogous to that of the *PA*. Revelation represents a very much larger corpus than does the *PA*, but even so, there are only 8 cases where **a-b** and **d-e** join against **c** (+ 6 others where one of the four is split), compared to over 100 each for **a-b** and **c** against **d-e** and for **c** and **d-e** against **a-b**. Again, being the common denominator, **c** was clearly the best of the three (see the apparatus of my Greek Text of the Apocalypse).

Now then, it so happens that $\mathbf{M}^{7}$ in the *PA* and $\mathbf{M}^{c}$ in Revelation equal Soden's $\mathbf{K}^{r}$, so I began to smell a rat.[3] Then the *Text und Textwert* series proved that $\mathbf{K}^{r}$ is independent of $\mathbf{K}^{x}$ throughout the NT. It follows that $\mathbf{K}^{r}$ cannot be a revision of $\mathbf{K}^{x}$. Then there are hundreds of places where $\mathbf{K}^{r}$

---

[1] Hort did the discipline a considerable disservice by positing theoretical text-types, devoid of evidence, and then treating them as established fact.

[2] Robinson's collations show that Soden 'regularized' the data.

[3] Why 'smelled a rat'? Because $\mathbf{M}^{7}$ is clearly older than $\mathbf{M}^{5}$ and $\mathbf{M}^{6}$ in the *PA*, and $\mathbf{M}^{c}$ than $\mathbf{M}^{a\text{-}b}$ and $\mathbf{M}^{d\text{-}e}$ in Revelation, but von Soden claimed $\mathbf{K}^{r}$ was a revision of $\mathbf{K}^{x}$ (how could it be a revision if it was older?).

has overt early attestation, against $\mathbf{K}^{x}$, but there is no pattern to that early attestation. There being no pattern then $\mathbf{K}^{r}$ must be early, as the picture in the *PA* and in Revelation has already implied. If $\mathbf{K}^{r}$ is early and independent, then it must be rehabilitated in the practice of NT textual criticism. **If it is the best line of transmission in the *PA* and Revelation, it just might be the best elsewhere as well.**

But there is an ingrained disdain/antipathy toward the symbol $\mathbf{K}^{r}$, so I have proposed a new name for the text-type. We should substitute $\mathbf{f}^{35}$ for $\mathbf{K}^{r}$—it is more objective, and will get away from the prejudice that attaches to the latter. Minuscule 35 contains the whole NT and reflects $\mathbf{K}^{r}$ throughout, and it is the MS with the smallest number that meets those qualifications[1] (just as cursives 1 and 13 are the smallest number in their families; and like them, 35 is not always the best representative [it is generally excellent]—but it is 11th century [and it is a copy of an older exemplar, not a new creation], so the text-type could not have been created in the 12th, Q.E.D.—this is an abbreviation for the Latin *quod erat demonstrandum*, 'the point to be proved has been proved'.)

Family 35 represents about 16% of the total of extant (known) Greek MSS, but it is almost never entirely alone. However, the roster of other MSS is almost never the same, and this throughout the NT. Does not this indicate that $\mathbf{f}^{35}$ is the common denominator? Because the roster of other MSS is almost never the same, it is possible to factor out the MSS that represent $\mathbf{f}^{35}$. As I stated at the end of Part I, the Original Text is the ultimate archetype, so any candidate must also be an archetype—a real, honest to goodness, objectively verifiable archetype; there is only one that has been identified so far—Family 35. Most of the words in the NT have virtually 100% attestation (from the extant Greek MSS), but where there is disagreement, it is the mosaic, or profile, of shared readings that define a family, or line of transmission. I now present the profile that defines Family 35.

Family 35 profile for the whole New Testament[2]

Key:

+++	around 20% = $\mathbf{f}^{35}$ virtually alone = diagnostic
++--	around 25% = quite good
++	around 30% = not bad
+--	around 35%
+	around 40%

[1] Minuscule 18 has a smaller number and also contains the whole NT, but it defects from the text-type in Revelation.

[2] This information was taken from my Greek Text and apparatus.

I have arbitrarily set the cutoff point at 40% (of the total of extant MSS), being sufficient for my present purpose, but of course higher percentages can also contribute to the family mosaic/profile. (Were I to include 45% and 50% the numbers would go up visibly, especially for some books. In some of Paul's epistles the other lines of transmission within the Byzantine bulk did not depart very much from the Family 35 norm.) Where the percentages do not add up to 100%, there are further variants; the interested reader may find them in the apparatus of my Greek Text. The reading of Family 35 is given first.

	Matthew	
++--	1:10	μανασσην [25%] ‖ μανασση [73%]
++	5:31	ερρεθη [30%] ‖ 1 δε [70%]
++	6:6	ταμειον [30%] ‖ ταμιειον [70%]
+++	6:25[a]	ενδυσεσθε [20%] ‖ ενδυσησθε [80%]
+++	6:25[b]	πλειων [20%] ‖ πλειον [80%]
++--	7:19	ουν [25%] ‖ --- [75%]
++--	8:4	προσενεγκαι [25%] ‖ προσενεγκε [75%]
++	8:13	εκατονταρχω [30%] ‖ εκατονταρχη [70%]
+++	8:20	λεγει [20%] ‖ και 1 [80%]
+++	8:21	μαθητων [20%] ‖ 1 αυτου [80%]
+--	9:4	ειδως (33.3%) ‖ ιδων (65.7%)
++	9:11	και πινει [30%] ‖ --- [70%]
+++	9:15	χρονον [20%] ‖ --- [80%]
++	9:18	τις [30%] ‖ εις [62%]
+++	9:28	αυτοις [20%] ‖ 1 ο ιησους [80%]
++--	9:33	οτι [25%] ‖ --- [75%]
++	10:2	εισιν [30%] ‖ εστιν [70%]
++	10:19	λαλησετε (1st) [30%] ‖ λαλησητε [70%]
++	10:25	απεκαλεσαν [30%] ‖ εκαλεσαν [49%] ‖ επεκαλεσαν [20%]
+++	10:31	πολλω [20%] ‖ πολλων [80%]
+--	11:20	ο ιησους [35%] ‖ --- [65%]
+++	11:21	χωραζιν [20%] ‖ χοραζιν [65%]
+--	11:23[a]	ἢ [35%] ‖ ἡ [64%]
+--	11:23[b]	υψωθης [35%] ‖ υψωθεισα [63%]
+++	12:15	απαντας [20%] ‖ παντας [80%]
++--	12:22	κωφον [25%] ‖ 1 και [75%]
+++	12:23	ο χριστος [20%] ‖ --- [80%]
++--	12:24	εν [25%] ‖ 1 τω [75%]
++	12:28	εγω εν πνευματι θεου [28%] ‖ ~ 2341 [70%]
+	12:29	διαρπαση [40%] ‖ διαρπασει [60%]
++	13:2	εις [30%] ‖ 1 το [70%]
++--	13:3	εν παραβολαις πολλα [25%] ‖ ~ 312 [75%]
++	13:24	σπειραντι [30%] ‖ σπειροντι [70%]
++	13:32	παντων [30%] ‖ --- [70%]
++	13:44	εν αγρω [30%] ‖ 1 τω 2 [70%]
+++	14:5	εφοβειτο [20%] ‖ εφοβηθη [80%]
++	14:22	αυτου [30%] ‖ --- [70%]

++--	14:28	δε [25%] ‖ 1 αυτω [73%]
+++	14:31	και ευθεως [20%] ‖ ~ 2 δε [80%]
++	14:34	γενησαρετ [30%] ‖ γεννησαρετ [55%]
+--	14:36	καν [35%] ‖ --- [65%]
++--	15:6	μητερα [25%] ‖ 1 αυτου [75%]
++	15:14	εμπεσουνται [30%] ‖ πεσουνται [70%]
++	15:31	εδοξαζον [30%] ‖ εδοξασαν [70%]
++	15:32[a]	ημερας [30%] ‖ ημεραι [70%]
++--	15:32[b]	νηστις [25%] ‖ νηστεις [75%]
++	15:39	ενεβη [30%] ‖ ανεβη [70%]
+--	16:20	εστιν [35%] ‖ 1 ιησους [65%]
+	17:2	εγενετο [40%] ‖ εγενοντο [60%]
+++	17:18	ιαθη [20%] ‖ εθεραπευθη [80%]
++--	17:25	εισηλθον [25%] ‖ εισηλθεν [72%]
+	17:27	αναβαντα [40%] ‖ αναβαινοντο [60%]
++--	18:15[a]	αμαρτη [25%] ‖ αμαρτηση [74%]
++	18:15[b]	υπαγε [30%] ‖ 1 και [70%]
+++	19:5	προς την γυναικα [20%] ‖ τη γυναικι [80%]
++--	19:16	τις [25%] ‖ --- [75%]
+++	20:26	εσται [20%] ‖ 1 εν [80%]
+--	20:27	εσται [35%] ‖ εστω [65%]
++	21:8	αυτων [30%] ‖ εαυτων [70%]
++--	21:35	εδηραν [25%] ‖ εδειραν [75%]
+	22:37	τη [40%] ‖ --- [60%]
++	22:46	αποκριθηναι αυτω [30%] ‖ ~ 21 [69%]
++	23:8	διδασκαλος [30%] ‖ καθηγητης [70%]
++	23:10	εστιν υμων [30%] ‖ ~ 21 [65%]
++--	23:11	εστω [25%] ‖ εσται [75%]
++--	24:1	αυτω [25%] ‖ --- [75%]
++--	24:6	μελησετε [25%] ‖ μελλησετε [72%]
++	24:18	το ιματιον [30%] ‖ τα ιματια [70%]
++--	24:32	γινωσκεται [25%] ‖ γινωσκετε [75%]
++	24:49	τε [30%] ‖ δε [70%]
++	25:29	δοκει εχειν [30%] ‖ εχει [70%]
++--	25:32	συναχθησονται [25%] ‖ συναχθησεται **f**^{35pt} [75%]
++--	26:1	ιησους [25%] ‖ 1 παντας [75%]
+	26:9	τοις [40%] ‖ --- [60%]
+	26:11	παντοτε γαρ τους πτωχους [40%] ‖ ~ 3421 [60%]
+	26:15	και εγω [40%] ‖ καγω [60%]
++	26:26	ευλογησας [30%] ‖ ευχαριστησας [70%]
++	26:29	γενηματος [30%] ‖ γεννηματος **f**^{35pt} [70%]
++	26:33[a]	και [30%] ‖ --- [70%]
+	26:33[b]	εγω [40%] ‖ 1 δε [60%]
+--	26:39	προελθων [35%] ‖ προσελθων [65%]
++	26:43	ευρεν [30%] ‖ ευρισκει [66%]
+++	26:46	ιδου [20%] ‖ 1 ηγγικεν [80%]
+	26:48	εαν [40%] ‖ αν [60%]
++	26:55	εν τω ιερω διδασκων [30%] ‖ ~ 4123 [69%]
+--	26:75	ρηματος [35%] ‖ 1 του [65%]
+++	27:1	πρεσβυτεροι [20%] ‖ 1 του λαου [80%]
++	27:12	και [30%] ‖ 1 των [70%]
++	27:33	λεγομενον [30%] ‖ λεγομενος [67%]

++--	27:35	βαλοντες [25%] || βαλλοντες **f**[35pt] [75%]
+--	27:55	και [35%] || --- [65%]
++--	27:64	οτι [25%] || --- [75%]

<u>Key</u>:

+++	around 20% = **f**[35] virtually alone = diagnostic (17)
++--	around 25% = quite good (22)
++	around 30% = not bad (34)
+--	around 35% (10)
+	around 40% (9)

Total: 92

A single diagnostic reading could be happenstance, but several presumably indicate that the MS is at least a fringe member of the family. Probably no two scholars would prepare identical lists—changing rank, adding or subtracting—but there is sufficient evidence here to establish that **f**[35] is a distinct family. The statements here apply to the remaining books as well.

<u>Mark</u>

+	1:12	ευθεως [40%] || ευθυς [60%]
++	1:30	του [30%] || --- [70%]
++	1:34	χριστον ειναι (28%) || --- (58.9%) || τον 12 (11.6%)
+	1:38	εληλυθα [40%] || εξεληλυθα [59%]
++--	1:44	προσενεγκαι [25%] || προσενεγκε [75%]
+	2:9	τον κραββατον σου [40%] || ~ 312 [59%]
++	3:20	μηδε [30%] || μητε [70%]
+--	3:35	μου [35%] || --- [65%]
++	4:24	αντιμετρηθησεται [30%] || μετρηθησεται [69%]
++	5:3a	οικησιν [30%] || κατοικησιν [70%]
+	5:3b	ηδυνατο [40%] || εδυνατο [60%]
++--	5:4	ισχυσεν [26%] || ισχυεν [74%]
+	5:5	μνημασιν και εν τοις ορεσιν [40%] || ~ 52341 [57%]
+++	6:20	ακουων [20%] || ακουσας [80%]
+	6:45	απολυσει [40%] || απολυση [59%]
++	6:53	γενησαρετ [30%] || γεννησαρετ [53%]
++	7:4	χαλκειων [30%] || χαλκιων [70%]
++	8:3	νηστις [30%] || νηστεις [70%]
+	8:6	και [40%] || --- [60%]
+--	8:14	οι μαθηται αυτου [35%] || --- [64%]
+	8:21	ουπω [41%] || ου [59%]
++--	9:3	κναφευς [25%] || γναφευς [75%]
++	9:20	ιδον [30%] || ιδων [70%]
++	9:48	σκωληξ [30%] || 1 αυτων [70%]
+--	10:8	σαρξ μια [35%] || ~ 21 [65%]
+++	10:17	τις [20%] || εις [70%] || --- [10%]
+++	10:25	γαρ [20%] || --- [80%]
+	10:30	πατερα και μητερα [40%] || μητερας [55%]
+	10:33	τοις [40%] || --- [60%]
+--	10:40	μου [35%] || --- [65%]

+--	10:51	ραβουνι [35%] ‖ ραββουνι [59%]
++	10:52	ηκολουθησεν [30%] ‖ ηκολουθει [69%]
++	11:5	εστωτων [30%] ‖ εστηκοτων [70%]
+--	11:14	φαγη [35%] ‖ φαγοι [65%]
+--	11:18	απολεσουσιν [35%] ‖ απολεσωσιν [65%]
+++	11:30	ανθρωπων [20%] ‖ 1 αποκριθητε μοι [80%]
++	12:3	εδηραν [30%] ‖ εδειραν [70%]
++	12:5	δαιροντες [30%] ‖ δεροντες [70%]
+++	12:26	μωυσεος [20%] ‖ μωσεως [50%] ‖ μωυσεως [30%]
++--	12:28	πασων [25%] ‖ παντων [72%]
++--	12:29a	πασων [25%] ‖ παντων [72%]
++--	12:29b	υμων [25%] ‖ ημων [74%]
+--	12:41	εβαλον [35%] ‖ εβαλλον [65%]
++	13:2a	αποκριθεις ο ιησους [30%] ‖ ~ 231 [68%]
+++	13:2b	ωδε (21.1%) ‖ --- (78.9%)
++	13:9	αχθησεσθε [30%] ‖ σταθησεσθε [70%]
+--	13:11a	αγωσιν [35%] ‖ αγαγωσιν [65%]
+--	13:11b	λαλησετε [35%] ‖ λαλησητε [65%]
++	13:21a	τοτε [30%] ‖ και 1 [70%]
+	13:21b	χριστος [40%] ‖ 1 η [60%]
++	13:28a	ηδη ο κλαδος αυτης (29%) ‖ ~ 4123 (50.2%)
++--	13:28b	γινωσκεται [25%] ‖ γινωσκετε [75%]
+++	13:33	προσευχεσθε [20%] ‖ και 1 [77%]
+	14:11	αγρυρια [40%] ‖ αγρυριον [60%]
++	14:15	ανωγεων [30%] ‖ ανωγεον [39%] ‖ ανωγαιον [25%]
++--	14:22	και [25%] ‖ --- [75%]
+++	14:28	μετα δε [20%] ‖ αλλα 1 [79%]
+--	14:32	προσευξομαι [35%] ‖ προσευξωμαι [65%]
++	14:36	παρενεγκαι [30%] ‖ παρενεγκε [70%]
+--	14:40	καταβαρυνομενοι [35%] ‖ βεβαρημενοι [64%]
++	15:18	και λεγειν [30%] ‖ --- [68%]
++--	15:42	παρασκευη ην [25%] ‖ ~ 21 [75%]
+--	15:43	ελθων [35%] ‖ ηλθεν [65%]
++	16:1	τον ιησουν [30%] ‖ αυτον [70%]
++	16:9	ο ιησους [30%] ‖ --- [70%]

Key:

+++	around 20% = **f**[35] virtually alone = diagnostic (8)
++--	around 25% = quite good (9)
++	around 30% = not bad (23)
+--	around 35% (13)
+	around 40% (12)

Total: 65

Luke

+--	1:55	εως αιωνος [35%] ‖ εις τον αιωνα [64%]
++--	1:63	εσται [26%] ‖ εστιν [74%]
+	2:40	αυτω [41%] ‖ αυτο [58%]
+	3:12	υπ αυτου [40%] ‖ --- [60%]
++++	3:18	τω λαω [15%] ‖ τον λαον [85%]

++--	3:30	ιωναμ [25%] ‖ ιωναν [48%]
+	3:34	θαρρα [40%] ‖ θαρα [60%]
++--	3:35	ραγαβ [25%] ‖ ραγαυ [70%]
++--	4:7	σοι [25%] ‖ σου [75%]
+	4:42	εζητουν [40%] ‖ επεζητουν [60%]
++++	5:1[a]	περι [18%] ‖ παρα [82%]
++	5:1[b]	γενησαρετ [29%] ‖ γεννησαρετ [60%]
++	5:14	προσενεγκαι [30%] ‖ προσενεγκε [70%]
+--	5:19	πως [35%] ‖ ποιας [57%]
++--	5:35	ημεραι [25%] ‖ 1 και [75%]
++--	6:7	ει [25%] ‖ 1 εν [75%]
+	6:10	ουτως [42%] ‖ --- [54.5%]
+++	6:26a	καλως ειπωσιν υμας (22%) ‖ ~ 132 (76.1%)
+	6:26b	παντες (39.1%) ‖ --- (60.5%)
++	6:49	την [30%] ‖ --- [70%]
+--	8:3	σωσαννα [35%] ‖ σουσαννα [65%]
++	8:24	και προσελθοντες [32%] ‖ ~ 2 δε [68%]
+--	8:26	αντιπεραν [33%] ‖ αντιπερα [60%]
++++	9:4	ην [15%] ‖ 1 αν [85%]
++	9:13	αγορασομεν [30%] ‖ αγορασωμεν [70%]
+	9:33	ο [40%] ‖ --- [60%]
+++	9:48	υμων [20%] ‖ υμιν [79%]
+	9:52	εαυτου [40%] ‖ αυτου [60%]
++--	10:4	μη [26%] ‖ μηδε [74%]
++--	10:6	μεν [25%] ‖ --- [75%]
+--	10:13	χωραζιν [35%] ‖ χοραζιν [29%] ‖ χοραζειν [20%]
+--	10:39	των λογων [37%] ‖ τον λογον [63%]
+	10:41	ο ιησους ειπεν αυτη [40%] ‖ ~ 3412 [59%]
++++	11:19	αυτοι υμων [18%] ‖ ~ 21 [52%] ‖
++	11:32	νινευι [32%] ‖ νινευιται [35%] ‖ ‖
+--	11:34	η [35%] ‖ 1 και [65%]
++--	11:53	συνεχειν [26%] ‖ ενεχειν [70%]
++++	12:7	πολλω [15%] ‖ πολλων [85%]
+--	12:11	απλογησεσθε [35%] ‖ απλογησησθε [63%]
++	12:22[a]	λεγω υμιν [28%] ‖ ~ 21 [72%]
++--	12:22[b]	ενδυσεσθε [25%] ‖ ενδυσησθε [74%]
++--	12:23	πλειων [23%] ‖ πλειον [77]
+++	12:27	λεγω [20%] ‖ 1 δε [80%]
+	12:56	του ουρανου και της γης [40%] ‖ ~ 45312 [60%]
++--	12:58	βαλη σε [24%] ‖ ~ 21 [76%]
++--	13:28	οψεσθε [27%] ‖ οψησθε [73%]
+++	14:9	συ [20%] ‖ σοι [80%]
+	14:21	τυφλους και χωλους [42%] ‖ ~ 321 [57%]
+--	14:26	μου ειναι μαθητης [36%] ‖ ~ 132 [60%]
+	15:20	εαυτου [42%] ‖ αυτου [58%]
++--	16:22	του [26%] ‖ --- [74%]
++	16:25	οδε [30%] ‖ ωδε [70%]
++	17:37	και [29%] ‖ --- [68%]
+--	19:15	βασιλειαν [37%] ‖ 1 και [63%]
++--	19:23	την [23%] ‖ --- [77%]
+++	20:10	δηραντες [20%] ‖ δειραντες [80%]
+++	20:11	δηραντες [20%] ‖ δειραντες [80%]

++--	20:15	εκβαλοντες [24%] ‖ 1 αυτον [76%]
+++	20:28	ο αδελφος αυτου λαβη [20%] ‖ ~ 4123 [80%]
++	21:6	λιθον (32.2%) ‖ λιθω (65.1%)
+--	21:12	απαντων [34%] ‖ παντων [66%]
++	21:15	η [30%] ‖ ουδε [68%]
++	21:30	προβαλλωσιν [28%] ‖ προβαλωσιν [66%]
++	21:33	παρελευσεται [32%] ‖ παρελευσονται [68%]
+--	22:27	ουχ [33%] ‖ ουχι [67%]
+--	22:52	προς [33%] ‖ επ [67%]
+--	22:54	εισηγαγον [37%] ‖ 1 αυτον [55%]
+--	22:63	δαιροντες [35%] ‖ δεροντες [65%]
++--	22:66	απηγαγον [24%] ‖ ανηγαγον [75%]
++	23:51	ος [32%] ‖ 1 και [67%]
++	24:19	ως [32%] ‖ ος [68%]
++	24:36	και [32%] ‖ --- [68%]
++	24:42	μελισσειου [30%] ‖ μελισσιου [70%]

Key:

+++	around 20% = **f**[35] virtually alone = diagnostic (12)
++--	around 25% = quite good (17)
++	around 30% = not bad (17)
+--	around 35% (15)
+	around 40% (12)

Total: 73

John

++--	1:28	βιθαβαρα [25%] ‖ βηθανια [65%] ‖
+	1:45	υιον [40%] ‖ 1 του [60%]
+	3:4	αυτον [40%] ‖ 1 ο [60%]
+++	4:1	ιησους (21.7%) ‖ κυριος (76.9%)
+	4:5	ου [40%] ‖ ο [60%]
+--	4:35	οτι [35%] ‖ 1 ετι [65%]
+++	5:44	ανθρωπων (22.6%) ‖ αλληλων (77.2%)
++--	5:46	εμου γαρ [25%] ‖ ~ 21 [75%]
++--	6:12	των κλασματων [25%] ‖ κλασματα [75%]
++	6:58	μου [30%] ‖ --- [70%]
++	7:3	εργα [30%] ‖ 1 σου [63.5%] ‖
+	7:31	σημεια [40%] ‖ 1 τουτων [55%]
++	7:39	ο [30%] ‖ ου [70%]
+	8:4	αυτοφωρω [40%] ‖ αυτοφορω [60%]
++++	8:7	τον λιθον επ αυτη βαλετω [18%] ‖ ‖ ‖ ‖ ‖ (5-way split)
+	8:14	η [40%] ‖ και [50%] ‖
++	8:33	και ειπον [30%] ‖ --- [70%]
++	9:17	ουν [30%] ‖ --- [70%]
++	9:26	ανεωξεν [30%] ‖ ηνοιξεν [63%]
++--	9:34	ολως [25%] ‖ ολος [75%]
++++	10:39	ουν παλιν πιασαι αυτον (18.9%) ‖ ~ 1243 (32.8%) ‖ ~ 243 (30.3%) ‖ ‖
+	11:2	εαυτης [40%] ‖ αυτης [60%]
++	11:46	οσα [29%] ‖ α [70%]

+--	11:51	ο [35%] || --- [65%]
+++	11:56	υμιν δοκει [20%] || ~ 21 [80%]
+	12:6	εμελεν [40%] || εμελλεν f^{35pt} [60%]
+	12:12	ο [40%] || --- [60%]
+	12:13	απαντησιν [38%] || υπαντησιν [60%]
++	12:14	αυτω [30%] || αυτο [70%]
+--	13:15[a]	δεδωκα [35%] || εδωκα [65%]
++--	13:15[b]	καθως [25%] || 1 εγω [75%]
+++	13:22[a]	δε [20%] || ουν [79.5%]
++--	13:22[b]	προς [25%] || εις [75%]
+--	18:23	δαιρεις [36%] || δερεις [64%]
+++	18:39	ημιν [20%] || υμιν [80%]
++	18:40	ουν [30%] || 1 παλιν [70%]
+	19:14	ην [40%] || δε [60%]
+	19:23	αρραφος [40%] || αραφος [60%]
++	19:28	ηδη παντα [30%] || ~ 21 [60%] ||
++	19:35	η μαρτυρια αυτου [30%] || ~ 312 [65%]
+++	21:1[a]	εαυτον [20%] || 1 παλιν [80%]
+	21:1[b]	αυτου [40%] || --- [60%]
++--	21:1[c]	εγερθεις εκ νεκρων [25%] || --- [75%]

<u>Key</u>:

+++	around 20% = **f**[35] virtually alone = diagnostic (8)
++--	around 25% = quite good (7)
++	around 30% = not bad (11)
+--	around 35% (4)
+	around 40% (13)

Total: 43 (The transmission of John was more conservative than that of the other Gospels.)

<u>Acts</u>

++--	1:8	και [25%] || 1 εν [75%]
+++	1:11	ουτος [20%] || 1 ο [80%]
++--	1:13	ιακωβος [25%] || 1 και [73%]
++-	1:18	ελακισεν [25%] || ελακησεν [75%]
++--	2:13	διαχλευαζοντες [25%] || χλευαζοντες [75%]
+++	2:14	επεφθεγξατο [20%] || απεφθεγξατο [80%]
+++	2:38	ειπεν δε πετρος [20%] || ~ 32 εφη [72%] ||
++--	3:23	αν [25%] || εαν [75%]
++--	3:24	προκατηγγειλαν [25%] || κατηγγειλαν [75%]
++	4:5	εν [30%] || εις [70%]
++	4:12[a]	ουδε [30%] || ουτε [70%]
++--	4:12[b]	ετερον εστιν [25%] || ~ 21 [75%]
+++	4:14	εστωτα [20%] || 1 τον [80%]
+++	4:17	ανθρωπω [20%] || ανθρωπων [80%]
++++	4:20	α [18%] || --- [82%]
+++	4:23	ανηγγειλαν [20%] || απηγγειλαν [80%]
++--	4:33[a]	δυναμει μεγαλη [25%] || ~ 21 [75%]
++-	4:33[b]	οι αποστολοι το μαρτυριον [25%] || ~ 3412 [75%]
++--	4:34	ην (24.5%) || υπηρχεν (74.8%)

++-	5:1	σαπφειρα [25%] || σαπφειρη [56%] || ||
+++	5:15	του [20%] || --- [80%]
++++	5:16	και [18%] || οιτινες [80%] ||
++--	5:22	παραγενομενοι υπηρεται [25%] || ~ 21 [75%]
++--	5:33	ακουοντες [25%] || ακουσαντες [75%]
+++	5:36[a]	προσεκλιθη [20%] || προσεκληθη [54%] || ||
+++	5:36[b]	ως [20%] || ωσει [80%]
++	5:39	δυνησεσθε [30%] || δυνασθε [58%] || ||
+++	5:40	δηραντες [20%] || δειραντες [80%]
++++	5:41	κατηξιωθησαν υπερ του ονοματος του χριστου [18%] || ~ 234561 [15%] || ~ 234 αυτου 1 [15%] || || || ||
++	5:42	τον χριστον ιησουν [30%] || ~ 312 [60%] || ||
++--	6:5	πληρη [25%] || πληρης [60%] ||
++--	7:5	δουναι αυτην εις κατασχεσιν αυτω [25%] || ~ 15342 [65%] ||
++--	7:14[a]	ιακωβ τον πατερα αυτου [25%] || ~ 2341 [75%]
++--	7:14[b]	αυτου [25%] || --- [75%]
++	7:14[c]	εβδομηκοντα πεντε ψυχαις [30%] || ~ 312 [63%] ||
+--	7:16	εμμωρ [33%] || εμμορ [60%] ||
+++	7:21	ανειλετο [22%] || 1 αυτον [60%] || ||
++++	7:27	τουτον [18%] || αυτον [82%]
+++	7:31[a]	μωσης [20%] || μωυσης [80%]
++--	7:31[b]	εθαυμασεν [25%] || εθαυμαζεν [75%]
+++	7:35	αρχηγον [20%] || αρχοντα [80%]
++--	7:37	ημων [25%] || υμων [75%] ||
+++	7:42	εν τη ερημω ετη τεσσαρακοντα [20%] || ~ 45123 [80%]
++--	8:6	δε [25%] || τε [75%]
++--	8:21	εναντιον [25%] || ενωπιον [70%] ||
++--	9:12	ανανιαν ονοματι [25%] || ~ 21 [75%]
++	9:18	παραχρημα [30%] || --- [70%]
+--	9:19	των [35%] || 1 οντων [65%]
++--	9:20	ιησουν [25%] || χριστον [75%]
++--	9:28[a]	και εκπορευομενος [25%] || --- [75%]
+++	9:28[b]	εν [20%] || εις [80%]
+++	9:28[c]	ιησου [20%] || κυριου 1 [70%] ||
++--	9:29	ανελειν αυτον [25%] || ~ 21 [75%]
+++	9:30	εξαπεστειλαν [20%] || 1 αυτον [80%]
++--	9:37	τω [25%] || --- [75%]
+++	9:43	αυτον ημερας ικανας μειναι [20%] || ~ 2341 [79%]
++--	10:5	ος επικαλειται πετρος [25%] || τον επικαλουμενον πετρον [75%]
++	10:17	υπο [30%] || απο [70%]
++++	10:22	αγγελου [18%] || 1 αγιου [80%] ||
+	10:26	ηγειρεν αυτον [40%] || ~ 21 [60%]
++--	10:47	ως [25%] || καθως [75%]
+++	10:48	ιησου [20%] || --- [67%] || ||
+++	11:3	εισηλθεις προς ανδρας ακροβυστιαν εχοντας και συνεφαγες [20%] || ~ 2345167 [71%] ||
+++	11:9	εκ δευτερου φωνη [20%] || ~ 312 [80%]
++	11:13[a]	δε [30%] || τε [70%]
++--	11:13[b]	ιοππην [25%] || 1 ανδρας [75%]
+--	11:16[a]	του [35%] || --- [65%]
++--	11:16[b]	οτι [25%] || --- [75%]

<table>
<tr><td>++++</td><td>11:17[a]</td><td>ιησουν [18%] || 1 χριστον [82%]</td></tr>
<tr><td>++--</td><td>11:17[b]</td><td>εγω [25%] || 1 δε [75%]</td></tr>
<tr><td>++--</td><td>11:26[a]</td><td>ευρων [25%] || 1 αυτον [75%]</td></tr>
<tr><td>+--</td><td>11:26[b]</td><td>ηγαγεν [35%] || 1 αυτον [65%]</td></tr>
<tr><td>+++</td><td>12:6</td><td>προαγειν αυτον [20%] || ~ 21 [63%] ||</td></tr>
<tr><td>++++</td><td>12:20</td><td>τε [18%] || δε [70%] ||</td></tr>
<tr><td>++</td><td>12:22</td><td>θεου φωνη [30%] || ~ 21 [68%]</td></tr>
<tr><td>+++++</td><td>12:25</td><td>εις αντιοχειαν (5.1%)+{19.5%} || 1 ιερουσαλημ (60%) || || || ||[1]</td></tr>
<tr><td>+++</td><td>13:4[a]</td><td>μεν [20%] || 1 ουν [80%]</td></tr>
<tr><td>++--</td><td>13:4[b]</td><td>τε [27%] || δε [72%]</td></tr>
<tr><td>++--</td><td>13:12</td><td>εκπληττομενος [24%] || εκπλησσομενος [76%]</td></tr>
<tr><td>+++</td><td>13:15</td><td>προς αυτους οι αρχισυναγωγοι [20%] || ~ 3412 [80%]</td></tr>
<tr><td>++</td><td>13:26</td><td>εξαπεσταλη [30%] || απεσταλη [70%]</td></tr>
<tr><td>++</td><td>13:27</td><td>κατοικουντες [30%] || 1 εν [70%]</td></tr>
<tr><td>+++</td><td>13:39[a]</td><td>εν [20%] || 1 τω [80%]</td></tr>
<tr><td>+++</td><td>13:39[b]</td><td>μωυσεος [20%] || μωυσεως [40%] || μωσεως [40%]</td></tr>
<tr><td>+++</td><td>13:41</td><td>ω [20%] || ο [80%]</td></tr>
<tr><td>++++</td><td>13:43</td><td>επιμενειν αυτους [18%] || ~ 21 [64%] ||</td></tr>
<tr><td>+++</td><td>14:10</td><td>ηλλατο [20%] || ηλλετο [35%] || ||</td></tr>
<tr><td>+++</td><td>14:15</td><td>υμιν εσμεν [20%] || ~ 21 [60%] ||</td></tr>
<tr><td>++--</td><td>14:20</td><td>των μαθητων αυτον [25%] || ~ 312 [55%] ||</td></tr>
<tr><td>+++</td><td>14:21</td><td>εις [20%] || 1 την [80%]</td></tr>
<tr><td>+++</td><td>15:1</td><td>μωυσεος [20%] || μωυσεως [63%] ||</td></tr>
<tr><td>++--</td><td>15:5</td><td>μωσεως [25%] || μωυσεως [70%] ||</td></tr>
<tr><td>++</td><td>15:7</td><td>υμιν [30%] || ημιν [70%]</td></tr>
<tr><td>+++</td><td>15:21</td><td>μωσης [20%] || μωυσης [80%]</td></tr>
<tr><td>+++</td><td>15:23</td><td>κατα [20%] || 1 την [80%]</td></tr>
<tr><td>++--</td><td>15:25</td><td>εκλεξαμενοις [25%] || εκλεξαμενους [75%]</td></tr>
<tr><td>++</td><td>15:37</td><td>και [30%] || τον [60%] ||</td></tr>
<tr><td>+++</td><td>15:39</td><td>χωρισθηναι [20%] || αποχωρισθηναι [75%] ||</td></tr>
<tr><td>++++</td><td>16:3</td><td>ηδεσαν [18%] || ηδεισαν [70%] ||</td></tr>
<tr><td>++++</td><td>16:9</td><td>την [18%] || --- [82%]</td></tr>
<tr><td>++++</td><td>16:11</td><td>την [18%] || --- [82%]</td></tr>
<tr><td>+++</td><td>16:15</td><td>αυτη [20%] || --- [80%]</td></tr>
<tr><td>+++</td><td>16:17</td><td>τω σιλα [20%] || ημιν [80%]</td></tr>
<tr><td>+--</td><td>16:26</td><td>δε [35%] || τε [65%]</td></tr>
<tr><td>+++</td><td>16:37</td><td>δηραντες [20%] || δειραντες [80%]</td></tr>
<tr><td>++--</td><td>16:38</td><td>δε [25%] || και [75%]</td></tr>
<tr><td>+++</td><td>16:40</td><td>απο [20%] || εκ [80%]</td></tr>
<tr><td>+++</td><td>17:3</td><td>ιησους ο χριστος [20%] || ~ 231 [75%] ||</td></tr>
<tr><td>++</td><td>17:4</td><td>πληθος πολυ [30%] || ~ 21 [70%]</td></tr>
<tr><td>++</td><td>17:5</td><td>ανδρας τινας [30%] || ~ 21 [65%] ||</td></tr>
<tr><td>++</td><td>17:7</td><td>ετερον λεγοντες [30%] || ~ 21 [70%]</td></tr>
</table>

[1] This is the only place in the whole NT where Family 35 splinters, there being five significant variants (plus two minor ones). Usually there are only two variants, where the family is divided. For a detailed discussion of this variant set please see my article, "Where to place a comma—Acts 12:25", available from my site: www.prunch.org. It is also in the "Appendix" of *The Sovereign Creator Has Spoken*, as well as "Appendix II" in *The Greek New Testament According to Family 35*.

++--	17:10	βερροιαν [25%] ‖ βεροιαν [75%]
++	17:11	προθυμιας [30%] ‖ 1 το [70%]
++--	17:13	βερροια [25%] ‖ βεροια [75%]
+++	18:6	τας κεφαλας [20%] ‖ την κεφαλην [80%]
++--	18:13	αναπειθει ουτος [25%] ‖ ~ 21 [65%] ‖
++	18:19	κακεινους [29%] ‖ και εκεινους [70%]
++	18:25	ιησου [30%] ‖ κυριου [70%]
+++	19:3	τε (18.3%)+{6.2%} ‖ 1 προς αυτους (61.6%)+{6.2%} ‖ ‖
+++	19:11	δε [21%] ‖ τε [79%]
++	19:13	ο [30%] ‖ --- [70%]
+++	19:17	εγενετο πασιν γνωστον [20%] ‖ ~ 132 [75%] ‖
+++	19:19	συνεψηφισαντο [20%] ‖ συνεψηφισαν [67%] ‖
++	19:27[a]	αρτεμιδος ιερον [30%] ‖ ~ 21 [70%]
++	19:27[b]	ουδεν [30%] ‖ ουθεν [70%]
++	19:40	αποδουναι [30%] ‖ δουναι [70%]
++--	20:3	επιβουλης αυτω [25%] ‖ ~ 21 [75%]
++--	20:4	βερροιαιος [25%] ‖ βεροιαιος [35%] ‖ ‖
++--	20:15	τρωγυλιω [25%] ‖ τρωγυλλιω [30%] ‖ ‖ ‖ ‖
++++	20:18	ημερας [18%] ‖ 1 αφ [82%]
++++	20:35	του λογου [18%] ‖ τον λογον [57%] ‖ των λογων [25%]
++	20:37	κλαυθμος εγενετο [30%] ‖ ~ 21 [70%]
+	21:8	ηλθομεν (38.8%) ‖ οι περι τον παυλον ηλθον (46.4%) ‖ ‖
+++	21:21	μωυσεος [20%] ‖ μωυσεως [50%] ‖ μωσεως [30%]
++--	21:27	ημελλον [25%] ‖ εμελλον [65%] ‖
++--	21:31	σπειρας [25%] ‖ σπειρης [75%]
+++	21:37	εις την παρεμβολην εισαγεσθαι [20%] ‖ ~ 4123 [80%]
+++	21:40	προσεφωνει [20%] ‖ προσεφωνησεν [80%]
+++	22:19[a]	δαιρων [20%] ‖ δερων [80%]
+++	22:19[b]	εις [20%] ‖ επι [80%]
++	22:20	και[4] [30%] ‖ --- [70%]
+++	22:24	ο χιλιαρχος αγεσθαι αυτον [20%] ‖ ~ 4123 [64%] ‖ ‖
++	22:25	προετειναν [30%] ‖ προετεινεν [30%] ‖ ‖
++	22:26	τω χιλιαρχω απηγγειλεν [30%] ‖ ~ 312 [63%] ‖
+--	22:30[a]	υπο [35%] ‖ παρα [65%]
++	22:30[b]	παν [30%] ‖ ολον [70%]
+++	23:6	φαρισαιων το δε ετερον σαδδουκαιων [20%] ‖ ~ 52341 [80%]
+	23:8	μητε [40%] ‖ μηδε [60%]
++--	23:12[a]	εαυτους [25%] ‖ 1 λεγοντες [75%]
++++	23:12[b]	ανελωσιν [18%] ‖ αποκτεινωσιν [80%] ‖
++--	23:15	καταγαγη αυτον [20%] +{6%} ‖ ~ 21 [74%]
+--	23:20	μελλοντες (33.1%) ‖ μελλοντα (27.2%) ‖ ‖ ‖ ‖
+--	23:24	φηλικα [35%] ‖ φιληκα [25%] ‖ φιλικα [40%]
+	23:26	φηλικι [40%] ‖ φιληκι [30%] ‖ φιλικι [17%] ‖
+++	23:35	του [18%] + {4%} ‖ --- [75%]
++++	24:4	πλεον [18%] ‖ πλειον [79%]
++	24:10	δικαιον [30%] ‖ --- [70%]
++	24:19	εδει [30%] ‖ δει [70%]
++++	24:26	πυκνοτερον [18%] ‖ 1 αυτον [75%] ‖
+--	25:2	οι αρχιερεις [35%] ‖ ο αρχιερευς [60%] ‖
++--	25:9	υπ [25%] ‖ επ [73%] ‖
++	25:13	ασπασομενοι [30%] ‖ ασπασαμενοι [70%]

++++	25:20[a]	περι την [18%] ‖ ~ 21 [80%]
+--	25:20[b]	τουτων [35%] ‖ τουτου [65%]
++--	26:12	εις [25%] ‖ 1 την [75%]
++	26:18	επιστρεψαι [30%] ‖ υποστρεψαι [35%] ‖ αποστρεψαι [35%]
+++	27:1	σπειρας [20%] ‖ σπειρης [80%]
+++	27:2	ατραμυτινω [21%] ‖ αδραμυττηνω [25%] ‖ ‖ ‖ ‖ ‖
+++	27:5	κατηχθημεν [21%] ‖ κατηλθομεν [75%] ‖
+++	27:6	εις [20%] ‖ 1 την [80%]
+++	27:10	φορτου [22%] ‖ φορτιου [78%]
++--	27:31	εν τω πλοιω μεινωσιν [25%] ‖ ~ 4123 [75%]
++	27:34	μεταλαβειν [30%] ‖ προσλαβειν [70%]
++	27:38	δε [30%] ‖ 1 της [70%]
+++	27:41	εμενεν [22%] ‖ εμεινεν [78%]
++	28:3[a]	εξελθουσα [30%] ‖ διεξελθουσα [70%]
++--	28:3[b]	καθηψατο [25%] ‖ καθηψεν [72%]
+++	28:21	πονηρον περι σου [20%] ‖ ~ 231 [80%]
+++	28:23	μωυσεος [20%] ‖ μωσεως [35%] ‖ μωυσεως [45%]
++--	28:27	ιασωμαι [25%] ‖ ιασομαι [75%]

Key:

+++	around 20% = **f**[35] virtually alone = diagnostic (78)
++--	around 25% = quite good (53)
++	around 30% = not bad (35)
+--	around 35% (10)
+	around 40% (4)

Total: 180

Of all the books, **f**[35] has the most distinct profile in Acts, with far and away the most diagnostic variants.

Pauline Corpus

++--	Rom. 1:23	ηλλαξαντο [26%] ‖ ηλλαξαν [74%]
++--	Rom. 1:27[a]	ομοιως [23%] ‖ 1 τε [70%] ‖
+++	Rom. 1:27[b]	εξεκαυθησαν [20%] ‖ 1 εν [80%]
+++	Rom. 4:16	εκ [20%] ‖ 1 του [80%]
+	Rom. 5:1	εχωμεν (43%) ‖ εχομεν (57%)
+	Rom. 5:11	καυχωμεθα [38%] ‖ καυχωμενοι [52%] ‖
++	Rom. 5:14	μωυσεος [30%] ‖ μωυσεως [50%] ‖ μωσεως [20%]
++--	Rom. 9:13	ήσαυ [25%] ‖ ἠσαυ [75%]
++	Rom. 10:5	μωσης [30%] ‖ μωυσης [70%]
+++	Rom. 10:19	μωσης [20%] ‖ μωυσης [80%]
++	Rom. 11:7	τουτου [32%] ‖ τουτο [68%]
++--	Rom. 15:9	κυριε [27%] ‖ --- [73%]
+++	Rom. 16:6	υμας (22.8%) ‖ ημας (76.4%)
++++	Rom. 16:24	ημων [18%] ‖ υμων [82%]

++--	1Cor. 1:2	υμων [25%] ‖ ημων [75%]
+	1Cor. 4:11	γυμνιτευομεν [40%] ‖ γυμνητευομεν [60%]
+++	1Cor. 5:8	είλικρινειας [20%] ‖ εἰλικρινειας [55%] ‖

+-- 1Cor. 6:8 αλλ [35%] || αλλα [65%]
+-- 1Cor. 6:11 αλλ[1] [35%] || αλλα [65%]
++ 1Cor. 9:9 ἁλοωντα [30%] || ἀλοωντα [70%]
++ 1Cor. 9:10 ἁλοων [30%] || ἀλοων [70%]
+-- 1Cor. 9:26 δαιρων [35%] || δερων [65%]
++ 1Cor. 10:13 δυνατος [30%] || πιστος [70%]
++ 1Cor. 11:6 κειρεσθαι [32%] || κειρασθαι [64%]
+ 1Cor. 12:26[a] συμπασχη [40%] || συμπασχει [60%]
+ 1Cor. 12:26[b] συγχαιρη [40%] || συγχαιρει [60%]
++-- 1Cor. 14:25 οντως ο θεος εν υμιν εστιν [23%] || ~ 231456 [75%]
++ 1Cor. 16:2 ευοδουται [30%] || ευοδωται [61%] ||

++-- 2Cor. 1:12 εἱλικρινεια [25%] || εἰλικρινεια [60%] || || (also at 2:17)
+++ 2Cor. 1:15 προς υμας ελθειν το προτερον (21.6%) || ~ 31245 (61.1%) || ||
+-- 2Cor. 3:7 μωυσεος [35%] || μωυσεως [55%] ||
+ 2Cor. 3:10 εινεκεν [43%] || ενεκεν [57%]
+ 2Cor. 3:15 μωσης [40%] || μωυσης [60%]
+-- 2Cor. 5:15 παντων [35%] || αυτων [55%] ||
++-- 2Cor. 7:11 αλλ[1] [27%] || αλλα [73%]
++ 2Cor. 8:4 δεξασθαι ημας [30%] || --- [70%]
+ 2Cor. 8:9 ημας [40%] || υμας [60%]
++ 2Cor. 8:12 καθὸ εαν [30%] || καθ ὃ εαν [58%] ||
+++ 2Cor. 11:7 εαυτον [22%] || εμαυτον [78%]
+ 2Cor. 11:20 δαιρει [40%] || δερει [60%]
++ 2Cor. 13:11 της [30%] || --- [70%]
+ 2Cor. 13:13 ημων [40%] || --- [60%]

++ Gal. 1:12 αποκαλυψεως [30%] || 1 ιησου [70%]
+ Gal. 3:6,etc. ἁβρααμ [40%] || ἀβρααμ [60%]
+ Gal. 3:16 ερρεθησαν [40%] || ερρηθησαν [55%] ||
+ Gal. 4:2 αλλ [40%] || αλλα [60%]

++ Eph. 1:12 της [30%] || --- [70%]
+ Eph. 2:17 ημιν [40%] || υμιν [60%]
+-- Eph. 4:32 υμιν [35%] || ημιν [65%]
++ Eph. 5:5 ιστε [30%] || εστε [70%]
+ Eph. 6:6 οφθαλμοδουλιαν [40%] || οφθαλμοδουλειαν [60%]

++ Phip. 1:10 εἱλικρινεις [30%] || εἰλικρινεις [70%]
++-- Phip. 1:20 καραδοκιαν [25%] || αποκαραδοκιαν [74%]
+-- Phip. 2:1 τι[2] [35%] || τις [60%] ||
+ Phip. 2:4 το [40%] || τα [45%] || των [15%]
+ Phip. 2:30 πληρωση [40%] || αναπληρωση [55%] ||
+ Phip. 3:1 το [40%] || --- [60%]
+ Phip. 3:13 ουπω [40%] || ου [60%]

+	Col. 1:22	αυτου [40%] || --- [60%]
+	Col. 1:27	τις ο [40%] || τι το [60%]
+	Col. 1:28	χριστω [40%] || 1 ιησου [60%]
+	Col. 3:22	οφθαλμοδουλιαις [40%] || οφθαλμοδουλειαις [43%] || ||

+	1Th. 1:7	και [40%] || 1 τη [30%] || 1 εν τη [30%]
+	1Th. 1:9	υμων [40%] || ημων [60%]
+	1Th. 3:8	στηκητε [40%] || στηκετε [60%]
++	1Th. 4:9	γαρ [30%] || 1 υμεις [70%]

None for 2 Thessalonians. (f^{35} is always accompanied by at least 40% of the Byzantine bulk.)

+	1Tm. 3:2	νηφαλιον [40%] || νηφαλεον [50%] ||
+	1Tm. 3:11	νηφαλιους [40%] || νηφαλεους [50%] ||
++	1Tm. 5:18	ἁλοωντα [30%] || ἀλοωντα [70%]
++--	1Tm. 5:21	προσκλισιν [25%] || προσκλησιν f^{35pt} [75%]
+	1Tm. 6:12	και [40%] || --- [60%]

+++	2Tm. 3:6	ενδυοντες [20%] || ενδυνοντες [77%]
+++	2Tm. 3:14	οις² [20%] || --- [80%]

+	Titus 2:1	νηφαλιους [40%] || νηφαλεους [40%] || νηφαλαιους [20%]
+++	Titus 3:9	ερις [20%] || ερεις [75%] ||

+	Phin. 1	ιησου χριστου [40%] || ~ 21 [60%]
+++	Phin. 25	ιησου [20%] || 1 χριστου [80%]

+--	Heb. 2:4	σημειοις [35%] || 1 τε [65%]
+	Heb. 2:16,etc.	ἁβρααμ [40%] || ἀβρααμ [60%]
+	Heb. 3:16	μωυσεος [40%] || μωυσεως [45%] || μωσεως [15%]
+	Heb. 3:19	δια [40%] || δι [60%]
+	Heb. 6:3	ποιησομεν [40%] || ποιησωμεν [59%]
+++	Heb. 8:3	προσενεγκοι [20%] || προσενεγκη [80%]
+	Heb. 8:6	τετευχεν [40%] || τετυχεν [50%] ||
+--	Heb. 8:11	πλησιον [35%] || πολιτην [65%]
+++	Heb. 9:12	ευρομενος [20%] || ευραμενος [80%]
++	Heb. 9:14	αγιου [29%] || αιωνιου [70%]
+--	Heb. 9:19	μωυσεος [35%] || μωυσεως [45%] || μωσεως [20%]
+	Heb. 10:1	δυναται [40%] || δυνανται [59%]
++	Heb. 10:28	μωυσεος [30%] || μωυσεως [55%] || μωσεως [15%]
++	Heb. 11:20	ἡσαυ [30%] || ἠσαυ [70%] (also 12:16)
+--	Heb. 12:7	ει [35%] || εις [65%]
++	Heb. 12:24	το [30%] || τον [70%]
+	Heb. 12:25	ουρανου [40%] || ουρανων [60%]

Key:

+++	around 20% = **f^{35}** virtually alone = diagnostic (14)
++--	around 25% = quite good (10)
++	around 30% = not bad (21)
+--	around 35% = (11)
+	around 40% = (38)

Total: 94

General Epistles

++	James 1:23	νομου [30%] ‖ λογου [69%]
+--	James 1:26	αλλ [35%] ‖ αλλα [65%]
++	James 2:3	λαμπραν εσθητα [30%] ‖ ~ 2 την 1 [70%]
++--	James 2:4	ου (26.8%) ‖ και 1 (72.2%)
+++	James 2:13	ανηλεος [20%] ‖ ανελεος [30%] ‖ ανιλεως [50%]
++--	James 3:2	δυναμενος [23%] ‖ δυνατος [76.5%]
+++	James 3:4	ιθυνοντος [21%] ‖ ευθυνοντος [79%]
++--	James 4:11	γαρ [26%] ‖ --- [74%]
++--	James 4:14[a]	ημων [26%] ‖ υμων [74%]
++	James 4:14[b]	επειτα [29.5%] ‖ 1 δε και [46%] ‖ 1 δε [15%] ‖ 1 και [9.5%]
+--	James 5:10[a]	αδελφοι [35%] ‖ 1 μου [62%] ‖
+	James 5:10[b]	εν τω [40%] ‖ 2 [58%]

+	1Peter 1:3	ελεος αυτου [38%] ‖ ~ 21 [60%]
+--	1Peter 1:7	δοξαν και τιμην [35%] ‖ ~ 321 [28%] ‖ ~ 32 εις 1 [37%]
+	1Peter 1:23	αλλ [40%] ‖ αλλα [60%]
+--	1Peter 2:6	ή [35%] ‖ εν τη [59%] ‖
++--	1Peter 2:21	και [23%] ‖ --- [77%]
++--	1Peter 3:10	ημερας ιδειν [26%] ‖ ~ 21 [74%]
+++	1Peter 3:16	τη αγαθη εν χριστω αναστροφη [20%] ‖ την αγαθην 34 αναστροφην [50%] ‖ ~ την 34 αγαθην αναστροφην [24%] ‖ ‖
+++	1Peter 4:2	του [22%] ‖ --- [78%]
+	1Peter 4:3[a]	υμιν (41.7%) ‖ ημιν (47.1%) ‖ --- (11.2%)
++--	1Peter 4:3[b]	χρονος [26%] ‖ 1 του βιου [74%]
+++	1Peter 4:11[a]	δοξαζηται θεος [20%] ‖ 1 ο 2 [73%] ‖
++--	1Peter 4:11[b]	αιωνας [27%] ‖ 1 των αιωνων [73%]
+	1Peter 4:14	αναπεπαυται [39%] ‖ αναπαυεται [52%] ‖ ‖
+--	1Peter 5:7	υπερ [35%] ‖ περι [65%]
++--	1Peter 5:8	περιερχεται [24%] ‖ περιπατει [76%]
++	1Peter 5:10	στηριξαι…σθενωσαι…θεμελιωσαι [30%] ‖ στηριξει…σθενωσει…θεμελιωσει [66%] ‖

+++	2Peter 2:2	ας [20%] ‖ ους [80%]
+--	2Peter 2:9	πειρασμων [33%] ‖ πειρασμου [67%]
++--	2Peter 2:12	γεγενημενα φυσικα [26%] ‖ ~ 21 [54%] ‖ ‖
++--	2Peter 2:17	εις αιωνας (25.1%) ‖ 1 αιωνα (70.3%) ‖ ‖
+	2Peter 2:18	ασελγειας [40%] ‖ ασελγειαις [60%]

+++	2Peter 3:1	είλικρινη [20%] || ειλικρινη [80%]
++--	2Peter 3:5	συνεστωτα [23%] || συνεστωσα [76%]
+--	2Peter 3:16	εισιν [33%] || εστιν [67%]
++--	2Peter 3:18	αυξανητε [27%] || αυξανετε [60%] || || ||

++	1John 1:6	περιπατουμεν [29%] || περιπατωμεν [71%]
+--	1John 2:24	πατρι και εν τω υιω [35%] || ~ 52341 [65%]
+--	1John 2:29	ειδητε [37%] || ιδητε [59%] ||
+--	1John 3:1	ημας [36%] || υμας [63.5%]
+++	1John 3:6	και [20%] || --- [80%]
++	1John 3:24	εν [30%] || και 1 [70%]
+--	1John 4:16	αυτω [37%] || 1 μενει [63%]
++--	1John 5:11	ο θεος ημιν [24%] || ~ 312 [76%]

++	2John 5	εχομεν [32%] || ειχομεν [68%]
+++	2John 9	δε [20%] || --- [80%]

++--	3John 11	δε [25%] || --- [75%]
++--	3John 12	οιδαμεν (23%) || οιδατε (61.5%) || οιδας (15.1%)

None for Jude. (**f**[35] is always accompanied by at least 40% of the Byzantine bulk.)

Key:

+++	around 20% = **f**[35] virtually alone = diagnostic (9)
++--	around 25% = quite good (16)
++	around 30% = not bad (7)
+--	around 35% (11)
+	around 40% (6)

Total: 49

Apocalypse

Due to Hoskier's collations, it is possible (and better) to state the evidence in terms of families, instead of percentages, as I have done in my apparatus—please consult it for the evidence.

+++	1:2	ἅ || ἅτινα || ---
+	1:5	εκ || ---
++	1:13	μαζοις || μαστοις || μασθοις
+--	2:2	κοπον || 1 σου
++--	2:7	δωσω || 1 αυτω
++--	2:24	βαλω || βαλλω
+++	3:2	εμελλες αποβαλειν || 1 αποβαλλειν || ημελλες αποβαλλειν || etc.
+--	3:5	ουτως || ουτος
++	3:18[a]	κολλουριον || κουλουριον || κολλυριον

+++	3:18b	εγχρισον επι || 1 || ινα εγχριση || ινα εγχρισαι || εγχρισαι || etc.
+	4:3	ομοια || ομοιος || ομοιως
+++	4:4	ειδον || ---
+	4:6	κρυσταλω || κρυσταλλω
+++	4:8	λεγοντα || λεγοντες
+	5:2	αξιος || 1 εστιν
++--	6:8	θανατος || ο 1 || ο αθανατος
+	6:9	των ανθρωπων || ---
+	6:12	και || ---
+	8:9	διεφθαρησαν || διεφθαρη
+	8:13	τρις || ---
+++	9:4	μονους || ---
+++	9:5	πληξη || παιση || πεση
+--	9:6	ζητουσιν || ζητησουσιν
+++	9:11	αββαδδων || αββαδων || αββααδων || αββααδδων || αβαδδων
+--	9:15	και την ημεραν || 1 εις 23 || 13 || ---
++	10:7a	τελεσθη || και 1 || και ετελεσθη
+	10:7b	ὅ || ως
++	10:7c	ευηγγελισατο || ευηγγελισεν || ευηγγελησε
++	11:1	και ειστηκει ο αγγελος λεγων || 1 φωνη λεγουσα || 5 || λεγει
+	11:11	επ αυτους || εις 2 || εν αυτοις || αυτοις
+	11:17	και ο ερχομενος || ---
+--	12:3	μεγας πυρρος || 1 πυρος || ~ 21 || ~ πυρος 1
+++	12:4	τικτειν || τεκειν
++--	12:5	ηρπαγη || ηρπασθη
++--	12:7	του πολεμησαι || 2 || επολεμησαν
+	13:7	φυλην || 1 και λαον
+	13:15	ινα2 || ---
+	14:6	αλλον αγγελον || 2 || ~ 21
+++	14:12	του ιησου || 2 || 2 χριστου
+	15:3	μωυσεος || μωυσεως || μωσεως
++--	15:4	αγιος ει || 1 || 2 || οσιος
+++	15:6	εκ του ουρανου || 12 ναου || ---
+	16:9	την || ---
+	17:8	βλεποντες || βλεποντων
+--	18:2	εν ισχυρα φωνη || 123 μεγαλη || 123 και μεγαλη || 23 || 23 μεγαλη || etc.
+	18:3	πεπωκεν || πεπωκασιν || πεπωτικεν || πεπτωκασιν || πεπτωκαν || πεπωκαν
+	18:7	βασανισμον || 1 και πενθος
+	18:14a	απωλοντο || απωλετο || απηλθεν
+	18:14b	ου μη ευρησεις αυτα || 12 ευρησης 4 || 12 ευρης 4 || 12 ευρησουσιν 4 || etc.
++--	18:17	ο επι των πλοιων πλεων || 2345 || 234 ομιλος || 234 ο ομιλος || etc.
+++	18:21	λεγων || 1 ουτως
+++	19:1	φωνην οχλου πολλου μεγαλην || ~ 1423 || 123 || φωνης 23
+	20:4	το μετωπον αυτων || 12 || των μετωπων 3 ||
++--	20:11	ο ουρανος και η γη || ~ 45312
+++	20:12a	ανεωχθησαν || ηνεωχθησαν || ηνοιχθησαν || ηνοιξαν
++--	20:12b	ανεωχθη || ηνεωχθη || ηνοιχθη

+++	20:14	εστιν ο θανατος ο δευτερος || ~ 1453 || ~ 23451 || ~ 2351 || --- || ~ 4531
+	21:5	καινα ποιω παντα || ~ 312 || ||
+	21:6	αρχη και τελος || η 12 το 3 || και η 12 το 3
++--	21:10	την μεγαλην την αγιαν || 12 και 4 || 34
+	21:24	την δοξαν και την τιμην αυτων εις αυτην || 12678 || αυτω 235 των εθνων 78 ||
+--	22:2	εκαστον αποδιδους || 1 αποδιδον || 1 αποδιδουν || ~ 21 || ~ 2 εκαστος

Key:

+++	$\mathbf{f}^{35}$ is alone, or virtually so (15)
++--	$\mathbf{f}^{35}$ is joined by part of another family (small) (10)
++	$\mathbf{f}^{35}$ is joined by a whole small family (not **a** or **e**) (5)
+--	$\mathbf{f}^{35}$ is joined by a whole small family (not **a** or **e**) plus (7)
+	$\mathbf{f}^{35}$ is joined by less than either of the other two main lines of transmission (25)

Total: 62

Here are the totals for the whole New Testament.

Key:

+++	around 20% = $\mathbf{f}^{35}$ virtually alone = diagnostic (161)
++--	around 25% = quite good (144)
++	around 30% = not bad (153)
+--	around 35% (81)
+	around 40% (119)

Total: 658

The evidence is clear. **Family 35** is an objectively/empirically defined entity throughout the New Testament. It remains to be seen if the same can be said for any other family or line of transmission—attention please: that is for all 27 books (a number of lines are confined to the Gospels, such as $\mathbf{f}^{1}$ and $\mathbf{f}^{13}$).

Family 35 is characterized by incredibly careful transmission (in contrast to other lines). I have a perfect copy of the Family 35 archetypal text for most NT books (22); I have copies made from a perfect exemplar (presumed) for another four (4); as I continue to collate MSS I hope to add the last one (Acts), but even for it the archetypal form is demonstrable. If God was preserving the original wording in some line of transmission other than Family 35, would that line be any less careful? I think not. So any line of transmission characterized by internal confusion is disqualified—this includes **all** the other lines of transmission that I have seen so far.

Epistemology

Kind reader, permit me to suggest that the matter of epistemology has not received the attention it deserves within the discipline of NT textual criticism. Epistemology deals with the nature of knowledge, including origin and foundations. Where does knowledge come from? "The fear of the Lord is the beginning of knowledge" (Proverbs 1:7). Is that correct? It can only be correct if the Sovereign Creator exists—to fear a nonexistent being will not result in true knowledge. Any evolutionist will naturally exclude the supernatural from any model that he creates, as did Fenton John Anthony Hort. Note that such a model does not allow for the possibility of a divinely inspired NT. The evolutionary hypothesis, as a theory of origins, is scientifically impossible; the evidence that surrounds us clearly points to the existence of an incredibly intelligent and powerful Creator.

If the Creator exists, and if He has delivered a written Revelation to our race, nothing should be more important to us than to know what He said. Of course, because He will be the Source of all true knowledge. Stop and think. If some Being created our planet with all it contains, including all forms of life (plants have life), and especially including our ability to reason,[1] He is obviously competent to give us correct information about what He created. He is the Source of objective truth about our planet. How do we 'know' anything? Only if we have experienced it, or if someone else has experienced it and tells us about it. But what happens if experiences conflict? And how can we know if or when we interpret an experience correctly? And how can we handle conflicting interpretations?

If there is no Creator to give us correct information, our 'knowledge' is condemned to be always partial and uncertain, when not dangerously mistaken. This is equally true for those who pretend that there is no Creator. The despair of relativism and unrelenting uncertainty about everything that is not hard science is the result. King Solomon was smart enough to figure that out 3,000 years ago: "Vanity of vanities, all is vanity!" (Ecclesiastes 1:2).

Satan has been filling the world with sophistries for 6,000 years, so there is no end of fake 'knowledge' out there—not least in the 'science' of NT textual criticism. For someone who claims to be a Christian to exclude the supernatural from his working model is to involve himself in a fundamental epistemological contradiction. He claims to be a Christian, but he works like an atheist. Anyone who excludes the supernatural from his

---

[1] Remember Descartes? "I think, therefore I am."

thinking obviously does not have the Holy Spirit, and is therefore wide-open to satanic interference in his mind.[1]

It will not do for someone to claim that he is only trying to be neutral; neither God nor Satan will allow neutrality. The Sovereign Creator, while He walked this earth as Jesus, was quite clear on the subject. "He who is not with me is against me, and he who does not gather with me scatters" (Matthew 12:30, Luke 11:23). Please note that this includes both what we believe and what we do: scattering is an activity. To work like an atheist is to be against Jesus. To practice atheistic textual criticism is to be against Jesus. Neutrality does not exist.

In 1881, when Westcott and Hort published their two-volume work, John William Burgon immediately began demonstrating that their theory and work was contrary to the empirical evidence. Burgon's biographer wrote this: "Burgon was in this country [England] the leading religious teacher of his time".[2] Burgon was a man of unquestioned scholarship; his biographer lists over fifty published works, on a considerable variety of subjects. His index of New Testament citations by early Christian leaders consists of sixteen thick manuscript volumes, to be found in the British Library; it contains 86,489 quotations.[3] Burgon's scholarship in this area of the total field has never been equaled. He may be the only person, living or dead, who personally collated each of the five great early uncials (known in his day)—א, A, B, C, D—in their entirety (NT). He catalogued 374 Greek MSS; in those days there were not even microfilms, he had to go personally to wherever a MS was held.

Because of Burgon's firsthand acquaintance with the empirical evidence, his refutation of Hort's theory has never been answered, at least based on the evidence. He was either ignored, or misrepresented: 'all he does is count MSS', a perverse (and grotesque) falsehood; 'he just doesn't understand genealogy', equally perverse and equally false.[4] But the most

---

[1] I have written extensively on the subject of biblical spiritual warfare. Most of it may be found in my book, *Essays on Discipleship, Missions and Spiritual Warfare*, 2nd edition, 2017. It is also available from my website, www.prunch.org (or www.prunch.com.br). For starters, you should meditate on Ephesians 2:2, along with Luke 8:12 and 2 Corinthians 4:3-4.

[2] E.M. Goulburn, Life of Dean Burgon (London: John Murray, 1892, 2 vols.), I, vii.

[3] Leo Vaganay, *An Introduction to the Textual Criticism of the New Testament*, trans. B.V. Miller (London: Sands and Co., Ltd., 1937), p. 48.

[4] Most 'scholars' and professors are really 'parrots', just repeating what they were taught—they have never gone back to the source to see if it is true. How many Greek NT 'scholars' have collated even one Greek manuscript? (Did Hort collate any MSS?) They blindly accept what has been written on the subject, perhaps not realizing that most of

strident, and ongoing, criticism was that his argumentation was theological, because he believed in, and defended, the divine inspiration of the NT. It is here that epistemology comes in: the attacks against Burgon were really a malignant epistemology attacking a godly epistemology.

It is impossible to work without presuppositions, in any discipline. It is therefore perverse to criticize someone for having them. That said, presuppositions can, and should be evaluated. Once evaluated, a presupposition may reasonably be criticized. The concrete (empirical) evidence is presumably the same for everyone, but the interpretation that one gives to the evidence will be controlled (or at least heavily influenced) by his presuppositions. It follows that every honest scholar should openly state his presuppositions. To fail to do so is reprehensible.[1] For someone who does not state his presuppositions to criticize someone else for doing so is worse than perverse—to pretend that he himself does not have any is depraved (well, maybe just brainwashed and blinded).

Although I am not in Burgon's class as a scholar (living in the Amazon jungle with an indigenous people did not permit scholarly research), I also have been constantly criticized for openly stating my belief that God both inspired and preserved the NT. It is even alleged that such a belief makes it impossible to do objective scholarly work. Well, well, well, if a servant of God cannot do objective scholarly work, then a servant of Satan most certainly cannot do so either. So on what basis does a servant of Satan criticize a servant of God? He does so on the basis of his presuppositions, his epistemology.

A brother who lives in Curitiba, the state capital of Paraná, recently wrote an introduction to a book in Portuguese that I am co-authoring. He praises my work from the point of view of epistemology. I found his argument to be so interesting (it inspired this article) that I translated it, sent the translation to him to be sure I got it right, and asked his permission to use it. His name is Carlos Eduardo Rangel Xavier. I ask you to concentrate on his argument, and not be distracted by the praise.

> Dr. Pickering's work within NT textual criticism (although he himself does not consider himself a textual critic[2]), especially in the collating of manuscripts, is impressive and incomparable.

---

what has been written was done by 'parrots'.

[1] While I was a student in theological seminary we were taught that we should never question someone else's motives. Now really, where do you suppose that 'doctrine' came from?

[2] True. I consider myself a textual student; the Text is above me. A critic is above the text. I do not have a theory of textual criticism; my theory is about textual preservation.

But more than that, his theory about the preservation of the New Testament by means of the group of manuscripts that he identifies as Family 35 is endowed with an epistemological solidity, with a methodological rigor and with an apologetic value that are equally impressive.

From an epistemological and apologetic point of view, his work starts with the presuppositional premise that God delivered a written revelation to the human race, and that would not make sense if His divine providence were not going to preserve that written revelation. As with every epistemological first principle, this point needs to be presupposed, and Dr. Pickering has always insisted upon making his presuppositions very clear, thereby demonstrating intellectual honesty.

But it is in the analysis of the empirical evidence that the impressive methodological rigor of Dr. Pickering's theory resides.

Although I insist upon emphasizing that his theory has a presuppositional epistemological base, I will nevertheless introduce a consideration of the empirical evidences using a completely different axis. As a consequence of the recent impact that scholars like Alvin Plantinga and William Lane Craig have contributed to my studies, I will now use modal logic to work on the base of an evidential apologetic.

Therefore, after making clear that the lines that follow refer exclusively to a work of persuasive argumentation, using modal logic, that I am here elaborating (and not to the way in which Dr. Pickering constructs his arguments), I can enunciate the following premises as a basis for reasoning about the preservation of the New Testament Text exemplified by Family 35.

1. It is possible that God delivered a written revelation to the human race.
2. If God delivered such a revelation to us, it is reasonable that it would be preserved.
3. The existence of a preserved text confirms 1) and 2).
4. The only type of text that objectively exemplifies 3) is that of Family 35.

To believe that God exists is a decision of faith. But it is not an irrational faith, since the Christian faith constitutes, as Alvin

Platinga has argued, a warranted belief, and that therefore corresponds to true knowledge, if the object of that belief is true. The traditional apologetic arguments for the existence of God function in this area.

On the other hand, the historical consideration of the person of Jesus is related to the question of revelation, since all the basic facts of the Christian faith lead to Christ as the culminating point in the process of self-revelation by God in History.

Therefore, if a God who created all things exists, and if He decided to reveal Himself to us in Christ, it is perfectly reasonable to infer that He also delivered and preserved a written revelation for us.

In other words, the only premise that is added to the basic facts of the Christian faith by inference is the preservation of the Text of the New Testament. That is to say, Dr. Pickering's Trinitarian theism presupposes not only the God who is Creator, Redeemer and Provider, but adds to God's Providence, by a simple rational inference, the preservation of the New Testament Text.

However all that may be, it is important to note that although I assigned the proof of 1) to traditional apologetics, and that in addition 2) may reasonably be inferred on the basis of 1), the fact remains that, for the purpose of analyzing the argument, proposition 3) follows from 1) and 2). Therefore, the whole validity of the argument depends only on proving 4); that is to say, that the text of Family 35 is the only text type of the New Testament that can be demonstrated objectively as having been preserved. It is here that Dr. Pickering's work comes into play.

It is precisely at this point, the demonstration of proposition 4), that Dr. Pickering's work ceases to be merely presuppositional and becomes empirical, analyzing the evidence in an objective way, something that any respectable contemporary scientist tries to do.

That is, the demonstration of the antiquity and the independence of the text of Family 35 is based on objective arguments and on a comparison of the evidences (all the extant manuscripts). In this area as well, Dr. Pickering's work is incomeparable.

Taking advantage of the correlation with apologetics, I can state that Dr. Pickering's work with the evidences, just like

Christian apologetics, uses a strategy of both defense and offence.

From the point of view of defense, his work consists in pointing out the inconsistency of the subjective postulates of the eclectic theory, and in demonstrating objectively the inferior quality of the earliest manuscripts.

From the point of view of offence, his work consists in looking at the possible lines of transmission of the text and in analyzing objectively the available evidences—that is, the manuscripts. The conclusion to which he has arrived is that Family 35 is the only archetype for the text of the whole New Testament that can be objectively demonstrated. [It is certainly the only one that has been demonstrated so far.]

Thank you, Professor Xavier! Anyone who deals fairly with my work[1] knows that I do not use supernatural or theological arguments to defend the divine preservation of the NT text. My claim that Family 35 preserves the Original wording is based entirely on empirical evidence, and logical deduction based on that evidence. If I use divine providence at all, it is only to explain the facts, not to arrive at them. The only way to explain the internal character of Family 35 is to understand that God was preserving His Text.

I insist that I am not a pure empiricist. My work is anchored in a transcendental premise. My collation of MSS has provided the empirical attestation of the premise. I do not use the premise to arrive at the facts; I arrive at the facts empirically. I use the premise to explain the facts, once they have been empirically determined. **My epistemology is based on the person and work of Sovereign Jesus.**[2]

The Dating of K^r (alias f^{35}, nee f^{18}) Revisited

When Hermann von Soden identified $\mathbf{K^r}$ and proclaimed it to be a revision of $\mathbf{K^x}$ made in the **XII** century, he rendered a considerable disservice to the Truth and to those with an interest in identifying the original wording of the NT Text. This section argues that if von Soden had really

---

[1] Since Satan obliges his servants to prevaricate, I do not expect to be treated fairly by them.

[2] Hebrews 1:10, John 1:10 and Colossians 1:16 make clear that of the three Persons who make up the Godhead, Jehovah the Son was the primary agent in the creation of our planet and our race. So He is the Source of all true knowledge relative to life on this planet, as Colossians 2:3 plainly states: "in whom all the treasures of the wisdom and the knowledge are hidden".

paid attention to the evidence available in his day, he could not have perpetrated such an injustice.

Those familiar with my work know that I began by using **f**[18] instead of **K**[r], because minuscule 18 is the family member with the smallest number. I then switched to **f**[35] for the following reasons: 1) although 18 is sometimes a purer representative of the texttype than is minuscule 35, in the Apocalypse 18 defects to another type, while 35 remains true [both MSS contain the whole NT]; 2) while 18 is dated to the **XIV** century, 35 is dated to the **XI**, thus giving the lie, all by itself, to von Soden's dictum that **K**[r] was created in the **XII** century. Further, if 35 is a copy, not a new creation, then its exemplar had to be older, and so on.

After doing a complete collation of 1,389 MSS that contain the whole *Pericope Adulterae* (there were a few others that certainly contain the pericope but could not be collated because the microfilm was illegible), Maurice Robinson concluded:

> Based upon the collated data, the present writer is forced to reverse his previous assumptions regarding the development and restoration/preservation of the Byzantine Textform in this sense: although textual transmission itself is a process, it appears that, for the most part, the lines of transmission remained separate, with relatively little mixture occurring or becoming perpetuated...
>
> Certainly, all the types of PA text are distinct, and reflect a long line of transmission and preservation in their separate integrities... ... ...
>
> ... ...
>
> It thus appears that the Byzantine minuscule MSS preserve lines of transmission which are not only independent but which of necessity had their origin at a time well before the 9th century.[1]

---

[1] "Preliminary Observations regarding the *Pericope Adulterae* based upon Fresh Collations of nearly all Continuous-Text Manuscripts and over One Hundred Lectionaries", presented to the Evangelical Theological Society, Nov., 1998, pp. 12-13. However, I have received the following clarification from Maurice Robinson: "I would request that if my name gets cited in regard to your various K[r] or M[7] articles that you make it clear that I do not concur with your assessment of K[r] or M[7]. This is particularly the case with the "Preliminary Considerations regarding the Pericope Adulterae" article; it should not be used to suggest that I consider the M[7] line or K[r] text to be early. This would be quite erroneous, since I hold with virtually all others that K[r]/M[7] are indeed late texts that reflect recensional activity beginning generally in the 12th century (perhaps with 11th century base exemplars, but nothing earlier)." [Assuming that he was sincere when he wrote that article, I wonder what new evidence came his way that caused him to change his mind—

Fair enough. If $\mathbf{K}^r$ ($\mathbf{M}^7$) was preserved in its 'separate integrity' during 'a long line of transmission' then it would have to have its origin 'at a time well before the 9th century'. Besides the witness of 35, Robinson's collations demonstrate that minuscule 1166 and lectionary 139, both of the **X** century, reflect $\mathbf{K}^r$. If they are copies, not new creations, then their exemplars had to be older, and so on. Without adducing any further evidence, it seems fair to say that $\mathbf{K}^r$ must have existed already in the **IX** century, if not the **VIII**.

For years, based on the *Text und Textwert* series, I have insisted that $\mathbf{K}^r$ is both ancient and independent. Robinson would seem to agree. "The lack of extensive cross-comparison and correction demonstrated in the extant MSS containing the PA precludes the easy development of any existing form of the PA text from any other form of the PA text during at least the vellum era."[1] "The vellum era"—does not that take us back to the **IV** century, at least? As a matter of fact, yes. Consider:

Acts 4:34—	τις ην	$\mathbf{K}^r$ ℵA (~21 B) [$\mathbf{K}^r$ is independent, and both $\mathbf{K}^r$ and $\mathbf{K}^x$ are **IV** century]
	τις υπηρχεν	$\mathbf{K}^x$ P^8D
Acts 15:7—	εν υμιν	$\mathbf{K}^r$ ℵABC,it^{pt} [$\mathbf{K}^r$ is independent, and both $\mathbf{K}^r$ and $\mathbf{K}^x$ are ancient]
	εν ημιν	$\mathbf{K}^x$ (D)lat
Acts 19:3—	ειπεν τε	$\mathbf{K}^r$ B(D) [$\mathbf{K}^r$ is independent, and both $\mathbf{K}^r$ and $\mathbf{K}^x$ are ancient]
	ο δε ειπεν	ℵA(P^{38})bo
	ειπεν τε προς αυτους	$\mathbf{K}^x$ sy^p,sa
Acts 21:8—	ηλθομεν	$\mathbf{K}^r$ ℵAC(B)lat,syr,cop [$\mathbf{K}^r$ is older than $\mathbf{K}^x$, very ancient]
	οι περι τον παυλον ηλθον	$\mathbf{K}^x$
Acts 23:20—	μελλοντες	(33.1%) $\mathbf{K}^r$ lat,syr,sa [$\mathbf{K}^r$ is independent and very ancient; there is no $\mathbf{K}^x$]
	μελλοντα	(27.2%) {HF,RP}
	μελλοντων	(17.4%)
	μελλων	(9.2%) AB,bo
	μελλον	(7.5%) {NU} ℵ
	μελλοντας	(5.4%)

---

his language there is certainly plain enough. Further, I had a copy of his collations in my hand for two months, spending much of that time poring over them, and saw no reason to question his conclusions in the Nov., 1998 article.]

[1] *Ibid.*, p. 13.

Rom. 5:1—	εχωμεν	(43%) $\mathbf{K}^r$ $\mathbf{K}^{x(1/3)}$ ℵABCD,lat,bo [did part of $\mathbf{K}^x$ assimilate to $\mathbf{K}^r$?]
	εχομεν	(57%) $\mathbf{K}^{x(2/3)}$
Rom. 16:6—	εις υμας	$\mathbf{K}^r$ P^{46}ℵABC [$\mathbf{K}^r$ is independent and very ancient, **II/III** century]
	εις ημας	$\mathbf{K}^x$
	εν υμιν	D
2 Cor. 1:15—	προς υμας ελθειν το προτερον	$\mathbf{K}^r$ [$\mathbf{K}^r$ is independent!]
	προς υμας ελθειν	ℵ
	προτερον προς υμας ελθειν	ABC
	προτερον ελθειν προς υμας	D,lat
	ελθειν προς υμας το προτερον	$\mathbf{K}^x$
2 Cor. 2:17—	λοιποι	$\mathbf{K}^r\mathbf{K}^{x(pt)}$ P^{46}D,syr [$\mathbf{K}^r$ is very ancient, **II/III** century]
	πολλοι	$\mathbf{K}^{x(pt)}$ ℵABC,lat,cop
James 1:23—	νομου	$\mathbf{K}^r$ [$\mathbf{K}^r$ is independent][1]
	λογου	$\mathbf{K}^x$ ℵABC
James 2:3—	την λαμπραν εσθητα	$\mathbf{K}^r$ [$\mathbf{K}^r$ is independent]
	την εσθητα την λαμπραν	$\mathbf{K}^x$ ℵABC
James 2:4—	— ου	$\mathbf{K}^r$ ℵABC [$\mathbf{K}^r$ is independent and ancient]
	και ου	$\mathbf{K}^x$
James 2:8—	σεαυτον	$\mathbf{K}^r$ ℵABC [$\mathbf{K}^r$ is independent and ancient]
	εαυτον	$\mathbf{K}^x$
James 2:14—	εχει	$\mathbf{K}^r$ [$\mathbf{K}^r$ is independent]
	εχη	$\mathbf{K}^x$ ℵABC
James 3:2—	δυναμενος	$\mathbf{K}^r$ ℵ [$\mathbf{K}^r$ is independent and ancient]
	δυνατος	$\mathbf{K}^x$ AB
James 3:4—	ιθυνοντος	$\mathbf{K}^r$ [$\mathbf{K}^r$ is independent; a rare classical spelling]
	ευθυνοντος	$\mathbf{K}^x$ ℵABC
James 4:11—	ο γαρ	$\mathbf{K}^r$ [$\mathbf{K}^r$ is independent]
	ο —	$\mathbf{K}^x$ ℵAB

[1] For the examples from James I also consulted *Editio Critica Maior*.

James 4:14—	ημων	$\mathbf{K}^r$ [$\mathbf{K}^r$ is independent]
	υμων	$\mathbf{K}^x$ ℵA(P^{100}B)
James 4:14—	επειτα	$\mathbf{K}^r$ [$\mathbf{K}^r$ is independent]
	επειτα και	ℵAB
	επειτα δε και	$\mathbf{K}^x$
1 Pet. 3:16—	καταλαλουσιν	$\mathbf{K}^r$ ℵAC,sy^p,bo [$\mathbf{K}^r$ is independent and ancient
	καταλαλωσιν	$\mathbf{K}^x$
	καταλαλεισθε	P^{72}B,sa
1 Pet. 4:3—	υμιν	$\mathbf{K}^r$ ℵbo [$\mathbf{K}^r$ is independent and ancient]
	ημιν	$\mathbf{K}^x$ C
	(omit)	P^{72}AB,lat,syr,sa
2 Pet. 2:17—	εις αιωνας	$\mathbf{K}^r$ [$\mathbf{K}^r$ is independent]
	εις αιωνα	$\mathbf{K}^x$ AC
	(omit)	P^{72}ℵB,lat,syr,cop
3 John 12—	οιδαμεν	$\mathbf{K}^r$ [$\mathbf{K}^r$ is independent]
	οιδατε	$\mathbf{K}^x$
	οιδας	ℵABC

So what conclusions may we draw from this evidence? $\mathbf{K}^r$ is independent of $\mathbf{K}^x$ and both are ancient, dating at least to the **IV** century.[1] A few of the examples could be interpreted to mean that $\mathbf{K}^r$ is older than $\mathbf{K}^x$, dating to the **III** and even the **II** century, but I will leave that possibility on the back burner and look at some further evidence. The following examples are based on *Text und Textwert* and the IGNTP *Luke*.

Luke 1:55—	εως αιωνος	$\mathbf{K}^r$ C [$\mathbf{K}^r$ is independent and **V** century]
	εις τον αιωνα	$\mathbf{K}^x$ ℵAB
Luke 1:63—	εσται	$\mathbf{K}^r$ C [$\mathbf{K}^r$ is independent and **V** century]
	εστιν	$\mathbf{K}^x$ ℵAB
Luke 3:12—	υπ αυτου και	$\mathbf{K}^r$ C [$\mathbf{K}^r$ is independent and **V** century]
	— — και	$\mathbf{K}^x$ ℵABD

[1] Someone may object that it is the readings that are ancient, not the text-types; but if a text-type is clearly independent, with constantly shifting alignments among the early witnesses, then it has ancient readings because it itself is ancient. And in the case of $\mathbf{K}^r$ there are many hundreds of variant sets where its reading has overt early attestation. (Recall that Aland's **M** and Soden's **K** include $\mathbf{K}^r$—the poor text-type itself should not be held responsible for the way modern scholars treat it.) If it can be demonstrated objectively that a text-type has hundreds of early readings, but it cannot be demonstrated objectively to have any late ones, on what basis can it be declared to be late?

Luke 4:7—	σοι	**K**^{r} [**K**^{r} is independent]
	σου	**K**^{x} ℵAB
Luke 4:42—	εζητουν	**K**^{r} [**K**^{r} is independent]
	επεζητουν	**K**^{x} ℵABCD
Luke 5:1—	περι	**K**^{r} [**K**^{r} is independent]
	παρα	**K**^{x} P^{75}ℵABC
Luke 5:19—	ευροντες δια	**K**^{r} [**K**^{r} is independent]
	ευροντες —	**K**^{x} ℵABCD
Luke 5:19—	πως	**K**^{r} [**K**^{r} is independent]
	ποιας	**K**^{x} ℵABC
Luke 6:7—	— τω	**K**^{r} D [**K**^{r} is independent and **V** century]
	εν τω	**K**^{x} ℵAB
Luke 6:10—	ουτως και	**K**^{r} [**K**^{r} is independent]
	—— και	**K**^{x} ℵABD
Luke 6:26—	καλως ειπωσιν υμας	**K**^{r} ℵA [**K**^{r} is independent and **IV** century]
	καλως υμας ειπωσιν	K^{x} D
	υμας καλως ειπωσιν	P^{75}B
Luke 6:26—	παντες οι	**K**^{r} P^{75}AB(ℵ) [**K**^{r} is independent and early **III** century]
	—— οι	**K**^{x} D,syr
Luke 6:49—	την οικιαν	**K**^{r} P^{75} [**K**^{r} is independent and early **III** century]
	— οικιαν	**K**^{x} ℵABC
Luke 8:15—	ταυτα λεγων εφωνει ο εχων ωτα ακουειν ακουετω	**K**^{r} [**K**^{r} is independent]
	(omit)	**K**^{x} ℵABC
Luke 8:24—	και προσελθοντες	**K**^{r} [**K**^{r} is independent]
	προσελθοντες και	**K**^{x} ℵABD
Luke 9:27—	εστηκοτων	**K**^{r} ℵB [**K**^{r} is independent and **IV** century]
	εστωτων	**K**^{x} ACD
Luke 9:56—	(have verse)	**K**^{r} **K**^{x} lat,syr,Diat,Marcion [**K**^{r} and **K**^{x} are **II** century]
	(omit verse)	P^{45,75}ℵABCDW,cop
Luke 10:4—	πηραν μη	**K**^{r} P^{75}ℵBD [**K**^{r} is independent and early **III** century]
	πηραν μηδε	**K**^{x} AC

Luke 10:6—	εαν μεν	**K**^{r} [**K**^{r} is independent]
	εαν —	**K**^{x} P^{75}ℵABCD
Luke 10:39—	των λογων	**K**^{r} [**K**^{r} is independent]
	τον λογον	**K**^{x} P^{45,75}ℵABC
Luke 10:41—	ο Ιησους ειπεν αυτη	**K**^{r} D [**K**^{r} is independent and **V** century]
	ο Κυριος ειπεν αυτη	P^{45} [the word order is **III** century]
	ειπεν αυτη ο Ιησους	**K**^{x} ACW,syr,bo
	ειπεν αυτη ο Κυριος	P^{75}ℵB,lat,sa
Luke 11:34—	— ολον	**K**^{r} CD [**K**^{r} is independent and **V** century]
	και ολον	**K**^{x} P^{45,75}ℵAB
Luke 11:53—	συνεχειν	**K**^{r} [**K**^{r} is independent!]
	ενεχειν	**K**^{x} P^{75}ℵAB
	εχειν	P^{45}D
	επεχειν	C
Luke 12:22—	λεγω υμιν	**K**^{r} P^{75}ℵBD,lat [**K**^{r} is independent and **II** century]
	υμιν λεγω	**K**^{x} AW
Luke 12:56—	του ουρανου και της γης	**K**^{r} P^{45,75}D [**K**^{r} is independent and early **III** century]
	της γης και του ουρανου	**K**^{x} ℵAB
Luke 12:58—	βαλη σε	**K**^{r} (D) [**K**^{r} is independent]
	σε βαλη	**K**^{x} A(P^{75}ℵB)
Luke 13:28—	οψεσθε	**K**^{r} BD [**K**^{r} is independent and **IV** century]
	οψησθε	**K**^{x} P^{75}AW
	ιδητε	ℵ
Luke 19:23—	επι την	**K**^{r} [**K**^{r} is independent]
	επι —	**K**^{x} ℵABD
Luke 21:6—	επι λιθον	**K**^{r} [**K**^{r} is independent]
	επι λιθω	**K**^{x} ℵAB
Luke 21:15—	αντειπειν η αντιστηναι	**K**^{r} A [**K**^{r} is independent and **V** century]
	αντειπειν ουδε αντιστηναι	**K**^{x} W

	— —	D, it, syr
	αντιστηναι	
	αντιστηναι η	ℵB, cop
	αντειπειν	
Luke 22:12—	αναγαιον	$\mathbf{K}^r$ ℵABD [$\mathbf{K}^r$ is independent and **IV** century]
	αναγεον	CW
	ανωγεον	$\mathbf{K}^x$
Luke 22:66—	απηγαγον	$\mathbf{K}^r$ P^{75}ℵBD [$\mathbf{K}^r$ is independent and early **III** century]
	ανηγαγον	$\mathbf{K}^x$ AW
Luke 23:51—	ος —	$\mathbf{K}^r$ P^{75}ℵBCD,lat [$\mathbf{K}^r$ is independent and **II** century]
	ος και	$\mathbf{K}^x$ AW

There are a number of further examples where $\mathbf{K}^r$ is alone against the world, showing its independence, but I 'grew weary in well doing', deciding I had included enough to make the point. Note that N-A^{27} mentions only a third of these examples from Luke—to be despised is to be ignored. This added evidence confirms that $\mathbf{K}^r$ is independent of $\mathbf{K}^x$ and both are ancient, only now they both must date to the **III** century, at least.

It will be observed that I have furnished examples from the Gospels (Luke, John), Acts, Paul (Romans, 2 Corinthians), and the General Epistles (James, 1 Peter, 2 Peter, 3 John), with emphasis on Luke, Acts and James.[1] Throughout the New Testament $\mathbf{K}^r$ is independent and ancient. Dating to the **III** century, it is just as old as any other text-type. Therefore, **it should be treated with the respect that it deserves!!**

I have cited Maurice Robinson twice and shown that the evidence vindicates his claims. Both $\mathbf{K}^r$ and $\mathbf{K}^x$ date to the beginning of the velum era. But he makes a further claim that is even bolder:

> Nor do the uncials or minuscules show any indication of any known line deriving from a parallel known line. The 10 or so "texttype" lines of transmission remain independent and must necessarily extend back to a point long before their separate stabilizations occurred—a point which seems buried (as Colwell and Scrivener suggested) deep within the second century.[2]

Well, well, well, we are getting pretty close to the Autographs! Objective evidence from the **II** century is a little hard to come by. For all that, the examples above taken from Acts 21:8, Acts 23:20, Romans 5:1, Luke

---

[1] I also have a page or more of examples from Revelation that confirm that $\mathbf{K}^r$ ($\mathbf{M}^c$) is independent and **III** century in that book as well.

[2] *Ibid.*

9:56, Luke 12:22 and Luke 23:51 might place $\mathbf{K^r}$ (and $\mathbf{K^x}$) in the **II** century. However, it is not the purpose of this section to defend that thesis. For the moment I content myself with insisting that $\mathbf{K^r}$ must date to the **III** century and therefore must be rehabilitated in the practice of NT textual criticism.

In conclusion, I claim to have demonstrated that $\mathbf{K^r}$ is independent and ancient, dating to the **III** century (at least). But there is an ingrained disdain/antipathy toward that symbol, so I have proposed a new name for the text-type. We should substitute $\mathbf{f^{35}}$ for $\mathbf{K^r}$—it is more objective and will get away from the prejudice that attaches to the latter.

Having criticized von Soden's dating of $\mathbf{K^r}$, I now ask: what led him to that conclusion and why has his conclusion been almost universally accepted by the scholarly community? I answer: the number of $\mathbf{K^r}$ type MSS first becomes noticeable precisely in the 12th century, although there are a number from the 11th. That number grows in the 13th and grows some more in the 14th, calling attention to itself. Those who had already bought into Hort's doctrine of a late 'Syrian' text would see no reason to question von Soden's statement, and would have no inclination or motivation to 'waste' time checking it out. If von Soden himself had bought into Hort's doctrine, then he was blinded to the evidence.

Those who catalog NT MSS inform us that the 12th and 13th centuries lead the pack, in terms of extant MSS, followed by the 14th, 11th, 15th, 16th and 10th, in that order. There are over four times as many MSS from the 13th as from the 10th, but obviously Koine Greek would have been more of a living language in the 10th than the 13th, and so there would have been more demand and therefore more supply. In other words, many hundreds of really pure MSS from the 10th perished. A higher percentage of the really good MSS produced in the 14th century survived than those produced in the 11th; and so on. That is why there is a progressive level of agreement among the Byzantine MSS, there being a higher percentage of agreement in the 14th than in the 10th. But had we lived in the 10th, and done a wide survey of the MSS, we would have found very nearly the same level of agreement (perhaps 98%). The same obtains if we had lived in the 8th, 6th, 4th or 2nd century. In other words, THE SURVIVING MSS FROM THE FIRST TEN CENTURIES ARE NOT REPRESENTATIVE OF THE TRUE STATE OF AFFAIRS AT THE TIME.

About 'Pattern' and 'Dependency'

When 100% of the known MSS are in agreement, the pattern and dependency among the MSS is total, or complete. Since **ALL** MSS received common influence from the Original, it is the divergences that require special attention.

When 100% of the known MSS are in agreement, there can be no reasonable question as to the original wording. This is probably true for at least 50% of the words in the NT. For many more of the words, only one MS disagrees—we call this a 'singular' reading. I agree with E.C. Colwell when he declared that all singular readings should be rigorously excluded from consideration[1]—even when a given reading is not an obvious mistake. It is simply unreasonable to imagine that a single MS could be correct against 1,700 in the Gospels, or against 700 in Paul. When all lines of transmission are in agreement, they must reflect the Original. If the MS containing a singular variant belongs to a line of transmission, that variant cannot be correct (it is internal to that line).

MSS that are so individually disparate that they cannot be grouped do not belong to any line of transmission. Any singular that they contain cannot be correct. The number of MSS containing the NT is so vast that any disparate MS was simply someone's private property; it is irrelevant to the history of the transmission of the Text.

When two or more MSS agree in a divergence, at least three questions need to be asked: 1) Were they produced in the same place? 2) Is it an easy copying mistake that different copyists could make independently? 3) Do they belong to the same line of transmission? When two or more MSS share a number of variants in common, there is probably some dependency: they share a common influence of some sort. The extent of such influence requires scrutiny.

Colwell opined that two MSS should agree at least 70% of the time, where there is variation, in order to be classed as representatives of the same family[2] [I would require 80%]. Since Codices Aleph and B agree less than 70% of the time, they fall below Colwell's threshold. That said, however, it cannot be denied that those two MSS suffered a common contamination, to be joined in varying degrees by A, C, D and W. That common contamination must have had a source; where? Within the discipline of NT textual criticism, that common contamination is called the 'Alexandrian' text-type. Since Alexandria is in Egypt, that text-type is also called

---

[1] "External Evidence and New Testament Criticism", *Studies in the History of the Text of the* New *Testament*, ed. B.L. Daniels and M.J. Suggs (Salt Lake City: University of Utah Press, 1967), p. 8.

[2] "The Significance of Grouping of New Testament Manuscripts," *New Testament Studies*, IV (1957-1958).

'Egyptian'. Each of the six codices mentioned above has a distinct conglomerate of variants; they are each rather different from all the others. Since they each have neither parents nor children (that we know of), they are individual productions, fabricated copies. We have no way of knowing what motivated each of the copyists who produced those fabricated copies. However, our ignorance on that point does not change the nature of those fabricated copies.

After I circulated a prior edition of this article, Dr. Michael C. Loehrer sent me a few thoughts about producing a 'text-type' without an archetype:

> While we cannot *know* what motivated the copyists to fabricate variations into the text, we can surmise what motivated them from where they lived and what they believed. They lived in Egypt and they held Gnostic beliefs in a Greco-Roman world. In their world, mixture of beliefs demonstrated mutual respect and a willingness to promote peace; one of their highest ideals. Jews and Christians believed such mixture diluted or compromised absolute truth. Egyptian Gnostics attempted to improve an imperfect text. Jews and Christians believed they began with a perfect text. Consequently, Jews and Christians sought to make copies faithful to their exemplar. Egyptian Gnostics sought to improve their exemplar. Several lines of reasoning influenced the conclusions above:
>
> 1. In the Roman Empire there were no copyright laws, so as soon as a text was released to the public it was vulnerable to free alteration—anyone could change it.
> 2. Gnostic copyists introduced intentional changes because they believed they were improving an imperfect text (they assumed all texts were imperfect, because they were of human origin).
> 3. They did not believe that divine authorship and inerrancy were possible in a material world (perfection existed only in the immaterial world).
> 4. They believed they had special knowledge and therefore an obligation to attempt improvements.
> 5. They believed they were superior (academically and religiously) to the common people who passed along inferior copies before them.

Thus, a loose Egyptian text-type was produced without an archetype by Egyptian Gnostics who had a very different world-view than the Jews and Christians who produced the original text. [I would say that his observations deserve consideration.]

Years ago, Colwell demonstrated that it is impossible to define an archetypal form for the so-called 'Alexandrian' text-type based on a vote of the participating MSS.[1] **A text-type without an archetype is a fiction**. That said, however, the common contamination attributed to Alexandria is not a fiction. Before he died, Kurt Aland, that great champion of the 'Egyptian' text, wrote that in 200 A.D. the gnostic presence and influence in Egypt was so pervasive that the manuscripts in Egypt could not be trusted![2] He also wrote that at that time the use of Greek in Egypt was dying out.[3] (So on what basis did he claim that the 'Egyptian' text was the best?)

Based on the objective evidence available to us, it seems to me that the production of MSS in Alexandria and environs was never more than a stagnant eddy on the fringe of the great river of NT transmission. The surviving MSS supposed to have been produced there are so disparate that they do not qualify as a line of transmission. Since we have the names of at least eleven gnostic 'denominations' in Egypt in 200 A.D., there was doubtless no lack of fabricated copies among them. The great age of a fabricated copy does not alter the fact that it is a fabricated copy! A fabricated copy is irrelevant to the history of the transmission of the Text.

Frederik Wisse collated and compared 1,386 MSS in Luke 1, 10 and 20 (three complete chapters); he reduced those MSS to 37 groups (families) (plus 89 "mavericks" [MSS that are so individually disparate that they cannot be grouped]).[4] It happens that 36 of the 37 fall within the broad Byzantine river of transmission. He found 70 subgroups within the 36, so felt able to define those relationships, based on the profiles. The 37th group is the 'Alexandrian', to which he assigned precisely ten MSS for the three chapters—10 out of 1,386, just what one might expect for a stagnant eddy. Wisse used pattern and dependency.

---

1 Colwell, "The Significance of Grouping of New Testament Manuscripts", *New Testament Studies*, IV (1957-1958), 86-87.

2 "The Text of the Church?", Trinity Journal, 1987, 8NS:138.

3 K. and B. Aland, *The Text of the New Testament* (Grand Rapids: Eerdmans, 1981), pp. 52-53.

4 The Profile Method for the Classification and Evaluation of Manuscript Evidence (Grand Rapids: Eerdmans, 1982).

Herman C. Hoskier collated about 220 MSS for the Apocalypse, and assigned them to nine families or groups, based on their affinities.[1] For the purposes of the following discussion, I will assign them letters: **a** through **i**. The critical apparatus of my Greek Text (Family 35) for the Apocalypse, based on Hoskier's collations, treats about 954 variant sets. I did a rough and ready count of all the internal divisions within the nine families, as given in my apparatus (for my present purpose, precision is not necessary). I now list the families in descending order of the number of divisions:

e—495

i—424

h—412

a—268

g—191

d—163

b—135

f—104

c—20

The total is 2,212, which gives an average of 2.3 per variant set! Strange to relate, in spite of all the fuzz, each of the groups has enough private property to permit identification. The top three have division around half of the time; evidently there was a great deal of comparison and mixture going on. Group **a** is by far the largest, and Hoskier identified five subgroups within it, so the high number should not surprise us. The number for the last one, **c**, is remarkably small, compared to the others. It happens that **c** equals my Family 35, and is perhaps the second largest group. I wish to explore the question: what do pattern and dependency tell us about the evidence presented above?

But first, I wish to analyze the Family 35 divisions. There are eleven numbers that are either spelled out or represented by the appropriate letters; since these are two ways of saying the same thing, they are not variants, and I did not count them. Nine are alternate spellings of the same word; I did count these, but they are not proper variants (for eight of them

---

[1] *Concerning the Text of the Apocalypse*, 2 vols. (London: Bernard Quaritch, 1929).

the difference is of a single letter, and the other is a diphthong). That leaves eleven proper variants, five of which involve a single letter, and three a diphthong; only one involves more than two letters. In short, Family 35 is very solid (internally coherent), much more so than any of the other groups. The proper variants involve only nineteen letters for the whole book of Revelation—astonishing!

What do pattern and dependency tell us about the evidence presented above? I begin with the following postulates:

1. When 100% of the known MSS are in agreement, the pattern and dependency among the MSS is total.
2. All MSS received common influence from the Original.
3. All singular readings should be rigorously excluded from consideration.
4. Any idiosyncratic MS was simply someone's private property, a fabricated copy; it is irrelevant to the history of the transmission of the Text.
5. Fragments do not contain enough text to permit classification, and like the idiosyncratic MSS are therefore irrelevant to the history of the transmission of the Text.[1]

Since all the extant MSS from the first five centuries (in Revelation) are either fragments or idiosyncratic, I will confine my analysis to the lines of transmission.

To begin, Hoskier used pattern and dependency to identify his nine groups. But obviously they cannot all represent the original, except when all are in agreement. Do wc have nine independent groups, or can some of the groups be grouped? I went through my apparatus and listed all the different combinations among the nine groups, with the number of times each combination occurred (a combination of two or more groups). I found **238** different combinations!! I counted only full groups (no divisions) except that I considered 2/3 or more to represent the full group. Because of the inordinate amount of fuzz, the statistics that I offer can only be a rough approximation, but they are good enough to allow defensible conclusions. However, 96 of the combinations occur only once, and 42 only twice, so I excluded them from the following tabulation. That still leaves one hundred!

---

[1] However, both fragments and idiosyncratic MSS demonstrate that any variants they contain existed at the time they were produced. They demonstrate existence, not value.

I am pleased to note that the recent *Text und Textwert* for the Apocalypse (2017) recognizes their Complutensian text as an independent line of transmission, along with the so-called Koine and Andreas texts. Their Complutensian is my Family 35; it corresponds to group **c** below. Their Koine corresponds to groups **a**, **b**, **f**, **g**, **i** below. Their Andreas corresponds to groups **d**, **e**, **h** below—well, that is to say, according to my evaluation. As you can see below, there is a good deal of 'promiscuity', the individual groups move around, some more than others. The most difficult case is **h**, that goes with the Koine almost as often as with Andreas.

Based on my analysis of Hoskier, the groups have the following 'size': **a** is represented by 65 MSS; **b** by 10; **c** by 33;[1] **d** by 15; **e** by 31; **f** by 11; **g** by 9; **h** by 13; **i** by 11. (**a** alone is larger than **b**, **f**, **g**, **i** combined.) (**d** is smaller than **e**, but **e** is by far the most fragmented group.)[2] Since I consider **c** to be the common denominator, I place it first; **a** leads the Koine and **d** the Andreas. Only combinations are listed; each group occurs by itself as well.

ca—10	cbdeg—5	ab—3	bd—9
cabdfgi—15	cbdegh—11	abdefghi—11	bde—12
cabdfi—3	cbdeh—6	abdfghi—10	bdeh—12
cabefgi—4	cbdfhi—3	abdfgi—4	bdf—4
cabf—5	cbefghi—3	abdfh—3	bdh—3
cabfg—8	cbegh—4	abefghi—4	be—7
cabfghi—28	cd—22	abefhi—3	beh—4
cabfgi—47	cde—49	abf—23	bf—4
cabfhi—7	cdef—13	abfg—15	bg—3
cabfi—13	cdefghi—3	abfgh—3	bh—5
cabghi—3	cdefhi—3	abfghi—20	
cadfghi—4	cdeg—11	abfgi—33	de—52
cadfgi—5	cdegh—14	abfh—4	def—8
caf—9	cdeghi—4	abfhi—8	deg—5

[1] I have added 10 MSS to the 33, based on research I did at the INTF. Of the 43, one is a mere fragment, but it contains the first diagnostic family reading.

[2] I should mention that Hoskier collated 14 MSS that I have not included in the nine groups (for various reasons). If they do not belong to a line of transmission, nor themselves form a separate group, they are irrelevant.

cafg—6	cdeh—32	abfi—17	degh—8
cafgh—5	cdehi—7	abgh—3	deh—25
cafgi—24	cdg—3	af—19	dei—3
cafhi—3	cdh—7	afg—15	df—6
cafi—5	ce—10	afghi—9	dg—3
cag—4	cef—4	afgi—7	dh—19
caghi—6	ceg—3	afh—5	
cb—5	ceh—5	afhi—3	eg—5
cbd—4	cf—4	afi—14	egh—3
cbde—15	cg—5	ag—19	eh—11
cbdefghi—3	ch—3	agh—5	
cbdefhi—6		agi—3	gh—4

Please remember that I have not listed 138 further combinations that occur only once or twice. The amount of 'mixture' is bewildering. In spite of all that, for at least 80 years the following canard has been standard fare within the discipline: the Complutensian group is a composite based on the Koine and Andreas groups. But how does that idea square with the evidence given above? **c** occurs in no fewer than 129 combinations with other groups, quite apart from the times when it is alone. However, it is almost never entirely alone; a sprinkling of unrelated MSS will agree with it; but the roster of such MSS is always different (if the roster were the same, such MSS would be part of the family). The incredible range of unrelated associations permits two conclusions: 1) the MSS that represent the group can be identified and factored out, giving us an empirically defined family; 2) that empirically defined family **must be independent** of all other lines of transmission.

So what do pattern and dependency tell us about the evidence? They operate at two levels: within a group and between groups. Within a group they define the level of consistency or internal coherence exhibited by that group. Thus, among the nine groups in the Apocalypse, **e**, **i** and **h** exhibit the most internal confusion, which reduces their credibility as lines of transmission. **a** is large, but it has five subgroups; without the subgroups, it drops from 65 to 18—the five subgroups, plus further internal confusion, detract from its credibility as a line of transmission. In contrast to the rest,

c is remarkably solid, internally consistent or coherent—the internal pattern and dependency are heavy, which enhances the group's credibility as a line of transmission.

And how about between groups? It is the comparatively high level of pattern and dependency that allows us to group **a**,**b**,**f**,**g**,**i** and to say that together they form a text-type (call it 'Koine'). The same obtains for **d**,**e**,**h** (call it 'Andreas'). In contrast to those eight, **c** is independent of them all, as shown by the lack of pattern and dependency. **c** and 'Koine' agree against 'Andreas' over 100 times, while **c** and 'Andreas' agree against 'Koine' over 100 times as well. The complete roster of 'Koine' and 'Andreas' agrees against **c** eleven times. I submit that the most reasonable explanation for the evidence before us is that **c** is the common denominator; it is the core of the transmission from which all the others departed, at different times and different ways.

So what do pattern and dependency tell us? They permit us to identify groups, or families, of MSS. They also define the level of internal consistency of each group. The lack of pattern and dependency permits us to identify independent lines of transmission. All MSS received common influence from the Original, but evidently independent lines of transmission cannot represent the Original equally. So what do we do when confronted with several such lines? Or, to take a concrete case, how can we choose between 'Koine', 'Andreas' and 'Complutensian' in Revelation? If we follow two against one, we will have a 'majority' text—as a guess, it will be at least 90% Complutensian (it is seldom alone).[1] (From my point of view, that would be a very good Text!)

There is not a single clear three-way split in the whole book, and only one that might be said to come fairly close (at 15:4). What does the lack of three-way splits tell us? It tells us that the three groups are not equally independent. It tells us that the Complutensian is the most independent of the three—independent with reference to the other two! Since all three are dependent on the Original, can we determine which one is most dependent, and therefore closest to the Original? If the evidence points to Complutensian as the common denominator, then the other two groups are at least partly dependent upon it; this would mean that Complutensian lies between them and the Original, and is therefore closest to the Original.

---

[1] Just for the record, the *TuT* edition uses a "relative majority". To arrive at that "*rM*" they added NA[28] as a fourth line, but also used 'internal' considerations. They followed 'Koine' 98 times, 'Complutensian' 95 times, 'Andreas' 79 times and NA[28] 41 times (extracted from twelve combinations). They followed 'Koine' by itself eleven times, the only line so treated.

But what about the few places where Koine and Andreas agree against Complutensian; did they do an 'end-run' and go back directly to the Original? [How could that be possible?] Did they 'pick and choose', consulting an exemplar different from the Complutensian? Such an exemplar would be a node above Koine and Andreas, since they both subsequently went their separate ways. [I suppose that would at least be possible.] But what if Complutensian correctly represents the Original? Then a stemma would perhaps look like this:

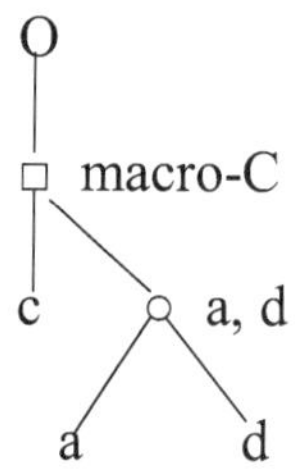

I suppose that one's final choice will be guided by considerations beyond pattern and dependency. But we need pattern and dependency to get us close to a final choice.

Early Uncial Support for f^{35} in the General Epistles

I take it that Klaus Wachtel, in his *Der Byzantinische Text der Katholischen Briefe* [*The Byzantine Text of the Catholic Letters*], recognizes that the Byzantine **text** is early (though often deciding against it on internal grounds), thereby bidding adieu to the prevailing canard that the Byzantine text is late. I believe that the evidence presented below demonstrates the same for the **text** of **f^{35}**.

I proceed to tabulate the performance of the early uncials (5th century and earlier) as they appear in the apparatus of my Greek text of the seven General Epistles, but supplemented from the *Editio Critica Maior* series.[1] I use **f^{35}** as the point of reference, but only tabulate variant sets where at least one of the extant early uncials (extant at that point) goes against **f^{35}** (this is necessary, since most words have unanimous attestation).

Thirteen early uncials appear in my apparatus: P^{20,23,72,78,81,100}, ℵ, A, B, C, 048, 0173, 0232. Only P^{72}, ℵ, A, B, C are not fragments (048 is a

[1] *Editio Critica Maior*, The Institute for New Testament Textual Research, ed (Sturrgart: Deutsche Bibelgesellschaft, 1997), vol. IV, Catholic Epistles.

variety of pieces, here and there). Codex C is missing basically chapters 4 and 5 of James, 1 Peter and 1 John [curiously, the same two chapters for all three books], as well as all of 2 John. Of course, P^{72} has only 1 & 2 Peter and Jude. 0173 is the only one of them that never sides with $\mathbf{f}^{35}$: Out of the total of 795 variant sets, $\mathbf{f}^{35}$ receives overt early attestation 77.9% of the time (619 ÷ 795).

Before drawing conclusions, I present the evidence (only combinations with at least one instance are tabulated). In passing, let me say that having neither secretary nor proof-reader, I do not guarantee complete accuracy, but a slip here or there will not alter the big picture, nor invalidate my conclusions.

	James	1 Peter	2 Peter	1 John	2 & 3 John	Jude	**total**
f^{35} alone	53	45	17	31	17	13	**176**
f^{35} P^{72}		7	1			1	**9**
f^{35} P^{100}	2						**2**
f^{35} א	9	9	7	11	3	1	**40**
f^{35} A	10	8	2	6		1	**27**
f^{35} B	2	3	1	7	3		**16**
f^{35} C	5	8	3	4	1	1	**22**
f^{35} 048	1		1	1			**3**
f^{35} P^{20}א	1						**1**
f^{35} P^{72}A		3					**3**
f^{35} P^{72}B		3	1				**4**
f^{35} P^{72}C		3					**3**
f^{35} P^{72}048		1					**1**
f^{35} P^{100}A	2						**2**
f^{35} אA	12	3	6	10		1	**32**
f^{35} אB	10	5		22	2		**39**
f^{35} אC		1	1	5		2	**9**
f^{35} א048			1		1		**2**
f^{35} AB	4	2	1	12		2	**21**
f^{35} AC	7	4	4	2		1	**18**
f^{35} A048			1	1	2		**4**
f^{35} BC	3			3			**6**
f^{35} B048	1			1	1		**3**
f^{35} P^{72}אA		8					**8**
f^{35} P^{72}אB		4				1	**5**
f^{35} P^{72}אC		2	1				**3**
f^{35} P^{72}AB		12	3			3	**18**
f^{35} P^{72}AC		2	1			1	**4**
f^{35} P^{72}BC		1	13				**14**
f^{35} P^{72}C048			1				**1**
f^{35} P^{81}BC		1					**1**
f^{35} P^{100}אA	1						**1**
f^{35} P^{100}אB	1						**1**
f^{35} P^{100}AB	2						**2**
f^{35} P^{100}AC	1						**1**

	James	1 Peter	2 Peter	1 John	2 & 3 John	Jude	**total**
f^{35} אAB	13	13	1	10	1	3	**41**
f^{35} אAC	8	4	1	11		2	**26**
f^{35} אA048			2	3	1		**6**
f^{35} אBC	17	1	2	17	2	2	**41**
f^{35} אB048				2			**2**
f^{35} אB0232					1		**1**
f^{35} אC048			1				**1**
f^{35} ABC	8	5	2	15	3	2	**35**
f^{35} AB048	2			4	1		**7**
f^{35} AB0232					1		**1**
f^{35} AC048			2				**2**
f^{35} BC048			1		1		**2**
f^{35} P^{23}ABC	1						**1**
f^{35} $P^{72,78}$AB						1	**1**
f^{35} P^{72}אAB		9	4			4	**17**
f^{35} P^{72}אAC		4	1			1	**6**
f^{35} P^{72}אBC		6	10			3	**19**
f^{35} P^{72}ABC		8	4			5	**17**
f^{35} P^{72}AB048			1				**1**
f^{35} P^{72}BC048			1				**1**
f^{35} P^{81}אAB		1					**1**
f^{35} P^{81}אAC		1					**1**
f^{35} P^{100}אBC	2						**2**
f^{35} P^{100}ABC	1						**1**
f^{35} אABC	1	11	4		2	7	**25**
f^{35} אAC048					1		**1**
f^{35} אBC048		1			1		**2**
f^{35} ABC048					2		**2**
f^{35} AB048,0232					2		**2**
f^{35} $P^{72,78}$אAB						1	**1**
f^{35} $P^{72,81}$אBC		1					**1**
f^{35} P^{72}אABC						1	**1**
f^{35} P^{72}אAB048			3		6		**9**
f^{35} P^{72}אAC048		2					**2**
f^{35} P^{72}אBC048			1				**1**
f^{35} P^{72}ABC048		1	2				**3**
f^{35} P^{78}אABC						1	**1**
f^{35} P^{81}אABC		3					**3**
f^{35} אABC048		3	3				**6**
Total w/ uncial	127	155	95	147	38	48	**619**

involving P^{20} -- **1**
involving P^{23} -- **1**
involving P^{72} -- **153**
involving P^{78} -- **3**
involving P^{81} -- **4**
involving P^{100} -- **12**
involving א -- **356**

involving A	--	**356**[1]
involving B	--	**378**
involving C	--	**285**
involving 048	--	**62**
involving 0232	--	**4**

Each of these twelve uncials is plainly independent of all the others.[2] The total lack of pattern in the attestation that these early uncials give to **f**^{35} shows just as plainly that **f**^{35} is independent of them all as well, quite apart from the 22.1% without them. But that 77.9% of the units receive early uncial support, without pattern or dependency, shows that the **f**^{35} **text** is early.

I invite special attention to the first block, where a single uncial sides with **f**^{35}; each of the seven uncials is independent of the rest (and of **f**^{35}) at this point, of necessity, yet together they attest 15% of the total (119 ÷ 795). Since there is no pattern or dependency for this 15%, how shall we account for these 119 early readings in **f**^{35}? Will anyone argue that whoever 'concocted' the first **f**^{35} MS had all these uncials in front of him, arbitrarily taking 9 readings from P^{72}, 2 from P^{100}, 40 from ℵ, etc., etc., etc.? Really now, how shall we account for these 119 early readings in **f**^{35}? (Should anyone demur that the 5th century MSS included really are not all that early, I inquire: are they copies, or original creations? If they are copies their exemplars were obviously earlier—all of these 119 readings doubtless existed in the 3rd century.)

Going on to the next block, we have another 148 readings where there is no pattern or dependency; 119 + 148 = 267 = 34%. Really now, how shall we account for these 267 early readings in **f**^{35}? Going on to the next

[1] This number is correct; it just happens to be the same.

[2] As further evidence of their indepence, I list the singular readings for each of these uncials (five have none):

	James	1Peter	2Peter	1John	2&3John	Jude	**TOTAL**
P^{72}		33	12			17	**62**
P^{78}						2	**2**
ℵ	11	25	13	18	5	4	**76**
A	8		5	10	2	2	**27**
B	7	10	3	8	4	5	**37**
C	3	7	7	5	2		**24**
048	1		1	4	3		**9**

block, we have another 224 readings where there is no pattern or dependency; 267 + 224 = 491 = 61.8%. Really now, how shall we account for these 491 early readings in $\mathbf{f}^{35}$? Going on to the next block, we have another 100 readings where there is no pattern or dependency; 491 + 100 = 591 = 74.3%. The final block brings the total to 77.9%.

To allege a dependency in the face of this EVIDENCE I consider to be dishonest. $\mathbf{f}^{35}$ is clearly independent of all these lines of transmission, themselves independent. If $\mathbf{f}^{35}$ is independent then it is early, of necessity. $\mathbf{f}^{35}$ has all those early readings for the sufficient reason that its **text** is early, dating to the 3rd century, at least. But if $\mathbf{f}^{35}$ is independent of all other lines of transmission (it is demonstrably independent of $\mathbf{K}^{x}$, etc.) then it must hark back to the Autographs. What other reasonable explanation is there? Should anyone wish to claim that $\mathbf{f}^{35}$ is a recension, I request (and insist) that he specify who did it, when and where, and furnish evidence in support of the claim. Without evidence, any such claim is frivolous and irresponsible.

Family 35 profile in Acts: ancient and independent

To my published profile for Acts, I have added the witnesses from the first five centuries, as recorded in the critical apparatus in my Greek Text. That is to say, I show only those that agree with Family 35, where that is the case. However, I also checked the evidence provided in the *Editio Critica Maior* for Acts, which lead me to make changes in around 60% of the following list of variant sets. So, I will have to revise my published profile. I have not collated any of those early witnesses; I simply copied the information from other sources. An occasional error that may exist will not change the force of my argument.

	Acts	
++--	1:8	και $\mathbf{f}^{35}$ A, C, D [25%] || 1 εν [75%]
+++	1:11	ουτος $\mathbf{f}^{35}$ [20%] || 1 ο [80%]
++--	1:13	ιακωβος $\mathbf{f}^{35}$ [25%] || 1 και [73%]
++--	1:18	ελακισεν $\mathbf{f}^{35}$ [25%] || ελακησεν [75%]
++--	2:13	διαχλευαζοντες $\mathbf{f}^{35}$ ℵ, A, B, C [25%] || χλευαζοντες [75%]
+++	2:14	επεφθεγξατο $\mathbf{f}^{35}$ [20%] || απεφθεγξατο [80%]
+++	2:38	ειπεν δε πετρος $\mathbf{f}^{35}$ [20%] || ~ 32 εφη [72%] ||
++--	3:23	αν $\mathbf{f}^{35}$ B,D [25%] || εαν [75%]
++--	3:24	προκατηγγειλαν $\mathbf{f}^{35}$ [25%] || κατηγγειλαν [75%]
++	4:5	εν $\mathbf{f}^{35}$ A, B, D(0165) [30%] || εις [70%]
++	4:12a	ουδε $\mathbf{f}^{35}$ ℵ, A, B, 0165 [30%] || ουτε [70%]
++--	4:12b	ετερον εστιν $\mathbf{f}^{35}$ A,0165 [25%] || ~ 21 [75%]
+++	4:14	εστωτα $\mathbf{f}^{35}$ [20%] || 1 τον [80%]
+++	4:17	ανθρωπω $\mathbf{f}^{35}$ [20%] || ανθρωπων [80%]
++++	4:20	α $\mathbf{f}^{35}$ [18%] || --- [82%]

+++	4:23	ανηγγειλαν $\mathbf{f}^{35}$ (א) [20%] || απηγγειλαν [80%]
++--	4:33[a]	δυναμει μεγαλη $\mathbf{f}^{35}$ P^{8}(א)A,B,D [25%] || ~ 21 [75%]
++--	4:33[b]	οι αποστολοι το μαρτυριον $\mathbf{f}^{35}$ A [25%] || ~ 3412 [75%]
++--	4:34	ην $\mathbf{f}^{35}$ א, A(B) (24.5%) || υπηρχεν (74.8%)
++--	5:1	σαπφειρα $\mathbf{f}^{35}$ B [25%] || σαπφειρη [56%] || ||
+++	5:15	του $\mathbf{f}^{35}$ [20%] || --- [80%]
++++	5:16	και $\mathbf{f}^{35}$ D [18%] || οιτινες [80%] ||
++--	5:22	παραγενομενοι υπηρεται $\mathbf{f}^{35}$ א, A, B [25%] || ~ 21 [75%]
++--	5:33	ακουοντες $\mathbf{f}^{35}$ P^{45} [25%] || ακουσαντες [75%]
+++	5:36[a]	προσεκλιθη $\mathbf{f}^{35}$ א, A, B [20%] || προσεκληθη [54%] || ||
+++	5:36[b]	ως $\mathbf{f}^{35}$ A, B, C, D [20%] || ωσει [80%]
++	5:39	δυνησεσθε $\mathbf{f}^{35}$ B [30%] || δυνασθε [58%] || ||
+++	5:40	δηραντες $\mathbf{f}^{35}$ [20%] || δειραντες [80%]
++++	5:41	κατηξιωθησαν υπερ του ονοματος του χριστου $\mathbf{f}^{35}$ [18%] || ~ 234561 [15%] || ~ 234 αυτου 1 [15%] || || || ||
++	5:42	τον χριστον ιησουν $\mathbf{f}^{35}$ א, A, B [30%] || ~ 312 [60%] || ||
++--	6:5	πληρη $\mathbf{f}^{35}$ B [25%] || πληρης [60%] ||
++--	7:5	δουναι αυτην εις κατασχεσιν αυτω $\mathbf{f}^{35}$ א, A [25%] || ~ 15342 [65%] ||
++--	7:14[a]	ιακωβ τον πατερα αυτου $\mathbf{f}^{35}$ א, A, B, C, D [25%] || ~ 2341 [75%]
++--	7:14[b]	αυτου $\mathbf{f}^{35}$ D [25%] || --- [75%]
++	7:14[c]	εβδομηκοντα πεντε ψυχαις $\mathbf{f}^{35}$ [30%] || ~ 312 [63%] ||
+--	7:16	εμμωρ $\mathbf{f}^{35}$ א, A, B, C, D [33%] || εμμορ [60%] ||
+++	7:21	ανειλετο $\mathbf{f}^{35}$ [22%] || 1 αυτον [60%] || ||
++++	7:27	τουτον $\mathbf{f}^{35}$ [18%] || αυτον [82%]
+++	7:31[a]	μωσης $\mathbf{f}^{35}$ A [20%] || μωυσης [80%]
++--	7:31[b]	εθαυμασεν $\mathbf{f}^{35}$ A, B, C [25%] || εθαυμαζεν [75%]
+++	7:35	αρχηγον $\mathbf{f}^{35}$ A [20%] || αρχοντα [80%]
++--	7:37	ημων $\mathbf{f}^{35}$ [25%] || υμων [75%] ||
+++	7:42	εν τη ερημω ετη τεσσαρακοντα $\mathbf{f}^{35}$ (A) [20%] || ~ 45123 [80%]
++--	8:6	δε $\mathbf{f}^{35}$ א, A, B, C [25%] || τε [75%]
++--	8:21	εναντιον $\mathbf{f}^{35}$ C [25%] || ενωπιον [70%] ||
++--	9:12	ανανιαν ονοματι $\mathbf{f}^{35}$ א, A, B, C [25%] || ~ 21 [75%]
++	9:18	παραχρημα $\mathbf{f}^{35}$ [30%] || --- [70%]
+--	9:19	των $\mathbf{f}^{35}$ א, A, B, C [35%] || 1 οντων [65%]
++--	9:20	ιησουν $\mathbf{f}^{35}$ P^{45} א, A, B, C [25%] || χριστον [75%]
++--	9:28[a]	και εκπορευομενος $\mathbf{f}^{35}$ א, A, B, C [25%] || --- [75%]
+++	9:28[b]	εν $\mathbf{f}^{35}$ [20%] || εις [80%]
+++	9:28[c]	ιησου $\mathbf{f}^{35}$ (C) [20%] || κυριου 1 [70%] ||
++--	9:29	ανελειν αυτον $\mathbf{f}^{35}$ א(A)B(C) [25%] || ~ 21 [75%]
+++	9:30	εξαπεστειλαν $\mathbf{f}^{35}$ A [20%] || 1 αυτον [80%]
++--	9:37	τω $\mathbf{f}^{35}$ P^{53}A,C [25%] || --- [75%]
+++	9:43	αυτον ημερας ικανας μειναι $\mathbf{f}^{35}$ A [20%] || ~ 2341 [79%]
++--	10:5	ος επικαλειται πετρος $\mathbf{f}^{35}$ א(A)B, C [25%] || τον επικαλουμενον πετρον [75%]
++	10:17	υπο $\mathbf{f}^{35}$ א,B [30%] || απο [70%]
++++	10:22	αγγελου $\mathbf{f}^{35}$ [18%] || 1 αγιου [80%] ||
+	10:26	ηγειρεν αυτον $\mathbf{f}^{35}$ א, A, B, C, D [40%] || ~ 21 [60%]
++--	10:47	ως $\mathbf{f}^{35}$ א, A, B [25%] || καθως [75%]
+++	10:48	ιησου $\mathbf{f}^{35}$ [20%] || --- [67%] || ||

+++	11:3	εισηλθες προς ανδρας ακροβυστιαν εχοντας και συνεφαγες $\mathbf{f}^{35}$ **א**, A, D [20%] ‖ ~ 2345167 [71%] ‖
+++	11:9	εκ δευτερου φωνη $\mathbf{f}^{35}$ B [20%] ‖ ~ 312 [80%]
++	11:13^{a}	δε $\mathbf{f}^{35}$ **א**, A, B, D [30%] ‖ τε [70%]
++--	11:13^{b}	ιοππην $\mathbf{f}^{35}$ **א**, A, B, D [25%] ‖ 1 ανδρας [75%]
+--	11:16^{a}	του $\mathbf{f}^{35}$ **א**, A, B, D [35%] ‖ --- [65%]
++--	11:16^{b}	οτι $\mathbf{f}^{35}$ [25%] ‖ --- [75%]
++++	11:17^{a}	ιησουν $\mathbf{f}^{35}$ [18%] ‖ 1 χριστον [82%]
++--	11:17^{b}	εγω $\mathbf{f}^{35}$ **א**, A, B, D [25%] ‖ 1 δε [75%]
++--	11:26^{a}	ευρων $\mathbf{f}^{35}$ **א**, A, B [25%] ‖ 1 αυτον [75%]
+--	11:26^{b}	ηγαγεν $\mathbf{f}^{35}$ P^{45}**א**, A, B, D [35%] ‖ 1 αυτον [65%]
+++	12:6	προαγειν αυτον $\mathbf{f}^{35}$ D [20%] ‖ ~ 21 [63%] ‖
++++	12:20	τε $\mathbf{f}^{35}$ [18%] ‖ δε [70%] ‖
++	12:22	θεου φωνη $\mathbf{f}^{35}$ **א**, A, B(D) [30%] ‖ ~ 21 [68%]
+++++	12:25	εις αντιοχειαν $\mathbf{f}^{35pt}$ (5.1%)+{19.5%} ‖ 1 ιερουσαλημ [60%] ‖ ‖ ‖ ‖[1]
+++	13:4^{a}	μεν $\mathbf{f}^{35}$ [20%] ‖ 1 ουν [80%]
++--	13:4^{b}	τε $\mathbf{f}^{35}$ **א**, A, B, C [27%] ‖ δε [72%]
++--	13:12	εκπληττομενος $\mathbf{f}^{35}$ B [24%] ‖ εκπλησσομενος [76%]
+++	13:15	προς αυτους οι αρχισυναγωγοι $\mathbf{f}^{35}$ [20%] ‖ ~ 3412 [80%]
++	13:26	εξαπεσταλη $\mathbf{f}^{35}$ **א**, A, B, C [30%] ‖ απεσταλη [70%]
++	13:27	κατοικουντες $\mathbf{f}^{35}$ C [30%] ‖ 1 εν [70%]
+++	13:39^{a}	εν $\mathbf{f}^{35}$ **א**, A, B, C, D [20%] ‖ 1 τω [80%]
+++	13:39^{b}	μωυσεος $\mathbf{f}^{35}$ [20%] ‖ μωυσεως [40%] ‖ μωσεως [40%]
+++	13:41	ω $\mathbf{f}^{35}$ [20%] ‖ ο [80%]
++++	13:43	επιμενειν αυτους $\mathbf{f}^{35}$ [18%] ‖ ~ 21 [64%] ‖
+++	14:10	ηλλατο $\mathbf{f}^{35}$ [20%] ‖ ηλλετο [35%] ‖ ‖
+++	14:15	υμιν εσμεν $\mathbf{f}^{35}$ C [20%] ‖ ~ 21 [60%] ‖
++--	14:20	των μαθητων αυτον $\mathbf{f}^{35}$ **א**, A, B, C [25%] ‖ ~ 312 [55%] ‖
+++	14:21	εις $\mathbf{f}^{35}$ D [20%] ‖ 1 την [80%]
+++	15:1	μωυσεος $\mathbf{f}^{35}$ [20%] ‖ μωυσεως [63%] ‖
++--	15:5	μωσεως $\mathbf{f}^{35}$ A, D [25%] ‖ μωυσεως [70%] ‖
++	15:7	υμιν $\mathbf{f}^{35}$ **א**, A, B, C [30%] ‖ ημιν [70%]
+++	15:21	μωσης $\mathbf{f}^{35}$ P^{45}A [20%] ‖ μωυσης [80%]
+++	15:23	κατα $\mathbf{f}^{35}$ [20%] ‖ 1 την [80%]
++--	15:25	εκλεξαμενοις $\mathbf{f}^{35}$ P^{45v}A,B [25%] ‖ εκλεξαμενους [75%]
++	15:37	και $\mathbf{f}^{35}$ A,C [30%] ‖ τον [60%] ‖
+++	15:39	χωρισθηναι $\mathbf{f}^{35}$ [20%] ‖ αποχωρισθηναι [75%] ‖
++++	16:3	ηδεσαν $\mathbf{f}^{35}$ [18%] ‖ ηδεισαν [70%] ‖
++++	16:9	την $\mathbf{f}^{35}$ [18%] ‖ --- [82%]
++++	16:11	την $\mathbf{f}^{35}$ [18%] ‖ --- [82%]
+++	16:15	αυτη $\mathbf{f}^{35}$ [20%] ‖ --- [80%]
+++	16:17	τω σιλα $\mathbf{f}^{35}$ [20%] ‖ ημιν [80%]
+--	16:26	δε $\mathbf{f}^{35}$ **א**, A, B, D [35%] ‖ τε [65%]
+++	16:37	δηραντες $\mathbf{f}^{35}$ [20%] ‖ δειραντες [80%]
++--	16:38	δε $\mathbf{f}^{35}$ P^{45}**א**, A, B [25%] ‖ και [75%]

[1] This is the only place in the whole NT where Family 35 splinters, there being five significant variants (plus two minor ones). Usually there are only two variants, where the family is divided. For a detailed discussion of this variant set please see the article, "Where to place a comma—Acts 12:25".

+++ 16:40 απο f^{35} א, B [20%] || εκ [80%]

+++ 17:3 ιησους ο χριστος f^{35} [20%] || ~ 231 [75%] ||

++ 17:4 πληθος πολυ f^{35} א, A, B, D [30%] || ~ 21 [70%]

++ 17:5 ανδρας τινας f^{35} A, B [30%] || ~ 21 [65%] ||

++ 17:7 ετερον λεγοντες f^{35} א, A, B [30%] || ~ 21 [70%]

++-- 17:10 βερροιαν f^{35} [25%] || βεροιαν [75%]

++ 17:11 προθυμιας f^{35} P^{45}א, A(D) [30%] || 1 το [70%]

++-- 17:13 βερροια f^{35} [25%] || βεροια [75%]

+++ 18:6 τας κεφαλας f^{35} [20%] || την κεφαλην [80%]

++-- 18:13 αναπειθει ουτος f^{35} א(A)B [25%] || ~ 21 [65%] ||

++ 18:19 κακεινους f^{35} א, A, B [29%] || και εκεινους [70%]

++ 18:25 ιησου f^{35} א, A, B(D) [30%] || κυριου [70%]

+++ 19:3 τε f^{35} B(D) (18.3%)+{6.2%} || 1 προς αυτους (61.6%)+{6.2%} || ||

+++ 19:11 δε f^{35} D [21%] || τε [79%]

++ 19:13 ο f^{35} P^{38} [30%] || --- [70%]

+++ 19:17 εγενετο πασιν γνωστον f^{35} [20%] || ~ 132 [75%] ||

+++ 19:19 συνεψηφισαντο f^{35} [20%] || συνεψηφισαν [67%] ||

++ 19:27[a] αρτεμιδος ιερον f^{35} א, A, B [30%] || ~ 21 [70%]

++ 19:27[b] ουδεν f^{35} D [30%] || ουθεν [70%]

++ 19:40 αποδουναι f^{35} א, A, B, D [30%] || δουναι [70%]

++-- 20:3 επιβουλης αυτω f^{35} א, A, B [25%] || ~ 21 [75%]

++-- 20:4 βερροιαιος f^{35} [25%] || βεροιαιος [35%] || ||

++-- 20:15 τρωγυλιω f^{35} [25%] || τρωγυλλιω [30%] || || || ||

++++ 20:18 ημερας f^{35} [18%] || 1 αφ [82%]

++++ 20:35 του λογου f^{35} [18%] || τον λογον [57%] || των λογων [25%]

++ 20:37 κλαυθμος εγενετο f^{35} א, A, B, C, D [30%] || ~ 21 [70%]

+ 21:8 ηλθομεν f^{35} א, A(B)C (38.8%) || οι περι τον παυλον ηλθον (46.4%) || ||

+++ 21:21 μωυσεος f^{35} [20%] || μωυσεως [50%] || μωσεως [30%]

++-- 21:27 ημελλον f^{35} [25%] || εμελλον [65%] ||

++-- 21:31 σπειρας f^{35} [25%] || σπειρης [75%]

+++ 21:37 εις την παρεμβολην εισαγεσθαι f^{35} [20%] || ~ 4123 [80%]

+++ 21:40 προσεφωνει f^{35} [20%] || προσεφωνησεν [80%]

+++ 22:19[a] δαιρων f^{35} [20%] || δερων [80%]

+++ 22:19[b] εις f^{35} [20%] || επι [80%]

++ 22:20 και f^{35} א, A, B, D [30%] || --- [70%]

+++ 22:24 ο χιλιαρχος αγεσθαι αυτον f^{35} [20%] || ~ 4123 [64%] || ||

++ 22:25 προετειναν f^{35} (א)B [30%] || προετεινεν [30%] || ||

++ 22:26 τω χιλιαρχω απηγγειλεν f^{35} (א)A(B)C(D) [30%] || ~ 312 [63%] ||

+-- 22:30[a] υπο f^{35} א,A,B,C [35%] || παρα [65%]

++ 22:30[b] παν f^{35} א,A,B,C [30%] || ολον [70%]

+++ 23:6 φαρισαιων το δε ετερον σαδδουκαιων f^{35} [20%] || ~ 52341 [80%]

+ 23:8 μητε f^{35} א,A,B,C [40%] || μηδε [60%]

++-- 23:12[a] εαυτους f^{35} C [25%] || 1 λεγοντες [75%]

++++ 23:12[b] ανελωσιν f^{35} (A) [18%] || αποκτεινωσιν [80%] ||

++-- 23:15 καταγαγη αυτον f^{35} [20%]+P^{48}א, A, B, C {6%} || ~ 21 [74%]

+-- 23:20 μελλοντες f^{35} (33.1%) || μελλοντα (27.2%) || || || ||

+-- 23:24 φηλικα f^{35} א, B [35%] || φιληκα [25%] || φιλικα [40%]

+ 23:26 φηλικι f^{35} P^{48}א, B [40%] || φιληκι [30%] || φιλικι [17%] ||

+++	23:35	του f^{35} [18%]+א, A {4%} || --- [75%] ||
++++	24:4	πλεον f^{35} [18%] || πλειον [80%]
++	24:10	δικαιον f^{35} [30%] || --- [70%]
++	24:19	εδει f^{35} א, A, B, C [30%] || δει [70%]
++++	24:26	πυκνοτερον f^{35} [18%] || 1 αυτον [75%] ||
+--	25:2	οι αρχιερεις f^{35} א, A, B, C [35%] || ο αρχιερευς [60%] ||
++--	25:9	υπ f^{35} [25%] || επ [73%] ||
++	25:13	ασπασομενοι f^{35} [30%] || ασπασαμενοι [70%]
++++	25:20^a	περι την f^{35} [18%] || ~ 21 [80%]
+--	25:20^b	τουτων f^{35} א, A, B, C [35%] || τουτου [65%]
++--	26:12	εις f^{35} A [25%] || 1 την [75%]
++	26:18	επιστρεψαι f^{35} א, B, C [30%] || υποστρεψαι [35%] || αποστρεψαι [35%]
+++	27:1	σπειρας f^{35} [20%] || σπειρης [80%]
+++	27:2	ατραμυτινω f^{35} [21%] || αδραμυττηνω [25%] || || || || ||
+++	27:5	κατηχθημεν f^{35} [21%] || κατηλθομεν [75%] ||
+++	27:6	εις f^{35} [20%] || 1 την [80%]
+++	27:10	φορτου f^{35} [22%] || φορτιου [78%]
++--	27:31	εν τω πλοιω μεινωσιν f^{35} א [25%] || ~ 4123 [75%]
++	27:34	μεταλαβειν f^{35} א, A, B, C [30%] || προσλαβειν [70%]
++	27:38	δε f^{35} א, A, B, C [30%] || 1 της [70%]
+++	27:41	εμενεν f^{35} A [22%] || εμεινεν [78%]
++	28:3^a	εξελθουσα f^{35} א, A, B, C [30%] || διεξελθουσα [70%]
++--	28:3^b	καθηψατο f^{35} C [25%] || καθηψεν [72%]
+++	28:21	πονηρον περι σου f^{35} [20%] || ~ 231 [80%]
+++	28:23	μωυσεος f^{35} [20%] || μωσεως [35%] || μωυσεως [45%]
++--	28:27	ιασωμαι f^{35} [25%] || ιασομαι [75%]

Key:

+++	around 20% = f^{35} virtually alone = diagnostic (78)
++--	around 25% = quite good (53)
++	around 30% = not bad (35)
+--	around 35% (10)
+	around 40% (4)

Total: 180

It should be obvious to any unbiased reader that f^{35} is entirely independent of the Byzantine bulk (Soden's K^x). Of the 180 variant sets, f^{35} is alone 75 times (42%), so it is independent of the lines of transmission represented by the early MSS that I included, as well. If f^{35} is independent of the Byzantine bulk, then it cannot be a revision based on that bulk—at any time! Before commenting further, I will list the early support for the readings that I classify as 'diagnostic' and 'quite good', identified as +++ and ++-- (25% or less), respectively.

P^{45} – 1	P^{53}A, C – 1	Total times each:
א – 2	א, A, B – 7	P^{8} – 1
A – 9	א, A, D – 1	P^{45} – 5

B – 4	A, B, C – 1	P^{48} – 1
C – 5	A, C, D – 1	P^{53} – 1
D – 5	P^{45}ℵ, A, B – 1	ℵ – 29
P^{45}A – 1	ℵ, A, B, C – 8	A – 42
ℵ, A – 2	ℵ, A, B, D – 2	B – 33
ℵ, B – 1	A, B, C, D – 1	C – 20
A, D – 1	P^{8}ℵ, A, B, D – 1	D – 16
A, 0165 – 1	P^{45}ℵ, A, B, C – 1	0165 – 1
B, D – 2	P^{48}ℵ, A, B, C – 1	
P^{45}A, B – 1	ℵ, A, B, C, D – 2	

Notice the support from the three great 'Alexandrian' codices. How could they support something produced in the 12th century? Let me say that again: how could IV century MSS support something that did not exist until the 12th? Out of a total of 131 sets, $\mathbf{f^{35}}$ is alone 68 times (52%) and has some early support 63 times (48%). Here again, $\mathbf{f^{35}}$ is independent of the lines of transmission represented by the early MSS that I included, so there is no pattern. Since there is no pattern, there is no dependency, so the **text** of $\mathbf{f^{35}}$ must be ancient, dating at least to the IV century. There being no pattern or dependency, it will not do to claim that only the individual readings are ancient. Again I say, the evidence indicates that it is impossible that $\mathbf{f^{35}}$ could be based on the Byzantine bulk. Anyone who continues to say so is uninformed, at best. Von Soden's $\mathbf{K^r}$ should be retired and be replaced by $\mathbf{f^{35}}$, or $\mathbf{f^{18}}$.

Down with Canards![1]

Once upon a time, a certain senior professor of Greek, at a certain Theological Seminary, sent me a personal communication affirming: "I hold with virtually all others that K^r/M^7 are indeed late texts that reflect recensional activity beginning generally in the 12th century (perhaps with 11th century base exemplars, but nothing earlier)." And then a different Greek professor sent me another personal communication: "all of this based upon the K^r strand, of all things? TC's who worked on this strand

[1] Dictionaries offer a variety of definitions for 'canard', but they all agree that it is false information, and imply that it was created with malicious intent. Of course those who repeat the canard may do so without malice, albeit they do so without checking the evidence.

before all said it was the oldest [*sic*, presumably he meant 'latest'], but now you say it represents the autograph perfectly? Are there K^r MSS which pre-date the 10-11th century?" (Both the men quoted above hold a PhD in New Testament textual criticism, and one would like to think that they had checked the evidence.)

Consider the following statement by Kirsopp Lake:

> Writers on the text of the New Testament usually copy from one another the statement that Chrysostom used the Byzantine, or Antiochian, text. But directly any investigation is made it appears evident, even from the printed text of his works, that there are many important variations in the text he quotes, which was evidently not identical with that found in the MSS of the Byzantine text.[1]

Having myself spent an occasional year in the arcane halls of academia, I have observed that the uncritical repetition of things that 'everyone knows' is really rather common, in almost any discipline. New Testament textual criticism is no exception, as Lake observed above.

I take it that Hermann von Soden was the first to formally identify his $\mathbf{K^r}$ as a distinct text-type, the 'r' standing for 'revision', since he considered it to be a revision based on his $\mathbf{K^x}$. Well now, by definition a 'revision' is perpetrated by a specific someone, at a specific time and in a specific place. Within our discipline I gather that 'revision' and 'recension' are synonyms. Consider: "The Syrian text must in fact be the result of a 'recension' in the proper sense of the word, a work of attempted criticism, performed deliberately by editors and not merely by scribes."[2] It is not my wont to appeal to Fenton John Anthony Hort, but his understanding of 'recension' is presumably correct. A recension is produced by a certain somebody (or group) at a certain time in a certain place. If someone wishes to posit or allege a recension/revision, and do so responsibly, he needs to indicate the source and supply some evidence.[3]

So, upon what basis did von Soden claim that his $\mathbf{K^r}$ (that I call Family 35) was a revision of his $\mathbf{K^x}$, and created in the 12th century? Had he really paid attention to the evidence available in his own *magnum opus*,

---

[1] Kirsopp Lake, *The Text of the New Testament*, sixth edition revised by Silva New (London: Rivingtons, 1959), p. 53.

[2] B.F. Westcott and F.J.A. Hort, *The New Testament in the Original Greek* (2 vols.; London: Macmillan and Co., 1881), *Introduction*, p. 133.

[3] Hort did suggest Lucian of Antioch as the prime mover—a suggestion both gratuitous and frivolous, since he had not really looked at the evidence available at that time. (Were he to repeat the suggestion today, it would be patently ridiculous.)

Die Schriften des Neuen Testaments (4 vols.; Göttingen: Vandenhoeck und Ruprecht, 1911-1913), he could not have done so, at least not honestly. But was he honest? At least with reference to John 7:53 - 8:11 (the *P.A.*), I think not. He claimed to have collated some 900 MSS for that pericope, and on that basis posited seven families, or lines of transmission, and even reproduced an alleged archetypal form for each one. Hodges and Farstad took his word for it and reflected his statement of the evidence in their critical apparatus; and I reflect the H-F apparatus in mine (for that pericope) for lack of anything better (except that I guarantee the witness of **M**^{7} [my Family 35], based on my personal examination of Robinson's collations; see below). However, some years ago now, Maurice Robinson did a complete collation of 1,389 MSS that contain the P.A.,[1] and I had William Pierpont's photocopy of those collations in my possession for two months, spending most of that time studying those collations. As I did so, it became obvious to me that von Soden 'regularized' the data, arbitrarily 'creating' the alleged archetypal form for his first four families, **M**^{1,2,3,4}— if they exist at all, they are rather fluid. His **M**$^{5\&6}$ do exist, having distinct profiles, but they are a bit 'squishy', with enough internal confusion to make the choice of <u>the</u> archetypal form to be arbitrary. In contrast to the above, his **M**^{7} (that I call Family 35) has a solid, unambiguous profile— the archetypal form is demonstrable, empirically determined.

Once upon a time I was led to believe that von Soden's work was reasonably reliable. This was important because his work is basic to both the Hodges-Farstad and Robinson-Pierpont editions of the Majority Text. However, the *Text und Textwert* (*TuT*)[2] collations demonstrate objectively that not infrequently von Soden is seriously off the mark. With reference to von Soden's treatment of codex 223 K.W. Clark wrote, "Furthermore, our collation has revealed sixty-two errors in 229 readings treated by von Soden".[3] 27% in error (62 ÷ 229) is altogether too much, and what is true of MS 223 may be true of other MSS as well. Please stop and think about that for a minute. 27% in error cannot be attributed to mere carelessness,

---

[1] 240 MSS omit the PA, 64 of which are based on Theophylact's commentary. Fourteen others have lacunae, but are not witnesses for total omission. A few others certainly contain the passage but the microfilm is illegible. So, 1389 + 240 + 14 + 7(?) = about 1650 MSS checked by Robinson. That does not include Lectionaries, of which he also checked a fair number. (These are microfilms held by the *Institut* in Münster. We now know that there are many more extant MSS, and probably even more that are not yet 'extant'.) Unfortunately, so far as I know, Robinson has yet to publish his collations, thus making them available to the public at large.

[2] *Text und Textwert der Griechischen Handschriften des Neuen Testaments* (Ed. Kurt Aland, Berlin: Walter de Gruyter).

[3] *Eight American Praxapostoloi* (Kenneth W. Clark, Chicago: The University of Chicago Press, 1941), p. 12.

or even sloppiness; mere carelessness should not exceed 5%. It really does look like the reader is being misled, deliberately, and that is dishonest. H.C. Hoskier was not entirely mistaken in his evaluation.

Furthermore, how could **K**^{r} be a revision of **K**^{x} if **K**^{x} does not even exist? Soden himself was perfectly well aware that there is no **K**^{x} in the *P.A.* H.C. Hoskier's collations prove that there certainly is no **K**^{x} in the Apocalypse. We are indebted to the *Institut für Neutestamentliche Textforschung* for their *Text und Textwert* series. A careful look at their collations indicates that there probably is no **K**^{x}, anywhere. Take, for example, the *TuT* volumes on John's Gospel, chapters 1-10. They examined a total of 1,763 MSS (for 153 variant sets) and included the results in the two volumes. Pages 54 - 90 (volume 1) contain "Groupings according to degrees of agreement" "agreeing more often with each other than with the majority text". Only one group symbol is used, precisely **K**^{r}—the first representative of the family, MS 18, heads a group of about 120 MSS, but all subsequent representatives have only a **K**^{r}. Of the 120, the last six show 98%, all the rest are 99% (74) or 100% (40). I would say that Family 35 in the Gospels has over 250 representatives; the ranking here is based on only 153 variant sets (but see what happens below).

The group headed by MS 18 numbers 120, and is the only one that receives a group symbol, being by far the largest. But are there any other groups of significant size? I will now list them in descending order, starting with those that have 40 or more:

group	size	coherence
2103	52	95% (15); 97% (20); 98% (13); 100% (4)
318	44	96% (1); 97% (24); 98% (6); 99% (10); 100% (4)
961	42	97% (1); 98% (4); 99% (34); 100% (3)
1576	42	97% (1); 98% (4); 99% (34); 100% (3)
1247	41	97% (1); 98% (4); 99% (33); 100% (3)
2692	41	97% (1); 98% (4); 99% (33); 100% (3)
1058	40	97% (1); 98% (17); 99% (15); 100% (7)
1328	40	98% (6); 99% (33); 100% (1)
1618	40	100% (all)
2714	40	98% (6); 99% (33); 100% (1)

Now then, 961, 1576, 1247, 2692, 1328, 1618 and 2714 all belong to Family 35 (**K**^{r}), which leaves only 2103, 318 and 1058. As we look at the 'coherence' column we note that 961, 1576, 1247 and 2692 are the same, and upon inspection we verify that the lists of MSS are virtually identical—so we may add 40 MSS to the 120 already designated **K**^{r}. 1618 and

2714 have heavy overlap, and 1328 partial overlap, so we may add at least another 20. Now let's look at the three that remain: 2103, 318 and 1058. Remembering that the threshold for **K**^{r} was 98%, we note that over half of the 2103 and 318 groups fall below it, so those groups are not solid. 1058 fares better, but almost half fall below 99% (all the **f**^{35} groups are heavily 99% or 100%). It may be relevant to observe that MS 1058 is probably fringe **f**^{35}. So where is **K**^{x}?

I will now list the groups between 25 and 39, in descending order:

group	size	coherence
1638	37	97% (2); 98% (2); 99% (29); 100% (4)
710	34	94% (18); 95% (1); 96% (13); 98% (2)
763	34	97% (1); 99% (33)
1621	32	98% (1); 99% (24); 100% (7)
1224	29	97% (1); 99% (28)
66	28	98% (1); 99% (26); 100% (1)
394	27	99% (all)
1551	26	99% (all)
1657	26	99% (all)
2249	26	99% (all)
685	25	99% (all)
1158	25	99% (all)

Guess what: they are all Family 35 except for 710; a glance at the coherence gives the clue. If 710 is really a group at all, it is rather 'squishy'. The last six lists are all but identical, and there is considerable overlap among the others. Even so, a few more MSS can probably be added to the Family 35 list, and an examination of the remaining 300+/- groups (depending on where the cutoff point is placed) will doubtless add even more. And so on. So where is **K**^{x}? Gentle reader, allow me to whisper in your ear: There is no **K**^{x}, it only existed in von Soden's imagination. Obviously **K**^{r} cannot be a revision of something that never existed.[1]

And then there is the matter of demonstrated independence. By definition a revision/recension is dependent upon its source. If there is no demonstrable source anywhere in the extant/available materials (which for the NT are really rather considerable), then it is dishonest, irresponsible and reprehensible to allege a revision/recension. Please see "Is **f**^{35} Ancient?" in Part III.

[1] See also the section, "Archetype in the General Epistles—**f**^{35} yes, **K**^{x} no" in Part III.

And then there is the matter of demonstrated antiquity. The crucial point here is the lack of pattern; without pattern there is no dependency. I invite attention to the following four paragraphs, that make up a single quote, reproduced from "Early Uncial Support for **f**^{35} in the General Epistles".

> Each of these twelve uncials is plainly independent of all the others. The total lack of pattern in the attestation that these early uncials give to **f**^{35} shows just as plainly that **f**^{35} is independent of them all as well, quite apart from the 22.1% without them. But that 77.9% of the units receive early uncial support, without pattern or dependency, shows that the **f**^{35} **text** is early.
>
> I invite special attention to the first block, where a single uncial sides with **f**^{35}; each of the seven uncials is independent of the rest (and of **f**^{35}) at this point, of necessity, yet together they attest 15% of the total (119 ÷ 795). Since there is no pattern or dependency for this 15%, how shall we account for these 119 early readings in **f**^{35}? Will anyone argue that whoever 'concocted' the first **f**^{35} MS had all these uncials in front of him, arbitrarily taking 9 readings from P^{72}, 2 from P^{100}, 40 from ℵ, etc., etc., etc.? Really now, how shall we account for these 119 early readings in **f**^{35}? (Should anyone demur that the 5th century MSS included really are not all that early, I inquire: are they copies, or original creations? If they are copies their exemplars were obviously earlier—all of these 119 readings doubtless existed in the 3rd century.)
>
> Going on to the next block, we have another 148 readings where there is no pattern or dependency; 119 + 148 = 267 = 34%. Really now, how shall we account for these 267 early readings in **f**^{35}? Going on to the next block, we have another 224 readings where there is no pattern or dependency; 267 + 224 = 491 = 61.8%. Really now, how shall we account for these 491 early readings in **f**^{35}? Going on to the next block, we have another 100 readings where there is no pattern or dependency; 491 + 100 = 591 = 74.3%. The final block brings the total to 77.9%.
>
> To allege a dependency in the face of this EVIDENCE I consider to be dishonest. **f**^{35} is clearly independent of all these lines of transmission, themselves independent. If **f**^{35} is independent then it is early, of necessity. **f**^{35} has all those early readings for the sufficient reason that its **text** is early, dating to the 3rd century, at least. But if **f**^{35} is independent of all other lines of

transmission (it is demonstrably independent of $\mathbf{K}^{x}$, etc.) then it must hark back to the Autographs. What other reasonable explanation is there? Should anyone wish to claim that $\mathbf{f}^{35}$ is a recension, I request (and insist) that he specify who did it, when and where, and furnish evidence in support of the claim. Without evidence, any such claim is frivolous and irresponsible.

So why don't we have $\mathbf{f}^{35}$ MSS from before the 11th century? Well, why do you suppose that with few exceptions only $\mathbf{f}^{35}$ MSS have the Lections marked in the margin? Could it be because the Greek speaking communities used them in their worship services and for reading at communal meals? And what effect does constant use have on any book? I suggest, for the calm, cool and collected consideration of all concerned, that any worthy MSS would be in constant use, and therefore could not survive for centuries. Copies that were considered to be of unacceptably poor quality would be left on the shelf to collect dust, and they are the ones that survived.

However that may be, I invite attention to the following list of $\mathbf{f}^{35}$ MSS from the 11th century:

MS	Location	Content	
35	Aegean	eapr	
83	Munich	e	
(125)	Wien	e	
(476)	London	e	($\mathbf{f}^{35}$ in John)
(516)	Oxford	e	
547	Karakallu	eap	
(585)	Modena	e	
746	Paris	e	
(1164)	Patmos	e	
1384	Andros	eapr	
1435	Vatopediu	e	
(1483)	M Lavras	e	
(1841)	Lesbos	apr	(IX/X—may be $\mathbf{f}^{35}$ in Paul)
1897	Jerusalem	ap	(I have done a complete collation, and it looks just as old)
2253	Tirana	e	(Introductory material indicates an 11th century date)
2587	Vatican	ap	
2723	Trikala	apr	
(2817)	Basel	p	

The MSS within ( ) appear to be marginal members of the family, or are mixed. To begin, we note that there are 18 MSS listed, and each in a distinct location (of course, some of those presently in Western Europe may have been acquired from the same monastery). Further, since they are internally distinct, they represent as many exemplars. Since exemplars must exist before any copies made from them, of necessity, and since many/most/(all?) of those exemplars must also have been based on distinct exemplars in their turn, even if someone were to allege a recension, it could not have been perpetrated later than the 8th century—simply impossible. Surely, because one must account for the geographical distribution.

Did someone concoct the **f**^{35} archetype in the 8th century? Who? Why? And how could it spread around the Mediterranean world? There are **f**^{35} MSS all over the place—Jerusalem, Sinai, Athens, Constantinople, Trikala, Kalavryta, Ochrida, Patmos, Karditsa, Rome, Sparta, Meteora, Venedig, Lesbos, and most monasteries on Mt. Athos (that represented different 'denominations'), etc. [If there were six monasteries on Cyprus—one Anglican, one Assembly of God, one Baptist, one Church of Christ, one Methodist and one Presbyterian—to what extent would they compare notes? Has human nature changed?] But the Byzantine bulk (**K**^{x}) controlled at least 60% of the transmissional stream (**f**^{35} = a. 18%); how could something concocted in the 8th century spread so far, so fast, and in such purity? How did it inspire such loyalty? Everything that we know about the history of the transmission of the Text answers that it couldn't and didn't. It is simply impossible that **f**^{35} could have been 'concocted' at any point subsequent to the 4th century. The loyalty with which **f**^{35} was copied, the level of loyalty for **f**^{35} being much higher than that for any other line of transmission, indicates that it was never 'concocted'—it goes back to the Original.[1]

And then there is the silence of history. Although I have already touched on this, it deserves specific attention. Allow me to borrow from my treatment of the 'Lucianic Recension'.[2] John William Burgon gave the sufficient answer to that invention.

> Apart however from the gross intrinsic improbability of the supposed Recension,—the utter absence of one particle of evidence, traditional or otherwise, that it ever did take place, must be held to be fatal to the hypothesis that it *did*. It is simply incredible that

---

[1] I have in mind an article that will take up the question of 'level of loyalty' and the 'quality quotient', comparing various lines of transmission on that basis. For example, why is it that an average **f**^{35} MS will have only one variant for every two pages of printed Greek text, while an average Byzantine bulk MS will have at least three variants per page, and an average Alexandrian MS will have over fifteen per page? Does that suggest anything about attitude, about taking one's work seriously? By 'attitude' I mean specifically toward the exemplar being copied—was it an object of respect or reverence?

[2] *The Identity of the New Testament Text IV*, p. 84.

> an incident of such magnitude and interest would leave no trace of itself in history.[1]

It will not do for someone to say that the argument from silence proves nothing. In a matter of this 'magnitude and interest' it is conclusive. Sir Frederick G. Kenyon, also, found this part of Hort's theory to be gratuitous.

> The absence of evidence points the other way; for it would be very strange, if Lucian had really edited both Testaments, that only his work on the Old Testament should be mentioned in after times. **The same argument tells against any theory of a deliberate revision at any definite moment** [emphasis added]. We know the names of several revisers of the Septuagint and the Vulgate, and it would be strange if historians and Church writers had all omitted to record or mention such an event as the deliberate revision of the New Testament in its original Greek.[2]

Come now, is there anything mysterious about what Burgon and Kenyon stated? Is it not obvious? Please stop and think about it for a minute. The silence of history 'must be held to be fatal to the hypothesis'. Selah.

And then there is the matter of 'supply and demand'. Those who catalog NT MSS inform us that the 12th and 13th centuries lead the pack, in terms of extant MSS, followed by the 14th, 11th, 15th, 16th and 10th, in that order. There are over four times as many MSS from the 13th as from the 10th, but obviously Koine Greek would have been more of a living language in the 10th than the 13th, and so there would have been more demand and therefore more supply. In other words, many hundreds of really pure MSS from the 10th perished. A higher percentage of the really good MSS produced in the 14th century survived than those produced in the 11th; and so on. That is why there is a progressive level of agreement among the Byzantine MSS, there being a higher percentage of agreement in the 14th than in the 10th. But had we lived in the 10th, and done a wide survey of the MSS, we would have found very nearly the same level of agreement (perhaps 98%). The same obtains if we had lived in the 8th, 6th, 4th or 2nd century. In other words, THE SURVIVING MSS FROM THE FIRST

---

1 J.W. Burgon, *The Revision Revised* (London: John Murray, 1883), p. 293.

2 F.G. Kenyon, *Handbook to the Textual Criticism of the Greek Bible*, 2nd ed. (Grand Rapids: Wm. B. Eerdmans Publishing Co., 1951), pp. 324-25. Whereas Burgon was a staunch defender of the Traditional Text of the NT, Kenyon most certainly was not, being an advocate of the so-called 'critical text'.

TEN CENTURIES ARE NOT REPRESENTATIVE OF THE TRUE STATE OF AFFAIRS AT THE TIME.

To conclude, I trust that the reader will not consider me to be unreasonable if I request that henceforth all informed persons cease and desist from calling Family 35 (**K**^{r}) a revision at any time. Enough is enough! **Down with canards!**

Von Soden's treatment of his K^r

I have been criticized because I have never answered, in an organized way, von Soden's 'arguments' whereby he called his **K**^{r} a late revision—I never did for him what I did for Hort. Since there are people today who still think that his 'arguments' are valid, I recognize that I should have. I appealed to Dr. Jakob van Bruggen for help with von Soden. He began his answer by saying that von Soden "makes statements and gives descriptions, but doesn't give arguments or proofs". Well now, how is it possible to refute 'arguments' that do not exist? But since an answer of some sort is being called for, I will evaluate the 'statements'.

1. Von Soden noted that there were relatively few **K**^{r} MSS in the libraries of Western Europe, probably true. But he went on to opine that it was a negative circumstance, a point against **K**^{r}.[1] He seems to have forgotten that until the Protestant Reformation the Roman Church dominated Western Europe, and that church used Latin, not Greek. Worse still, only the Pope could interpret the Scriptures, and only the clergy were permitted to even read them. The common people, the laity, were forbidden to do so. So in the 14th century, who in all of Western Europe would have any use for Greek MSS? They were curiosities, museum pieces, to be found only in libraries or museums. All the NT MSS in those libraries came from the east. The British Museum (now Library) has a considerable collection; how did it get them? They were donated by travelers who had bought them in the east. All said and done, I submit to the reader that the number of **K**^{r} MSS in the west is irrelevant to the age and nature of the text-type, and should not be adduced.
2. Von Soden repeatedly mentioned the well-known fact that the **K**^{r} MSS are characterized by an elaborate liturgical apparatus in the margins, including 'begin' and 'end' written within the Text itself, but in ink of a different color, usually red, so the reader would know

---

[1] Soden, Hermann F. von. *Die Schriften des Neuen Testaments.* 2 vols. Göttingen: Vandenhoeck und Ruprecht, 1911, pages 757-765. (His German is difficult to read.)

precisely where to start and stop. Although some non-**K**^{r} MSS have some indication of lections in their margins, none are so elaborate as **K**^{r}, with the exception of what Frederik Wisse[1] called Cluster 17 in Luke, composed of fewer than ten MSS (**K**^{r} has over 250 in the Gospels). So far as I know, they are the only two groups that have the elaborate apparatus, so the presence of that apparatus is virtually diagnostic of his **K**^{r} (my Family 35, **f**^{35}). That much is fact, but what does it mean?

Von Soden gave it as his opinion that the circumstance indicated that his **K**^{r} was a liturgical revision produced in Constantinople in the XII century, but did not offer so much as a shred of evidence in support of his opinion. (He did try to defend the XII century by re-dating the three **K**^{r} MSS that he knew of from the XI.) (I hold copies of at least ten such MSS, and there are others, but I will argue that the point is irrelevant.) Now then, it should be obvious to everyone that preparing a copy in two colors with an elaborate apparatus will take more time and effort than a copy in one color without that apparatus. So why would people do it? There had to be a demand for such copies. But what factor, or factors, could drive such a demand?

A MS with a liturgical apparatus was obviously prepared to be used for public reading, to be read aloud to an audience. For private reading and study you want a text without interruptions. Von Soden actually noted that the individual letters in his **K**^{r} MSS tended to be somewhat larger than in non-**K**^{r} MSS. So why would that be? Presumably to facilitate the public reading. So why is **K**^{r}/**f**^{35} by far the largest family within the broad Byzantine tradition? And why are its representatives scattered all around the Mediterranean world? And how many people could read Koine Greek, and how many of them could afford a private copy of the NT? After all, 'supply and demand' operates within the Church as well as in the world.

In 2014 I spent nine nights on the Mt. Athos peninsula, with its twenty independent monasteries. I visited five of them (including the top four in the hierarchy), slept in three of them and ate meals in two of them. To this day, the monks and visitors eat in silence, while one monk reads Scripture aloud. The monasteries pride themselves on being ruled by tradition, which they affirm goes back to the earliest centuries. Is it not reasonable to conclude that that tradition includes the reading of Scripture during meals? Would they not use MSS that were precisely prepared for public

---

[1] *The Profile Method for the Classification and Evaluation of Manuscript Evidence* (Grand Rapids: Eerdmans, 1982).

reading? And to what text-type do those MSS belong? And why did they use that text-type?

Quite apart from the Talmud, we know from the NT that it was the custom in the Jewish synagogues to read from the OT writings in their Sabbath meetings. The Lord Jesus Himself did this, as recorded in Luke 4:16-19. At the 'Jerusalem Council' James concluded his decision with: "For from ancient generations Moses has in every city those who preach him, being read in the synagogues every Sabbath" (Acts 15:21). The apostle Paul always began his ministry in a new city with the Jewish synagogue, when there was one. Notice what Acts 13:15 says: "After the reading of the Law and the Prophets, the synagogue leaders sent to them..." In a synagogue Paul usually began his speech with: "Men of Israel and you who fear God", the 'you who fear God' referring to Gentiles who were present.

Now in the very beginning the Christian community was mainly made up of Jews and such Gentiles, and they would naturally continue the practice of reading Scripture in their weekly meetings. Recall what gave rise to the office of deacon in Acts 6. "It is not advantageous that we should forsake the Word of God to serve at tables" (verse 2). "We will give ourselves continually to prayer and to the ministry of the Word" (verse 4). Of course, at that time their Bible was the OT; the first Gospel, Matthew, not being published until 38/39. However, since the NT writings were recognized as Scripture from the very first, it was natural that they would be added to the OT, and in time probably took the lead. Notice what Justin Martyr wrote in his First Apology (around 150 AD):

> On the day called Sunday, all who live in cities or in the country gather together in one place, and the memoirs of the Apostles or the writings of the prophets are read, as long as time permits; then, when the reader has ceased, the president [presiding minister] verbally instructs and exhorts to the imitation of these good things.[1]

The "memoirs of the Apostles" were the Gospels as we know them (First Apology 66). If one considers Justin's use of the phrase "memoirs of the Apostles" in all of his writings, one may safely conclude that he accurately refers to two apostles (Matthew and John) and two followers of the apostles (Mark and Luke), which he delineated. Justin used the phrase

---

[1] Roberts, Alexander and Donaldson, James, eds. *The Ante-Nicean Fathers.* American Edition. New York: Christian Literature Co., 1906. I. p. 186.

"memoirs of the Apostles" to reference the four Gospels, but he never used this phrase to reference gnostic or apocryphal gospels.[1]

Notice that the Gospels are mentioned first, before the 'writings of the prophets', that would refer to the OT. Justin makes clear that the practice of reading Scripture in the weekly meetings was continued by the Christians, and, as was to be expected, the NT writings came to be preferred. We have no evidence that the practice of reading Scripture in public meetings was ever dropped, at least in the east. Indeed, the very existence of Lectionary manuscripts would be evidence that the practice continued. If the 'Eusebian Canons' were actually produced by Eusebius of Caesarea (d. 339), we have evidence from the early fourth century, and he certainly was merely standardizing what was already being practiced in the churches. So then, when the Mt. Athos monks claim that their practice goes back to the earliest times, they are correct. However, **none of the above tells us what text-type was used**, and it is incumbent upon me to address that question.

But first, the lectionary evidence flatly contradicts von Soden's claim that the system was created in Constantinople in the 12th century. According to the *Kurzgefasste Liste*[2] (Feb., 2018), we have one extant lectionary from the IV century, two from the V, two from the VI, two from the VII, fifteen from the VIII, 113 from the IX, 162 from the X and 303 from the XI. Even if we reduce all those numbers by half (to preclude quibble), they demonstrate that von Soden was completely mistaken. It happens that among the extant Lectionaries, the second largest family contains the **K^{r}/f^{35}** text, but it is small, compared to the dominant family; but please note: the difference is in the wording, not the selection of lections. Von Soden also claimed that the **K^{r}/f^{35}** text was imposed by ecclesiastical authority. In that event, how is it that the vast majority of Lectionaries have a different text? And how could something created in the 12th century supplant an ancient practice? Again, von Soden was completely mistaken.

It should be obvious to everyone that books that are used wear out; the more they are used, the faster they wear. The earliest manuscripts survived because no one wanted to use them; nor were they copied (why waste good parchment?). If the communities used **K^{r}/f^{35}** for public reading, those copies would be worn out and could not survive physically. So the lack of early **K^{r}/f^{35}** MSS is not necessarily an argument against the text-type.

---

[1] Personal communication from Dr. Michael C. Loehrer.

[2] Kurt Aland, ed., *Kurzgefasste Liste der Grieshischen Handschriften des Neuen Testaments* (Berlin: Walter de Gruyter, 1994).

3. Von Soden noted, correctly, that **K**^{r}/**f**^{35} MSS are characterized by far fewer variants than MSS of other types. His explanation was that his **K**^{r} was a revision imposed by ecclesiastical authority; it was a controlled text. Within the discipline, the notion of a controlled text was extended to the whole Byzantine text. For example, on page 11* of the English 'Introduction', the editors of the *Editio Critica Maior* of James[1] refer to the Byzantine text (which includes **K**^{r}/**f**^{35}) as being "carefully controlled". **K**^{r}/**f**^{35} is by far the largest, and most cohesive (internally consistent), line of transmission within the broad Byzantine river, so if the Byzantine bulk was controlled, **K**^{r}/**f**^{35} would be more so.

Now then, if a text is 'controlled', someone has to do the controlling—if there is no controll**er**, there can be no controll**ing**. So who are the possible candidates? I see three possibilities: human beings, Satan, God. So far as I know, all those who refer to the Byzantine text as 'controlled' exclude the supernatural from their model; so for them, the controlling is done by human beings, independent of supernatural influence. Since the alleged control had to operate for more than a millennium, it could not be done by a single individual. But who could control the whole Mediterranean world? For over a thousand years the Roman Church used Latin, not Greek. Was there ever a functioning central authority among the Orthodox Churches? Certainly not for a thousand years, and not for the whole Mediterranean world. So who did the controlling?

Not only that, but the supposed controlling was evidently rather lax, since the MSS are full of random mistakes, quite apart from shared dependencies. Consider the conclusion reached by F. Wisse after he collated and analyzed 1,386 Greek MSS containing chapters 1, 10 and 20 of Luke (three complete chapters). He described 37 lines of transmission, plus 89 "mavericks", MSS so individually disparate that they could not be grouped. Of the 37 groups, 36 fall within the broad Byzantine river, and within them Wisse described 70 subgroups. So what kind of 'control' could permit such a situation? I trust that my readers will not think me unreasonable when I say that in the face of such concrete evidence I find the thesis of a 'controlled' Byzantine text (excluding the supernatural) to be less than convincing. But then, how shall we account for the comparative uniformity found within it?

I hope that my readers are aware that I personally insist that the supernatural should be included in any model of NT textual criticism. Both God

---

[1] Aland, Barbara, Mink, Gerd, and Wachtel, Klaus (eds.). *Novum Testamentum Graecum, Editio Critica Maior*. Stuttgart: Deutsche Bibelgesellschaft, 1997.

and Satan certainly exist, and both have an ongoing interest in the fortunes of the NT Text. For some time I have been defending the divine preservation of the NT Text in concrete terms. Curiously, those who allege a controlled Byzantine text usually reject any notion of divine preservation. But of course, if they do not believe in divine inspiration, they will not believe in preservation. Someone who denies the existence of a Sovereign Creator will logically insist that a nonexistent being cannot do anything. But how then can such a person explain the Byzantine text? I submit that no naturalistic hypothesis can account for Family 35 (**K**^{r}).

Satan would certainly do nothing to help preserve the NT Text; any involvement of his would be with a view to pervert the text, thereby undermining its authority. (I would say that he concentrated his efforts in Egypt.) I have argued elsewhere that the transmission of the NT Text was predominately 'normal', and that normality was defined by the Christian Church. Why were copies made? Because the congregations needed them. Why did the congregations 'need' them? Because they understood that the NT writings were divinely inspired, and they were read and discussed in their weekly meetings. To argue that the early Christians were mistaken in that understanding would be beside the point. That understanding (mistaken or not) determined their attitude toward the NT writings, which controlled their production of copies. If the majority of persons producing copies was made up of sincere (more or less) Christians, they would do their work with reasonable care (some more, some less). Those who held a strong view of inspiration would be especially careful.

I submit that the surviving MSS reflect my description above. **K**^{r}/**f**^{35}, by far the largest and most cohesive group (perhaps the only group that exists in all 27 books), represents the core of the transmission, its representatives having been produced by copyists with a high view of inspiration (as evidenced by the extreme care in their work). Outside that core are a large number of tangents, or rivulets, that diverge from the core in varying degrees, and that began at different times and places. A monk who was merely carrying out a religious obligation would produce a 'run of the mill' Byzantine copy; good enough for virtually all practical purposes, but not up to the **f**^{35} standard.

So was the Byzantine text 'controlled'? Obviously not in any strict sense. The control was exercised by a common belief (within the Christian community) that the NT was divinely inspired. It was that belief that dictated the proliferation of copies made with reasonable care. That reasonable care is reflected in the basic uniformity within the Byzantine bulk. But to explain the incredibly careful transmission reflected in the **f**^{35} representatives, requires something more.

Of $\mathbf{f}^{35}$ MSS that I myself have collated, I hold perfect copies of the family archetype (empirically determined) as follows: 29 for Philemon, 15 for 2 Thessalonians, 9 for Titus, 6 for Galatians, 4 for Ephesians, and at least one for 22 of the 27 NT books (and many more are off by a single letter!). These are MSS from all over the Mediterranean world, and representing five centuries. So what kind of control could produce such an incredible level of perfection—a control exercised in isolated monasteries scattered around the Mediterranean world and during five centuries? We know of no human agency that could do it. If the agency was not human, then it had to be divine. Since von Soden certainly was not thinking of supernatural control, once more he was completely mistaken.

4. Von Soden was obsessed with the adulterous woman passage (John 7:53-8:11) (apparently he thought that it would provide a key for the whole NT). He and his team collated over 900 MSS for those twelve verses (far more than for any other NT passage). He reduced those 900 MSS to seven families, or lines of transmission, that he called $\mathbf{M}^{1,2,3,4,5,6,7}$ (the M being the first letter in 'adultery', in Greek). On page 524 he offered a stemma, wherein his M^1 was closest to the Source and $\mathbf{M}^7$ the farthest from that Source. The last three families were by far the largest, any one of them being larger than the first four combined; so much so that any two of the three represented a majority of the total. Von Soden argued that his $\mathbf{M}^7$ was a composite based on his $\mathbf{M}^6$ and $\mathbf{M}^5$, and therefore was subsequent and inferior to them.

This is reminiscent of Hort's treatment of his 'Syrian' text. However, Hort produced eight alleged 'conflations' within his Syrian text and condemned it for the whole NT on that basis. Now then, a genuine conflation is by definition secondary (if you can prove that the two shorter readings are not independent simplifications of the original longer reading). But in the 'Pericope', $\mathbf{M}^7$ does not contain any 'conflations', so on what objective basis did von Soden claim that it was based on $\mathbf{M}^6$ and $\mathbf{M}^5$? Within the Pericope there are 32 variant sets that are relevant to the three large groups, that I will now reproduce. I ask the reader to try to analyze the evidence without preconceived notions.

The information offered below is based on Maurice A. Robinson's complete collation of 1,389 MSS that contain the Pericope, John 7:53 - 8:11.[1] I attempted to establish a profile of readings for each of the three main groups of MSS, $\mathbf{M}^{5,6,7}$.

---

[1] 240 MSS omit the *PA*, 64 of which are based on Theophylact's commentary. Fourteen

		M^7	M^6	M^5
7:53	01	απηλθεν	απηλθεν / απηλθον	**επορευθη / επορευθησαν
8:1	02	Ιησους δε	**και ο Ιησους δε / και ο Ιησους	Ιησους δε
8:2	03	(βαθεως) = <u>omit</u>	**βαθεως / βαθεος	(βαθεως)
8:2	04	παρεγενετο	**ηλθεν ο Ιησους	παρεγενετο
8:2	05	προς αυτον	προς αυτον	**(προς αυτον)
8:3	06	προς αυτον	(προς αυτον) / προς αυτον	προς αυτον
8:3	07	επι	επι	**εν
8:3	08	κατειλημμενην	κατειλημμενην	**καταληφθεισαν
8:3	09	εν μεσω	εν τω μεσω / εν μεσω	εν μεσω
8:4	10	λεγουσιν	**ειπον	λεγουσιν
8:4	11	(πειραζοντες)	(πειραζοντες)	**πειραζοντες
8:4	12	ταυτην ευρομεν	ταυτην ευρομεν	**αυτη η γυνη κατεληφθη / ειληπται / κατειληπται
8:4	13	επαυτοφωρω	επαυτοφωρω / -φορω / -φορως	επαυτοφωρω / -φορω
8:4	14	μοιχευομενην	μοιχευομενην / -νη	**μοιχευομενη
8:5	15	ημων Μωσης	ημων Μωσης / υμων Μωσης / Μ. ενετ. ημιν / Μωση	**Μωσης ημιν
8:5	16	λιθοβολεισθαι	**λιθαζειν	λιθοβολεισθαι
8:5	17	(περι αυτης)	(περι αυτης) / περι αυτης	(περι αυτης)
8:6	18	κατηγοριαν κατ	κατηγοριαν κατ	**κατηγορειν
8:6	19	μη προσποιουμενος	(μη προσποιουμενος) / μη προσποιουμενος	μη προσποιουμενος
8:7	20	ερωτωντες	ερωτωντες / επερωτωντες	ερωτωντες
8:7	21	ανακυψας	αναβλεψας / ανακυψας	ανακυψας
8:7	22	προς αυτους	**αυτοις	προς αυτους
8:7	23	**τον λιθον επ αυτη βαλετω	**λιθον βαλετω επ αυτην	**επ αυτην τον λιθον βαλετω
8:9	24	και υπο της συνειδησεως ελεγχομενοι	(και υπο της συνειδησεως ελεγχομενοι) /και υπο της συνειδησεως ελεγχομενοι	και υπο της συνειδησεως ελεγχομενοι
8:9	25	εως των εσχατων	εως των εσχατων	**(εως των εσχατων)
8:9	26	μονος ο Ιησους	ο Ιησους μονος / μονος	μονος ο Ιησους
8:10	27	και μηδενα θεασαμενος πλην της γυναικος	**ειδεν αυτην και	και μηδενα θεασαμενος πλην της γυναικος
8:10	28	αυτη	**(αυτη) γυναι	αυτη / αυτη γυναι
8:10	29	εκεινοι οι κατηγοροι σου	εκεινοι οι κατηγοροι σου / οι κατηγοροισου	εκεινοι οι κατηγοροι σου
8:11	30	ειπεν δε αυτη ο Ιησους	ειπεν δε αυτη ο Ιησους	**ειπεν δε ο Ιησους

---

others have lacunae, but are not witnesses for total omission. A few others certainly contain the passage but the microfilm is illegible. So, 1389 + 240 + 14 + 7(?) = about 1650 continuous text MSS checked by Robinson. He also checked a number of Lectionaries.

8:11	31	κατακρινω	κατακρινω	**κρινω / κατακρινω
8:11	32	και απο του νυν	και απο του νυν/ απο του νυν και	**και

$\mathbf{M}^7$ has a single, clear-cut, unambiguous profile/mosaic, as defined by 127 MSS—there is no internal variation among them (the 127 are precisely the same for all twelve verses). This contrasts dramatically with $\mathbf{M}^6$ and $\mathbf{M}^5$. It is possible to come up with a partial profile for both **5** and **6**, for purposes of distinguishing them from each other and from **7**, but they have so much internal variation that I see no way to come up with a family archetype that is objectively defined. I used ** to distinguish variants that might be called the 'backbone' of the family, for the purpose of distinguishing it from the others. As the reader can verify, **6** has internal division no less than 15 times out of 32, which does not improve its credibility quotient. **5** has 'only' four, so it is far less 'squishy' than 6, but the nature of those four does not allow a single archetypal form. (I did not include set 13 in the above because there is generalized confusion among the MSS.)

Now then, **7** and **6** join against **5** fourteen times; **7** and **5** join against **6** nine times; **6** and **5** join against **7** not one single time. Does this mean that **7** is dependent on **5** and **6** (von Soden), or does it mean that **5** and **6** are independent departures from **7** (WNP)? Only for set 23 are all three groups entirely distinct, but at least for this set **7** does not depend on the other two. (Curiously, the MSS present us with at least seven different arrangements of the five words in set 23, and the main lectionary group goes with a fourth reading, not one of the big three.) To my mind, **7** is the lowest common denominator, and therefore older and better than the other two. So what is the point? The point is that $\mathbf{M}^7$ equals von Soden's $\mathbf{K}^r$ (my $\mathbf{f}^{35}$), and he used his analysis of $\mathbf{M}^7$ to characterize his $\mathbf{K}^r$ for the whole NT! He repeatedly offered $\mathbf{M}^7$ as 'proof' that $\mathbf{K}^r$ was late. As anyone who is even remotely acquainted with the MSS knows, to characterize even one book, not to mention the whole NT, on the basis of twelve verses is just plain wrong.[1]

5. For some mysterious reason von Soden seemed determined that his $\mathbf{K}^r$ should have been created in the XII century, so he exerted himself to re-date the three $\mathbf{K}^r$ MSS from the XI that he knew of. But since the three are copies, not original creations, their exemplars were older, of necessity (as were the exemplars of the exemplars), so what did von Soden think he was 'proving'? To his mind, apparently, a

---

[1] Since it is impossible to demonstrate objectively that $\mathbf{M}^7$ is dependent on $\mathbf{M}^6$ and $\mathbf{M}^5$, that imagined dependency should not be alleged as being relevant to the age and nature of the text-type.

text-type could not have existed before its earliest extant represent-tative [!]. For many years, I have heard people repeating the evident stupidity that because there are no early Byzantine MSS the Byzantine text cannot be early, and they are still doing it. This is based on the obviously false assumption that the surviving MSS from the earliest centuries are representative of the total manuscript situation at that time.

The only surviving 'edifices' in Egypt that are 4,000 years old are the pyramids. Will anyone be so ridiculous as to argue that a pyramid was the only type of structure used in Egypt at that time? How many Egyptians at that time lived in pyramids? Absolutely none, because pyramids were only for the dead. But did ordinary people get a pyramid for a tomb? Only a pharaoh could afford one. We can say with total certainty that pyramids are not representative of the totality of structures in Egypt 4,000 years ago, even though they are the only ones that have survived. I would say that it is equally certain that the earliest MSS are not representative of the manuscript situation at the time. (They are the resting place of 'dead' forms of the NT Text, much like the pyramids.)

I do not know even the name of any of my great, great grandfathers, and I have no artifacts that they used. Yet I can state with total certainty that they existed. How can I do that? I can do that because I am here, because I exist. I could not exist without great, great grandfathers. My body contains some of their genes, their DNA. Just because I did not exist 400 years ago, does not mean that none of my ancestors did. Is that not perfectly obvious?

In 1976 Dr. Jakob van Bruggen published *The Ancient Text of the New Testament* (Winnipeg: Premier Printing Ltd.). It contains a chapter on 'The Age of the Byzantine Type' that occupies pages 22 – 29. He marshals a variety of arguments to show that the Byzantine text-type must be older than its surviving representatives. I will limit myself to quoting just one paragraph (page 25).

> What conditions must be satisfied if we wish to award the prize to the older majuscules? While asking this question we assumed wittingly or unwittingly that we were capable of making a fair comparison between manuscripts in an earlier period and those in a later period. After all, we can only arrive at positive statements if that is the case. Imagine that someone said: in the Middle Ages mainly cathedrals were built, but in modern times many small and plainer churches are being built. This statement seems completely true when we today look around in the cities and

villages. Yet we are mistaken. An understandable mistake: many small churches of the Middle Ages have disappeared, and usually only the cathedrals were restored. Thus a great historical falsification of perspective with regard to the history of church-building arises. We are not able to make a general assertion about church-building in the Middle Ages on the basis of the surviving materials. If we would still dare to make such an assertion, then we wrongly assumed that the surviving materials enabled us to make a fair comparison. But how is the situation in the field of New Testament manuscripts? Do we have a *representative* number of manuscripts from the first centuries? Only if that is the case do we have the right to make conclusions and positive statements. Yet it is just at this point that difficulties arise. The situation is even such that we know with certainty that we *do not* possess a representative number of manuscripts from the first centuries. This is due to three reasons, which now deserve our attention successively [emphasis in the original].

He then goes on to discuss those three reasons. (I know Dr. van Bruggen personally, and may say that he is an authority on the subject of cathedrals.) Pages 137 – 154 of my *The Identity of the New Testament Text IV* give a detailed discussion of the evidence for an early Byzantine text-type.

I continue to insist that most of the early MSS survived because they were intolerably bad; it was psychologically impossible to use them, besides being a criminal waste of good parchment to copy them (is not uncial 06 the only one with an extant 'child'?). A while ago I collated cursive GA 789 (Athens: National Library) for John, having already done so for Luke. Although the copyist made an occasional mistake, I judge that his exemplar was a very nearly perfect representative of Family 35. However, 789 is presently lacking John 19:12 to the end. A later hand, 789^s, has 19:26 to the end, but that copyist was a terrible speller, averaging nearly one mistake per verse—reminiscent of P^{66} (although P^{66} is worse, averaging around two mistakes per verse). I found myself becoming angry with the copyist—I was prepared to call down curses on his head! Assuming that the cause of the mistakes was ignorance, rather than perversity, the copyist should not have undertaken a task for which he was so pitifully unqualified. It would be psychologically impossible for me to use 789^s for devotion or study. I would become too angry to continue. I assume that sincere Christians in the early centuries would have reacted in the same way.

Strange to relate, the very INTF that Kurt Aland founded—he who declared that the Byzantine MSS were irrelevant to the search for the original text—that INTF has now published the following:

Since the Textus Receptus was overcome by the scholarly textual criticism of the 19th century, there is tenacious negative bias against the Byzantine majority text. Wherever well-known, older textual witnesses like Vaticanus and Sinaiticus, and even more so in combination with a papyrus, stand against the majority of minuscules, the decision against the majority text was often made easily, without seriously considering the quality of the variants in question. Therefore, the editors of the present edition have taken two factors as paramount.

First, it is often overlooked that in the vast majority of variant passages only a few witnesses differ from all the others. As a rule, the popular witnesses from the 4th / 5th centuries and, if extant, from even earlier papyri, agree with the majority of all witnesses. This implies that at all these passages the old age of the majority text is not in doubt.

Second, it is necessary to distinguish consistently between a manuscript and the text transmitted in it. "*Recentiores non deteriores*" is a principle widely accepted in editing philology, but in New Testament scholarship it was applied only to a few younger manuscripts featuring similar textual peculiarities as Vaticanus and Sinaiticus. For the reason given above, it is undoubtedly true that the textual tradition as a whole goes back to a very early period and that the coherent transmission of the majority of all textual witnesses provides a strong argument *for*, not *against*, the variant in question [emphasis in the original]. (Page 30* of the recent [2017] *Editio Critica Maior* for Acts.)

Well, well, well, better late than never! "The textual tradition as a whole" includes $\mathbf{f^{35}}$/$\mathbf{K^r}$, of necessity. The *Text und Textwert* series[1] is now complete for the whole NT, except for John 11-21. The objective evidence it provides shows clearly, empirically, that Family 35 ($\mathbf{K^r}$) is independent of the Byzantine bulk (Soden's $\mathbf{k^x}$) throughout the NT. It follows that it **cannot** be a revision of that bulk. Anyone who continues to affirm that von Soden's $\mathbf{K^r}$ was a revision of his $\mathbf{K^x}$ is either uninformed or perverse.[2]

6. It remains to take up the question of the liturgical apparatus characteristic of $\mathbf{f^{35}}$/$\mathbf{K^r}$. A lectionary copy would be far easier and faster to

---

[1] *Text und Textwert der Griechischen Handschriften des Neuen Testaments* (Ed. Kurt Aland, Berlin: Walter de Gruyter).

[2] To ignore clear evidence that has been called to your attention and to continue to promote a claim that you know is false, is to be perverse.

produce than a full continuous text copy, quite apart from an apparatus in a different color. Since we have extant lectionaries from the IV and all subsequent centuries, why would anyone go to the extra work of adding a liturgical apparatus to a continuous text copy? And why was that apparatus added to only one text-type?

But first, why were lectionaries prepared, instead of continuous text MSS? As the practice of reading and expounding established passages on specific Sundays became generalized, having to use a full text MS became cumbersome; why not prepare MSS containing only the established lections? Recall that most people could not read and were limited to hearing Scripture during the weekly meetings. Very few people were able to read and study the Scriptures at home. Fewer still would be in a position to make written copies of anything. Scribe was a profession. However, I submit for the consideration of the reader that the very mentality that would consider a lectionary to be a good thing, in itself represented a relaxing of a devout commitment to the precise form of the Sacred Text.

From the fourth century on, if not before, the Roman Church used Latin, not Greek. So who preserved the Greek NT during the middle ages? Increasingly it would have been the Greek speaking monastic communities. By definition a monastery is a religious community; its daily life and very existence derives from and depends upon its religion. For Christian communities, the NT writings would be central to their faith. However, as time went on, tradition took over, and there would be a relaxing of a devout commitment to the precise form of the Sacred Text. This would be reflected in the level of quality control that prevailed in each monastery with reference to the copying of NT MSS. It would also be reflected by the increased production of lectionaries in the monasteries.

The relaxing of quality control in the copying of NT MSS is reflected in the variety of readings to be found among the MSS that make up the Byzantine tradition. For three chapters of Luke, F. Wisse identified 36 lines of transmission within that tradition. An average Byzantine MS will have 3 to 5 variants per page of a printed Greek Text (as compared to 15 to 20 for an Alexandrian MS). The monk was performing a religious duty, but without a personal commitment to the Text. A merely 'ho-hum' **f^{35}/K^r** MS will have one variant per two pages of a printed Greek Text, while the better ones will only have one variant per four or more pages of a printed Greek Text (the really good ones will be perfect for the shorter books). I have collated a MS with just one variant for the 21 chapters of John; the same MS (GA 586) has just one variant for the 16 chapters of Mark. What does that picture tell us about the mentality of the copyists? How can we account for the extreme care demonstrated by the **f^{35}/K^r** copyists?

The extant f^{35}/**K**^{r} MSS come from isolated monasteries around the Mediterranean world and were produced during five centuries (XI-XV). (I ignore, for the moment, the generations of exemplars that they represent.) There simply was no human agency that could exercise such control. Evidently some monasteries would be more conservative in doctrine and attitude than others, and within a conservative monastery an individual copyist could be committed to the divine authority of the exemplar he was copying. Apart from supernatural participation in the process, the prevailing attitude in certain monasteries plus the personal conviction of individual copyists is the only explanation that I can see for the incredible internal consistency that the f^{35}/**K**^{r} MSS demonstrate.

But why would anyone go to the extra work of adding a liturgical apparatus to a continuous text copy, since lectionaries were in plentiful supply? And why was that apparatus added to only one text-type, precisely the one with the greatest internal consistency? Well, what would a conservative monastery do if it wanted to use the established lections for the reading aloud at the community meals, but doing so with a continuous text MS (because of respect for the Text)? The beginning and the ending of the lections would have to be marked somehow. But respect for the Text dictates that such lection markers must not be confused with the Text itself—therefore ink of a different color (which would also help the reader to start and stop at the correct spots).

Well and good, but why choose f^{35}/**K**^{r}? Well, if it is respect for the Text that motivates you to use continuous text MSS, rather than lectionaries, what kind of text are you going to use? If you are aware that the different MSS offer some differences in wording, how will you choose? That very awareness will derive from a conviction within the monastery as to which line of transmission within the MSS has the best pedigree, and it will be that line that deserves your greatest respect. So that is the type of text that you will use. But how is it that isolated monasteries made the same choice? Aye, there's the rub, how is it that isolated monasteries made the same choice? Von Soden opined that a central authority ordered a revision and imposed it on the monasteries. Since it is demonstrable that f^{35}/**K**^{r} is not a revision, on what basis would that imaginary authority make a choice of what text to impose? If that authority was a sincere Christian, would he not choose what he considered to be the best text? Since there was no such authority, we are still left with the question: how is it that isolated monasteries made the same choice?

The only answer that I can see is that there was a generalized conviction throughout the global Christian community as to the identity of the line of transmission with the best pedigree. Since the transmission of the NT Text down through the centuries was essentially normal, from the very start, the conviction about pedigree would be based upon historical evidence. When the Autographs were penned, there were no NT lections. The idea of adding lection markers had to come later; just how much later we have no way of knowing. Somewhere along the line, the first such MS was produced. Was the idea so brilliant that it spread like wild fire? Or did the idea spread slowly? We have no way of knowing.

It should be obvious to everyone that preparing a copy in two colors with an elaborate apparatus will take more time and effort than a copy in one color without that apparatus. So why would people do it? There had to be a demand for such copies. A MS with a liturgical apparatus was obviously prepared to be used for public reading, to be read aloud to an audience. For private reading and study you want a text without interruptions. Von Soden actually noted that the individual letters in his $\mathbf{K^r}$ MSS tended to be somewhat larger than in non-$\mathbf{K^r}$ MSS. So why would that be? Presumably to facilitate the public reading. In any case, books that are used wear out. So much so, that monasteries that used a specific text-type for their public reading would be sure to make and keep a number of back-up copies on hand. There would not be the same motivation for text-types that were not used. That may be why $\mathbf{f^{35}/K^r}$ is by far the largest family within the Byzantine tradition, and is the only family that has so far been demonstrated to exist in all 27 books.[1]

CONCLUSION: Von Soden's characterization of his $\mathbf{K^r}$ as a late revision is simply false. It follows that all informed persons should stop using the symbol $\mathbf{K^r}$.

Copyist Care Quotient

For some time I have been of the opinion that the question of the mentality that a copyist brought to his task deserves far more attention than it has so far received. If we can agree that the job of a copyist is to reproduce the exemplar that he is copying, then it should be possible to evaluate his failures in so doing. Of course such evaluation depends on the known existence of his exemplar, or of the archetype of the family to which the copy belongs (as determined by its mosaic or profile). Where there is a line of transmission descending from an archetype, a given variant could have been in the exemplar, of course, but I see no way of controlling for that possibility, at the moment. A 'variant' is defined by its departure from

---

[1] Just by the way, it is common knowledge that the Lectionaries contain no lections from the Apocalypse. What few people know is that some $\mathbf{f^{35}}$ MSS do contain a liturgical apparatus in the Apocalypse. Might this be something that deserves further study?

the archetypal form, as empirically determined by the consensus of the family representatives.[1] The variant can be evaluated, whenever it was introduced.

However, thought needs to be given to the exact definition of a 'variant'. I am of the opinion that ultimately the term 'variant' should be reserved for readings that make a difference in the meaning, and even so, only if they were made deliberately. Of course, since an unintentional change can also alter meaning, we must proceed slowly, which is why I used the term 'ultimately'. In the meantime, in the chart below I have omitted alternate spellings of the same word, but they are duly recorded in my full **f**[35] apparatus for Mark.

Mark

I invite attention to the following evidence from the Gospel of Mark. I will use E.C. Colwell's analysis of thirteen 'Alexandrian' MSS in the first chapter, and my own collation of fifty-three Family 35 MSS throughout the entire book.[2] Here is Colwell's own statement.

> After a careful study of all alleged Beta Text-type witnesses in the first chapter of Mark, six Greek manuscripts emerged as primary witnesses: א, B, L, 33, 892, 2427. Therefore, the weaker Beta manuscripts C, D, 157, 517, 579, 1241 and 1342 were set aside. Then on the basis of the six primary witnesses an 'average' or mean text was reconstructed including all the readings

---

[1] I have determined the archetypal form of **f**[35] for Mark on the basis of complete collations of the 53 family representatives plotted on the chart below. The results are recorded in my full **f**[35] apparatus for Mark. There are seven splits that hover around 20%, four of them being alternate spellings of the same word. There are two splits that hover around 25%. None of the nine is a serious candidate for the archetypal form. There is but one serious split, hovering around 40%, it is in 13:31. Is the verb that goes with "the heaven and the earth" singular, or plural? In English the translation for either is "will pass away", so they are two ways of saying the same thing. Although the plural has a considerable geographic distribution, the singular has far more. There are good representatives on both sides, but the five best copies have the singular. Of the five XI MSS, four have the singular. Adding it all up, the singular gets the nod.

[2] To someone who has never collated a Greek manuscript, I may say that it is slave labor, plain drudgery. To collate one copy of a book the size of Mark takes several days. So why do I do it? The underlying consideration is the belief that the NT books are divinely inspired, a written revelation from the Sovereign Creator. Such a revelation has objective authority, and it becomes important to have the precise original wording. If Mark were just a bit of ordinary ancient literature, the precise original wording would be of little interest. So what? What difference would it make?

supported by the majority of the primary witnesses.[1] Even on this restricted basis the amount of variation recorded in the apparatus was dismaying. In this first chapter, each of the six witnesses differed from the 'average' Beta Text-type as follows: L, nineteen times (Westcott and Hort, twenty-one times); Aleph, twenty-six times; 2427, thirty-two times; 33, thirty-three times; B, thirty-four times; and 892, forty-one times. These results show convincingly that any attempt to reconstruct an archetype of the Beta Text-type on a quantitative basis is doomed to failure. The text thus reconstructed is not reconstructed but constructed; it is an artificial entity that never existed.[2] [A text-type with no archetype cannot represent the Original.]

Let us consider carefully what Colwell did, recalling that he was a partisan of the 'Alexandrian' text-type (his 'Beta Text-type'). He attempted to arrive at the archetypal form of that text-type, for one chapter, by a majority vote of its known representatives, that he presumed to be the thirteen listed.[3] The result was so impossibly bad that he discarded the seven 'weaker' representatives and tried again, using only the six 'primary' witnesses. In his own words: "Even on this restricted basis the amount of var-

---

1 Note that his 'mean' text would not include a reading where the internal division was such that there was no majority; and since he only used six MSS, what did he do when they were evenly divided?

2 Colwell, "The Significance of Grouping of New Testament Manuscripts", *New Testament Studies*, IV (1957-1958), 86-87. Cf. also Colwell, "Genealogical Method", pp. 119-123. Colwell follows Kenyon and uses "Beta text-type" to refer to today's 'Alexandrian' text, whereas Hort used "b group" to refer to his 'Western' text.

3 Notice that the total representation of the text-type is just thirteen MSS (in the Gospels), and that number has not increased significantly since Colwell's day (sixty years ago)—but recall that it has no demonstrable archetype. In contrast, the fifty-one **f**[35] MSS I have collated represent only some 20% of the extant family representatives, in the Gospels (around 250 MSS). It remains to be seen how many further families, within the Byzantine bulk, can be identified that have a single demonstrable archetypal form, based on a complete collation of all its representatives (or at least a sufficient proportion to establish the archetype). For the *TuT* volumes covering the first ten chapters of John, the *INTF* collated some 1875 MSS for 153 variant sets. Pages 54-90 in the first volume contain a list of 'groupings' of MSS; aside from their **K**[r], the largest group has 53 MSS, headed by MS 2103. The number of groups is bewildering. Further, with few exceptions, the groups or families identified by von Soden and others are limited to the Gospels; they do not exist throughout the 27 books that form our NT Canon. But if God inspired all 27 books, then He must have preserved all 27 books (or else why bother inspiring). Since the Autograph is the quintessential archetype, any candidate for that preservation should have an archetype, an empirically determined archetype, and for all 27 books—as of this writing, there is only one: Family 35.

iation recorded in the apparatus was dismaying." The great Codex Vaticanus differed from its archetypal form no less than thirty-four times, in one chapter. Come now, can a MS that differs from its archetype 34 times in one chapter be called a good copy? What objective basis could anyone have for so doing? By way of comparison, or contrast, I invite attention to the following evidence from Family 35, covering all sixteen chapters of Mark, including the last twelve verses.

Key:

s =	singular reading (until all MSS have been collated, this is just an assumption; also, easy transcriptional errors could be made by more than one copyist, independently);
c =	corrected variant (variation of any kind corrected to the presumed archetype);
x =	uncorrected variant ('variant' here means that it is attested by MSS outside the family, but by no other family members; this could indicate mixture);
y =	family is divided, but the variant is also attested by MSS outside the family (this could be mixture on the part of whoever introduced the variant);
/ =	family is divided, and the variant has no outside attestation (a splinter group);
h =	an obvious case of homoioteleuton (or –arcton) [I do not consider this to be a proper 'variant', but it is included below];
i =	sheer inattention (often repeating a syllable from one line to the next);
--- =	no departures from the presumed profile.

It will be observed that I attribute a smaller number of variants to the presumed exemplar than to the copy—I discount 'c', 's', 'h' and 'i', ascribing them to the copyist; 'c' could have been done by someone else, but the result is correct. Of course, any of them might have been in the exemplar, and the exemplar might have had an error that the copyist corrected, so the numbers under 'exemplar' are only an approximation (but probably not far off). It is also true that a variant classed under 'x', 'y' or '/' could be an independent mistake by the copyist, not in the exemplar. For all that, I consider that the general contour of the evidence given below is valid and relevant.

f^{35} in Mark—raw data

MS	stats	total	exemplar	date	location[1]	content
18	5y, 1/, 7s, 2i	15	6	1364	Constantinople	eapr
35	5c	5	---	XI	Aegean	eapr
128	1y, 1/, 2s, 1h, 2i	7	2	XIII	Vatican	e
141	2x, 2y, 4/, 3c, 9s, 2h	22	8	XIII	Vatican	eapr
204	3y, 2/, 3s, 1i	9	5	XIII	Bologna	eap
510	1x, 1y, 9s, 3i	14	2	XII	Oxford-cc	e
547	10y, 1/, 4s	15	11	XI	Karakallu	eap
553	2x, 9y, 2/, 1c, 4s, 3i	21	13	XIII	Jerusalem	e

[1] I give the location where a MS was acquired, when this differs from where it is presently held, on the basis of available information.

MS	stats	total	exemplar	date	location[1]	content
586	1i	1	---	XIV	Modena	e
645	2x, 8y, 4/, 3c, 16s, 2h, 13i	48	14	1304	Cyprus	e
689	5x, 5y, 1/, 1c, 7s, 3i	22	11	XIII	London	e
789	1y, 2s	3	1	XIV	Athens	e
824	2x, 3y, 3s, 2i	10	5	XIV	Grottaferrata	eapr
928	3y, 1/, 1c, 1s	6	4	1304	Dionysiu	eap
1023	1x, 4y, 2/, 1c, 1s, 1i	10	7	1338	Iviron	e
1040	2x, 3y, 1/, 2s, 1h	9	6	XIV	Karakallu	eap
1072	1y, 2i	3	1	XIII	M Lavras	eapr
1075	4y, 2/, 1s, 2i	9	6	XIV	M Lavras	eapr
1111	4y, 3/, 1c, 1s	9	7	XIV	Stavronikita	e
1117	1x, 3y, 7s, 1i	12	4	XIV	Philotheu	e
1133	10y, 12/, 1c, 10s, 1h	34	22	XIV	Philotheu	e
1145	1x, 9y, 3/, 5c, 2s, 2i	22	13	XII	Constantinople	e
1147	1y, 3/, 1c, 5s, 2h, 3i	15	4	1370	Constantinople	e
1199	8x, 12y, 10/, 24s, 19i	73	30	XII	Sinai	e
1251	1x, 9y, 4/, 7s, 1h, 7i	29	14	XIII	Sinai	eap
1339	2x, 1y, 1/, 1s, 1i	6	4	XIII	Jerusalem	e
1384	1x, 8y, 1/, 1c, 7s, 1h, 4i	23	10	XI	Andros	eapr
1435	4y, 1/, 10s	15	5	XI	Vatopedi	e
1461	1y, 3s	4	1	XIII	M Lavras	e
1496	1y, 2s, 1i	4	1	XIII	M Lavras	e
1503	2/, 1c, 2s, 1i	6	2	1317	M Lavras	eapr
1572	3y, 1/, 3s	7	4	1304	Vatopedi	e
1628	1y, 5s, 1h, 2i	9	1	1400	M Lavras	eap
1637	2y, 2s, 2i	6	2	1328	M Lavras	eapr
1652	1y, 1s, 2i	4	1	XVI	M Lavras	eapr
1667	5y, 2/, 1c, 8s	16	7	1309	Panteleimonos	e
1705	1x, 15y, 4/, 13s, 1h, 4i	38	20	XIV	Tirana	e
1713	1y, 2c, 2s	5	1	XV	Lesbos	e
2122	5y, 5s	10	5	XII	Athens	e
2221	6x, 15y, 1/, 2s, 1h	25	22	1432	Sparta	eap
2253	1y, 1s, 1i	3	1	XI	Tirana	e
2261	10y, 9/, 3c, 1s, 3i	26	19	XIV	Kalavryta	eap
2323	10y, 2/, 4c, 4s	20	12	XIII	Athens	er
2352	2y, 2/, 4c, 4i	12	4	XIV	Meteora	eapr
2382	1/	1	---	XII	Constantinople	e
2466	3y, 1/, 3c, 12s, 4i	23	4	1329	Patmos	eap
2503	3y, 1/, 5s, 1i	10	4	XIV	Sinai	e
2554	1/, 1c	2	1	1434	Bucharest	eapr
2765	4y, 1/, 1i	6	5	XIV	Corinth?(Oxford)	e
2875	1x, 37, 2/, 1c, 5s, 1i	13	6	1314	Valopedi	e
2876	2x, 2y, 3/, 13s	20	7	XIV	Vatopedi	e
l.2110	2y, 2/, 2c, 1s, 1i	8	4	1322	Iviron	e
L.65	2x, 3y, 2/, 2c, 9s, 2i	20	7	XIV	Leukosia	e

How did I choose which MSS to collate? I used the *TuT* volumes for Mark. The *INTF* collated some 1,700 MSS for 196 variant sets (not all MSS are extant for all sets). The distinctive $\mathbf{f}^{35}$ profile is made up of just four of those 196 sets, but it is enough to identify any $\mathbf{f}^{35}$ MS that they collated. Within the list of MSS presumed to belong to $\mathbf{f}^{35}$, I first chose those that would give me the widest geographical distribution. I next concentrated on MSS with a 'perfect' profile. Of course, I was limited by the availability of MSS in PDF. With my family profile for the whole NT, I can quickly identify any **f**^{35} MS that has yet to be studied. That is how Iviron 2110 and Leukosia 65 got in (they have not yet been assigned a number by INTF, as of this writing).

Looking at the chart, eleven MSS have an average of only one variant per three chapters or more—exceptional! (MS 586 is all but perfect as it stands.) Another nine MSS have only one variant per two chapters—excellent. Virtually 40% are excellent or better. Another seventeen have only one variant per chapter—good. Another twelve have two variants per chapter—fair. Another three have three variants per chapter—poor. One MS has five variants per chapter—marginal. Note that the very worst of the fifty-three **f**^{35} representatives (1199, e, XII, Sinai) is four times 'better' than Colwell's very best Alexandrian representative, Codex L. Stop for a moment and think about the implications. How can any sane person defend the proposition that the Alexandrian text-type represents the best line of transmission?[1]

A representative case

In the opening paragraph I stated that variants can be evaluated. I will now take one of the merely 'fair' **f**^{35} representatives—MS 1384, eapr, XI, Andros—list its variants and evaluate them.

1:17	γενεσθαι ‖ --- 1384 [the verb must be understood in any case; the meaning is not altered]
1:44	προσενεγκαι ‖ προσενεγκε [75%] 1384 + five [these forms were used interchangeably, so they are virtually alternate spellings of the same word]
2:17	εχοντες ‖ 1 και 1384 [he merely supplied an implied conjunction; there is no change in the basic meaning]
3:12	πολλα ‖ --- 1384 [this does not change the basic meaning]

[1] I here repeat a sentence from Colwell's paragraph: "These results show convincingly that any attempt to reconstruct an archetype of the Beta Text-type on a quantitative basis is doomed to failure." "These results show convincingly" something else: those copyists were not encumbered with any special respect or consideration for what they were copying. Obviously, they did not believe that they were copying a sacred text, which makes one wonder why they would expend time and material in so doing. I see one explanation that makes sense: they were deliberately perverting the text, presumably under Satanic or demonic influence. By way of contrast, the care with which most **f**^{35} copyists did their work implies a high degree of respect for the text being copied. If God were concerned to preserve His Text, what sort of copyist would He use? What sort of copyist would the Holy Spirit protect and bless? [Since both God and Satan exist, someone who excludes the supernatural from his model is being naïve in the extreme.]

3:28 υιοις των ανθρωπων || ανθρωποις 1384 [this is a synonym, it does not change the basic meaning]

4:24 μετρειτε || μετρειται 1384 [an itacism resulting in a misspelling]

5:4 αλυσεσιν || αλισεσιν 1384^{1x} [a misspelling; he got it right elsewhere]

5:13 τα ακαθαρτα || --- [1%] 1384 + one [an easy case of homoioteleuton and –arcton]

5:19 αναγγειλον || αναγκειλον 1384 [an alternate spelling]

5:27 ακουσασα || ακουσα 1384 [from one line to the next]

6:13 εξεβαλλον || εξεβαλον [10%] 1384 + three [imperfect, or 2nd aorist? one 'l' could have been dropped accidentally, but there is little difference in meaning, in any case]

6:20 ακουων 1384^{alt} || ακουσας [80%] 1384 + nine [present, or aorist? the first hand placed the present above the aorist as an alternate; there is little difference in meaning]

(1384 is missing 6:20-45)

6:53 γενησαρετ || γεννησαρετ [53%] 1384 + three [an alternate spelling]

7:4 χαλκειων || χαλκιων [70%] 1384 + one [an itacism, or an alternate spelling]

7:26 εκβαλη || εκβαλλη [30%] 1384 + two [2nd aorist, or present? in the context it makes little difference]

8:7 παραθειναι || παραθηναι [15%] 1384 + one [an itacism resulting in a misspelling]

8:35 απολεση || απολεσει [5%] 1384 [aorist subjunctive, or future indicative? in the context it makes little difference]

8:38 μοιχαλιδι || μοιχαλιδη 1384 [an itacism resulting in a misspelling]

9:19 φερετε || 1 μοι 1384 [an unnecessary repetition of the pronoun that does not alter the meaning]

9:20 ιδον || ιδων [70%] 1384 + eight [is the subject of the verb the demon, or the boy? in the context it makes little difference]

9:40 υμων || ημων [12%] 1384 + three [the variant is inferior, but in the context it makes little difference]

(1384 is missing 10:23-46, 12:16-41)

12:43 βαλλοντων || βαλοντων [39%] 1384 + six [present, or 2nd aorist? in the context it makes little difference]

13:28 γινωσκεται || γινωσκετε [75%] 1384^{alt} + two [see 1:44, only here it is the alternate]

14:36 παρενεγκαι || παρενεγκε [70%] 1384 + three [see 1:44]

(1384 is missing 15:29-16:7)

16:9a μαγδαληνη || μαγδαλινη 1384 [an itacism resulting in a misspelling]

16:9b εκβεβληκει || εκβεβληκη 1384 [an itacism resulting in a misspelling]

16:14 ωνειδισεν || ωνειδησε 1384 [an itacism resulting in a misspelling]

With four exceptions, only a single letter or syllable is involved, and nowhere is the meaning seriously affected. If the missing pages were available and collated, a number of variants would presumably be added, but they would not differ in kind from the rest. **Someone reading MS 1384 would not be misled as to the intended meaning at any point in the book**. I say this is noteworthy, and it is typical of almost all $\mathbf{f}^{35}$ MSS. Down through the centuries of transmission, anyone with access to a $\mathbf{f}^{35}$ representative could know the intended meaning of the Autograph.[1] Not only that, most lines of transmission within the Byzantine bulk would be reasonably close, good enough for most practical purposes. This is also true of the much maligned *Textus Receptus*; it is certainly good enough for most practical purposes. Down through the centuries of Church history, most people could have had reasonable access to God's written revelation.

1 Since $\mathbf{f}^{35}$ MSS are scattered all over, or all around, the Mediterranean world, such access would have been feasible for most people.

Incredibly careful transmission

I will now evaluate the variants in the eleven 'exceptional' representatives.

MS 586 has one: 10:35—ημιν || υμιν 510,586. Since MS 510 has fourteen variants, and 586 never joins it elsewhere, there is evidently no dependency, so these are independent variants. But there is a curious aspect to this variant: it is nonsense! The sons of Zebedee say, "Teacher, we want you to do <u>for us</u> whatever we may ask". So the variant, 'to do <u>for you (pl)</u>', is manifest nonsense. Was it a mere case of itacism? If so, it is the only one in the whole book (for 586). On several occasions, with different copyists in different books, I have observed a similar situation: the copyist has done perfect work to that point and then introduces an impossible variant, where the reader will almost automatically make the necessary correction, as here. It makes me wonder if the copyist felt unworthy to produce a perfect copy, and introduced an obvious error on purpose.

MS 2382 has one: 13:1—εις || 1 εκ 510, 1117, 2382. As with the example above, there is evidently no dependency, so these are independent variants. (MS 1117 has twelve variants.) "One of His disciples said to Him"—the preposition is implicit, and making it overt does not alter the meaning; the translation remains the same.

MS 2554 has two: 2:23—ποιειν 2554^{c} || πιειν 1251, 2554, 2765; 15:46—επι την θυραν || 1 τη θυρα 2554 + eleven family representatives. The first one is manifest nonsense, independent instances of itacism. The copyist of 2554 caught his mistake and corrected it himself, so this is not a proper variant. The second one represents a split in the family. The preposition takes three cases—genitive, dative, accusative—so there is little difference in meaning.

MSS 789, 1072 and 2253 have three, to be discussed in that order. MS 789: 1:20—αυτων || αυτον 789, 1199; 13:31—παρελευσεται || παρελευσονται [40%] 789 + twenty-one family representatives; 16:9—πρωτη || πρωτον 789. The first one is an independent itacism, resulting in nonsense. (MS 1199 has 73 variants.) The second one has already been explained in the first footnote, under "Copyist Care Quotient". The third one is a silly mistake, where apparently the copyist became confused and assimilated the suffix to that of the following noun, only then it doesn't make sense—perhaps he was hurrying to finish, being so near the end of the book. In any case, it is not a valid variant.

MS 1072: 6:22—ορχησαμενης || ωρχησαμενης 1072; 7:37—εξεπλησσοντο || εξεπληστο 1072; 9:20—ιδον || ιδων [70%] 1072 +

seven family representatives. The first one is presumably an itacism, resulting in an alternate spelling for the same word. The second one is a mistake, going from one line to the next, and is not a proper variant. As for the third one, is the subject of the verb the demon, or the boy? In the context, it makes little difference.

MS 2253: 5:36—ευθεως ακουσας || ~ 21 [1%] 547,2253; 8:24—περιπατουντες || περιπαπατουντες 2253; 15:46—επι την θυραν || 1 τη θυρα 2253 + eleven family representatives. The first one is presumably an independent mistake, that does not affect the meaning. (MS 547 has fifteen variants.) The second one is an accidental repetition of a syllable, going from one line to the next, and is not a proper variant. The third one is discussed above.

MSS 1461, 1496 and 1652 have four, to be discussed in that order. (Curiously, they all three come from M. Lavras, but have different sets of variants.) MS 1461: 5:13—αυτοις || --- 1461; 6:15—δε || --- 1461; 12:6—οτι || --- 824, 1461; 13:31—παρελευσεται || παρελευσονται [40%] 1461 + twenty-one family representatives. The first one is an accidental omission, presumably, that does not change the meaning. The second omission does not affect the meaning either. The third omission, presumably independent, does not affect the meaning either. (MS 824 has ten variants.) The fourth variant has been discussed above.

MS 1496: 10:43—εν || --- 1496, 2323; 11:10—υψιστοις || υυψιστοις 1496; 13:31—(see above); 14:43—παραγινεται || 1 ο 1496. The first one is an independent omission, making the preposition implicit. (MS 2323 has twenty variants.) The second one is an accidental repetition of the vowel, going from one line to the next, and is not a proper variant. The third variant has been discussed above. The fourth one is a 'natural' addition of the article, that does not affect the meaning.

MS 1652: 8:32—προσλαβομενος || προσλαβομενον 1652; 11:13—αυτην || αυτη 1652; 13:6—πολλοι || πολοι 1652; 13:31—(see above). The first one is an obvious error that any reader would correct in his mind. For the second one, the preposition takes both cases, with no change in meaning, in this context. The third one is an obvious misspelling. The fourth one has been discussed above.

MSS 35 and 1713 have five, to be discussed in that order. MS 35: all five of them were corrected to the archetype.

MS 1713: the first two were corrected to the archetype; 9:5—ηλια || ηλιαν 1705, 1713, 2503; 9:50—αρτυσετε || αρτυσητε 1713; 13:31—(see above). The third one appears to be an independent change, from dative to accusative, although the dative is clearly correct. The meaning is not altered. (MS 1705 has 38 variants; MS 2503 has ten.) The fourth one could be an itacism, although it changes the mood. The meaning is not altered. The fifth one has been discussed above.

Out of a total of thirty-five variants, for eleven MSS, for the whole book of Mark,[1] eight were corrected, which leaves twenty-seven. At least six are not a proper variant, which leaves twenty-one. Five are repetitions of a variant in common, which leaves sixteen.[2] Most of these involve a single letter or syllable, as is typical of **f**[35] variants. None of them changes the meaning. Now I call that **incredibly careful transmission**.

I venture to predict, if all extant MSS are ever collated, that no other line of transmission will come anywhere close to this level of precision, or copyist care quotient.

Observations

1. Two-thirds of the collated MSS above have no extra-family variants = no mixture. The monks faithfully reproduced what was in front of them.
2. The sloppiest MS, 1199, also has the most extra-family variants = the copyist was comparatively careless and not concerned for purity. (But if it represented any other line of transmission within the Byzantine bulk it would probably be a good copy.)
3. The five XI MSS evidently reflect distinct exemplars (which themselves probably had distinct exemplars), so the archetype certainly existed in the uncial period.
4. Although the precise profile of the archetype is clear, it is also clear that the extant MSS reflect a number of separate lines of transmission within the family.
5. Any attempt at reconstructing a family tree will require the positing of a fair number of intervening nodes, nodes that could well be separated by centuries.
6. It follows that any claim that the **f**[35] archetype was created after the

---

[1] 11 MSS x 16 chapters = 171 chapters; it took these eleven MSS together no less than 171 chapters to introduce as many variants as Codex B managed to do in one! That means that Codex B is 171 times worse than the eleven **f**[35] representatives taken together. And yet there are those who have stated that B is our 'best' MS!

[2] That is to say, between them the eleven MSS have sixteen variants for the whole book, or an average of 1.5 variants each, for the whole book.

beginning of the minuscule period is either uninformed or perverse.

Romans

I invite attention to the following evidence from Paul's letter to the Romans. I will use Reuben Swanson's collation of the three great 'Alexandrian' MSS—Codex Aleph (01), Codex A (02) and Codex B (03)[1]—and my own collation of thirty-seven Family 35 MSS, throughout the entire book in both cases.[2]

I simply followed Swanson religiously; I did not check any of his MSS for myself. I did a rough count; I generally counted a phrase as one variant, and so for a long omission. I did not count *nomina sacra*, movable *nu*, accents, and *καθως/καθω*. Swanson collated against both UBS[4] and the Oxford 1873 TR. The difference between the 3rd and 4th UBS editions is in the apparatus; the text is the same, the text that Kurt Aland was pleased to call the 'standard' text. It is basically an 'Alexandrian' text, and I will use it to represent the hypothetical 'Alexandrian' archetype (I take that to be the judgment of the editors).

Based on the rough count described above, Codex B differed from UBS[4] 271 times, Aleph 308 times, and Codex A 333 times; this for the entire book of Romans. Even if my rough count were off by 10, 20, or even 50, it would make little difference to the point of this exercise: **these three great codices are pitifully poor representatives of their Alexandrian text-type**. However, I then did a second count, also eliminating alternate spellings of the same word (most of them involved ei/i/e). Based on this second count, Codex B differed from UBS[4] 170 times, Aleph 133 times, and Codex A 204 times. There were a great many itacisms, especially in Aleph. The picture has improved considerably, but these three great codices are still rather poor representatives of their Alexandrian text-type.

---

[1] *New Testament Greek Manuscripts—Romans* (Pasadena, CA: William Carey International University Press, 2001). In the Gospels, Codex A is marginally Byzantine, but in the Epistles it is considered to be good quality Alexandrian. (I think I recall seeing the opinion expressed that it is better than Aleph, and even B.)

[2] To someone who has never collated a Greek manuscript, I may say that it is slave labor, plain drudgery. To collate one copy of a book the size of Romans can take two full days. So why do I do it? The underlying consideration is the belief that the NT books are divinely inspired, a written revelation from the Sovereign Creator. Such a revelation has objective authority, and it becomes important to have the precise original wording. If Romans were just a bit of ordinary ancient literature, the precise original wording would be of little interest. So what? What difference would it make?

By way of comparison, or contrast, I invite attention to the following evidence from Family 35, also covering all of Romans.

f[35] *in Romans—raw data*

MS	stats	total	exemplar	date	location[1]	content
18	2y, 1s, 1h, 1i	5	2	1364	Constantinople	eapr
35	3c	3	---	XI	Aegean	eapr
141	1x, 1c, 4s, 2h, 1i	9	1	XIII	Vatican	eapr
201	2x, 2/, 1c, 3s, 1i	9	4	1357	Constantinople	eapr
204	1/, 1h, 1i	3	1	XIII	Bologna	eap
386	2y, 2s, 1h	5	2	XIV	Vatican	eapr
394	2y, 3/, 4s, 1i	10	5	1330	Rome	eap
757	1y, 1/, 1c, 3s, 1h	7	2	XIII	Athens	eapr
824	1x, 1y, 1/, 1s	4	2	XIV	Grottaferrata	eapr
928	2/	2	2	1304	Dionysiu	eap
986	2y, 1/, 4s, 1i	8	3	XIV	Esphigmenu	eapr
1040	2x, 1y, 1/	4	4	XIV	Karakallu	eap
1072	1x, 1y, 1/, 4s	7	3	XIII	M Lavras	eapr
1075	1x, 1y, 1/, 1s, 1h	5	3	XIV	M Lavras	eapr
1100	1y, 1s	2	1	1376	Dionysiu	ap
1249	1c, 3s, 1i	5	---	1324	Sinai	ap
1482	---	---	---	1304	M Lavras	eap
1503	1y, 1/, 1i	3	2	1317	M Lavras	eapr
1548	1x, 2/, 6s, 3i	12	3	1359	Vatopediu	eap
1637	1y, 1/, 1s, 1i	4	2	1328	M Lavras	eapr
1652	1y, 1/, 1s	3	2	XIV	M Lavras	eapr
1704	1y, 5s, 2h, 5i	13	1	1541	Kutlumusiu	eapr
1725	1/, 3s, 4i	8	1	1367	Vatopediu	ap
1732	1x, 1y, 1s, 2h	5	2	1384	M Lavras	apr
1761	2x, 2y, 1c, 3s, 1h	9	4	XIV	Athens	ap
1855	1s	1	---	XIII	Iviron	ap
1856	6x, 1y, 2/, 6s, 1h	16	9	XIV	Iviron	ap
1858	1y, 1/, 1s, 1i	4	2	XIII	Konstamonitu	ap
1864	1y, 1/	2	2	XIII	Stavronikita	apr
1865	1s	1	---	XIII	Philotheu	apr
1876	2x, 2/, 12s, 2h, 5i	23	4	XV	Sinai	apr
1892	3y, 2/, 1c, 12s, 1h, 2i	21	5	XIV	Jerusalem	ap
1897	1/, 4s, 2h, 1i[2]	8	1	XII	Jerusalem	ap
2466	2c, 11s, 2i	15	---	1329	Patmos	eap
2554	---	---	---	1434	Bucharest	eapr
2587	1/, 2s	3	1	XI	Vatican	ap
2723	---	---	---	XI	Trikala	apr

Looking at the chart, eighteen MSS have an average of only one variant per four chapters or more—exceptional! (MSS 1482, 2554 and 2723 are perfect as they stand.) Another nine MSS have only one variant per two chapters—excellent. Over 70% are excellent or better. Another

[1] I give the location where a MS was acquired, when this differs from where it is presently held, on the basis of available information.

[2] Only has 1:1 – 11:22.

eight have only one variant per chapter—good. Another two have two variants per chapter—fair. Note that the very worst of the thirty-seven **f**^{35} representatives (1876, apr, XV, Sinai) is almost six times 'better' than the very best Alexandrian representative, Codex Aleph. Stop for a moment and think about the implications. **How can any sane person defend the proposition that the Alexandrian text-type represents the best line of transmission?**[1]

A representative case

In the opening paragraph I stated that variants can be evaluated. I will now take one of the just two merely 'fair' **f**^{35} representatives—MS 1892, ap, XIV, Jerusalem—list its variants and evaluate them.

1:6	ημων 1892^{c} ‖ --- 1892 [an accidental omission that was corrected]
2:5	του ‖ --- (group 1) 1892 [the case being genitive, the meaning is not touched]
4:21	πληροφορηθεις ‖ πληρωφορηθεις 1892 [an itacism resulting in a misspelling; they would be pronounced the same way]
5:11	νυν ‖ --- 1892 [a careless omission that does not change the basic meaning]
5:13	ελλογειται ‖ ελλογειτο 1892 [was the copyist trying to change present to imperfect? The meaning is not changed]
9:15	μωυση ‖ μωυσει 1892 [merely an alternate spelling of the proper name]
9:27	ως η ‖ ωσει 1892 [an itacism resulting in a misspelling; they would be pronounced the same way]
12:8	1892 supplies ο μεταδιδους εν απλοτητι in the margin (a clear case of homoioarcton, and/or -teleuton)
13:11	γαρ ‖ --- 1892 [a careless omission that does not change the basic meaning]
14:8	αποθνησκομεν ‖ αποθνησκωμεν 1725,1876,1892 [an itacism that changes Indicative to Subjunctive, that makes little difference in the context; they would be pronounced the same way; the other two MSS do not belong to group 1, so this is an independent change]
14:15	χριστος ‖ 1 δωρεαν 1892 [a gratuitous addition that makes little difference]

[1] If I may borrow a statement from Colwell: "These results show convincingly that any attempt to reconstruct an archetype of the Beta Text-type [Alexandrian] on a quantitative basis is doomed to failure." "These results show convincingly" something else: those copyists were not encumbered with any special respect or consideration for what they were copying. Obviously, they did not believe that they were copying a sacred text, which makes one wonder why they would expend time and material in so doing. I see one explanation that makes sense: they were deliberately perverting the text, presumably under Satanic or demonic influence. By way of contrast, the care with which most **f**^{35} copyists did their work implies a high degree of respect for the text being copied. If God were concerned to preserve His Text, what sort of copyist would He use? What sort of copyist would the Holy Spirit protect and bless? [Since both God and Satan exist, someone who excludes the supernatural from his model is being naïve in the extreme.]

15:7 αλληλους || αλληλοις 1892 [apparently—working from a black and white film it is hard to be sure; changes accusative to dative, but does not alter the meaning]

15:9 ψαλω || ψαλλω 1892 [probably a careless change, but it changes future to present, that makes little difference in the meaning; they would be pronounced the same way]

15:13 περισσευειν || περησσευειν 1892 [apparently—working from a black and white film it is hard to be sure; an itacism resulting in a misspelling; they would be pronounced the same way]

15:29 του χριστου || της ειρηνης 1892 [perhaps the exemplar was damaged; in the context the change makes little difference]

15:30 συναγωνισασθαι || συναγωνισασθε 141,1892 [changes Indicative to Subjunctive, but they have the same effect; they are two ways to say the same thing;; the other MS does not belong to group 1, so this is an independent change]

16:2 και γαρ || 121 1892 [a careless repetition of the coordinating conjunction that does not change the meaning]

16:3 πρισκαν || πρισκιλλαν [30%] 394,1249[c],1761,1892 [alternate names for the same person]

16:6 υμας || ημας (75.5%) 394,1732,1761,1892 [a change that dominated the general transmission; it makes little difference in the context]

16:20 συντριψει || συντριψοι 1652[alt],1892 [a change from future Indicative to Optative that weakens the force of the verb]

16:24 ημων || υμων [82%] (group 1)+ 1892 [a change that dominated the general transmission and would be made almost automatically if the copyist did not notice that Tertius is speaking; it makes little difference in the context]

With five exceptions, only a single letter or syllable is involved, and nowhere is the meaning seriously affected.[1] **Someone reading MS 1892 would not be misled as to the intended meaning at any point in the book**. I say this is noteworthy, and it is typical of all **f**[35] MSS. <u>Down through the centuries of transmission, anyone with access to a **f**[35] representative could know the intended meaning of the Autograph</u>.[2] Not only that, most lines of transmission within the Byzantine bulk would be reasonably close, good enough for most practical purposes. This is also true of the much maligned *Textus Receptus*; it is certainly good enough for most practical purposes. Down through the centuries of Church history,

---

[1] Looking at the list above, it is evident that the care quotient of the copyist fluctuated; about half of the changes occurred in the last two chapters; between 5:13 and 9:15 there are no changes, so he did perfect work for four chapters. In chapter 16 he appears to have suffered some outside influence. For all that, 1892 is an adequate representative of the original wording of Romans.

[2] Since **f**[35] MSS are scattered all over, or all around, the Mediterranean world, such access would have been feasible for most people.

most people could have had reasonable access to God's written revelation.[1]

Incredibly careful transmission

I will now evaluate the variants in the eighteen 'exceptional' representatives. (Eighteen out of thirty-seven is virtually half.)

MSS 1482, 2554 and 2723 are perfect as they stand.

MSS 1855 and 1865 have one, to be discussed in that order. MS 1855: 13:1—υπο || 1 του 1855, 1856. Both MSS are held by the same monastery, so they may have had a common exemplar. They add the article before "God", but the case being genitive the meaning is not touched.

MS 1865: 16:18—ευλογιας || ευλογολογιας 1865 (apparently—working from a black and white film it is hard to be sure). It is obvious that something went wrong here, and the result is nonsense; a reader would presumably make the necessary correction.

MSS 928, 1100 and 1864 have two, to be discussed in that order. MS 928: 11:1—αβρααμ || 1 εκ 394, 928, 1856. The three MSS belong to group 2, and may point to a subgroup. The preposition is implicit, and making it overt does not alter the meaning; the translation remains the same. 16:19—ειναι 1249[c] || --- 201, 394, 928, 1249, 1856. All but 201 belong to group 2. The verb must be understood in any case, so the meaning is not affected.

MS 1100: 15:6—δοξαζητε || δοξαζηται 1100. This change is quite common, evidently being regarded as two ways of saying the same thing. 16:24—ημων || υμων [82%] (group 1)+ 1100. MS 1100 is not part of either group 1 or 2. This is a change that dominated the general transmission and would be made almost automatically if the copyist did not notice that Tertius is speaking; it makes little difference in the context.

MS 1864: 2:5—του || --- (group 1) 1864. The group omits the article before "God", but the case being genitive the meaning is not touched. 16:24—ημων || υμων [82%] (group 1)+ 1864. MS 1864 is part of group 1. This is a change that dominated the general transmission and would be made almost automatically if the copyist did not notice that Tertius is speaking; it makes little difference in the context.

[1] However, it is well to remember what is written in 2 Corinthians 4:7: we have the 'treasure' in 'earthen vessels'. Even with a perfect Text in hand, because of our inherent limitations we are incapable of taking full advantage of that Text. Who among us can guarantee a perfect interpretation of that perfect Text? Humility is called for.

MSS 35, 204, 1503, 1652 and 2587 have three, to be discussed in that order. MS 35: 1:27—εξεκαυθησαν 35^c || 1 εν [70%] 35. The preposition is implicit, but in any case the variant was corrected. 2:4—αυτου και της 35^c || --- 35. This may be a instance of homoioteleuton, but in any case the variant was corrected. 15:31—γενηται τοις αγιοις 35^c || ~ 231 [5%] 35, 2466. The change in word order does not affect the meaning, but the variant was corrected in any case. As corrected, this manuscript is perfect.

MS 204: 2:25—σου || 11 204. The word is repeated from one side of the sheet to the other. It is obviously an unintentional mistake that would be automatically corrected by a reader. 6:8—πιστευομεν || πιστευωμεν (group 2)+ 204. This may be an itacism, but it changes the mood from Indicative to Subjunctive, that weakens the force of the verb a little. Since MS 204 is not part of group 2, it may have been an independent slip. 10:15—ειρηνην των ευαγγελιζομενων || --- 204. This appears to be a clear case of homoioteleuton, that I do not consider to be a proper variant; but since the result makes good sense, the copyist evidently didn't notice it (it is part of a quote from the OT).

MS 1503: 2:5—του || --- (group 1) 1503. The group omits the article before "God", but the case being genitive the meaning is not touched. 11:4—1503 repeats ὁ from one line to the next. It is obviously an unintentional mistake that would be automatically corrected by a reader. 16:24—ημων || υμων [82%] (group 1)+ 1503. MS 1503 is part of group 1. This is a change that dominated the general transmission and would be made almost automatically if the copyist did not notice that Tertius is speaking; it makes little difference in the context.

MS 1652: 1:15—και || 1 εν 1652. This appears to be a careless mistake that a reader would probably ignore. 2:5—του || --- (group 1) 1652. The group omits the article before "God", but the case being genitive the meaning is not touched. 16:24—ημων || υμων [82%] (group 1)+ 1652. MS 1652 is part of group 1. This is a change that dominated the general transmission and would be made almost automatically if the copyist did not notice that Tertius is speaking; it makes little difference in the context.

MS 2587: 3:20—δικαιωθησεται || δικαιουται 2587. This changes the person from plural to singular, and the tense from future to present. In the context the meaning is not changed. 6:8—πιστευομεν || πιστευωμεν (group 2)+ 2587. This may be an itacism, but it changes the mood from Indicative to Subjunctive, that weakens the force of the verb a little. 12:2—μεταμορφουσθε || μεταμορφουσθαι 2587. This changes Subjunctive to Indicative, but they have the same effect; they are two ways to say the same thing.

MSS 824, 1040, 1249, 1637 and 1858 have four, to be discussed in that order. MS 824: 2:5—του || --- (group 1) 824. The group omits the article before "God", but the case being genitive the meaning is not touched. 11:17—αγριελαιος || αγριελεος 824. This appears to be an itacism resulting in an alternate spelling. 15:14—αλλους || αλληλους [7%] 824. 'Admonish one another' perhaps seemed more natural than 'admonish others', but the difference in meaning is slight. 16:24—ημων || υμων [82%] (group 1)+ 824. MS 824 is part of group 1. This is a change that dominated the general transmission and would be made almost automatically if the copyist did not notice that Tertius is speaking; it makes little difference in the context.

MS 1040: 11:17—πιοτητος || ποιοτητος 1040,1072[c],1548. This appears to be a careless spelling mistake, since the result is not a word. In the context a reader would make the necessary correction. 15:2—ημων || υμων [22%] 1040. That this was a 'natural' alteration is seen by the 22%, but in the context it makes little difference. 15:7—ημας || υμας [38%] 757[c],1040. That this also was a 'natural' alteration is seen by the 38%, but in the context it makes little difference. 16:24—ημων || υμων [82%] (group 1)+ 1040. MS 1040 is part of group 1. This is a change that dominated the general transmission and would be made almost automatically if the copyist did not notice that Tertius is speaking; it makes little difference in the context.

MS 1249: 2:14—ποιη || ποιει 1249. Although this was probably an itacism, it changes the mood, but the meaning is not affected. 9:12—τω || το 1249. This looks like another itacism, but it mistakenly changes the case. A reader would make the necessary correction, and since the two forms are pronounced the same, a listener would understand correctly. 9:20—το || τω 1249, 1876. This looks like a reverse itacism; see the comment above. 16:19—ειναι 1249[c] || --- 201, 394, 928, 1249, 1856. All but 201 belong to group 2. The verb must be understood in any case, so the meaning is not affected, but the variant was corrected.

MS 1637: 2:5—του || --- (group 1) 1637. The group omits the article before "God", but the case being genitive the meaning is not touched. 15:20—δε || --- 1637. This appears to be a careless omission that does not affect the meaning. 16:2—και || 11 1637. This is a careless mistake; the word is repeated from one line to the next. A reader would automatically correct it. 16:24—ημων || υμων [82%] (group 1)+ 1637. MS 1637 is part of group 1. This is a change that dominated the general transmission and would be made almost automatically if the copyist did not notice that Tertius is speaking; it makes little difference in the context.

MS 1858: 1:25—κτισει || κτιση 1858. This appears to be an itacism that misspells the word; a reader would make the necessary correction. 2:15—κατηγορουντων || κατοιγορουντων 1858. Repeat the comment above. 6:8—πιστευομεν || πιστευωμεν (group 2)+ 1858. This may be an itacism, but it changes the mood from Indicative to Subjunctive, that weakens the force of the verb a little. 8:28—εις || 1 το [27%] 986, 1732[c], 1858. The article is not called for, but it makes little difference.

Out of a total of forty-three variants, for eighteen MSS, for the whole book of Romans,[1] five were corrected, which leaves thirty-eight. At least ten are not a proper variant, which leaves twenty-eight. Thirteen are repetitions of a variant in common, which leaves fifteen.[2] Over 30 of the 43 involve a single letter or syllable, as is typical of **f**^{35} variants. None of them changes the meaning. Now I call that **incredibly careful transmission**.

I venture to predict, if all extant MSS are ever collated, that no other line of transmission will come anywhere close to this level of precision, or copyist care quotient.

Observations

1. Two-thirds of the collated MSS above have no extra-family variants = no mixture. The monks faithfully reproduced what was in front of them.
2. The three XI MSS evidently reflect distinct exemplars (which themselves probably had distinct exemplars), so the archetype certainly existed in the uncial period.
3. Although the precise profile of the archetype is clear, it is also clear that the extant MSS reflect a number of separate lines of transmission within the family.
4. Any attempt at reconstructing a family tree will require the positing

---

[1] If we divide 43 by 18 we get an average of about 2.4 variants for each of the eighteen MSS, for the whole book. If we take an average MS like 204 (of the 18), with its three variants, and compare it to Codex Aleph, with its 133 variants, it would take 204 no less than 44 books the size of Romans to produce as many deviations from its archetype as Aleph did from its hypothetical archetype, for one book. It would take 204 no less than 56 such books to produce as many such deviations as Codex B, and 68 for Codex A!! Now really, gentle reader, what objective basis can anyone allege for preferring the 'Alexandrian' text? To do so on the basis of subjective preference is mere superstition.

[2] That is to say, between them the eighteen MSS have fifteen variants for the whole book, or an average of .83 variant each, for the whole book—verily, incredibly careful transmission.

of a fair number of intervening nodes, nodes that could well be separated by centuries.

5. It follows that any claim that the **f**[35] archetype was created after the beginning of the minuscule period is either uninformed or perverse.

Postscript

Family 35 readings are attested by early witnesses, but without pattern, and therefore without dependency. But there are many hundreds of such readings. So how did the **f**[35] archetype come by all those early readings? Did its creator travel around and collect a few readings from Aleph, a few from B, a few from $P^{45,66,75}$, a few from W and D, etc.? Is not such a suggestion patently ridiculous? The only reasonable conclusion is that the **f**[35] text is ancient (also independent).

I claim to have demonstrated the superiority of Family 35 based on size (number of representatives), independence, age, geographical distribution, profile (empirically determined), care (see above) and range (all 27 books). I challenge any and all to do the same for any other line of transmission!

Incredibly Careful Transmission

This section focuses on the Thessalonian epistles, generally thought to have been the first of the apostle Paul's canonical writings (at least in conservative circles). If so, his prestige and authority as an apostle would not yet have reached its full stature, and in consequence such early writings might not have been accorded as much respect as later ones. As I continue collating more and more **f**[35] MSS I have been surprised by a different picture. I have collated the following thirty-four representatives of the family and invite attention to the results.

Performance of f[35] MSS in the Thessalonian Epistles

MS	1 Thess.	2 Thess.	Location	Date[1]	Exemplar
18	---	---	Constantinople[2]	1364	---
35	2c	---	Aegean[3]	XI	---
201	2y,2/	2x	London	1357	2x,2y,2/
204	1	---	Bologna	XIII	1/
328	1/,1s	2s	Leiden	XIII	1/

[1] I give the location and date as in the *Kurzgefasste Liste* (1994), although I must admit to an occasional doubt as to the accuracy of the dating.

[2] Although presently in Paris, 18 was produced in Constantinople.

[3] Although presently in Paris, 35 was acquired in the Aegean area.

MS	1 Thess.	2 Thess.	Location	Date[1]	Exemplar
386	1y,1/,1s	1s	Vatican	XIV	1y,1/
394	1s	---	Rome	1330	---
444	1s	2s	London	XV	---
604	1x,1y	1s	Paris	XIV	1x,1y
757	1s	1y,1c	Athens	XIII	1y
824	---	1i	Grottaferrata	XIV	---
928	---	---	Dionysiu (Athos)	1304	---
986	1s	1s	Esphigmenu (Athos)	XIV	---
1072	1i	---	M. Lavras (Athos)	XIII	---
1075	1x,1	---	M. Lavras	XIV	1x,1/
1100	1y,1s	1y	Dionysiu	1376	2y
1248	3x,1/,4s	2s,2i	Sinai	XIV	3x,1/
1249	1y	---	Sinai	1324	1y
1503	2s	---	M. Lavras	1317	---
1548	2x,1s	1s	Vatopediu (Athos)	1359	2x
1637	1/	---	M. Lavras	1328	1/
1725	2/	1/	Vatopediu	1367	3/
1732	1y,2s	1/	M. Lavras	1384	1y,1/
1761	2x,2y,1s	1s,1i	Athens	XIV	2x,2y
1855	---	1s	Iviron (Athos)	XIII	---
1864	---	---	Stavronikita (Athos)	XIII	---
1865	1c	---	Philotheu (Athos)	XIII	---
1876	4y,1/	1y,1/	Sinai	XV	5y,2/
1892	10s	3s	Jerusalem	XIV	---
1897	1/,1c	3s,1h	Jerusalem	XII	1/
2466	1x,2y,1s	1s	Patmos	1329	1x,2y
2554	1c	---	Bucharest	1434	---
2587	1s	1s	Vatican	XI	---
2723	---	---	Trikala	XI	---

Key:

x = an uncorrected variant that it is attested by MSS outside the family;
y = a split that is not limited to the family;
/ = a split within the family (no outside attestation);
c = a variant of any kind that has been corrected to the presumed archetype;
s = singular reading / private variant (until all MSS have been collated, this is just an assumption);
h = an obvious case of homoioteleuton (or –arcton), often involving a line or more, but can be just three or four words;
i = sheer inattention;
--- = no departures from the presumed profile.

Implications

I begin with the last column in the chart, 'Exemplar'. Except for 18, 928, 1864 and 2723 that are themselves perfect, most of the others have a different rating. All singular readings should be discounted (including homoioteleuton and inattention); if not introduced by the copyist it was done by the 'father' or 'grandfather'—an ancestor was free of all 'singulars', so they contribute nothing to the history of the transmission, are not relevant to the tracing of that transmission. All variants that were corrected to the presumed family profile should also be discounted—whoever did the correcting, it was done on the basis of a correct exemplar (correct at that point). So I only attribute 'x', 'y' and '/' to the exemplar—of course some of these could be the work of the copyist as well, which would make the exemplar even better, but I have no way of knowing when that occurred.

Notice that of thirty-four MSS, sixteen of their exemplars (almost half) were 'perfect', and another six were off by only one variant (the worst was only off by seven, for two books). If there were no splinters, we could be looking at thirty-four independent lines of transmission, within the family, which to me is simply fantastic.[1] But what about the splinters? There are a few very minor ones in 1 Thessalonians, and only a few pairs in 2 Thessalonians.

I conclude that all thirty-four MSS were independent in their generation, and I see no evidence to indicate a different conclusion for their exemplars. Please note that I am not claiming that all thirty-four lines remain distinct all the way back to the archetype. I cheerfully grant that there would be a number of convergences before getting back to the source. However all that may be, we are looking at very careful transmission.

I now invite attention to location. The MSS come from all over the Mediterranean world. The thirteen Mt. Athos MSS were certainly produced in their respective monasteries (seven). Ecclesiastical politics tending to be what it tends to be, there is little likelihood that there would be collusion between the monasteries on the transmission of the NT writings—I regard the thirteen as representing as many exemplars. MSS from Trikala, Patmos, Jerusalem and Sinai were presumably produced there; cursive 18 was certainly produced in Constantinople; cursive 35 was acquired in the Aegean area. The MSS at the Vatican and Grottaferrata may very well have been produced there.

I now invite special attention to minuscule 18, produced in Constantinople in **1364**! As it stands it is a perfect representative of the presumed family profile for the Thessalonian epistles (I say 'presumed' only out of deference to all the family representatives that I haven't collated yet, but given the geographical distribution of the thirty-four above, I have no doubt that the profile as given in my Text is correct).[2] How many

---

1 18, 928, 1864 and 2723 were produced in Constantinople, Dionysiu, Stavronikita and Trikala, respectively—I consider it to be virtually impossible that they should have a common exemplar (of course they could join somewhere back down the line).

2 Actually I have now collated 39 family representatives for 1 Thessalonians and 38 for 2 Thessalonians. They probably represent at least 40% of the total extant membership, so there can really be no doubt that they correctly represent the family archetype.

generations of copies would there have been between MS 18 and the family archetype? Might there have been fifteen, or more? I would imagine that there were at least ten. However many there actually were, please note that every last one of them was perfect! *The implications of finding a perfect representative of any archetypal text are rather powerful. All the 'canons' of textual criticism become irrelevant to any point subsequent to the creation of that text* (they could still come into play when studying the creation of the text, in the event). For MS 18 to be perfect, all the generations in between had to be perfect as well. Now I call this **incredibly careful transmission.** Nothing that I was taught in Seminary about New Testament textual criticism prepared me for this discovery! Nor anything that I had read, for that matter. But MS 18 is not an isolated case; all the thirty-four MSS in the chart above reflect an **incredibly careful transmission**—even the worst of the lot, minuscules 1761 and 1874, with their seven variants [the 'singulars' in 1893 and 1248 are careless mistakes {unhappy monks}], are really quite good, considering all the intervening generations.

This point deserves some elaboration. A typical 'Alexandrian' MS will have over a dozen variants per page of printed Greek text. A typical 'Byzantine' MS will have 3-5 variants per page. MSS 1761 and 1876 have about one per page, and one of the better **f**[35] MSS will go for pages without a variant. There is an obvious difference in the mentality that the monks brought to their task. A monk copying an 'Alexandrian' MS evidently did not consider that he was handling Scripture, in stark contrast to one copying an **f**[35] MS. For those who do not exclude the supernatural from their model, I submit that the information above is highly significant: obviously God was not protecting any 'Alexandrian' type of MS, probably because it contained 'tares' (Matthew 13:28). A monk copying a 'Byzantine' bulk type MS did far better work than the Alexandrian, but still was not being sufficiently careful—he was probably just doing a religious duty, but without personal commitment to the Text. Since God respects our choices (John 4:23-24), the result was a typical 'Byzantine' MS. It is also true that not all **f**[35] MSS were carefully done, but I conclude that the core representatives were done by copyists who believed they were handling God's Word and wanted their work to be pleasing to Him[1]—just the kind that the Holy Spirit would delight to aid and protect.

---

[1] It is not at all uncommon to find a colophon at the end of a MS where the copyist calls on God for His mercy, and even for His recognition and blessing.

Performance of f^{35} MSS in 2 & 3 John and Jude

This section focuses on 2 & 3 John and Jude. I have collated forty-six representatives of Family 35, so far (for these three books), and invite attention to the results. I have so far identified 84 MSS as belonging to **f**[35] in the General Epistles (plus another 10 or 12 on the fringes), so this sample is certainly representative, considering also the geographic distribution.

MS	2 John	3 John	Jude	Location	Date	Exemplar
18	---	1s	---	Constantinople	1364	---
35	---	---	2c	Aegean	XI	---
141	---	---	---	Vatican	XIII	---
149	---	1/	1/,1c	Vatican	XV	2/
201	---	1/	1/	London	1357	2/
204	---	---	---	Bologna	XIII	---
328	---	---	1x,1s	Leiden	XIII	1x
386	---	---	---	Vatican	XIV	---
394	---	1i	---	Rome	1330	---
432	2s	1/	3s	Vatican	XV	1/
444[1]	---	---	1s	London	XV	---
604	1x	1/	---	Paris	XIV	1x,1/
664	1x,1s	3s	3s	Zittau	XV	1x
757	2s	---	---	Athens	XIII	---
824	---	---	---	Grottaferrata	XIV	---
928	---	---	---	Dionysiu (Athos)	1304	---
986	1s	---	1s,1i	Esphigmenu (Athos)	XIV	---
1072	---	---	---	M Lavras (Athos)	XIII	---
1075	---	---	---	M Lavras	XIV	---
1100	---	---	---	Dionysiu	1376	---
1247	1x,1/,1s	1/,1s	1x,1/,6s	Sinai	XV	2x,3/
1248	2/	1/,3s	4s	Sinai	XIV	3/
1249	1/,1c	---	1/	Sinai	1324	2/
1503	1s	---	---	M. Lavras	1317	---
1548	---	---	1s	Vatopediu (Athos)	1359	---
1628	---	---	1s	M. Lavras	1400	---
1637	---	---	---	M. Lavras	1328	---
1725	---	---	1s	Vatopediu	1367	---
1732	1/	---	1x,1s	M. Lavras	1384	1x,1/
1754	1s	1/,1s	2s	Panteleimonos (Athos)	XII	1/
1761	1s	2s	---	Athens	XIV	---
1768	---	1y	1s	Iviron (Athos)	1516	1y
1855	---	---	---	Iviron	XIII	---
1864	---	---	---	Stavronikita (Athos)	XIII	---
1865	---	1/	---	Philotheu (Athos)	XIII	1/
1876	2/,1s	1/	1/,2s	Sinai	XV	4/
1892	1x	---	---	Jerusalem	XIV	1x
1897	---	---	1s	Jerusalem	XII	---
2221	---	---	---	Sparta	1432	---

[1] 444 is a mixed MS. In James, 1&2 Peter it is not at all **f**[35], while in 1 John it is a very marginal member of the family.

MS	2 John	3 John	Jude	Location	Date	Exemplar
2352	1c,1i	---	---	Meteora	XIV	---
2431	---	---	1i	Kavsokalyvia (Athos)	1332	---
2466	---	1/	2s	Patmos	1329	1/
2554	---	---	---	Bucharest	1434	---
2587	---	---	1c	Vatican	XI	---
2626	1/	1/,1s	2/	Ochrida	XIV	4/
2723	---	---	---	Trikala	XI	---

Implications

In 2 John, 2/3 (thirty) of the MSS are perfect representatives of the family as they stand; in 3 John the percentage is also 2/3 (thirty, but a different selection); in Jude just under ½ (twenty-two); and for all three under 1/3 (fourteen). Over half (twenty-nine) of the exemplars were presumably perfect. Since I have the figures for all seven books of the General Epistles, I can assure the reader that all forty-six MSS are independent in their generation, as were their exemplars. Cursives 149 and 201 are clearly related, as are 432 and 604, and all four probably come from a common source short of the archetype. I see no evidence of collusion, of 'stuffing the ballot box'—there was no organized effort to standardize the Text. We are looking at a normal transmission, except that it was **incredibly careful.** The fourteen MSS that are perfect in all three books had perfect ancestors all the way back to the archetype, and so for the twenty-nine perfect exemplars. I refer the reader to the prior section for the explanation of how I arrive at the classification of the exemplars.

As I keep on collating MSS I have observed a predictable pattern. For the first 2 or 3, even 4, pages the MSS tend to have few mistakes, or none. If the scribe is going to make mistakes, it tends to be after he has been at it long enough to start getting tired, or bored. Quite often most of the mistakes are on a single page, or in a single chapter; then the scribe took a break (I suppose) and returning to his task refreshed did better work. I would say that the high percentage of 'perfect' copies is largely due to the small size of our three books—the copyists didn't have a chance to get tired. For all that, this observation does not change the fact that there was **incredibly careful transmission** down through the centuries.[1] Considering the size of my sample and the geographic distribution of the MSS, I am cheerfully certain that we have the precise original wording, to the

[1] I have already demonstrated this for the Thessalonian epistles, above, and am in a position to do the same for all the books of the NT. Of course, the longer the book the greater the likelihood that a copyist would make an inadvertent mistake or two. Even so, I have a perfect copy of Romans (fair size and complexity) and one of Matthew (a Gospel, no less!).

letter, of the f^{35} archetype for 2 and 3 John and Jude. It is reproduced in my Greek Text.

Given my presuppositions, I consider that I have good reason for declaring the divine preservation of the precise original wording of the complete New Testament Text, to this day. That wording is reproduced in my edition of the Greek NT, *The Greek New Testament According to Family 35*, available from Amazon.com, as well as from my site, www.prunch.org. BUT PLEASE NOTE: whether or not the archetype of f^{35} is the Autograph (as I claim), the fact remains that the MSS collated for this study reflect an incredibly careful transmission of their source, and this throughout the middle ages. My presuppositions include: God exists; He inspired the Biblical Text; He promised to preserve it for a thousand generations (1 Chronicles 16:15); so He must have an active, ongoing interest in that preservation [there have been fewer than 300 generations since Adam, so He has a ways to go!]. **If He was preserving the original wording in some line of transmission other than f^{35}, would that transmission be any less careful than what I have demonstrated for f^{35}?** I think not. So any line of transmission characterized by internal confusion is disqualified—this includes **all** the other lines of transmission that I have seen so far![1]

The Best Complete NT I Have Seen, so Far!

GA 2554 is one of a number of complete NT manuscripts representing Family 35 that are available to the academic community. It is dated at 1434 AD and is held by the Romanian Academy in Bucharest. I wish to register my sincere thanks to the Institute for New Testament Textual Research in Münster for making available a digital copy of their microfilm of this manuscript. Although from the fifteenth century, the hand is very neat. Of the eighteen complete NT manuscripts representing Family 35 of which I hold a copy (there are others), 2554 is easily the best—I have collated it from cover to cover. I will now list all the places where it deviates from the family archetype, including some doubtful cases, for the whole NT.[2] There are only 49,[3] not all of which are proper variants.

---

[1] Things like $\mathbf{M}^6$ and $\mathbf{M}^5$ in John 7:53-8:11 come to mind.

[2] For the Family 35 profile please see Appendix B in my *Identity IV*, freely available from my site, www.prunch.org, but it is also included as the second section in this Part II. The complete archetype is printed in my *The Greek New Testament according to Family 35*.

[3] To have no more than 49 for the whole NT is simply astonishing.

1. Mt. 11:8 *βασιλειων* || *βασιλεων* (36.4%)[1] 2554^c [the first hand clearly had the *iota*, that was subsequently erased, so this is not a variant; in any case, within the context the two forms are synonymous]
2. Mt. 13:15 *ιασωμαι* || *ιασομαι* [50%] 2554^c [traces of the erased right side of the omega remain, so the first hand was correct, so this is not a variant; in any case, within the context the change in tense does not affect the meaning]
3. Mt. 25:32 *συναχθησονται* || *συναχθησεται* [70%] [I include this case only because, of the 51 family representatives I have collated for Matthew so far, a slight majority have the singular rather than the plural (27/24); because of the quality of the minority, including 2554, I have chosen it as the archetype; in any case, whether the mass noun is viewed as singular or plural, the meaning remains the same—they are two ways of saying the same thing]
4. Mt. 26:29 *γενηματος* || *γεννηματος* [70%] 2554^c [the extra *nu* was added above the line, but the first hand was correct, so this is not a variant; in any case, within the context the two forms are synonymous]

Comment: I consider that the first hand gives us a perfect copy of the archetype for Matthew.

5. Mk. 2:23 *ποιειν* 2554^c || *πιειν* 2554 [it looks like 2554's exemplar had πιειν, and the copyist duly copied it, but then realized that it was a nonsensical mistake and corrected it; if the correction was made by the first hand, then we do not have a proper variant, but working from a microfilm it is difficult to tell if the ink is the same]
6. Mk. 5:41 *κουμι* || *κουμ* (17.4%) 2554 [this is a transliteration from another language, so a spelling difference does not affect the meaning, the more so since it is followed immediately with the translation; I do not consider this to be a proper variant]
7. Mk. 14:25 *γενηματος* || *γεννηματος* [25%] 2554^c [the extra *nu* was added above the line, but the first hand was correct, so this is not a variant; in any case, within the context the two forms are synonymous]
8. Mk. 15:46 *επι την θυραν* || 1 *τη θυρα* [1%] 2554 [about a fourth of the family representatives join 2554 here; the preposition works with

[1] Percentages within parentheses are taken from *Text und Textwert*, while those within brackets are my own extrapolation.

three cases—genitive, dative, accusative—within this context the change in case does not affect the meaning]

Comment: I consider that the first hand has only one proper variant in Mark, the last one, and it does not affect the meaning.

9. Lk. 1:36 *συγγενης* || *συγγενις* [10%] 2554 [instead of the adjective functioning as a generic noun, 2554 uses the feminine noun; within the context the two forms are synonymous]

10. Lk. 1:55 *εως αιωνος* || *εις τον αιωνα* [64%] 2554 [the variant is by far the more common, and therefore expected, but within the context the two forms are virtually synonymous; any difference in nuance does not alter the basic meaning]

11. Lk. 3:1 *αβιληνης* || *αβιλινης* 2554 [perhaps an itacism that resulted in an alternate spelling for the place name; the two forms would receive the same pronunciation; I do not consider this to be a proper variant]

12. Lk. 3:18 *τω λαω* || *τον λαον* [85%] 2554 [since the direct object, 'good news', is implicit in the verb, 'the people' functions as the indirect object, and the dative case is correct; however, the accusative case does occur, and within the context there is no difference in meaning]

13. Lk. 12:18 *γενηματα* || *γεννηματα* [7%] 2554[c] [the extra *nu* was added above the line, but the first hand was correct, so this is not a variant; in any case, within the context the two forms are synonymous]

14. Lk. 21:33 *παρελευσεται* || *παρελευσονται* [68%] 2554 [whether the compound subject of the verb is viewed as singular or plural, the meaning is the same; in English the translation is the same]

15. Lk. 22:18 *γενηματος* || *γεννηματος* [15%] 2554[c] [the extra *nu* was added above the line, but the first hand was correct, so this is not a variant; in any case, within the context the two forms are synonymous]

Comment: I consider that the first hand has four proper variants in Luke, and they do not affect the meaning.

16. Jn. 6:55 *αληθως* || *αληθης* (24.5%) 2554[2x] [whether an adverb or an adjective, within the context they have the same meaning; I treat the repetition as a single variant]

17. Jn. 12:6 *εμελεν* || *εμελλεν* [60%] [taking account of the corrections, the MSS I have collated (57) are about evenly divided. Is the verb μελω or μελλω? μελει as an impersonal form is most common; however the verb is also used in a personal/active sense. μελλω ('to be about to') does not make sense here. μελλω is about ten times as frequent in the NT and some copyists may have put the more customary spelling without thinking. They had just written μελλων two lines above and may have repeated the form by attraction. However, since both forms have the same pronunciation, someone hearing the Text read aloud would understand it correctly, being guided by the context. Precisely for this reason, it may be that the semantic area of the longer form came to be regarded as including that of the shorter form; in which case we would have alternate spellings of the same verb. (It is not my custom to appeal to the early uncials, but all of them have the shorter form here, which would go along with my hypothesis above.) The first hand of 2554 left space for the second *lambda*, so he was aware of the variant, but he correctly did not copy it.]

18. Jn. 12:40 *ιασωμαι* || *ιασομαι* [20%] 2554 [the first hand of 2554 left space to complete the *omega*, so he was aware of the variant; within the context the change in tense does not affect the meaning]

Comment: I consider that the first hand has two proper variants in John, and they do not affect the meaning. 2 + 4 + 1 = 7; a manuscript with only seven variants for all four Gospels is surely a paragon of virtue. I call that extraordinarily careful transmission, since it would also be true of the preceding generations, of necessity.

19. Acts 1:11 *ουτος* || 1 *ο* [70%] 2554 [a demonstrative pronoun defines, even more than a definite article, so the article is redundant here; in any case, the meaning is not affected]

20. Acts 11:26 *συναχθηναι* || 1 *εν* [20%] 2554 [the family is divided here, a bare majority of the 35 MSS that I have collated add the preposition, that is a 'natural' but is redundant; in any case, the meaning is not affected]

21. Acts 12:25 *εις αντιοχειαν* || *απο ιερουσαλημ* 2554 [this is the only place in the whole NT where Family 35 splinters, there being a six-way split (usually there are only two main contenders); for a detailed discussion please see my article, "Where to place a comma—Acts 12:25", available from my site, www.prunch.org; within the context, the two readings given here have the same effect; the article is also the last item in the Appendix of my translation of the N.T., *The*

Sovereign Creator Has Spoken, second edition]

22. Acts 16:9 *την* 2554c || --- [80%] 2554 [Family 35 is virtually unanimous for the article, so the first hand may have omitted it on his own, to be corrected by someone else; in any case, the meaning is not affected]

23. Acts 18:17 *εμελλεν* || *εμελεν* [14%] 2554c [Family 35 is divided here; 2554 has a single *lambda* in a space that is too large for it, so I assume the first hand had the double but was erased. Is the verb *μελλω* or *μελω*? If the former, the meaning is not common and could easily give rise to the latter. Render: 'None of this was a delay to Gallio'; Gallio is in the dative. Gallio presumably considered himself to be a busy man and did not appreciate the interruption; he was not about to allow himself to be further delayed. In 22:16 the same verb has the sense of 'delay'. Although there is some difference in meaning, the point of the narrative is not altered.]

24. Acts 25:7 *καταβεβηκοτες* || 1 *οι* 2554 [this appears to be a careless mistake on the part of the copyist, but which still makes sense; the meaning is not affected]

25. Acts 28:27 *ιασωμαι* || *ιασομαι* [60%] 2554 [the first hand of 2554 left space to complete the *omega*, so he was aware of the variant; within the context the change in tense does not affect the meaning]

Comment: I consider that the first hand has six proper variants in Acts, one of which was corrected, leaving five. Of the five, four do not affect the meaning. In Acts 12:25, within the context, the two variants are virtually two ways of saying the same thing, the point of the narrative is not affected.

26. Rom. 7:13 *αλλα* || *αλλ* [30%] 2554 [these are alternate spellings of the same word, so this is not a proper variant]

27. Rom. 16:24 *ημων* || *υμων* [82%] 2554c [if verse 24 was not dictated by Paul, the first person is especially appropriate, coming from Tertius; within the context, the meaning is scarcely affected]

Comment: I consider that the first hand gives us a perfect copy of the archetype for Romans, there being no proper variants. 1 Corinthians also gives us a perfect copy of the archetype.

28. 2 Cor. 8:9 *ημας* || *υμας* [60%] [Family 35 is divided here, but the better representatives, including 2554, are with the first person, that is more inclusive; within the context there is no real difference in meaning]

29. 2 Cor. 9:10 *γενηματα* || *γεννηματα* [6%] 2554[c] [the extra *nu* was added above the line, but the first hand was correct, so this is not a variant; in any case, within the context the two forms are synonymous]

30. 2 Cor. 11:7 *εαυτον* || *εμαυτον* [78%] 2554[c] [the *mu* was added above the line by a later hand, so this is not a variant; in any case, within the context the two forms are synonymous]

Comment: I consider that the first hand gives us a perfect copy of the archetype for 2 Corinthians. Galatians, Ephesians, Philippians and Colossians also give us a perfect copy of the archetype.

31. 1 Thes. 2:8 *ιμειρομενοι* || *ομειρομενοι* [30%] 2554[c] [it appears that an *omicron* was written around an *iota*, but it is difficult to tell from a microfilm; in any case, since these appear to be alternate spellings of the same word, this is not a proper variant]

Comment: I consider that the first hand gives us a perfect copy of the archetype for 1 Thessalonians. 2 Thessalonians also gives us a perfect copy of the archetype.

32. 1 Tim. 1:9a *πατραλοιαις* || *πατρολωαις* [34%] [Family 35 is divided here, but a majority, including 2554, have the first reading. Liddell & Scott give it and the feminine counterpart as the basic forms, their meaning being 'striker', rather than 'killer', which makes better sense]

33. 1 Tim. 1:9b *μητραλοιαις* || *μητρολωαις* [40%] [same as above]

34. 1 Tim. 5:21 *προσκλισιν* || *προσκλησιν* [75%] [Family 35 is divided here, but a majority, including 2554, have the first reading; the two forms were pronounced the same way; within the context the meaning is not affected.]

Comment: I consider that the first hand gives us a perfect copy of the archetype for 1 Timothy.

35. 2 Tim. 3:14 *επιστωθης* || *επιστευθης* [10%] 2554 [the two forms represent different verbs, but within the context they act as synonyms; the meaning is not affected]

36. Titus 2:7 *αδιαφθοριαν* || *αδιαφοριαν* (8%) 2554 [this is just an alternate spelling of the same word, and therefore not a proper variant]

Comment: I consider that the first hand has only one proper variant in 2 Timothy, and it does not affect the meaning. Titus and Philemon give us a perfect copy of the archetype.

37. Heb. 3:13 *καλειται* || *καληται* 2554[c] [an itacism produced by a later hand, resulting in nonsense]

38. Heb. 9:1 *πρωτη* || 1 *σκηνη* [30%] [Family 35 is divided here, but with corrections a majority, including 2554, have the first reading; in any case, within the context the meaning is not affected]

Comment: I consider that the first hand gives us a perfect copy of the archetype for Hebrews. James and 1 and 2 Peter also give us a perfect copy of the archetype. A manuscript with only one proper variant for the whole Pauline corpus is surely a paragon of virtue. I call that extraordinarily careful transmission, since it would also be true of the preceding generations, of necessity.

39. 1 Jn. 1:6 *περιπατουμεν* || *περιπατωμεν* [71%] [Family 35 is divided here; I follow a minority, made up of the better MSS, including 2554. The verb 'say' is properly Subjunctive, being controlled by εαν, but the verbs 'have' and 'walk' are part of a statement and are properly Indicative—only if we are in fact walking in darkness do we become liars for claiming to be in fellowship. So περιπατουμεν is correct. In any case, within the context the meaning is not affected.]

40. 1 Jn. 3:23 *πιστευσωμεν* || *πιστευωμεν* (26.5%) 2554[c] [traces of the *sigma* are visible; in any case, within the context the change in tense does not affect the meaning]

Comment: I consider that the first hand gives us a perfect copy of the archetype for 1 John. 2 and 3 John and Jude also give us a perfect copy of the archetype. A manuscript with not a single variant for all seven General Epistles is surely a paragon of virtue. I call that extraordinarily careful transmission, since it would also be true of the preceding generations, of necessity. Up to here there have only been thirteen proper variants, but let us see what happens in Revelation.

41. Rev. 1:17 *επεσα* || *επεσον* 2554 [these appear to be alternate forms of the same word, so this is not a proper variant][1]

42. Rev. 4:8 *λεγοντα* || *λεγοντες* 2554[alt] [Is the subject of the verb just the living creatures, or are the elders included? On the basis of verses 9-11, it would be just the living creatures. In any case, a translation

---

[1] In Revelation I do not give percentages because I state the evidence in terms of families; the interested reader should consult my Greek Text for the evidence.

into English will be the same for the two forms.]

43. Rev. 7:17a *ποιμαινει* 2554[alt] || *ποιμανει* 2554 [well over half of the family representatives that have the future tense have the present form as an alternate above the line, as does 2554; this appears to have been standard procedure in Revelation, when there was doubt between two forms, so the archetype is always represented; within the context the meaning is not affected]
44. Rev. 7:17b *οδηγει* 2554[alt] || *οδηγησει* 2554 [same as above]
45. Rev. 9:5 *πληξη* 2554[alt] || *παιση* 2554 [same as above, except that here it is the verb that is changed; within the context the meaning is not affected]
46. Rev. 14:14 *καθημενος ομοιος* 2554[alt] || *καθημενον ομοιον* 2554 [same as above, except that here it is just the case that is changed; within the context the meaning is not affected]
47. Rev. 14:19 *τον μεγαν* || *την μεγαλην* 2554 [Is the phrase modifying 'wrath' or 'wine-press'? Within the context, they are two ways of saying the same thing.]
48. Rev. 16:12 μεγαν || 1 τον 2554 [the variant does not affect the meaning]
49. Rev. 19:18 *και*[7] || --- 2554 [this appears to be a singular reading; it does not affect the meaning]

Comment: I consider that the first hand has seven variations from the archetype, four of which are corrected with the alternate; that leaves three proper variants, none of which affects the meaning. None of the alternates affects the meaning either. For all practical purposes, 2554 is a perfect representative of the archetype in Revelation.

Conclusion

Out of the 49 cases listed above, only sixteen may be classed as a 'proper variant', and only one of them may be said to affect the meaning: Acts 12:25.[1] Even here, within the context, the two readings listed have the same effect. Manuscript GA 2554 is a virtually perfect representative of its archetype for the whole New Testament, and this in the fifteenth

[1]This holds true for all the 49 cases above. A reader would not be misled as to the intended meaning at any point, for the whole NT!

century! This means that all the preceding generations also had to be virtually perfect. Now I call that extraordinarily careful transmission. **God has preserved His Text!**

Major f[35] splits in Matthew

There are only five splits that might be called 'major' in Matthew. The reading listed first is the one that I have chosen as representing the family archetype, for reasons explained at the end of this article.

9:17 απολουνται [80%] || απολλυνται [20%]—the verb is the same and both are Indicative; the first is future middle and the second is present passive. In the immediately prior clauses, both εκχεται and ρηγνυνται are present passive and go together; so why the second reference to the wineskins? Any difference in meaning is almost too slight to translate.

19:29 οικιας [66%] || οικιαν [30%]—plural or singular? As with the brothers, if you only have one, that is all that you can leave; and if you have none, you leave none.

25:32 συναχθησονται [25%] || συναχθησεται [75%]—plural or singular; mass noun or not? The translation is the same.

26:29 γενηματος [30%] || γεννηματος [70%]—the nouns are different, the first referring to plant produce and the second to animal offspring; if the second is used of plants, it is a secondary meaning. The translation is the same.

27:35 βαλοντες [25%] || βαλλοντες [75%]—aorist or present? In the context any difference in meaning is so slight that the translation is the same.

As is typical of variation within the family, the difference is of one letter, except for the syllable, and Matthew is not a small book. I call this incredibly careful transmission—at no point will a reader be misled as to the intended meaning. The original wording of Matthew has been precisely preserved to our day. (The percentages within brackets are estimates, referring to the total of extant MSS for Matthew.)

I checked 114 representatives of Family 35, with reference to the five major splits, and the result is plotted on the chart below. I trust that any reasonable person will grant that the sample is adequate for my purpose (the extant Family 35 representatives for Matthew number at least 250). ++ stands for the first reading, — for the second.

MS	9:17	19:29	25:32	26:29	27:35	location	date	content
18	++	—	—	—	++	Constantinople	1364	eapr
35	—	illegible	—	++	—	Aegean	XI	eapr
55	—	—	—	++	++	Bodleian	XIV	e
83	++	++	++	++	++	Munich	XI	e
125	++	++	++	++	—	Wien	XI	e
128	—	—	—	++	—	Vatican	XIII	e
141	missing	—	—	—	—	Vatican	XIII	eapr
155	—	—	—	++	—	Vatican	XIII	e
189	—	—	++	—	—	Florence	XIII	eap
201	++	—	—	—	++	Constantinople	1357	eapr
204	++	—	—	—	—	Bologna	XIII	eap
214	++	—	—	—	++	Venedig	XIV	e
246	++	++	++	—	++	Moscow	XIV	e
363	—	++	—	++	—	Florence	XIV	eap
386	++	—	—	—	++	Vatican	XIV	eapr
394	—	++	—	—	—	Rome	1330	eap
402	++	—	—	++	—	Neapel	XIV	e
415	missing	++	—	—	—	Venedig	1356	e
479	—	—	—	++	—	Birmingham	XIII	eap
480	++	—	—	—	++	Constantinople	1366	e
510	++	—	—	++	—	Oxford-cc	XII	e
516	++	++	++	++	—	Oxford-cc	XI	e
520	—	—	++	—	—	Oxford-cc	XII	e
536	—	—	—	++	—	Ann Arbor	XIII	ea
547	—	—	—	++	—	Karakallu	XI	eap
553	—	++	—	—	—	Jerusalem	XIII	e
586	++	—	—	++	—	Modena	XIV	e
645	—	—	++	++	—	Cyprus	1304	e
676	++	—	++	—	—	Munster	XIII	eap
685	—	—	++	—	++	Ann Arbor	XIII	e
689	missing	++	—	++	++	London	XIII	e
691	++	—	—	—	++	London	XIII	e
696	—	—	—	++	—	London	XIII	e
757	++	missing	++	++	++	Athens	XIII	eapr
758	++	—	—	—	—	Athens	XIV	e
763	++	++	++	++	++	Athens	XIV	e
781	—	—	—	++	—	Athens	XIV	e
789	++	++	++	++	++	Athens	XIV	e
824	++	++	++	++	++	Grottaferrata	XIV	eapr
867	—	—	—	++	—	Vatican	XIV	e
897	missing	—	—	++	—	Edinburgh	XIII	e
928	—	—	—	—	—	Dionysiu	1304	eap
938	—	++	—	++	—	Dionysiu	1318	e
959	++	++	++	++	++	Dionysiu	1331	eap
986	++	—	—	++	—	Esphigmenu	XIV	eapr
1023	—	++	—	++	—	Iviron	1338	e
1040	++	++	++	++	++	Karakallu	XIV	eap
1062	++	—	—	++	++	Kutlumusiu	XIV	e
1072	++	++	++	—	++	M Lavras	XIII	eapr
1075	++	++	++	++	++	M Lavras	XIV	eapr
1111	—	—	++	++	++	Stavronikita	XIV	e
1117	++	++	++	++	++	Philotheu	XIV	e
1133	—	—	++	—	—	Philotheu	XIV	e
1145	++	++	++	—	++	Constantinople	XII	e

MS	9:17	19:29	25:32	26:29	27:35	location	date	content
1147	missing	—	—	—	—	Constantinople	1370	e
1158	++	—	—	++	—	Lesbos	XIV	e
1189	—	—	—	—	—	Sinai	1346	e
1199	—	—	++	++	—	Sinai	XII	e
1234	++	—	++	—	++	Sinai	XIV	e
1247	++	++	—	—	++	Sinai	XV	eap
1248	++	—	—	—	++	Sinai	XIV	eapr
1250	++	—	++	++	++	Sinai	XV	eap
1251	—	—	—	++	—	Sinai	XIII	eap
1323	—	—	++	—	—	Jerusalem	XII	e
1328	++	++	++	++	++	Jerusalem	XIV	er
1334	—	++	—	—	—	Jerusalem	XIII	e
1339	++	++	++	++	++	Jerusalem	XIII	e
1384	++	—	—	++	—	Andros	XI	eapr
1435	—	—	—	++	—	Vatopediu	XI	e
1445	++	—	—	—	—	M Lavras	1323	e
1461	++	++	++	++	++	M Lavras	XIII	e
1482	—	—	—	—	—	M Lavras	1304	eap
1490	—	—	—	++	—	M Lavras	XII	eap
1496	++	++	++	++	++	M Lavras	XIII	e
1503	++	++	++	++	++	M Lavras	1317	eapr
1548	++	++	++	—	++	Vatopediu	1359	eap
1551	++	++	++	—	++	Vatopediu	XIII	er
1559	++	++	++	++	++	Vatopediu	XIV	e
1560	++	++	++	++	++	Vatopediu	XIV	e
1572	—	—	—	—	—	Vatopediu	1304	e
1614	missing	++	++	++	++	M Lavras	1324	e
1617	++	++	++	++	++	M Lavras	XIV	eapr
1628	++	++	++	—	++	M Lavras	1400	eap
1637	++	++	++	++	++	M Lavras	1328	eapr
1652	++	++	++	++	++	M Lavras	XVI	eapr
1667	missing	++	++	++	—	Panteleimonos	1309	e
1686	++	++	++	++	++	Athens	1418	e
1694	—	—	++	—	—	Athens	XIII	e
1698	—	—	—	++	—	Athens	XIV	e
1705	++	++	++	—	—	Tirana	XIV	e
1713	++	++	++	++	++	Lesbos	XV	e
1813	—	++	++	++	—	Duke	XII	e
2122	illegible	—	—	++	—	Athens	XII	e
2175	++	++	—	—	—	St Petersburg	XIV	eap
2221	++	++	++	—	++	Sparta	1432	eap
2253	++	++	—	++	++	Tirana	XI	e
2261	—	—	—	—	—	Kalavryta	XIV	eap
2284	—	—	—	—	—	Manchester	XIII	e
2322	—	++	—	—	—	Prinkipos Is	XII	e
2323	++	++	++	—	++	Benaki (Athens)	XIII	er
2352	++	++	++	++	++	Meteora	XIV	eapr
2367	—	—	—	++	—	Princeton	XII	e
2382	++	—	—	++	—	Constantinople	XII	e
2399	missing	++	—	++	++	Chicago	XIV	e
2407	—	—	++	—	—	Chicago	1332	e
2466	—	—	—	—	—	Patmos	1329	eap
2503	++	—	—	—	++	Sinai	XIV	e
2554	++	++	++	++	++	Bucharest	1434	eapr

MS	9:17	19:29	25:32	26:29	27:35	location	date	content
2559	missing	—	—	—	missing	Benaki (Athens)	XII	e
2765	—	—	—	++	—	Corinth? (Oxford)	XIV	e
2897	++	++	++	—	++	Orlando	XIII	e
2916	++	—	++	—	missing	Athens	XIII	e
I.2110	++	++	++	++	++	Iviron	1322	e
L.65	++	++	missing	++	missing	Leukosia	XIV	e

I will now plot the patterns for the five variant sets. I noticed eight 'corrections' and nine 'alternates', scattered here and there; I ignored them for the purpose of this exercise (although 12 of the 17 change a '—' to a '++'). That purpose is to evaluate whether the patterns indicate independent lines of transmission within Family 35. Here are the patterns. The numbers stand for the first reading (++), — for the second.

PATTERNS

1	2	3	4	5	——	23**	[+2]
1	2	3	4	—	——	2	
1	2	3	—	5	——	9*	
1	2	—	4	5	——	1	
1	—	3	4	5	——	1	
—	2	3	4	5	——	0	
miss	2	3	4	5	——	1	[the exemplar presumably had all five]
1	miss	3	4	5	——	1	[the exemplar presumably had all five]
1	2	miss	4	miss	——	1	
miss	2	—	4	5	——	2	
miss	2	3	4	—	——	1	

1	2	3	—	—	——	1
1	2	—	—	5	——	1
1	—	—	4	5	——	1
—	—	3	4	5	——	1
—	2	3	4	—	——	1
1	—	3	—	5	——	1
1	—	3	—	miss	——	1

1	—	—	—	5	——	8*
—	—	—	4	5	——	1
—	2		4	—	——	3
1	—	—	4	—	——	7*
—	—	3	4	—	——	2
1	—	3	—	—	——	1
—	—	3	—	5	——	1
1	2	—	—	—	——	1
miss	2	—	—	—	——	1
miss	—	—	4	—	——	1
Illeg	—	—	4	—	——	1
—	Illeg	—	4	—	——	1

1	—	—	—	—	——	3
—	2	—	—	—	——	4
—	—	3	—	—	——	6*
—	—	—	4	—	——	14*

—	—	—	—	5	——	0	
—	—	—	—	—	——	7*	[+3]
miss	—	—	—	—	——	2	[the exemplars probably had none]
miss	—	—	—	miss	——	1	[the exemplar probably had none][1]

Setting aside the 14 incomplete MSS, another 12 have a private pattern (so far). Two patterns show 2 MSS, another two show 3 MSS, while one shows 4 MSS. I will disregard all of these. I invite attention to the following seven patterns:

1. 1 , 2 , 3, 4, 5 = 23 [+2] MSS
2. —,—,—, 4, — = 14 MSS
3. —,—,—,—,— = 7 [+3] MSS
4. 1 , 2 , 3 ,—,5 = 9 MSS
5. 1 ,—,—,—,5 = 8 MSS
6. 1 ,—,—, 4,— = 7 MSS
7. —,—, 3 ,—,— = 6 MSS

I consider that pattern 1) represents the family archetype; it is by far the strongest pattern and of necessity represents a line of transmission. But what of pattern 2); did 14 copyists just happen to make the same set of choices independently? Is it not far more likely that they represent an independent line of transmission? Indeed, I have collated many dozens of **f**[35] MSS, and with few exceptions the copyists were faithful to their exemplar. For example, consider the following evidence for six of the patterns listed above:

Pattern 1)— GA 2554 (Bucharest, 1434, eapr) is a precisely perfect copy of the line of transmission that has Pattern 1). There are several others that are all but perfect.

Pattern 2)— GA 867 (Vatican, XIV, e) is missing the first five chapters of Matthew, but otherwise is a precisely perfect copy of the line of transmission that has Pattern 2). GA 128 (Vatican, XIII, e) is almost perfect.

Pattern 3)— GA 1189 (Sinai, 1346, e) is a virtually perfect copy of the line of transmission that has Pattern 3). GA 928 (Dionysiu, 1304, eap), GA 1572 (Vatopediu, 1304, e) and GA 2466 (Patmos, 1329, eap) are all good.

---

[1] Do not all the solitary patterns, indeed the wide variety of patterns (at least 24), indicate that the transmission was normal? There was no enforced conformity.

Pattern 4)— GA 1072 (M Lavras, XIII, eapr) is an all but perfect copy of the line of transmission that has Pattern 4). GA 246 (Moscow, XIV, e) is almost perfect.

Pattern 5)— GA 18 (Constantinople, 1364, eapr) and GA 2503 (Sinai, XIV, e) are almost perfect copies of the line of transmission that has Pattern 5).

Pattern 6)— GA 586 (Modena, XIV, e) is a perfect copy of the line of transmission that has Pattern 6). GA 2382 (Constantinople, XII, e) is almost perfect, and GA 510 (Oxford-cc, XII, e) is virtually so.

Clearly the copyists were faithfully reproducing their exemplars, that represented distinct lines of transmission. Three of the patterns have overt XI century attestation, and another has overt XII, and all have scattered geographic distribution. The evidence before us simply requires the conclusion that the Family 35 archetype had to exist in the uncial period, and probably well back in that period. I have argued elsewhere that the evidence in hand indicates that it already existed in the III century, if not earlier still. **All preconceived notions concerning von Soden's K^r need to be discarded.**

Should anyone bother to count the MSS, pro and con, he will discover that the form I have chosen as archetypal has a numerical majority in only two of the five cases. Counting only the MSS included in the seven leading patterns, my choice is ahead in four of the five. Aside from the dominant nature of pattern 1), my choice was dictated by quality of MS and geographic distribution, in each case. But as pointed out at the beginning, the difference in meaning is so slight that a single translation can cover both readings, in every case. **God has preserved His Text!**

The Divine Preservation of the Original Wording of the General Epistles

As a point of departure for this discussion I will use a definition of 'preservation' written by Bart D. Ehrman:

> Any claim that God preserved the text of the New Testament intact, giving His church actual, not theoretical, possession of it, must [emphasis added] mean one of three things—either 1) God preserved it in all the extant manuscripts so that none of them contain any textual corruptions, or 2) He preserved it in a group of manuscripts, none of which contain any corruptions, or 3) He

preserved it in a solitary manuscript which alone contains no corruptions.[1]

He limits the concept of preservation in a way that verges on the creation of a straw man, but his definition serves my present purpose very nicely. It is obvious that option 1) cannot stand, but what of 2) and 3)? As the title indicates, this section is limited to the General Epistles; this group of seven books is one of the sections into which scribes divided the New Testament for the purpose of making copies.[2] Since of Ehrman's three options the third would appear to be the easiest to meet, if we can, I will begin with it.[3]

We must first define the scope—are we looking for a manuscript that is perfect for a whole book,[4] a whole section, or the whole New Testament? I think it is reasonably clear that the correct answer is a whole book; after all, that is how the New Testament was written; it follows that the very first copies were made book by book (and all subsequent copies are dependent upon them). So far as I know, no one claims divine inspiration for the division into sections—over the centuries of copying this became an accepted response to the constraints of materials and time. However, since most of the extant copies reflect that division, it will be interesting to see if we can find a manuscript that is perfect for a whole section. The formal recognition of the complete canon of the New Testament did not take place until the end of the fourth century, although informally it was known in the second (and many hundreds, if not thousands, of copies were in existence by that time—in fact, the main lines of transmission had been established long since), but the question there was the precise roster of books to be included, not the precise wording of the several books. Although many of us believe that God certainly superintended that choice of books, the wording was not at issue. So, we are looking for manuscripts that are perfect for a whole book.

---

1 "New Testament Textual Criticism: Search for Method", M.Div. thesis, Princeton Theological Seminary, 1981, p. 40—from a copy he sent to me personally.

2 There are comparatively few MSS (about 60) of the complete New Testament (and about 150 more that have all but Revelation); because of the bulk (and the physical and financial difficulty of gathering enough leather) the four Gospels were copied as a unit, and so for the letters of Paul (including Hebrews) and the General Epistles. Acts was usually joined to the Generals, but not always, and there are many MSS (over 300) that join Acts, Paul and the Generals. Revelation was added here and there.

3 At first glance, but when properly redefined the second may be easier.

4 Since the Autographs did not contain chapter or verse divisions, or even division between words (to judge by the earliest extant MSS), anything less than a whole book will not be convincing.

We must next define the text—precisely what profile are we looking for; how can we know if a MS is 'perfect'? This question lands us squarely in the snake pit of NT textual criticism [and most of the snakes are poisonous]. What I think on that subject began to appear in print in 1977[1] and I will not repeat here what is available elsewhere. As a tactical withdrawal I will retreat to an easier question (but I will return to the main one): How can we know if a MS is a perfect representative of its text-type, that is, of its family archetype? To gain time I will illustrate the theory with a concrete example. I invite attention to the chart that follows:

Performance of f^{35} MSS in Individual Books for the General Epistles[2]

Key:

s = singular reading (until all MSS have been collated, this is just an assumption);
c = corrected variant (variation of any kind corrected to the presumed archetype);
x = uncorrected variant ('variant' here means that it is attested by MSS outside the family);
/ = family is divided (a splinter group);
h = an obvious case of homoioteleuton (or –arcton), involving a line or more;
i = sheer inattention (usually repeating a syllable from one line to the next);
--- = no departures from the presumed profile.

MS	James	1 Peter	2 Peter	1 John	2 John	3 John	Jude	date	location	corpus exemplar
18	---	1x,2/	1s	1x,2/	---	1s	---	1364	Constantinople	2x,4/
35	2c	2c	---	2c	---	---	2c	XI	Aegean	---
141	1/,2s	1x,4/, 2s	1c,1s	1/,3s, 2h	---	---	---	XIII	Vatican	1x,6/
149	1x,5/, 1c,7s	1x,8/, 3s	5/,2s	4/,1c, 3s	---	1/	1/,1c	XV	Vatican	2x,24/
201	5/,1s	7/	3/	2/	---	1/	1/	1357	London	19/
204	1x	1/	2/,2s	---	---	---	---	XIII	Bologna	1x,3/
328	1x,5/, 2s	5/,4s	1x,2/, 1s	2x,4/, 1c,1s	---	---	1x, 1s	XIII	Leiden	5x,16/
386	2/	1/,1s	1/,2s	3/,3s, 1h	---	---	---	XIV	Vatican	7/
394	2/	4/,1c, 1i	4/	4/,1s	---	1i	---	1330	Rome	14/
432	5/,3s, 1h	10/,6s	1x,2/, 1c,1s	1x,5/, 1c,1s, 1h	2s	1/	3s	XV	Vatican	2x,23/
604	6/,1s	1x,11/, 1s	4/,1c, 1s	7/,1s	1x	1/	---	XIV	Paris	2x,29/
664[3]	4x,5/, 21s	5x,9/, 1c,25s	4/,1c, 14s	6x,6/, 14s,1h	1x,1s	3s	3s	XV	Zittau	16x,24

[1] *The Identity of the New Testament Text* (Nashville: Thomas Nelson Inc., Publishers, 1977)—but now please see the present edition, *The Identity of the New Testament Text IV*.

[2] I collated all forty-three of these manuscripts myself.

[3] For all its wildness, 664 has all the diagnostic **f^{35}** readings, and thus is clearly a family member (albeit sloppy and promiscuous).

MS	James	1 Peter	2 Peter	1 John	2 John	3 John	Jude	date	location	corpus exemplar
757	1x	3/,1c, 1s	1x,1s	1/	2s	---	---	XIII	Athens	2x,4/
824	1x,2s	1s	1s	---	---	---	---	XIV	Grottaferrata	1x
928	2/	3/	3/	1/,1c	---	---	---	1304	Dionysiu	9/
986[1]	4/,2s,1i	6/,4s	1/,1s	3/,3s	1s	---	1s,1i	XIV	Esphigmenu	14/
1072	2/,1h, 1i	3/,2c, 1s	1s	1/,1c	---	---	---	XIII	M Lavras	6/
1075	1/,1s	7/,2s	1s	1/	---	---	---	XIV	M Lavras	9/
1100	2x,1s	1/,1i	1/	---	---	---	---	1376	Dionysiu	2x,2/
1248	1x,2/, 2c,2s, 2h	1x,5/, 2c,3s, 1h	2x,1/, 7s	4s,2h	2/	1/, 2s, 1h	2s, 2h	XIV	Sinai	4x,11/
1249	3/	1x,5/, 2s	4/	1x,3/	1/,1c	---	1/	1324	Sinai	2x,17/
1503	1s	3/,1c	1s	1s	1s	---	---	1317	M Lavras	3/
1548	2/,2s	1x,6/, 1c,2s	1/,2s	1/,1s	---	---	1s	1359	Vatopediu	1x,10/
1637	1/,1s	4/,1c, 1s	1/	1c	---	---	---	1328	M Lavras	6/
1725	2/	1/,1c	---	1s,1i	---	---	1s	1367	Vatopediu	3/
1732	2s	1/,2s	1/,1i	2s	1h	---	1s,1i	1384	M Lavras	2/
1754[2]	2/,16s	3/,8s	2/,9s	2x,1/, 13s,3h	1s	1/,1s	2s	XII	Panteleimonos	2x,9/
1761	2x,2s	2x,4/, 3s	1/	1/,1s, 1h	1s	2s	---	XIV	Athens	4x,6/
1768	7/,2c, 1s	12/,1i	6/,2i	2c	---	1/	1s	1516	Iviron	26/
1855	1/,1s	1x,2/	2/	1/,1c	---	---	---	XIII	Iviron	1x,6/
1864	---	3/,2c	---	1c,2s	---	---	---	XIII	Stavronikita	3/
1865	1s	---	2s	1c	---	1/	---	XIII	Philotheu	1/
1876	1x,4/, 3s	2x,4/, 3s,1h	4/,1s	1x,3/, 1c,2s	2/,1s	1/	1/,2s	XV	Sinai	4x,19/
1892	1x,4/, 2c,1s	3x,4/, 4s	1x,2/, 1c	1/,1c, 2s	1x	---	1c, 1s	XIV	Jerusalem	6x,11/
1897	2/,3s	1/,3s	2s	2s	---	---	1/	XII	Jerusalem	4/
2221	1s	2x	1x,3/, 1s	1x,1/	---	---	---	1432	Sparta	4x,4/
2352	1/,1c, 1i	6/,1c, 1s,1i	3/,1c	2/,1c	1c,1i	---	---	XIV	Meteora	12/
2431	4/,4s,1i	11/,2s, 2i	2/,1c, 2s,2i	2/,2s,2i	---	---	1i	1332	Kavsokalyvia	19/
2466	1/,1s	1x,1/, 1c,4s	1x,2s	3/,1s	---	1/	2s	1329	Patmos	2x,6/
2554	---	---	---	---	---	---	---	1434	Bucharest	---
2587	2/	3/	3/	1/	---	---	1c	XI	Vatican	9/
2626	1/,1s	1x,5/	1/,1s	2/	1/	1/,1s	2/	XIV	Ochrida	1x,13/
2723	---	---	---	1h	---	---	---	XI	Trikala	---

Interpretation

Now then, the text-type that I call Family 35 (**f**^{35}) is represented by some 84 MSS (extant) in the General Epistles. This sample of forty-three family members is certainly representative of the whole text-type, being fully half of its representatives, and taking into consideration the geographic distribution as well. The question immediately before us is: How can

1 986 is lacking 1 Peter 1:23 - 2:15.

2 MS 1754 is second only to 664 in sloppiness, but is clearly a family member.

we know if a MS is a perfect representative of its text-type? The answer must obtain for a whole book.

The first book in the section is James. Looking at the chart we observe that cursives 18, 1864, 2554 and 2723 are presumed to be perfect representatives, as they stand—they have no deviations from the presumed archetypal profile.[1] Since 35 has been systematically corrected, its exemplar was also perfect. If we ascribe singular readings to the copyist, then the exemplars of 1503, 1732, 1865 and 2221 were perfect as well. If 18, 1864, 2554 and 2723 are copies, not original creations, then their exemplars were also perfect; and the exemplars of the exemplars were also perfect, and so on. The implications of finding a perfect representative of any archetypal text are rather powerful. All the 'canons' of textual criticism become irrelevant to any point subsequent to the creation of that text (they could still come into play when studying the creation of the text, in the event). Of the other MSS, 204 and 757 have only one deviation; 386, 394, 928, 1075, 1637, 1725, 1732, 1855, 2466 and 2587 have only two; and so on. (MS 664 has thirty, most of them being careless mistakes; 664 attests the basic profile [the diagnostic variants that distinguish it from all other profiles] and is thus clearly a member of the family, albeit sloppy.)

I have referred to 'the presumed archetypal profile'. So how did I identify it? I did so on the basis of a fundamental principle. If we have a family made up of 50 MSS, wherever they are all in agreement there can be no question as to the family reading. Where a single MS goes astray against all the rest, there still can be no question—which is what I argue for James above. Wherever so many as two agree (against the rest) then we have a splinter group—off hand I would say that anything up to 20% of the family total would remain a splinter group, with virtually no chance of representing the archetypal reading (if the other 80% are unanimous). Where the attestation falls below 80%, the more so if there are several competing variants, other considerations must come into play.

Returning to James, I claim that we have reasonable certainty as to the precise family profile for that book.[2] That being so, we can now evaluate the individual MSS. That is why I affirm that the exemplars of 18, 35, 1503, 1732, 1864, 1865, 2221, 2554 and 2723 are perfect representatives of the family. To have nine perfect exemplars out of forty-three is probably

---

[1] Before I collated cursive 18 for myself, I was limited to the collation reflected in *TuT* (*Text und Textwert der Griechischen Handschriften des Neuen Testaments* [Ed. Kurt Aland, Berlin: Walter de Gruyter, 1987], volumes 9 and 11), which evidently assigns two errors to the copyist; I am satisfied that there are none.

[2] There are only two significant family splits in James, that I discuss in "**f**[35] sub-groups in the General Epistles", to be found in the Appendix.

more than most of us would expect! So in James we have several MSS that meet Ehrman's option 3), with reference to the archetypal text.

But what about Ehrman's second option? When he speaks of a 'group' of MSS, as distinct from a 'solitary' MS (option 3), he presumably is thinking of a family, since they would all have the same profile, of necessity. But if he is thinking of a family, then I submit that option 2) needs to be restated. I suggest: "He preserved it in a family of manuscripts whose archetypal text contains no corruptions—provided that its precise profile can be affirmed beyond reasonable doubt." (Recall that we are speaking of actual possession of the profile.) The obvious mistakes in individual representatives can cheerfully be factored out, leaving the witness of the family unscathed. As restated, Ehrman's second option is met by **f**^{35} in James, with reference to the archetypal text. Let's move on to 1 Peter.

Looking at the chart, cursives 1865, 2554 and 2723 are perfect representatives of the presumed archetypal profile, but since 35 has been systematically corrected, its exemplar was also perfect.[1] If we ascribe singular readings to the copyist, then the exemplar of 824 was perfect as well. Of the other MSS, 204 has only one deviation; 386, 1100, 1725 and 2221 have only two; and so on. Arguing as I did for James, in 1 Peter we have five exemplars that meet Ehrman's option 3) and again **f**^{35} meets his option 2), with reference to the archetypal text. Let's move on to 2 Peter.

Looking at the chart, cursives 35, 1725, 1864, 2554 and 2723 are perfect representatives of the presumed archetypal profile.[2] If we ascribe singular readings to the copyist, then the exemplars of 18, 824, 1072, 1075, 1503, 1865 and 1897 were perfect as well. Of the other MSS, 1100, 1637 and 1761 have only one deviation; 141, 757, 986, 1732, 1855 and 2626 have only two; and so on. Arguing as I did for James, in 2 Peter we have twelve exemplars that meet Ehrman's option 3) and again **f**^{35} meets his option 2), with reference to the archetypal text. Let's move on to 1 John.

Looking at the chart, cursives 204, 824, 1100 and 2554 are perfect representatives of the presumed archetypal profile, but since 35, 1637, 1768 and 1865 have been systematically corrected, their exemplars were also perfect.[3] The single variation in 2723 is the omission of a whole line

---

[1] There are eight significant family splits in 1 Peter, that I discuss in "**f**^{35} sub-groups in the General Epistles".

[2] There are two significant family splits in 2 Peter, that I discuss in "**f**^{35} sub-groups in the General Epistles".

[3] There are two significant family splits in 1 John, that I discuss in "**f**^{35} sub-groups in the General Epistles".

in an obvious case of homoioteleuton, which to my mind does not constitute a proper variant reading. In any case its exemplar would be perfect. If we ascribe singular readings to the copyist, then the exemplars of 1503, 1725, 1732 and 1897 were perfect as well. Of the other MSS, 757, 1075 and 2587 have only one deviation; 201, 928, 1072, 1548, 1855, 2221 and 2626 have only two; and so on. Arguing as I did for James, in 1 John we have thirteen exemplars that meet Ehrman's option 3) and again **f**^{35} meets his option 2), with reference to the archetypal text. Let's move on to 2 John.

Looking at the chart, most of the cursives are perfect representatives of the presumed archetypal profile. Arguing as I did for James, in 2 John we have thirty-six exemplars that meet Ehrman's option 3) and again **f**^{35} meets his option 2), with reference to the archetypal text. Let's move on to 3 John.

Looking at the chart, most of the cursives are perfect representatives of the presumed archetypal profile. Arguing as I did for James, in 3 John we have thirty-two exemplars that meet Ehrman's option 3) and again **f**^{35} meets his option 2), with reference to the archetypal text. Let's move on to Jude.

Looking at the chart, half of the cursives are perfect representatives of the presumed archetypal profile. Arguing as I did for James, in Jude we have thirty-six exemplars that meet Ehrman's option 3) and again **f**^{35} meets his option 2), with reference to the archetypal text.

The section that follows should be viewed as a continuation of this one.

But is the archetypal text of f^{35} the Autograph?

As they used to say in another world, long departed, "That's the $64 question". In Part III I present further objective evidence in support of the claim that the text of **f**^{35} is ancient and independent of all other lines of transmission. If **f**^{35} is independent of all other lines of transmission then it must hark back to the Autographs. What other reasonable explanation is there? If anyone has a different explanation that accounts for the evidence better than (or as well as) mine does, I would like to see it.[1]

[1] Should anyone wish to claim that **f**^{35} is a recension, I request (and insist) that he specify who did it, when and where, and furnish evidence in support of the claim. Without evidence any such claim is frivolous and irresponsible—Hort's claim that his 'Syrian' text was the result of a 'Lucianic' recension is a classic example (Burgon protested at the complete lack of evidence, at the time, and no one has come up with any since). I remind

Family 35 readings are attested by early witnesses, but without pattern, and therefore without dependency. But there are many hundreds of such readings. So how did the $\mathbf{f}^{35}$ archetype come by all those early readings? Did its creator travel around and collect a few readings from Aleph, a few from B, a few from $P^{45,66,75}$, a few from W and D, etc.? Is not such a suggestion patently ridiculous? The only reasonable conclusion is that the $\mathbf{f}^{35}$ text is ancient (also independent).

I claim to have demonstrated the superiority of Family 35 based on size (number of representatives), independence, age, geographical distribution, profile (empirically determined), care (see above) and range (all 27 books). I challenge any and all to do the same for any other line of transmission!

So then, if the archetypal text of $\mathbf{f}^{35}$ is the Autograph then we have met two of Ehrman's three options for each of the seven General Epistles. I maintain that in this year of our Lord we have actual (not theoretical) possession of the precise original wording of James, 1 Peter, 2 Peter, 1 John, 2 John, 3 John and Jude!! Furthermore, I am prepared to offer the same sort of demonstration for each of the 27 books that make up our NT. In consequence thereof, I maintain that in this year of our Lord we have actual (not theoretical) possession of the precise original wording of the whole New Testament!!! It is reproduced in my published Greek Text, *The Greek New Testament According to Family 35*.

I have argued above that preservation is to be demonstrated book by book, but would it not be interesting if we could do the same for a whole section? But of course we have—Ehrman's option 2), as restated, obtains for the whole section of seven books. Not just interesting but astonishing it would be to find a single MS that is perfect throughout a section of seven books![1] And again we have!! 2554 fills the bill, as do the exemplars of 35 and 2723, and as does 2723 itself, virtually. So recently as twelve years ago I would not have dreamed of such a thing.

If God demonstrably preserved the precise wording of a text throughout two millennia, this implies rather strongly that He inspired it in the first place—otherwise, why bother with it? And if He went to such pains, I rather suspect that He expects us to pay strict attention to it. When we stand before the Just Judge—who is also Creator, Savior and Inspirer—He will require an accounting based on the objective authority of that Text.

---

the reader that evidence must be rigorously distinguished from presupposition and interpretation.

[1] This would be true for the archetypal text of any group of 70-80 MSS, or even fewer. If the archetype is the Autograph, all the more so.

PART III: Some Further Considerations

Is f^{35} Ancient?

I have received feedback that goes something like this: "ok, the evidence you have presented indicates that $\mathbf{f}^{35}$ is independent, but it doesn't prove that it's ancient" [I affirm both]. I consider that the point deserves a bit of 'chewing'. For instance: minuscules 35, 2587 and 2723 are generally dated to the 11th century; although minuscule 1897 is generally dated to the 12th, I have collated it and must say that it looks older to me, just as old as the other three, so I claim it for the 11th as well. What about their provenance? 35 is presently in Paris, but was acquired in the Aegean area [18, also in Paris, was done in Constantinople]; 1897 is in Jerusalem and presumably was produced there; 2587 is in the Vatican and may well have been produced there; 2723 is in Trikala and was doubtless produced there.

I now consider their performance in the seven General Epistles (a corpus of sufficient size and diversity to preclude reasonable challenge—I have done a complete collation of all four MSS throughout that corpus). As best I can tell, the exemplars of 35 and 2723 were perfect representatives of the presumed family archetype—not one variant in all seven books. The exemplar of 1897 participates in a splinter group (within the family) at three points, with no further variants. The exemplar of 2587 participates in a splinter group at six points, with no further variants. So the four monks who produced our four 11th century copies were each looking at a perfect (virtually) representative of the family's ($\mathbf{f}^{35}$) archetypal text. But how old were the exemplars?

If a MS was not in constant or regular use it would easily last for a century or more, even several. Would Greek MSS in Rome be likely to be much in use at that time? Probably not, so the exemplar of 2587 could easily have been an uncial. How about Jerusalem? The chances of greater use there were probably little better than in Rome. In Constantinople (35?) and Trikala Greek was certainly still in use. But do we know to what extent Christians were actually reading Scripture in those years? I think we may reasonably assume that the exemplars were at least a century older than their copies. But 1897 and 2587 join splinter groups, so we are looking at some transmissional history—there must be the parent of the splinter between our exemplar and the archetype.

So, the exemplars were presumably no later than 10th century. If we allow one generation for the creation of splinters, that generation would be no later than the 9th and the archetype no later than the 8th. (I have given an absolute minimum, but obviously there could have been any number of further intervening generations, which would place the archetype much earlier.) But what are the implications of perfect representatives of a family in the tenth century in four diverse locations? How could there be **perfect** copies of *anything* in the 10th century?? That there were four perfect (virtually) representatives of the $\mathbf{f^{35}}$ archetype in diverse locations in the 10th century is a fact. That they were separated from that archetype by at least one intervening generation is also a fact. So how can we explain them?

Did someone concoct the $\mathbf{f^{35}}$ archetype in the 8th century? Who? Why? And how could it spread around the Mediterranean world? There are $\mathbf{f^{35}}$ MSS all over the place—Jerusalem, Sinai, Athens, Constantinople, Trikala, Kalavryta, Ochrida, Patmos, Karditsa, Rome, Sparta, Meteora, Venedig, Lesbos, and most monasteries on Mt. Athos (that represented different 'denominations'), etc. [If there were six monasteries on Cyprus—one Anglican, one Assembly of God, one Baptist, one Church of Christ, one Methodist and one Presbyterian—to what extent would they compare notes? Has human nature changed?] But the Byzantine bulk ($\mathbf{K^x}$) controlled at least 60% of the transmissional stream ($\mathbf{f^{35}}$ = about 16%); how could something concocted in the 8th century spread so far, so fast, and in such purity? How did it inspire such loyalty? Everything that we know about the history of the transmission of the Text answers that it could not and did not. It is simply impossible that $\mathbf{f^{35}}$ could have been 'concocted' at any point subsequent to the 4th century. The loyalty with which $\mathbf{f^{35}}$ was copied, the level of loyalty for $\mathbf{f^{35}}$ being much higher than that for any other line of transmission, indicates that it was never 'concocted'—it goes back to the Original.

However, although $\mathbf{f^{35}}$ has been demonstrated to be independent of $\mathbf{K^x}$ (Byzantine bulk), they are really very close and must have a common source. (I would say that $\mathbf{K^x}$ represents a departure from $\mathbf{f^{35}}$, that $\mathbf{f^{35}}$ is therefore older.) In the General Epistles $\mathbf{f^{35}}$ does not differ from the H-F Majority Text all that much. For instance, in James $\mathbf{f^{35}}$ differs from H-F nineteen times, only two of which affect the meaning (not seriously). If $\mathbf{f^{35}}$ and $\mathbf{K^x}$ have a common source, but $\mathbf{f^{35}}$ is independent of $\mathbf{K^x}$, then $\mathbf{f^{35}}$ must be at least as old as $\mathbf{K^x}$—Q.E.D. [*quod erat demonstrandum*, for those who read Latin; "which was to be proved", for the rest of us; and in yet plainer English, "the point to be proved has been proved"].

Further, if $\mathbf{f^{35}}$ is independent of all other known lines of transmission, then it must hark back to the Autographs. If it was created out of existing materials at some point down the line, then it is dependent on those materials and it should be possible to demonstrate that dependence. So far as I know, no such dependence has been demonstrated, and to the extent that I have analyzed the evidence, it cannot be demonstrated.

The Importance of Objective Evidence

Even when MSS are collated by persons with a negative bias (bias against the MSS), if they will record the collation accurately, the result is valuable. The continuous text MSS are the primary witnesses to the NT Text. To be able to trace the transmissional history of individual readings, we need complete collations of a large number of extant MSS, the more the better. I wish to illustrate what I have affirmed with the *Editio Critica Maior* (*ECM*) collations for James and 1 John. They were done while Kurt Aland was still directing the Institute for New Testament Textual Research in Münster (*INTF*), and the work reflects his bias against the Byzantine MSS. (By the time the *ECM* for the General Epistles was published, 1997, Kurt had died, but since his wife, Barbara, succeeded him as director of the Institute, *INTF*, there would be no change in the theoretical orientation.)[1]

As of May, 1988, Kurt and Barbara Aland had excluded "more than 1,175 minuscules" (p. 138) as exhibiting "a purely or predominately Byzantine text". They go on to say, "they are all irrelevant for textual criticism, at least for establishing the original form of the text and its development in the early centuries" (p. 142). (*The Text of the New Testament*, Eerdmans, 1989.) That this bias prevailed in the *Editio Critica Maior* for James is quite clear. Without apology the editors excluded some 340 of the 522 MSS they evaluated because they "attest the Majority text in at least 90% of the test passages" (p. 12). The "test passages" refers to the 98 variant sets taken from the seven General Epistles presented in *Text und Textwert*. However, they did include GA 18 and 35 to represent Soden's **K**^{r} (my Family 35), and GA 1, 424, 607, 617 and 2423 to represent the core Byzantine MSS that were excluded. Apart from those seven, they class another 70 (of the included MSS) as being Byzantine, albeit falling below the 90% threshold.

So why do I say that their work is valuable, in spite of their bias? I hasten to explain. In the critical apparatus of my *The Greek New Testament According to Family 35*, I list eight **f**^{35} readings (for James) as having 30% overall attestation, or less, which would make them more or less diagnostic

---

[1] Indeed, for James the editors included 70 MSS that they classed as Byzantine; but for 1 Peter they reduced the number to 51, and for 2 Peter to 44. For 1 John it was reduced to 41—one might conclude that Barbara was even more radical than Kurt in her disdain for the Byzantine MSS.

f[35] readings. Family 35 represents about 16% of the total of extant MSS, but it is almost never entirely alone. However, as illustrated below, the sprinkling of other MSS is almost never the same. So I ask: **How is that diverse sprinkling to be explained?** In the chart below, the eight readings form the first line, and below each reading I list the MSS that *ECM* gives as supporting each one. Since GA 18 and 35 have them all, of course, they are not listed. I will discuss the implications below, but first, the evidence (numbers with an asterisk are classed as Byzantine):

3:4 ιθυνοντος	1:23 νομου	4:14 ημων	4:14 επειτα	3:2 δυναμενος	2:3 λαμπ. εσθ.	4:11 γαρ	2:4 ου
---	---	---	---	ℵ	---	---	ℵ
---	---	---	---	---	---	---	A
---	---	---	---	---	---	---	C
---	---	33	---	---	---	---	33
---	---	---	---	---	---	---	81
---	88	88	---	---	---	---	---
---	104*	---	---	---	---	---	---
---	---	206	206	206	206	206	206
---	---	254*	---	254	---	254	254
---	---	321*	321	---	---	---	---
---	378*	---	---	---	---	378	---
400	---	---	---	---	400	---	---
---	---	429	429	429	429	429	429
---	---	---	---	---	---	---	436
442*	---	---	---	---	---	---	442
---	459*	---	---	---	---	---	---
---	467*	---	---	---	---	---	---
---	---	---	522	522	522	522	522
---	<u>607</u>	---	---	---	---	---	---
---	---	---	614	614	614	614	614
---	---	---	---	621	---	621	621
---	---	630	630	630	630	630	630
---	---	---	---	---	720*	---	---
---	---	---	---	---	876*	---	---
---	915	915	---	---	---	---	---
---	---	---	---	---	---	---	945
---	---	999*	---	---	---	---	---
---	---	---	---	---	---	---	1067
---	1127	---	---	---	---	---	---
---	---	---	---	---	---	---	1175
---	---	---	---	---	---	---	1241
---	---	---	---	---	---	---	1243
1270	---	---	---	---	---	---	---
---	---	---	1292	---	1292	1292	1292
1297	---	---	---	---	---	---	---
---	---	---	---	---	1367*	1367	---
---	---	---	---	1448	1448	1448	1448
---	---	1490	---	1490	1490	1490	1490

3:4	1:23	4:14	4:14	3:2	2:3	4:11	2:4
ιθυνοντος	νομου	ημων	επειτα	δυναμενος	λαμπ. εσθ.	γαρ	ου
---	1501*	---	---	---	---	---	---
---	---	---	1505	1505	1505	1505	1505
---	---	1524	---	1524	---	1524	1524
1595*	---	---	---	---	---	---	---
1598	---	---	---	---	---	---	---
---	---	---	1611	---	1611	1611	1611
---	---	1678	---	---	---	---	---
---	---	1729*	---	---	---	---	---
---	---	---	---	---	---	---	1735
---	---	---	---	---	---	---	1739
---	---	---	---	---	---	1751	---
---	---	---	---	---	1765*	---	---
---	---	---	1799	---	1799	1799	1799
---	---	---	---	1827*	---	---	---
---	---	1831	1831	1831	1831	1831	1831
---	---	---	---	---	1832*	---	---
---	1838*	1838	---	---	---	---	---
---	1842	---	---	1842	---	---	---
---	1848*	---	---	---	---	---	---
---	---	---	---	1852	---	1852	---
---	---	---	---	---	---	---	1874*
---	1890	---	1890	1890	1890	1890	1890
1893*	---	---	---	---	---	---	---
2080*	2080	---	2080	---	2080	2080	2080
---	---	---	2138	2138	2138	2138	2138
---	2147	---	2147	---	2147	2147	---
---	---	---	---	---	---	---	2180*
---	---	2200	2200	2200	2200	2200	2200
---	---	---	---	---	---	---	2298
---	---	---	---	---	---	---	2344
---	---	---	---	2374	---	2374	2374
---	---	---	2412	2412	2412	2412	2412
---	---	---	---	---	---	---	2492
---	---	---	---	---	2494*	---	---
---	---	---	2495	2495	2495	2495	2495
---	---	---	---	---	2523	---	---
---	---	---	---	---	---	---	2541
---	---	---	2652	---	2652	2652	---
---	---	2674*	---	---	---	---	---
---	---	2774*	---	---	---	---	---
---	---	---	---	2805	---	2805	2805
---	---	---	---	---	---	---	2818*
8	16	18	19	23	28	29	44

So what can we learn from this evidence? To begin, the sole underlined MS that appears in the chart, 607, is the only one of the five core representatives to appear, and it does so only once. This shows clearly that **f**^{35} is distinct from the Byzantine bulk, or Soden's **K**^{x}. Further, there are 43 MSS that are alone in attesting a **f**^{35} reading: A, C, 81, 104*, 436, 459*,

467*, 607, 720*, 876*, 945, 999*, 1067, 1127, 1175, 1241, 1243, 1270, 1297, 1501*, 1595*, 1598, 1678, 1729*, 1735, 1739, 1751, 1765*, 1827*, 1832*, 1848*, 1874*, 1893*, 2180*, 2298, 2344, 2492, 2494*, 2523, 2541, 2674*, 2774*, 2818*. Twenty-one of them, or virtually half, are classed as Byzantine, but since they only appear once, they are evidently independent of the Byzantine bulk. (Actually, all of the MSS that appear here are independent of the Byzantine bulk, except 607.) So we have 43 independent witnesses to **f**^{35} readings that **are certainly not part of that family**.

Twelve MSS appear only twice, but there is no pattern, no overlap, except for three with the same distribution; so we have ten more independent witnesses. Those that appear more than twice generally reflect some dependency, but even so, they add another ten independent witnesses. When I say 'independent', I mean in their generation. There will presumably be grouping as we move back through the centuries. Still, would the 63 independent witnesses in their generation reduce by more than half by the time we got back to the fifth century? I very much doubt it; I would expect at least 30 lines[1] still in the fifth century. Would they reduce by more than half in two centuries? If not, we would still have 15 lines in the third century; which would mean that **f**^{35} is very early.

Going back to the chart, I note that ιθυνοντος and νομου share only one MS out of 23; but ιθυνοντος and ημων share none at all out of 26! ιθυνοντος and επειτα share only one out of 26; ιθυνοντος and δυναμενος share none at all out of 31! νομου and ημων share three out of 31; νομου and επειτα share two out of 35; νομου and δυναμενος share only two out of 37. ου is the champion, having 18 MSS by itself. So what does this evidence tell us? Does it not indicate that **f**^{35} is the core from which a great many tangents departed? There is very little pattern, which indicates that **f**^{35} must be both ancient and independent. The MSS that agree with **f**^{35} six times out of the eight may prove to be on the fringe of the family; those that agree five times would be farther away, and so on.

Now let us look at 1 John. Whereas in James they included 77 Byzantine MSS (including **f**^{35}), for 1 John they included only 48, so the bias is stronger. Again they included seven to represent the excluded MSS, GA

[1] I understand that someone may well say: "Wait just a minute; on what basis do you say that all those independent MSS represent lines of transmission?" Well, the readings that they attest are not the sort that a copyist would invent on his own initiative. If the copyist did not invent it, then the reading was in his exemplar. If the reading was in his exemplar, then you have a line of transmission. To attempt to gage the length of the 'lines', and any relationship between lines, we need complete collations of a great many more MSS.

18 and 35 to represent Soden's **K**[r], and GA 319, 424, 468, 617 and 2423 to represent the core Byzantine MSS that were excluded.

I list four **f**[35] readings (for 1 John) as having 30% overall attestation, or less, which would make them more or less diagnostic **f**[35] readings. In the chart below, those readings form the first line, and below each reading I list the MSS that *ECM* gives as supporting each one. Since GA 18 and 35 have them all, of course, they are not listed. I will discuss the implications below, but first, the evidence (numbers with an asterisk are classed as Byzantine):

3:6 και	5:11 ο θεος ημιν	1:6 περιπατουμεν	3:24 --- εν
---	---	---	א
---	B	---	---
---	---	0142*	---
---	0296	---	---
---	---	33	---
---	---	61	---
---	69*	---	---
---	---	---	94
---	---	180*	180
254	---	---	---
---	323	---	---
---	---	378	---
---	---	607*	607
---	614	---	614
---	630	---	---
915	---	---	---
---	1292	---	---
---	---	1501*	---
---	1505	1505	---
1523	---	---	---
1524	---	---	---
---	1611	---	---
---	1739	---	---
1827*	---	---	---
---	---	---	1836
---	---	1842*	---
1844	---	---	---
1852	---	---	---
---	1881	---	---
---	---	1890*	1890
---	2138	---	---
---	---	2147	---
---	2200	---	---
---	2298	---	---
2374	---	---	---
---	2412	---	2412
---	---	---	2423

3:6	5:11	1:6	3:24
και	ο θεος ημιν	περιπατουμεν	--- εν
---	2492	---	---
---	---	2544	---
---	---	2652	---
---	---	---	2805
8	16	13	10

As with James, there is no overlap between the first two columns (in James the 1st column does share one MS with the 2nd, but none with the 3rd and 5th), and only one MS in common between the 2nd and 3rd! It follows that **f**[35] is independent of all the lines of transmission represented by the MSS in those columns. There are no Byzantine MSS in the 1st column and only one (not very strong—69) in the 2nd. In contrast, the 3rd column has one very strong Byzantine MS (607), one strong one (180), two fair ones (0142, 1890), and two weak ones (1501, 1842); for all that, they obviously do not represent the bulk of the Byzantine tradition. As in James, **f**[35] is clearly early and independent of **K**[x]. If it is independent of all other lines of transmission as well, as I believe I can demonstrate, then it harks back to the Original—what other reasonable explanation is there?

Family 35 represents about 16% of the total of extant MSS, but it is almost never entirely alone. However, as illustrated above, the sprinkling of other MSS is almost never the same. So again I ask: How is that diverse sprinkling to be explained? Does it not indicate that **f**[35] is the core from which a great many tangents departed? What other reasonable explanation is there? If it is the core, then it represents the Original. (I am assuming a reasonably normal transmission, which I have defended elsewhere.)

I invite the reader to pause and really think about the implications of the evidence presented above (trying to set aside preconceived ideas). It has been standard procedure for partisans of a certain theoretical orientation to insist upon the difference between individual readings and a text-type. I agree that these must be distinguished. However, it is the mosaic, or profile, or selection of individual readings that define a text-type, or family, or line of transmission. **If all the individual readings that define a family are demonstrably ancient, then perforce the family itself is ancient!**

I suppose it could be theoretically possible for someone in the eighth century to concoct a new archetype, using only early readings; but what possible reason could anyone have for doing so? And how could such a concocted text spread throughout the Mediterranean world? And how could it achieve a level of loyalty far exceeding that in any other line of transmission, including far older ones? How could an archetype concocted in the eighth century supplant all of the older archetypes? I refer to fidelity of transmission. (In our day a concocted text, based on early MSS, has taken over the academic world, but there is no analogy—we know who did it, when, how and why. I have written a page or two on that subject elsewhere.)

Anyone who wishes to advance a theory that Family 35 was concocted by someone in the twelfth century, or the eighth, or the fourth, and do so responsibly, must produce the evidence that gives rise to the theory. He must show who did it, when and where. There are many hundreds of extant copies of NT writings. If all those MSS do not furnish the requisite evidence, then the theory is patently false. To advance a theory that is patently false is to be perverse.

Concerning the Text of the *Pericope Adulterae*

The information offered below is based on Maurice A. Robinson's complete collation of 1,389 MSS that contain the Pericope, John 7:53 - 8:11.[1] I attempted to establish a profile of readings for each of the three main groups of MSS, **M**[5,6,7] (as in the apparatus of the H-F Majority Text). I take it that the smaller groups are all mixtures based on the big three. This section presents the results, along with my interpretation of their significance.

M[7] Profile

7:53	01	απηλθεν
8:1	02	Ιησους δε
8:2	03	(βαθεως) = omit
8:2	04	παρεγενετο
8:2	05	προς αυτον
8:3	06	προς αυτον
8:3	07	επι
8:3	08	κατειλημμενην
8:3	09	εν μεσω
8:4	10	λεγουσιν
8:4	11	(πειραζοντες)

[1] 240 MSS omit the PA, 64 of which are based on Theophylact's commentary. Fourteen others have lacunae, but are not witnesses for total omission. A few others certainly contain the passage but the microfilm is illegible. So, 1389 + 240 + 14 + 7(?) = about 1650 MSS checked by Robinson. (These are microfilms held by the *Institut* in Münster. We now know that there are many more extant MSS, and probably even more that are not yet 'extant'.)

8:4	12	ταυτην ευρομεν
8:4	13	επαυτοφωρω
8:4	14	μοιχευομενην
8:5	15	ημων Μωσης
8:5	16	λιθοβολεισθαι
8:5	17	(περι αυτης)
8:6	18	κατηγοριαν κατ
8:6	19	μη προσποιουμενος
8:7	20	ερωτωντες
8:7	21	ανακυψας
8:7	22	προς αυτους
8:7	23	τον λιθον επ αυτη βαλετω
8:9	24	και υπο της συνειδησεως ελεγχομενοι
8:9	25	εως των εσχατων
8:9	26	μονος ο Ιησους
8:10	27	και μηδενα θεασαμενος πλην της γυναικος
8:10	28	αυτη
8:10	29	εκεινοι οι κατηγοροι σου
8:11	30	ειπεν δε αυτη ο Ιησους
8:11	31	κατακρινω
8:11	32	και απο του νυν

Comment: This is a single, clear-cut, unambiguous profile/mosaic, as defined by 127 MSS—there is no internal variation among them. This contrasts dramatically with **M**^{6} and **M**^{5}, and I suppose with the lesser groups (though I haven't checked them). As given below, it is possible to come up with a profile for both **5** and **6**, for purposes of distinguishing them from each other and from **7**, but they have so much internal variation that I see no way to come up with an archetype that is objectively defined; both will have to be subdivided. The profile above defines the archetypal text of **M**^{7}.

M^{6} Profile

7:53	01	απηλθεν / απηλθον
8:1	02	**και ο Ιησους δε / και ο Ιησους
8:2	03	**βαθεως / βαθεος
8:2	04	**ηλθεν ο Ιησους
8:2	05	προς αυτον
8:3	06	(προς αυτον) / προς αυτον
8:3	07	επι
8:3	08	κατειλημμενην
8:3	09	εν τω μεσω / εν μεσω
8:4	10	**ειπον

8:4	11	(πειραζοντες) = omit
8:4	12	ταυτην ευρομεν
8:4	13	επαυτοφωρω / –φορω / –φορως
8:4	14	μοιχευομενην / –νη
8:5	15	ημων Μωσης / υμων Μωσης / Μ. ενετ. ημιν / Μωσης
8:5	16	**λιθαζειν
8:5	17	(περι αυτης) / περι αυτης
8:6	18	κατηγοριαν κατ
8:6	19	(μη προσποιουμενος) / μη προσποιουμενος
8:7	20	ερωτωντες / επερωτωντες
8:7	21	αναβλεψας / ανακυψας
8:7	22	**αυτοις
8:7	23	**λιθον βαλετω επ αυτην
8:9	24	(και υπο της συνειδησεως ελεγχομενοι) /και υπο της συνειδησεως ελεγχομενοι
8:9	25	εως των εσχατων
8:9	26	ο Ιησους μονος / μονος
8:10	27	**(και μηδενα θεασαμενος πλην της γυναικος)
8:10	28	**ειδεν αυτην και ειπεν
8:10	29	**(αυτη) γυναι
8:10	30	(εκεινοι) / (εκεινοι οι κατηγοροι σου) / (που εκεινοι οι κατηγοροι σου)
8:11	31	ειπεν δε αυτη ο Ιησους
8:11	32	κατακρινω
8:11	33	και απο του νυν / απο του νυν και

Comment: I checked the **M**^{6} MSS from the **XI** century (over 80) and to my surprise no two of them had an identical mosaic of variants. No matter what contrastive set one uses as a basis (e.g. βαθεως X βαθεος), as soon as you look down the roster of other variants the MSS wander back and forth, producing a bewildering array of variation, shifting alliances, or whatever. If all the centuries are checked, there will presumably be a few small groups wherein the member MSS share identical mosaics, but no single definitive profile for **M**^{6} will emerge (in contrast to **M**^{7}). If there is no single profile, then there is no objective way to define / establish / re-construct an archetype for **M**^{6}. Without a definable archetype, **M**^{6} is not a viable candidate for the original form of the Text. However, the ten variants marked by ** do distinguish **M**^{6} from both **M**^{5} and **M**^{7}, forming its 'backbone'. But two of the ten, plus another fourteen, have internal variation (besides a variety of further variation not recorded in this list). The individual MSS meander around the plethora of internal (within the group) variation in a bewildering manner, all of which diminishes the credibility of the group. I take it that **M**^{6} reflects Alexandrian influence.

M^5 Profile

7:53	01	**επορευθη / επορευθησαν
8:1	02	Ιησους δε
8:2	03	(βαθεως) = omit
8:2	04	παρεγενετο
8:2	05	**(προς αυτον)
8:3	06	προς αυτον
8:3	07	**εν
8:3	08	**καταληφθεισαν
8:3	09	εν μεσω
8:4	10	λεγουσιν
8:4	11	**πειραζοντες
8:4	12	**αυτη η γυνη
8:4	13	**κατεληφθη / ειληπται / κατειληπται
8:4	14	επαυτοφωρω / –φορω
8:4	15	**μοιχευομενη
8:5	16	**Μωσης ημιν
8:5	17	λιθοβολεισθαι
8:5	18	(περι αυτης)
8:6	19	**κατηγορειν
8:6	20	μη προσποιουμενος
8:7	21	ερωτωντες
8:7	22	ανακυψας
8:7	23	προς αυτους
8:7	24	**επ αυτην τον λιθον βαλετω
8:9	25	και υπο της συνειδησεως ελεγχομενοι
8:9	26	**(εως των εσχατων)
8:9	27	μονος ο Ιησους
8:10	28	και μηδενα θεασαμενος πλην της γυναικος
8:10	29	αυτη / αυτη γυναι
8:10	30	εκεινοι οι κατηγοροι σου
8:11	31	**ειπεν δε ο Ιησους
8:11	32	**κρινω / κατακρινω
8:11	33	και

Comment: Setting aside the splits in #1, 13, 14, 29, 32 there is a group of MSS with this profile. There is an equally large group that changes εγραφεν to κατεγραφεν in verse 6 and changes πρωτος to πρωτον in verse 7. Both of these groups have a core of MSS that have a 'perfect' profile, except that both groups split on -φωρω/-φορω. Both groups have 'fuzzy' edges with numerous MSS showing various degrees of variation. There is a large number of mixed MSS, clustering around several roughly defined mosaics. Also there is a three-way split in variant #24, plus a fourth lesser variant (205 MSS x 191 x 104 x 21). However, the variants with ** do distinguish **M**^{5} from both **M**^{6} and **M**^{7}, forming its 'backbone', although there is internal variation in three of them, besides #24. There is further internal variation not recorded in this list. **M**^{5} is not as 'squishy' as **M**^{6}, but not as solid as **M**^{7}. I take it that **M**^{5} reflects Latin influence. In any event, it looks to be scarcely possible to establish a single archetype for **M**^{5}, which it must have to be a viable candidate for the original form of the Text. Evidently the original form is the ultimate archetype.

Unambiguous M^7 (f^{35}) representatives = 245 MSS

a) Perfect match (core representatives)—**XI**: 35, 83, 547, 1435; **XII**: 510, 768, 1046, 1323, 1329, 1489, 1490, 2296, 2367, 2382; **XIII**: 128, 141, 147, 154, 167, 170, 204, 361, 553, 676, 685, 696, 757, 825, 897, 1072, 1251, 1339, 1400, 1461, 1496, 1499, 1550, 1551, 1576, 1694, 2284, 2479, 2510; **XIV**: 18, 55, 66, 201, 246, 363, 386, 402, 415, 480, 586, 645, 758, 763, 769, 781, 789, 797, 824, 845, 867, 928, 932, 938, 960, 986, 1023, 1075, 1092, 1111, 1117, 1119, 1133, 1146, 1189, 1236, 1328, 1390, 1482, 1488, 1492, 1493, 1548, 1560, 1572, 1584, 1600, 1619, 1620, 1628, 1633, 1637, 1650, 1659, 1667, 1688, 1698, 1703, 2261, 2355, 2407, 2454, 2503, 2765, 2767; **XV**: 955, 958, 962, 1003, 1180, 1250, 1508, 1625, 1636, 1648, 1686, 1713, 2131, 2554; **XVI**: 1596, 1652, 2496, 2636, 2806 = 127 MSS

b) Major subgroup: in 8:4 it has επαυτοφορω (only change)—**XII**: 660, 1145, 1224; **XIII**: 479, 689, 691, 940, 1334, 1487, 1501, 1601, 2584, 2598; **XIV**: 189, 290, 394, 521, 890, 959, 1025, 1165, 1234, 1445, 1462, 1476, 1543, 1559, 1614, 1618, 1622, 1634, 1657, 1658, 2309, 2399, 2466, 2621, 2689; **XV**: 285, 961, 1017, 1059, 1132, 1158, 1247, 1649, 1656, 2204, 2221, 2352, 2692; **XVI**: 1680, 1702, 2255; **XVII**: 1700 = 55 MSS

c) Minor subgroup: in 8:9 it has κατεληφθη (only change)—**XIII**: 155, 2520; **XIV**: 588, 1185; **XV**: 1617; **XVI**: 1088 = 6 MSS

d) Minor subgroup: in 8:7 it has τον λιθον βαλετω επ αυτην (only change)—**XII**: 1199; **XIV**: 953, 1020, 1147; **XV**: 1389 = 5 MSS

e) Other MSS with a single change—**XII**: 520, 1401, 2122, 2322; **XIII**: 2647; **XIV**: 1095, 1503, 2273, 2508; **XV**: 575, 2673; **XVI**: 1030; **XVII**: 2136, 2137, 2497 = 15 MSS

+2) MSS with two changes:
- b) + c)—**XII**: 1453, 2559; **XV**: 1131; **XVIII**: 1325
- b) + d)—**XII**: 387, 1813; **XIII**: 1552
- b) + e)—**XII**: 2260; **XIV**: 1599, 1638, 1544
- b) + odd—<u>X: 1166</u>; **XIV**: 952,978,1062; **XVI**: 1591,2714
- d) + e)—**XIII**: 1477,1497; **XIV**: 1181,1248; **XVI**: 2635
- + 2 odd—**XI**: 1314,1384; **XIV**: 2265; **XV**: 1116,1348

= 27 MSS

+3) MSS with three changes:
- b) + c) + odd—**XII**: 105; **XVI**: 2715
- b) + d) + e)—**XIV**: 806
- b) + d) + odd—**XII**: 353; **XIII**: 966
- b) + e) + odd—**XV**: 664
- b) + 2 odd—**XII**: 2632; **XV**: 56; **XVI**: 61
- + 3 odd—**XV**: 58

= 10 MS

Comment: b) and c) differ from a) only in a similar sounding vowel, while variants 8 and 14 involve a single letter. There is a small sub-group (with fuzzy edges) based on variants 17, 20, 29. There is a larger, fuzzier group that has variants 1, 16, 17, 28, 29 as sort of a basis, with 9, 19 on the fringes, and then further variation. There are 40-50 MSS with varying amounts of mixture added to an $\mathbf{M}^7$ base (adding these to the unambiguous ones and dividing by 1650 we come out with about 18%). Actually, I believe that $\mathbf{M}^7$ was the base from which the creators of $\mathbf{M}^5$ and $\mathbf{M}^6$ (and all other groups) departed.

Interpretative comment: The progressive 'purification' of the stream of transmission through the centuries (from a Byzantine priority perspective) has been recognized by all and sundry, their attempts at explaining the phenomenon generally reflecting their presuppositions. From my point of view the evident explanation is this: All camps recognize that the heaviest attacks against the purity of the Text took place during the second century. But 'the heartland of the Church', the Aegean area, by far the best qualified in every way to watch over the faithful transmission, simply refused to copy the aberrant forms. MSS containing such forms were not used (nor copied), so many survived physically for over a millennium. Less bad forms were used (copies were hard to come by) but progressively were not copied. Thus the surviving IX century uncials are fair, over 80% Byzantine, but not good enough to be copied and recycled (when the better MSS were put into minuscule form). Until the advent of a printed text, MSS were made to be used. Progressively only the best were used, and thus worn out, and copied. This process culminated in the XIV century, when the Ottoman shadow was advancing over Asia Minor, but the Byzantine empire still stood.

Please note the 'from a Byzantine priority perspective'. **Family 35 was copied faithfully from beginning to end**. For seventeen books I myself have a single perfect copy done in the 15th century (besides a variety of copies that are perfect for one or more books, from the 14th, 13th, 12th and 11th). For a copy done in the 15th to be perfect, <u>all of its 'ancestors' had to be perfect as well</u>. Please note that a perfect copy makes all the 'canons' of textual criticism irrelevant to any point subsequent to the creation of the archetype. But how can we know that a given copy is 'perfect'? The archetypal profile can be empirically established by comparing all the extant family representatives (I am referring to $\mathbf{f}^{35}$ only). A copy that matches the archetype perfectly is a perfect copy, of necessity. But perfect copies tell us something important about the attitude of the copyists. That they should do their work with such care presumably indicates at least respect, if not reverence toward what they were copying—they believed they were copying God's Word. **Since MSS from all other lines of transmission were copied with less care, presumably the copyists made a distinction in their minds, evidently considering f^{35} to be the best line.**

When Is a 'Recension'?

"The Syrian text must in fact be the result of a 'recension' in the proper sense of the word, a work of attempted criticism, performed deliberately by editors and not merely by scribes."[1] It is not my wont to appeal to Fenton John Anthony Hort, but his understanding of 'recension' is presumably correct. A recension is produced by a certain somebody (or group) at a certain time in a certain place. If someone wishes to posit or allege a recension, and do so responsibly, he needs to indicate the source and supply some evidence.[2]

Are there any recensions among the MSS that contain the Catholic Epistles? I will base my response on the collations presented in *Text und Textwert* (*TuT*).[3] They collated about 555 MSS, some 30 of which are fragmentary; this represents around 85% of the total of extant MSS. I will use Colwell's requirement of 70% agreement in order for MSS to be classified in the same text-type (although for myself I require at least 80%). Since *TuT* presents 98 variant sets, spread over the seven epistles, we have a corpus that presumably is reasonably representative. Although the *Institut* has never divulged the criteria by which they chose the sets, so far as I know, the chosen sets are significant (not trivial).

An Alexandrian Recension?

Is there an Egyptian or Alexandrian recension, or text-type? *TuT* follows the 'standard' text, which it calls LESART 2. No single MS has this profile. The closest is Codex B, that diverges from it 13 times out of 98, three being sub-variants and four being singulars (including two of the sub-variants)—the agreement is 86.7% [ignoring the sub-variants it is 89.8%]. Next is cursive 1739 that diverges 29 times out of 98, four being sub-variants and no singulars—the agreement is 70.4% [ignoring the sub-variants it is 74.5%]. Next is P^{74} [7th century] that diverges 3 times out of 10, one being a sub-variant and one being a singular—the agreement is

---

1 B.F. Westcott and F.J.A. Hort, *The New Testament in the Original Greek* (2 vols.; London: Macmillan and Co., 1881), *Introduction*, p. 133.

2 Hort did suggest Lucian of Antioch as the prime mover—a suggestion both gratuitous and frivolous, since he had not really looked at the evidence available at that time. (Were he to repeat the suggestion today, it would be patently ridiculous.)

3 *Text und Textwert der Griechischen Handschriften des Neuen Testaments* (Ed. Kurt Aland, Berlin: Walter de Gruyter, 1987), volumes 9 and 11.

70% [ignoring the sub-variant it is 80%]. Next is Codex A that diverges 34 times out of 98, four being sub-variants and no singulars—the agreement is 65.3% [ignoring the sub-variants it is 69.4%]. Next is Codex C that diverges 24 times out of 66, one being a sub-variant and four being singulars—the agreement is 63.6% [ignoring the sub-variant it is 65.2%]. Next is cursive 1852 that diverges 36 times out of 95, two being sub-variants and no singulars—the agreement is 62.1% [ignoring the sub-variants it is 64.2%]. Next is Codex א that diverges 40 times out of 98, seven being sub-variants and nine being singulars (including four of the sub-variants)—the agreement is 59.2% [ignoring the sub-variants it is 66.3%]. Next is Codex 044 [a. 800] that diverges 40 times out of 97, four being sub-variants and seven being singulars (including three of the sub-variants)—the agreement is 59% [ignoring the sub-variants it is 62.9%]. Next is Codex 048 [5th century] that diverges 8 times out of 18, one being a sub-variant and no singulars—the agreement is 55.6% [ignoring the sub-variant it is 61.1%]. Not next is P^{72} that diverges 18 times out of 38, six being sub-variants and nine being singulars (including three of the sub-variants)—the agreement is 52.6% [ignoring the sub-variants it is 68.4%]. Codex B is clearly the most important MS in Aland's scheme of things; and the 'standard' text is a composite.

But is there an Egyptian text-type here? Well, **B** and **א** disagree in 44 out of 98 sets, so their agreement is 55.1%. **B** and **A** disagree in 43 out of 98 sets, so their agreement is 56.1%. **B** and **P^{72}** disagree in 19 out of 38 sets, so their agreement is 50%. **B** and **C** disagree in 27 out of 66 sets, so their agreement is 59.1%. **B** and **P^{74}** disagree in 5 out of 10 sets, so their agreement is 50%. **B** and **1739** disagree in 37 out of 98 sets, so their agreement is 62.2%. **A** and **א** disagree in 35 out of 98 sets, so their agreement is 64.3%. **A** and **P^{72}** disagree in 24 out of 38 sets, so their agreement is 36.8%. **A** and **C** disagree in 26 out of 66 sets, so their agreement is 60.6%. **A** and **P^{74}** disagree in 4 out of 10 sets, so their agreement is 60%. **A** and **1739** disagree in 36 out of 98 sets, so their agreement is 63.3%. **א** and **P^{72}** disagree in 26 out of 38 sets, so their agreement is 31.6%. **א** and **C** disagree in 30 out of 66 sets, so their agreement is 54.5%. **א** and **P^{74}** disagree in 5 out of 10 sets, so their agreement is 50%. **א** and **1739** disagree in 46 out of 98 sets, so their agreement is 53.1%. **C** and **P^{72}** disagree in 18 out of 31 sets, so their agreement is 41.9%. **C** and **P^{74}** disagree in 3 out of 7 sets, so their agreement is 57.1%. **C** and **1739** disagree in 23 out of 66 sets, so their agreement is 65.2%. **1739** and **P^{72}** disagree in 22 out of 38 sets, so their agreement is 42.1%. **1739** and **P^{74}** disagree in 3 out of 7 sets, so their agreement is 57.1%. Based on this evidence Colwell would not allow us to claim a text-type. The early MSS evidently suffered a common influence, but each wandered off on a private path. No two sets have the same roster of disagreements. They each are certainly independent in their own generation. The common influence observable in the early MSS must have had a source, but that source is really too shadowy to qualify as a recension.

A Byzantine Recension?

LESART 1 is a majority text in the strictest sense. Aland followed the majority reading in every case, except for two variant sets where there is no majority variant and there he followed the plurality (set 32, 1 Peter 3:16—καταλαλωσιν has 49.8%, against καταλαλουσιν with 44.6%) (set 34, 1 Peter 4:3—ημιν has 47.1%, against υμιν with 41.7%). As a byproduct of that procedure no single MS has that precise profile—I found four MSS that come within two variants (607, 639, 1730, 2423) and five that miss by three. The basic **f**[35] profile diverges by five.

Having analyzed the profiles for the ± 555 MSS, apart from **f**[35] I found precisely one cluster of four MSS (82, 699, 1668, 2484), with a few hangers-on, and one cluster of three MSS (390, 912, 1594), also with a few hangers-on, and nine pairs—all the rest have private profiles (including the 'hangers-on').

Within **f**[35] 31 MSS have the basic profile; there is a sub-group of 6 MSS, another of 4, another of 3, plus two pairs—these 17 MSS, plus another 10, differ from the basic profile in only one variant. There are 15 MSS that differ by two and 7 by three, making a total of 80 MSS (32 of which have private profiles), plus a few others on the fringes.

Setting aside all the MSS with a shared profile, plus about 30 that have less than 11% of the total, we are left with around 450 MSS that have a private profile (based on the 98 variant sets), the heavy majority of which are Byzantine. We are looking at a normal transmission; no mass production of a single exemplar.

Setting aside the fragmentary MSS, there are about 40 that fall below Colwell's 70% threshold; all the rest (± 485) would qualify as members of one text-type, which we may call Byzantine. Using my 80% threshold we lose another 17 MSS, leaving ± 470. But I would really rather have 90%, and with that threshold we lose another 46—call it ± 420 MSS. Setting aside the 30 fragmentaries, dividing 420 by 525 we have 80% of the MSS that are strongly Byzantine[1] (using the 80% threshold gives almost 90%)

---

[1] For a 95% threshold we lose another 35 MSS; 385 ÷ 525 gives 73%. 75% of the MSS

[using the 70% threshold gives 92%]. 345 of the 420 have private profiles—with the possible exception of **f**[35] there was no 'stuffing the ballot box'.

Although **f**[35] obviously falls within the Byzantine stream, I will factor it out and treat it separately. 420 less 80 equals 340 strongly Byzantine MSS, only 25 of which share a profile. We obviously have a text-type, but is it a recension? To posit a recension we need a source—who did it, when and where? And using what? Did he merely edit existing materials or did he invent some of the variants? If he invented, is there an observable pattern to explain his attitude?

We have 315 strongly Byzantine MSS (without **f**[35]) with private profiles—they are independent in their own generation, presumably representing as many exemplars, also presumably independent in their own generation, etc. Which is at least partly why scholars from Hort to Aland have recognized that any Byzantine 'recension' could not have been created later than the 4th century.

As a preliminary to taking up the question of **f**[35] (**K**[r]) as possibly a recension, I wish to consider other aspects of the general evidence presented in *TuT*. Of the MSS that were collated, 78 are dated. There are nine pairs of MSS with the same date (but no more than two MSS to a year—so 60 have a private year); in eight of them the two MSS are quite different in profile; in the ninth pair both MSS are **f**[35] but differ in one variant. Both are at Mt. Athos, but in different monasteries—it is highly improbable that they had the same exemplar. There is no evidence here of mass production. But why would a monk on Mt. Athos produce a copy in 1280 AD? <u>If the copy is still there</u>, it was not to fill an order from the city. So why did he do it, as a religious exercise or duty? But what would he copy? It seems to me most likely that he would copy an aged exemplar that was showing signs of wear, to preserve its text. I will demonstrate below that the MSS produced in a single monastery were based on distinct exemplars (as Lake, Blake and New indicated some 85 years ago).[1]

Mt. Athos

I have heard it said that the MSS at Mt. Athos are under suspicion of having been mass produced, and of being made to conform to an arbitrary standard. I suspect that the speaker was not aware that there are a number

---

reflect a very strong consensus, and yet most have private profiles.

1 K. Lake, R.P. Blake and Silva New, "The Caesarean Text of the Gospel of Mark", *Harvard Theological Review*, XXI (1928), 348-49.

of distinct monasteries in that area. *TuT* lists a mere twenty.[1] Recall that these monasteries represented different patriarchates, orders, countries and even languages. An average small city in the U.S. will likely have an Assembly of God, a Baptist church, a Bible church, a Congregational church, an Episcopal church, a Methodist church, a Presbyterian church, some kind of neo-pentecostal church, among others. How do they relate to each other? To what extent do they join forces? Even a citywide evangelistic campaign will not get them all together. Were monks in the Byzantine empire any different than pastors in the U.S.? Has human nature changed? The point I am making is that there was probably very little comparing of notes between monasteries on a subject like copying MSS.

Consider: Grigoriu, Pavlu and Protatu are listed with one MS each (for the Catholic Epistles),[2] none of which are **f**^{35}. Karakallu and Kavsokalyvion are listed with one each that is **f**^{35}. Konstamonitu, Philotheu and Stavronikita are listed with two MSS, one **f**^{35} and one not. Xiropotamu has two MSS, neither being **f**^{35}. Pantokratoros has three, one of which is **f**^{35}. Dochiariu has five MSS, none being **f**^{35}. Esphigmenu also has five, one being **f**^{35}. Panteleimonos is listed with seven MSS, two being **f**^{35}. Dionysiu is listed with nine MSS, three being **f**^{35}. Kutlumusiu is listed with ten MSS, two being **f**^{35}. Iviron is listed with twelve MSS, five being **f**^{35}. Vatopediu is listed with 28 MSS, five being **f**^{35}. M Lavras is listed with 52 MSS, 22 being **f**^{35}. With the possible exception of M Lavras, there was evidently no **f**^{35} 'steamroller' at work.

But what about within a single monastery? Although MSS presently located at places like London or Paris were presumably produced elsewhere, those located at places like Mt. Athos, Patmos, Jerusalem and Sinai were probably produced right there. The monastery at Mt. Sinai is sufficiently isolated that we might expect that a good deal of 'inbreeding' took place. So let's take a look at the Sinai MSS listed by *TuT*.

Mt. Sinai

I will list the MSS in a descending order of 'Alexandrishness',[3] with the proviso that such an ordering is only relevant for the first seven or eight:[4]

---

[1] I personally visited the Mt. Athos peninsula in 2014, and can guarantee that there are twenty independent monasteries, plus a number of subordinate ones.

[2] *TuT* lists a MS each for Andreas and Dimitriu, but did not collate them. Esphigmenu has an added three MSS that were not collated.

[3] I consider a high 'erraticity' quotient to be a defining feature of 'Alexandrishness'.

[4] *TuT* includes two 6th century uncial fragments: 0285 has one reading (of the 98) and 0296 has two. Such a scant basis only allows us to guess that they are not Byzantine.

1. ℵ,01[1]– IV, eapr (2 = 57 [2 subs],[2] 1/2 = 5 [1 sub], 1 = 19 [3 subs], sing = 9, odd = 8) = 98 variants;
2. 1243 – XI, eap (2 = 51, 1/2 = 6, 1 = 22 [5 subs], sing = 2, odd = 16) = 97;
3. 1241 – XII, eap (2 = 47 [5 subs], 1/2 = 4, 1 = 17 [2 subs], sing = 5, odd = 18) = 91;
4. 1881 – XIV, ap (2 = 42 [3 subs], 1/2 = 3 [1 sub], 1 = 16 [1 sub], sing = 1, odd = 11) = 73;
5. 2495 – XIV, eapr (2 = 37 [2 subs], 1/2 = 4, 1 = 37 [4 subs], sing = 2, odd = 17) = 97;
6. 2492 – XIII, eap (2 = 17 [2 subs], 1/2 = 8, 1 = 58 [2 subs], sing = 1, odd = 9) = 93;
7. 2494 – 1316, eapr (2 = 11, 1/2 = 4, 1 = 73 [2 subs], odd = 10) = 98;

   From here on down all the MSS fall within the Byzantine stream.

8. 1874 – X, ap (2 = 4, 1/2 = 9, 1 = 78 [2 subs], sing = 1, odd = 6) = 98;
9. 1877 – XIV, ap (2 = 2, 1/2 = 9, 1 = 81 [5 subs], sing = 2, odd = 4) = 98;
10. 2086 – XIV, ap (2 = 2, 1/2 = 8, 1 = 82 [2 subs], sing = 1, odd = 5) = 98;
11. 1251 – XIII, eap (2 = 2, 1/2 = 9, 1 = 82 [3 subs], odd = 4) = 97;
12. 1245 – XII, ap (2 = 3, 1/2 = 10 [1 sub], 1 = 83 [6 subs], odd = 2) = 98;
13. 1240 – XII, eap (2 = 1, 1/2 = 7, 1 = 82 [7 subs], odd = 4) = 94;
14. 2356 – XIV, eap (2 = 1, 1/2 = 9, 1 = 76 [2 subs], odd = 4) = 90;
15. 1880 – X, ap (2 = 2, 1/2 = 10, 1 = 84 [5 subs], odd = 2) = 98;
16. 2502 – 1242, eap (2 = 1, 1/2 = 9, 1 = 73 [6 subs], odd = 2) = 85;
17. 1242 – XIII, eap (2 = 1, 1/2 = 9, 1 = 86 [4 subs], odd = 2) = 98;

---

[1] Of course Aleph is presently located in London, but it became extant in Sinai; to this day the monks at St. Catharine's refer to Tischendorf as 'the thief'.

[2] 'subs' stands for sub-variants, which are included in the larger number. Where a 'sub' is also a singular I list it only as a singular—each variant is counted only once.

18. 1250 – XV, eap (2 = 1, 1/2 = 10, 1 = 77 [3 subs], odd = 3) = 91; [**f**^{35} ± 2]

19. 1247 – XV, eap (2 = 1, 1/2 = 10, 1 = 81 [3 subs], odd = 3) = 95; [**f**^{35} ± 2]

20. 1876 – XV, apr (2 = 1, 1/2 = 11, 1 = 83 [3 subs], odd = 3) = 98; [**f**^{35} ± 2]

21. 1249 – 1324, ap (2 = 1, 1/2 = 10, 1 = 84 [3 subs], odd = 2) = 97; [**f**^{35} ± 1]

22. 1248 – XIV, eap (2 = 1, 1/2 = 11, 1 = 84 [3 subs], sing = 1, odd = 1) = 98; [**f**^{35} ± 1]

23. 2501 – XVI, ap (2 = 1, 1/2 = 11, 1 = 83 [5 subs], odd = 1) = 96; [**f**^{35} ± 4]

24. 2085 – 1308, ap (2 = 0, 1/2 = 11, 1 = 84 [3 subs], sing = 1, odd = 2) = 98;

25. 1244 – XI, ap (2 = 0, 1/2 = 10, 1 = 85 [3 subs], odd = 2) = 97;

26. 2799 – XIV, ap (2 = 0, 1/2 = 3, 1 = 28 [2 subs], sing = 1, odd = 1) = 33.[1]

Absolutely no two MSS are identical; even the six **f**^{35} MSS all differ by at least one variant. The rest of the Byzantine MSS are all distinct, some really so,[2] yet all clearly fall within the Byzantine tradition.[3] These 26 MSS represent as many exemplars; there was no 'inbreeding', no stuffing the ballot box; each copyist tried to reproduce what was in front of him, regardless of the type of text. Since the MSS were still there in 1800, they were not made to fill an order from elsewhere. Given its isolation, some

---

1 The last three MSS have very different profiles.

2 Notice that no MS scores a perfect 87 for LESART 1, and only four score a perfect 11 for LESART 1/2.

3 Remember that we are only looking at 98 variant sets—if we had complete collations for the seven books it is almost certain that no two MSS would be identical (from all sources); perhaps for a single book, the smaller the better, a few might be found. [I wrote the above in 2004, when I was just beginning to really pay attention to **f**^{35}—in fact, <u>within that family</u>, considering only the MSS that I myself have collated, we can say the following: I have in my possession copies of thirty identical MSS for both 2 and 3 John (not identical lists), twenty-nine for Philemon, twenty-two for Jude, fifteen for 2 Thessalonians, nine for Titus, six each for Galatians, Colossians and 1 Thessalonians, five each for Philippians and 2 Peter, four each for Ephesians, James and 1 John, three each for 2 Timothy and 1 Peter, and two each for Romans and 1 Timothy. It is not the same selection of MSS in each case, and they come from all over.] Apart from **f**^{35} I would still be surprised to find identical copies of any book with over 3 chapters.

of the ancestors of the 26 extant MSS may well have been brought to the monastery before the Islamic conquest.

The profiles of the first five MSS in the above list are **very** different, distinct from each other; none is a copy of א, which I find to be curious. Evidently א was not copied—why?[1]

Megistis Lavras

Well, ok, but what about M Lavras? Isn't the disproportionate percentage of **f**[35] MSS suspicious? To find out we must do for M Lavras what we did for Sinai, which will be twice as much work (52 X 26). Again, I will list the MSS in a descending order of 'Alexandrishness', with the proviso that such an ordering is only relevant for the first nine or ten:

1. 1739 – X, ap (2 = 66 [4 subs], 1/2 = 7, 1 = 12 [2 subs], odd = 13) = 98;
2. 044 – VIII, ap (2 = 52 [1 sub], 1/2 = 7, 1 = 20, sing = 7, odd = 11) = 97;
3. 1735 – XI, ap (2 = 43 [2 subs], 1/2 = 7 [1 sub], 1 = 35 [2 subs], sing = 1, odd = 12) = 98;
4. 1505 – XII, eap (2 = 41 [3 subs], 1/2 = 4, 1 = 35 [3 subs], odd = 18) = 98;
5. 1448 – XI, eap (2 = 23, 1/2 = 7 [1 sub], 1 = 58 [2 subs], sing = 1, odd = 8) = 97;
6. 1490 – XII, eap (2 = 13, 1/2 = 7 [1 sub], 1 = 69 [4 subs], odd = 9) = 98;
7. 1751 – 1479, ap (2 = 7 [1 sub], 1/2 = 11 [1 sub], 1 = 69 [3 subs], sing = 5, odd = 6) = 98;
8. 1501 – XIII, eap (2 = 8 [1 sub], 1/2 = 8, 1 = 73 [1 sub], sing = 1, odd = 8) = 98;
9. 1661 – XV, eap (2 = 6, 1/2 = 9 [1 sub], 1 = 73 [5 subs], sing = 3, odd = 7) = 98;

From here on down all the MSS fall within the Byzantine stream.

10. 1609 – XIV, eap (2 = 9 [1 sub], 1/2 = 9, 1 = 76 [4 subs], odd = 3) =

---

[1] But over ten people did try to correct it, down through the centuries, so they knew it was there. 1243 and 1241 are almost as bad, and they were produced in the 11th and 12th centuries, respectively.

97;

11. 1646 – 1172, eap (2 = 3, 1/2 = 10, 1 = 77 [6 subs], sing = 5, odd = 3) = 98;
12. 1509 – XIII, eap (2 = 3, 1/2 = 9, 1 = 77 [5 subs], sing = 3, odd = 5) = 97;
13. 1744 – XIV, ap (2 = 2, 1/2 = 8, 1 = 81 [2 subs], sing = 2, odd = 5) = 98;
14. 1643 – XIV, eap (2 = 3, 1/2 = 7, 1 = 82 [3 subs], odd = 6) = 98;
15. 1626 – XV, eapr (2 = 2, 1/2 = 9, 1 = 81 [6 subs], sing = 1, odd = 5) = 98;
16. 1743 – XII, ap (2 = 1, 1/2 = 7 [1 sub], 1 = 83 [2 subs], odd = 7) = 98;
17. 1622 – XIV, eap (2 = 4, 1/2 = 10, 1 = 81 [4 subs], odd = 3) = 98;
18. 2194 – 1118, ap (2 = 2, 1/2 = 8, 1 = 83 [2 subs], odd = 5) = 98;
19. 1495 – XIV, eap (2 = 4, 1/2 = 10, 1 = 82 [5 subs], odd = 2) = 98;
20. 1642 – 1278, eap (2 = 1, 1/2 = 10, 1 = 82 [6 subs], sing = 1, odd = 3) = 97;
21. 1738 – XI, ap (2 = 2, 1/2 = 10, 1 = 82 [8 subs], odd = 3) = 97;
22. 1649 – XV, eap (2 = 2, 1/2 = 9, 1 = 84 [5 subs], odd = 3) = 98;
23. 1734 – 1015, apr (2 = 1, 1/2 = 9, 1 = 82 [1 sub], odd = 4) = 96;
24. 049 – IX, ap (2 = 1 [1 sub], 1/2 = 9, 1 = 84 [4 subs], odd = 3) = 97;
25. 1741 – XIV, ap (2 = 0, 1/2 = 7 [1 sub], 1 = 87 [4 subs], odd = 4) = 98;
26. 1456 – XIII, eap (2 = 0, 1/2 = 8 [1 sub], 1 = 69 [2 subs], odd = 4) = 81;
27. 1747 – XIV, ap (2 = 1, 1/2 = 9, 1 = 84 [6 subs], odd = 2) = 96;
28. 1736 – XIII, ap (2 = 1, 1/2 = 10, 1 = 83 [4 subs], odd = 2) = 96;
29. 2511 – XIV, eap (2 = 1, 1/2 = 10 [1 sub], 1 = 76 [I sub], odd = 2) = 89;
30. 1750 – XV, ap (2 = 0, 1/2 = 9, 1 = 87 [3 subs], odd = 2) = 98;
31. 1733 – XIV, apr (2 = 1, 1/2 = 11, 1 = 83 [3 subs], odd = 3) = 98; [**f^{35}** ± 2] (16, 91)

32. 1732 – 1384, apr (2 = 2, 1/2 = 11 [1 sub], 1 = 83 [3 subs], odd = 1) = 97; [$\mathbf{f}^{35}$ ± 2] (1, 72)

33. 1508 – XV, eap (2 = 1, 1/2 = 10, 1 = 85 [4 subs], odd = 2) = 98; [$\mathbf{f}^{35}$ ± 2] (21, 65)

34. 1482 – 1304, eap (2 = 1, 1/2 = 10, 1 = 85 [2 subs], odd = 2) = 98; [$\mathbf{f}^{35}$ ± 2] (45, 65)

35. 1656 – XV, eap (2 = 1, 1/2 = 11, 1 = 84 [2 subs], odd = 2) = 98; [$\mathbf{f}^{35}$ ± 2] (8, 45)

36. 1748 – 1662, ap (2 = 1, 1/2 = 11, 1 = 85 [4 subs], odd = 1) = 98; [$\mathbf{f}^{35}$ ± 2] (32, 62)

37. 1737 – XII, ap (2 = 1, 1/2 = 11, 1 = 85 [3 subs], odd = 1) = 98; [$\mathbf{f}^{35}$ ± 2] (32, 77)

38. 1749 – XVI, ap (2 = 2, 1/2 = 11, 1 = 78 [3 subs], odd = 1) = 92; [$\mathbf{f}^{35}$ ± 1] (29)

39. 1637 – 1328, eapr (2 = 2, 1/2 = 11, 1 = 84 [3 subs], odd = 1) = 98; [$\mathbf{f}^{35}$ ± 1] (17)

40. 1740 – XIII, apr (2 = 1, 1/2 = 11, 1 = 85 [4 subs], odd = 1) = 98; [$\mathbf{f}^{35}$ ± 1] (39)

41. 1617 – XV, eapr (2 = 1, 1/2 = 11, 1 = 85 [4 subs], odd = 1) = 98; [$\mathbf{f}^{35}$ ± 1] (21)

42. 1618 – 1568, eap (2 = 1, 1/2 = 11, 1 = 85 [2 subs], odd = 1) = 98; [$\mathbf{f}^{35}$ ± 1] (32)

43. 1072 – XIII, eapr (2 = 1, 1/2 – 11, 1= 85 [3 subs], odd = 1) = 98; [$\mathbf{f}^{35}$ ± 0]

44. 1075 – XIV, eapr (2 = 1, 1/2 = 11, 1= 85 [3 subs], odd = 1) = 98; [$\mathbf{f}^{35}$ ± 0]

45. 1503 – 1317, eapr (2 = 1, 1/2 = 11, 1= 85 [3 subs], odd = 1) = 98; [$\mathbf{f}^{35}$ ± 0]

46. 1619 – XIV, ea(p) (2 = 1, 1/2 = 11, 1= 85 [3 subs], odd = 1) = 98; [$\mathbf{f}^{35}$ ± 0]

47. 1628 – 1400, eap (2 = 1, 1/2 = 11, 1= 85 [3 subs], odd = 1) = 98; [$\mathbf{f}^{35}$ ± 0]

48. 1636 – XV, eap (2 = 1, 1/2 = 11, 1= 85 [3 subs], odd = 1) = 98; [$\mathbf{f}^{35}$

± 0]

49. 1745 – XV, apr (2 = 1, 1/2 = 11, 1= 85 [3 subs], odd = 1) = 98; [**f**^{35} ± 0]

50. 1746 – XIV, apr (2 = 1, 1/2 = 11, 1= 85 [3 subs], odd = 1) = 98; [**f**^{35} ± 0]

51. 1652 – XVI, eap (2 = 1, 1/2 = 3, 1= 21) = 25; [**f**^{35} frag]

52. 1742 – XIII, ap (2 = 1, 1/2 = 11, 1= 85 [3 subs]) = 97; [**f**^{35} ± 5]

Again, setting aside the **f**^{35} MSS for the moment, absolutely no two MSS are identical. The rest of the Byzantine MSS are all distinct, some really so, yet all clearly fall within the Byzantine tradition. These 30 MSS represent as many exemplars; there was no 'inbreeding', no stuffing the ballot box; each copyist tried to reproduce what was in front of him, regardless of the quality of text. Since the MSS were still there in 1800, they were not made to fill an order from elsewhere.

Also, where did the monasteries get the parchment for their ongoing production of MSS? Did they have money to go out and buy from tanneries? It seems to me more probable that they made their own from the skins of the sheep and goats that they ate. In such an event it could easily take several years to get enough for a single New Testament. The problem of finding enough parchment mitigates against the mass production of copies at any time in the vellum era. Three of the dated MSS at Sinai are eight years apart (1308, 1316, 1324)—might it have taken that long to gather enough vellum?

Now let's consider the **f**^{35} group. Seven are **f**^{35} ± 2, but no two of them have an identical profile—I have put the deviant variants within ( ) at the end of the line, so the reader can check that at a glance. Five are **f**^{35} ± 1, but no two of them have an identical profile either, as the reader can see at a glance. So these twelve MSS must also have been copied from as many exemplars—we now have 44 MSS that were copied from distinct exemplars. Ah, but there are eight MSS with a perfect **f**^{35} profile; what of them? Well, let's start with the contents: three contain **eapr**, three contain **eap**, two contain **apr**—at the very least, these three groups must represent distinct exemplars. So now we are down to a maximum of five MSS that might not represent a distinct exemplar. Setting aside preconceived ideas, what objective basis could anyone have for affirming that these five were not copied on the same principle as the rest, namely to preserve the text of the exemplar? It seems to me only fair to understand that the 52 extant MSS at M Lavras represent as many distinct exemplars.[1]

An f^{35} (K^r) Recension?

Since **f**^{35} is the only group of consequence, with a significant number of MSS, with an empirically defined profile, we can determine its archetypal text with certainty—we have the most cohesive of all text-types. But is it a 'recension'? Von Soden claimed that it was, assigning it to the 12th century; I am not aware that he named a source, but if he did he was wrong. Minuscule 35, along with other 11th century MSS, belongs to this group—their exemplars were presumably 10th century or earlier. I have demonstrated elsewhere[2] that **f**^{35} (**K**^{r}) is independent of **K**^{x}, throughout the NT—if it is independent it cannot have been based upon **K**^{x}. Repeatedly **f**^{35} has overt early attestation, against **K**^{x}, but there is no pattern to the alignments, they are haphazard. It is supported (against K^x) by P^{45,46,47,66,75},א, A, B, C, D, W, lat, syr, cop—sometimes just by one, sometimes by two, three, four or more of them, but in constantly shifting patterns. If there is no pattern then there is no dependency; **f**^{35} has ancient readings because it itself is ancient.

Returning to *TuT* and the Catholic Epistles, I will list the present location of **f**^{35} MSS by century:

XI — Paris, Trikala, Vatican;
XII — Athos (Kutlumusiu, M Lavras, Panteleimonos, Stavronikita, Vatopediu), Jerusalem;
XIII — Athens, Athos (Iviron, Konstamonitu, M Lavras, Pantokratoros, Philotheu), Bologna, Kalavryta, Leiden, Vatican;
XIV — Athens, Athos (Dionysiu, Esphigmenu, Iviron, Karakally, Kavsokalyvion, M Lavras, Vatopediu), Grottaferrata, Jerusalem, Karditsa, London, Ochrida, Paris, Patmos, Rome, Sinai, Vatican;
XV — Athens, Athos (Iviron, M Lavras), Bucharest, London, Meteora, Sinai, Sparta, Vatican, Venedig, Zittau;

---

1 I remind the reader again that we are only looking at 98 variant sets—if we had complete collations for the seven books it is almost certain that no two MSS would be identical (for the seven books; I have identical copies for a single book). With full collations these five will doubtless prove to be distinct as well. [Having now collated 43 Family 35 MSS for the seven general epistles, I have two that are perfect for all seven books, and four of the exemplars may have been so—they come from different locales.]

2 See "The Dating of K^r (alias **f**^{35}, nee f^{18}) Revisited", above. (See also "Concerning the Text of the *Pericope Adulterae*" in Part II.)

XVI— Athens, Athos (Iviron, Kuthumusiu, M Lavras), Lesbos, Sinai;
XVII— Athos (Dionysiu, M Lavras).

Manuscripts at Vatican, Grottaferrata, Jerusalem, Patmos, Sinai, Athos, Trikala, Meteora, Lesbos, at least, are most probably based on a line of ancestors held locally; any importing of exemplars probably took place in the early centuries. If there are **f^{35}** MSS in those places today, it is presumably because there have been **f^{35}** MSS there from the beginning.

I reject as totally unfounded the allegation that **f^{35}** is a recension. If anyone wishes to claim that it is, I request that they state who did it, when and where, and that they furnish evidence in support of the claim. Without evidence any such claim is frivolous and irresponsible.

Archetype in the General Epistles—f^{35} yes, K^x no

If you want to be a candidate for the best plumber in town, you need to be a plumber; the best lawyer, you need to be a lawyer; the best oncologist, you need to be an oncologist; and so on. Similarly, if you want to be a candidate for Autograph archetype, you need to be an archetype; a real, honest to goodness, objectively verifiable archetype. This section addresses the following question: are there any objectively identifiable archetypes in the General Epistles?

I invite attention to the following evidence taken from my critical apparatus of those books. I will take the books one at a time. The reading of **f^{35}** will always be the first one, and the complete roster defines that family's archetype.[1]

James

1:05 ουκ **f^{35}** (70.3%) || μη ℵA,B,C (29.7%); ?[no **K^x**][2]
1:23 νομου **f^{35}** [30%] || λογου ℵA,B,C [69%] || λογων [1%];
1:26 αλλ **f^{35}** [35%] || αλλα ℵA,B,C,0173 [65%];
2:03 λαμπραν εσθητα **f^{35}** [30%] || εσθητα την λαμπραν ℵA,B,C [70%];
2:04 ου **f^{35}** ℵA,C (26.8%) || και ου (72.2%) || και (0.6%) || --- B (0.4%);
2:08 σεαυτον **f^{35}** ℵA(B)C [50%] || εαυτον [50%]; [no **K^x**]

---

[1] Setting aside singular readings, over 50% of the words in the Text will have 100% attestation; 80% of the words will have over 95% attestation; 90% of the words will have over 90% attestation; only for some 2% of the words will the attestation fall below 80%. I regard **f^{35}** as the base from which all other streams of transmission departed, to one extent or another, so in general the Byzantine bulk will have stayed with **f^{35}**. It follows that the roster only includes cases where there is a serious split in the Byzantine bulk, or where **f^{35}** is alone (or almost so) against that bulk.

[2] For the purposes of this section I use **K^x** to represent the Byzantine bulk.

2:13	ανηλεος $\mathbf{f^{35}}$ [20%] ‖ ανελεος ℵA,B,C [30%] ‖ ανιλεως [50%];	[no $\mathbf{K^x}$]
2:14	λεγη τις $\mathbf{f^{35}}$ ℵB [70%] ‖ ~ 21 A,C [1%] ‖ λεγει τις [28%];	?[no $\mathbf{K^x}$]
2:14	εχει $\mathbf{f^{35}}$ [46%] ‖ εχη ℵA,B,C [47%] ‖ εχειν [4.5%] ‖ σχη [2.5%];	[no $\mathbf{K^x}$]
3:02	δυναμενος $\mathbf{f^{35}}$ ℵ [23%] ‖ δυνατος A,B [76.5%];	
3:03	ιδε $\mathbf{f^{35}}$ [60%] ‖ ει δε [38.5%] ‖ ιδου [0.5%];[1]	[no $\mathbf{K^x}$]
3:04	ανεμων σκληρων $\mathbf{f^{35}}$ ℵB,C [44%] ‖ ~ 21 A [56%];	?[no $\mathbf{K^x}$]
3:04	ιθυνοντος $\mathbf{f^{35}}$ [21%] ‖ ευθυνοντος ℵA,B,C [79%];	
3:18	δε $\mathbf{f^{35}}$ A,B,C [56.6%] ‖ δε της [42%] ‖ δε ο ℵ [0.4%] ‖ --- [1%];	[no $\mathbf{K^x}$]
4:02	ουκ εχετε $\mathbf{f^{35}}$ P^{100}A,B [64%] ‖ και 12 ℵ [35%] ‖ 12 δε [1%];	[no $\mathbf{K^x}$]
4:04	ουν $\mathbf{f^{35}}$ ℵA,B [58%] ‖ --- [42%];	[no $\mathbf{K^x}$]
4:07	αντιστητε $\mathbf{f^{35}}$ [47.5%] ‖ 1 δε ℵA,B [50%] ‖ 1 ουν [2.5%];	[no $\mathbf{K^x}$]
4:11	γαρ $\mathbf{f^{35}}$ [26%] ‖ --- ℵA,B [74%];	
4:12	και κριτης $\mathbf{f^{35}}$ ℵA,B [62%] ‖ --- [38%];	[no $\mathbf{K^x}$]
4:14	ημων $\mathbf{f^{35}}$ [26%] ‖ υμων (P^{100})ℵA(B) [74%]	
4:14	εστιν $\mathbf{f^{35}}$ [52%] ‖ εσται (A) [41%] ‖ εστε B [7%] ‖ --- ℵ;	[no $\mathbf{K^x}$]
4:14	επειτα $\mathbf{f^{35}}$ [29.5%] ‖ 1 δε και [46%] ‖ 1 δε [15%] ‖ 1 και ℵA,B [9.5%];	[no $\mathbf{K^x}$]
5:07	αν $\mathbf{f^{35}}$ ℵ [53%] ‖ --- A,B,048 [45.5%] ‖ ου [1.5%];	[no $\mathbf{K^x}$]
5:10	αδελφοι $\mathbf{f^{35}}$ (A)B [35%] ‖ αδελφοι μου (ℵ) [62%] ‖ --- [3%];	
5:10	εν τω $\mathbf{f^{35}}$ B [40%] ‖ τω A [58%] ‖ εν ℵ [0.6%] ‖ επι τω [1.4%];	
5:11	ειδετε $\mathbf{f^{35}}$ ℵB [53%] ‖ ιδετε A [45%];	[no $\mathbf{K^x}$]
5:11	πολυσπλαγχνος $\mathbf{f^{35}}$ ℵA,B [65%] ‖ πολυευσπλαγχνος [35%];	[no $\mathbf{K^x}$]
5:19	αδελφοι $\mathbf{f^{35}}$ [72%] ‖ αδελφοι μου ℵA,B,048 [28%].	?[no $\mathbf{K^x}$]

The archetypal profile of $\mathbf{f^{35}}$ in James is defined by the 28 readings above. It is clear and unambiguous, so we have at least one objectively defined archetype in James. In contrast, there are 14 + ?4 variant sets where $\mathbf{K^x}$ is seriously divided, placing an objectively defined archetype beyond our present reach.[2] (I did not include a number of lesser splits—25%, 20%, 15%—that conceivably could complicate any attempt to come up with an archetype for $\mathbf{K^x}$.) As Colwell observed for Mark's Gospel, there is no objectively definable 'Alexandrian' archetype;[3] the same applies to any 'Western' archetype, unless we follow the Alands and take a single MS as such, their "D text" (which only includes the Gospels and

---

1 Since $\mathbf{f^{35}}$ ($\mathbf{K^r}$) is distinct from $\mathbf{K^x}$, its 20% must be subtracted from the 60%, leaving an even split in $\mathbf{K^x}$.

2 If all the MSS are ever collated, some smaller groups (in the 5% - 10% range) with an objectively defined archetype may emerge, but I very much doubt that there will be a majority of the MSS with a single archetype; as in the Apocalypse, where there simply is no $\mathbf{K^x}$ (but there is indeed an objectively defined $\mathbf{f^{35}}$ [K^r]).

3 E.C. Colwell, "The Significance of Grouping of New testament Manuscripts", *New Testament studies*, IV (1957-1958), 86-87. What he actually said was: "These results show convincingly that any attempt to reconstruct an archetype of the Beta Text-type [Alexandrian] on a quantitative basis is doomed to failure. The text thus reconstructed is not reconstructed but constructed; it is an artificial entity that never existed." [Amen!]

Acts, however, so there would be no 'D text' for Romans - Revelation).[1] Let's go on to 1 Peter.

1 Peter

1:03	ελεος αυτου $\mathbf{f}^{35}$ P^{72} [38%] ‖ ~ 21 ℵA,B,C [60%] ‖ 1 [2%];	[no $\mathbf{K}^{x}$]
1:07	δοξαν και τιμην $\mathbf{f}^{35}$ P^{72}ℵA,B,C [35%] ‖ ~ 321 [28%] ‖ ~ 32 εις 1 [37%];	[no $\mathbf{K}^{x}$]
1:16	γινεσθε $\mathbf{f}^{35}$ [52%] ‖ γενεσθε [36%] ‖ εσεσθε P^{72}ℵA,B,C [12%];	[no $\mathbf{K}^{x}$]
1:23	αλλ $\mathbf{f}^{35}$ C [40%] ‖ αλλα P^{72}ℵA,B [60%];	
2:02	εις σωτηριαν $\mathbf{f}^{35}$ (P^{72})ℵA,B,C [65%] ‖ --- [35%];	[no $\mathbf{K}^{x}$]
2:03	χρηστος $\mathbf{f}^{35}$ ℵA,B,C [48%] ‖ χριστος P^{72} [52%];	[no $\mathbf{K}^{x}$]
2:06	η $\mathbf{f}^{35}$ C [35%] ‖ εν τη [59%] ‖ εν P^{72}ℵA,B [6%];	?[no $\mathbf{K}^{x}$]
2:11	απεχεσθαι $\mathbf{f}^{35}$ ℵB [65%] ‖ απεχεσθε P^{72}A,C [35%];	[no $\mathbf{K}^{x}$]
2:12	καταλαλουσιν $\mathbf{f}^{35}$ P^{72}ℵA,B,C [52%] ‖ καταλαλωσιν [48%];	[no $\mathbf{K}^{x}$]
2:14	μεν $\mathbf{f}^{35}$ C [52%] ‖ --- P^{72}ℵA,B [48%];	[no $\mathbf{K}^{x}$]
2:17	αγαπησατε $\mathbf{f}^{35}$ [71%] ‖ αγαπατε P^{72}ℵA,B,C [24%] ‖ --- [5%];	?[no $\mathbf{K}^{x}$]
2:20	τω $\mathbf{f}^{35}$ A [47%] ‖ --- $P^{72,81v}$ℵB,C [53%];	[no $\mathbf{K}^{x}$]
2:21	και $\mathbf{f}^{35}$ P^{72} [23%] ‖ --- ℵA,B,C [77%];	
2:24	αυτου $\mathbf{f}^{35}$ ℵ [71%] ‖ --- $P^{72,81v}$A,B,C [29%];	[no $\mathbf{K}^{x}$]
2:25	ημων $\mathbf{f}^{35}$ [50%] ‖ υμων P^{72}ℵA,B,C [50%];	[no $\mathbf{K}^{x}$]
3:06	εγενηθητε $\mathbf{f}^{35}$ P^{81v}ℵA,B,C [63%] ‖ εγεννηθητε P^{72} [35%] ‖ εγεννηθη [2%];	[no $\mathbf{K}^{x}$]
3:07	χαριτος ζωης $\mathbf{f}^{35}$ P^{81v}B,C [58%] ‖ 1 ζωσης [35%] ‖ ποικιλης 12 ℵA [7%] ‖ 12 αιωνιου P^{72};	[no $\mathbf{K}^{x}$]
3:07	εγκοπτεσθαι $\mathbf{f}^{35}$ P^{81}(ℵ)A,B [70%] ‖ εκκοπτεσθαι P^{72}C [30%];	?[no $\mathbf{K}^{x}$]
3:10	ημερας ιδειν $\mathbf{f}^{35}$ C [26%] ‖ ~ 21 $P^{72,81v}$ℵA,B [74%];	
3:16	καταλαλουσιν $\mathbf{f}^{35}$ ℵA,C (44.4%) ‖ καταλαλωσιν (50%) ‖ καταλαλεισθε P^{72}B (5%);	[no $\mathbf{K}^{x}$]
3:16	τη αγαθη εν χριστω αναστροφη $\mathbf{f}^{35}$ [20%] ‖ την αγαθην 34 αναστροφην (ℵ)A,B [50%] ‖ την 34 αγαθην αναστροφην P^{72} [24%] ‖ την 34 αγνην αναστροφην C [1%] ‖ την καλην 34 αναστροφην [4%] ‖ --- [1%];	[no $\mathbf{K}^{x}$]
3:18	ημας $\mathbf{f}^{35}$ A,C [64%] ‖ υμας P^{72}B [36%] ‖ --- ℵ;	[no $\mathbf{K}^{x}$]
4:02	του $\mathbf{f}^{35}$ [22%] ‖ --- P^{72}ℵA,B,C [78%];	
4:03	υμιν $\mathbf{f}^{35}$ ℵ (41.7%) ‖ ημιν C (47.1%) ‖ --- P^{72}A,B (11.2%);	[no $\mathbf{K}^{x}$]
4:03	χρονος $\mathbf{f}^{35}$ P^{72}ℵA,B,C [26%] ‖ χρονος του βιου [74%];	
4:03	ειδωλολατριαις $\mathbf{f}^{35}$ ℵA,C [70%] ‖ ειδωλολατρειαις B [30%];	?[no $\mathbf{K}^{x}$]
4:07	τας $\mathbf{f}^{35}$ [70%] ‖ --- P^{72}ℵA,B [30%];	?[no $\mathbf{K}^{x}$]
4:08	η $\mathbf{f}^{35}$ [49%] ‖ --- P^{72}ℵA,B [51%];	[no $\mathbf{K}^{x}$]
4:08	καλυπτει $\mathbf{f}^{35}$ A,B [60%] ‖ καλυψει P^{72}ℵ [40%];	[no $\mathbf{K}^{x}$]
4:11	ως $\mathbf{f}^{35}$ [69%] ‖ ης P^{72}ℵA,B [28%] ‖ --- [3%];	[no $\mathbf{K}^{x}$]
4:11	δοξαζηται Θεος $\mathbf{f}^{35}$ [20%] ‖ 1 ο 2 P^{72}ℵA,B [73%] ‖ ~ο 21 [6%];	
4:11	αιωνας $\mathbf{f}^{35}$ P^{72} [27%] ‖ αιωνας των αιωνων ℵA,B [73%];	
4:14	αναπεπαυται $\mathbf{f}^{35}$ [39%] ‖ επαναπαυεται A [6%] ‖ επαναπεπαυται P^{72} [2%] ‖ αναπαυεται ℵB [52%] ‖ αναπεμπεται [1%];	?[no $\mathbf{K}^{x}$]

---

[1] K. and B. Aland, *The Text of the New Testament* (Grand Rapids: Eerdmans, 1967), pp. 55, 64. They speak of "the phantom 'Western text'".

5:03 μηδε $\mathbf{f}^{35}$ P^{72} [49%] || μηδ ℵA [50%]; [no $\mathbf{K}^{x}$]
5:07 υπερ $\mathbf{f}^{35}$ [35%] || περι P^{72}ℵA,B [65%];
5:08 οτι $\mathbf{f}^{35}$ P^{72} [50%] || --- ℵA,B [50%]; [no $\mathbf{K}^{x}$]
5:08 περιερχεται $\mathbf{f}^{35}$ [24%] || περιπατει P^{72}ℵA,B [76%];
5:08 καταπιειν $\mathbf{f}^{35}$ (ℵ)B [53%] || καταπιει [25%] || καταπιη P^{72}A [22%]; [no $\mathbf{K}^{x}$]
5:10 στηριξαι $\mathbf{f}^{35}$ [33%] || στηριξει P^{72}ℵA,B [66%] || στηριξοι [1%];
5:10 σθενωσαι $\mathbf{f}^{35}$ [30%] || σθενωσει ℵA,B [66%] || σθενωσοι [1%] || --- P^{72} [3%];
5:10 θεμελιωσαι $\mathbf{f}^{35}$ [30%] || θεμελιωσει P^{72}ℵ [66%] || θεμελιωσοι [1%] || --- A,B [3%];
5:11 η δοξα και το κρατος $\mathbf{f}^{35}$ ℵ (59.6%) || 125 (31.3%) || ~ 45312 (7%) || 4 (-το P^{72}) 5 P^{72}A,B (0.8%). [no $\mathbf{K}^{x}$]

The archetypal profile of $\mathbf{f}^{35}$ in 1 Peter is defined by the 42 readings above. It is clear and unambiguous, so we have at least one objectively defined archetype in 1 Peter. In contrast, there are 24 + ?6 variant sets where $\mathbf{K}^{x}$ is seriously divided, placing an objectively defined archetype beyond our present reach. (I did not include a number of lesser splits—25%, 20%, 15%—that conceivably could complicate any attempt to come up with an archetype for $\mathbf{K}^{x}$. Please go back to James for other comments.) Let's go on to 2 Peter.

<u>2 Peter</u>

1:02 ιησου του κυριου ημων $\mathbf{f}^{35}$ (P^{72})B,C [68%] [234 1.4%] || 1 χριστου 234 ℵA [15%] || χριστου 1234 [8%] || σωτηρος 1 χριστου 234 [1.2%] || ~ 2341 χριστου [6%]; [no $\mathbf{K}^{x}$]
1:05 δε τουτο $\mathbf{f}^{35}$ ℵ [66%] || ~ 21 P^{72}B,C [32%] || 1 A [1%] || 2 [0.8%]; [no $\mathbf{K}^{x}$]
2:02 ας $\mathbf{f}^{35}$ [20%] || ους P^{72}ℵA,B,C [80%];
2:09 πειρασμων $\mathbf{f}^{35}$ ℵ [33%] || πειρασμου (P^{72})A,B,C [67%];
2:12 γεγενημενα φυσικα $\mathbf{f}^{35}$ ℵ [26%] || ~ 21 [54%] || γεγεννημενα 2 A,B,C [3%] || ~ 2 γεγεννημενα [12%] || 1 [4.2%] || 2 P^{72} [0.4%]; ?[no $\mathbf{K}^{x}$]
2:17 εις αιωνας $\mathbf{f}^{35}$ (25.1%) || 1 αιωνα A,C (70.3%) || 1 τον αιωνα (2.4%) || --- P^{72}ℵB (2.2%);
2:18 ασελγειας $\mathbf{f}^{35}$ [40%] || ασελγειαις P^{72}ℵA,B,C [60%];
3:02 υμων $\mathbf{f}^{35}$ P^{72}ℵA,B,C [70%] || ημων [28.8%] || --- [1.2%]; ?[no $\mathbf{K}^{x}$]
3:05 συνεστωτα $\mathbf{f}^{35}$ ℵ [23%] || συνεστωσα P^{72}A,C(048) [76%];
3:10 η $\mathbf{f}^{35}$ ℵ,048 [67%] || η οι P^{72}A,B,C [33%]; [no $\mathbf{K}^{x}$]
3:15 αυτω δοθεισαν $\mathbf{f}^{35}$ [60%] || ~ 21 P^{72}(ℵ)A,B,C,048 [40%]; [no $\mathbf{K}^{x}$]
3:16 εισιν $\mathbf{f}^{35}$ A [33%] || εστιν P^{72}ℵB,C [67%];
3:18 αυξανητε $\mathbf{f}^{35}$ [27%] || αυξανετε ℵA,B [60%] || αυξανεσθε P^{72}C [5%] || αυξανησθε [3%] || αυξανοιτε [5%].

The archetypal profile of $\mathbf{f}^{35}$ in 2 Peter is defined by the 13 readings above. It is clear and unambiguous, so we have at least one objectively defined archetype in 2 Peter. $\mathbf{K}^{x}$ is in unusually good shape here, so the diagnostic readings are comparatively fewer. The 4 + ?2 variant sets where

$\mathbf{K}^x$ is seriously divided are sufficiently few in number that it might be possible to posit an archetype. (I did not include a number of lesser splits—25%, 20%, 15%—that conceivably could complicate any such attempt. Please go back to James for other comments.) Let's go on to 1 John.

1 John

1:04	ημων $\mathbf{f}^{35}$ ℵB [59%] ‖ υμων A,C [41%];	[no $\mathbf{K}^x$]
1:06	περιπατουμεν $\mathbf{f}^{35}$ [29%] ‖ περιπατωμεν $\mathbf{f}^{35pt}$ ℵA,B,C [71%];	
2:16	αλαζονεια $\mathbf{f}^{35}$ C [72%] ‖ αλαζονια ℵA,B [28%];	?[no $\mathbf{K}^x$]
2:24	πατρι και εν τω υιω $\mathbf{f}^{35}$ ℵ [35%] ‖ ~ 52341 A(B)C [65%];	
2:27	διδασκη $\mathbf{f}^{35}$ ℵA,B [71%] ‖ διδασκει C [28%];	?[no $\mathbf{K}^x$]
2:29	ειδητε $\mathbf{f}^{35}$ ℵB,C [37%] ‖ ιδητε A [59%] ‖ οιδατε [4%];	
2:29	γεγεννηται $\mathbf{f}^{35}$ ℵA,B,C [70%] ‖ γεγενηται [30%];	[no $\mathbf{K}^x$]
3:01	ημας $\mathbf{f}^{35}$ A,B [36%] ‖ υμας ℵC [63.5%] ‖ --- [0.5%];	
3:06	και $\mathbf{f}^{35}$ [20%] ‖ --- ℵA,B,C [80%];	
3:15	εαυτω $\mathbf{f}^{35}$ ℵA,C [70%] ‖ αυτω B [30%];	[no $\mathbf{K}^x$]
3:17	θεωρη $\mathbf{f}^{35}$ ℵA,B,C [47%] ‖ θεωρει [53%];	?[no $\mathbf{K}^x$]
3:18	εν $\mathbf{f}^{35}$ ℵA,B,C [65%] ‖ --- [35%];	[no $\mathbf{K}^x$]
3:19	πεισωμεν $\mathbf{f}^{35}$ [43%] ‖ πεισομεν ℵA,B,C [56%];	
3:21	καταγινωσκη $\mathbf{f}^{35}$ ℵB,C [71%] ‖ καταγινωσκει A [29%];	?[no $\mathbf{K}^x$]
3:23	πιστευσωμεν $\mathbf{f}^{35}$ B (66.9%) ‖ πιστευωμεν ℵA,C (26.5%) ‖ πιστευομεν (5.4%) ‖ πιστευσομεν (1.2%);	[no $\mathbf{K}^x$]
3:24	εν $\mathbf{f}^{35}$ ℵ [30%] ‖ και εν A,B,C^v [70%];	
4:02	γινωσκεται $\mathbf{f}^{35}$ [67%] ‖ γινωσκετε A,B,C [25%] ‖ γινωσκομεν ℵ [8%];	[no $\mathbf{K}^x$]
4:03	ομολογει $\mathbf{f}^{35}$ ℵ (73.5%) ‖ ομολογει τον A,B (24.2%);	?[no $\mathbf{K}^x$]
4:03	εκ $\mathbf{f}^{35}$ ℵA,B [70%] ‖ --- [30%];	[no $\mathbf{K}^x$]
4:16	αυτω $\mathbf{f}^{35}$ A [37%] ‖ αυτω μενει ℵB [63%];	
5:04	ημων $\mathbf{f}^{35}$ ℵ,A,B (56.4%) ‖ υμων (43.2%) ‖ --- (0.4%);	[no $\mathbf{K}^x$]
5:06	και $\mathbf{f}^{35}$ ℵ [70%] ‖ και εν (A)B [30%];	[no $\mathbf{K}^x$]
5:10	εαυτω $\mathbf{f}^{35}$ ℵ [48%] ‖ αυτω A,B [52%];	?[no $\mathbf{K}^x$]
5:11	ο θεος ημιν $\mathbf{f}^{35}$ B [24%] ‖ ~ 312 ℵA [76%];	
5:20	γινωσκωμεν $\mathbf{f}^{35}$ [66%] ‖ γινωσκομεν ℵA,B [34%];	[no $\mathbf{K}^x$]
5:20	η ζωη η $\mathbf{f}^{35}$ [60%] ‖ 2 ℵA,B [26%] ‖ 12 [6%] ‖ 23 [4%] ‖ --- [4%].	[no $\mathbf{K}^x$]

The archetypal profile of $\mathbf{f}^{35}$ in 1 John is defined by the 26 readings above. It is clear and unambiguous, so we have at least one objectively defined archetype in 1 John. In contrast, there are 11 + ?6 variant sets where $\mathbf{K}^x$ is seriously divided, placing an objectively defined archetype beyond our present reach. (I did not include a number of lesser splits—25%, 20%, 15%—that conceivably could complicate any attempt to come up with an archetype for $\mathbf{K}^x$. Please go back to James for other comments.) Let's go on to 2 & 3 John.

2 John

02 εσται μεθ υμων $\mathbf{f^{35}}$ [58%] || εσται μεθ ημων ℵB,0232 [40%] || --- A [2%]; [no $\mathbf{K^x}$]
05 αλλ $\mathbf{f^{35}}$ A [35%] || αλλα ℵB [65%];
05 εχομεν $\mathbf{f^{35}}$ [30%] || ειχομεν ℵA,B [70%];
09 δε $\mathbf{f^{35}}$ [20%] || --- ℵA,B [80%];
12 αλλ $\mathbf{f^{35}}$ [30%] || αλλα ℵA,B [70%].

3 John

11 δε $\mathbf{f^{35}}$ [25%] || --- ℵA,B,C [75%];
12 οιδαμεν $\mathbf{f^{35}}$ (23%) || οιδατε (61.5%) || οιδας ℵA,B,C,048 (15.1%) || οιδα (0.4%).

The archetypal profile of $\mathbf{f^{35}}$ in 2 & 3 John is defined by the 7 readings above. It is clear and unambiguous, so we have at least one objectively defined archetype in these books. $\mathbf{K^x}$ is in unusually good shape here, so the diagnostic readings are comparatively fewer. With only one variant set where $\mathbf{K^x}$ is seriously divided it may be possible to posit an archetype. Let's go on to Jude.

Jude

06 αλλ $\mathbf{f^{35}}$ C [30%] || αλλα P^{72}ℵA,B [70%];
16 εαυτων $\mathbf{f^{35}}$ C [35%] || αυτων ℵA,B [65%];
24 αυτους $\mathbf{f^{35}}$ (68.8%) || υμας ℵB,C (29.2%) || ημας A (1%). ?[no $\mathbf{K^x}$]

The archetypal profile of $\mathbf{f^{35}}$ in Jude is defined by the 3 readings above. It is clear and unambiguous, so we have at least one objectively defined archetype in this book. $\mathbf{K^x}$ is in unusually good shape here, so the diagnostic readings are comparatively fewer. With only one variant set where $\mathbf{K^x}$ is seriously divided it may be possible to posit an archetype.

Conclusion

Taking the seven epistles as a block or group, the evidence presented furnishes an answer to the opening question: there is only one objectively identifiable archetype in the General Epistles—precisely $\mathbf{f^{35}}$. Its distinctive profile is defined by the 119 readings listed above. In contrast, there are 54 + ?18 variant sets where $\mathbf{K^x}$ is seriously divided, making it highly doubtful that a single $\mathbf{K^x}$ archetype exists for these books. (I did not include a number of lesser splits—28 around 25%, 53 around 20%, 57 around 15%—that conceivably could complicate any attempt to establish an archetype for $\mathbf{K^x}$, especially if the membership in the splits is not constant or predictable.) I am not aware of any other possible contenders. Granting the present state of our ignorance, in the General Epistles there is only one qualified candidate for Autograph archetype: $\mathbf{f^{35}}$. (If there is only one candidate for mayor in your town, who gets elected?)

'*Concordia discors*' and f^{35} minority readings in the General Epistles

Over a century ago, and throughout his works, John William Burgon repeatedly called attention to the *concordia discors*, the prevailing confusion and disagreement, which the early uncials (ℵABCD—he personally collated each) display between/among themselves. Luke 11:2-4 offers one example.

> "The five Old Uncials" (ℵABCD) falsify the Lord's Prayer as given by St. Luke in no less than forty-five words. But so little do they agree among themselves, that they throw themselves into six different combinations in their departures from the Traditional Text; and yet they are never able to agree among themselves as to one single various reading: while only once are more than two of them observed to stand together, and their grand point of union is no less than an omission of the article. Such is their eccentric tendency, that in respect of thirty-two out of the whole forty-five words they bear in turn solitary evidence.[1]

James

Concordia discors

Four of those uncials are extant in James (ℵABC), to which I add $P^{20,100}$ and 048,[2] and what Burgon calls their 'eccentric tendency' is plainly visible. Their eccentricity, viewed from the perspective of the normal transmission, is sufficient to warm the cockles of the heart of the most obdurate iconoclast. However, their very eccentricity establishes their independence, which is of special interest in what follows. I proceed to tabulate their performance in the 120 relevant variant sets (excluding 5 with *rell*) included in the critical apparatus of my edition of the Greek Text of James. I do so using **f^{35}** as the point of reference.

f^{35} alone	53	[In these cases the uncials are usually together, but not always.]
f^{35} P^{100}	2	
f^{35} ℵ	6	
f^{35} A	9	

---

[1] Burgon, *The Traditional Text of the Holy Gospels Vindicated and Established*, arranged, completed, and edited by Edward Miller (London: George Bell and Sons, 1986), p. 84.

[2] P^{23}, 0173 and 0246, all fragmentary, are also cited in my apparatus, but they never agree with **f^{35}** against the rest.

f^{35} B	1
f^{35} C	5
f^{35} 048	1

f^{35} P^{20}ℵ	1
f^{35} P^{100}A	1
f^{35} ℵA	7
f^{35} ℵB	2
f^{35} AB	2
f^{35} AC	6

f^{35} P^{100}ℵA	1
f^{35} P^{100}AB	1
f^{35} P^{100}AC	1
f^{35} ℵAB	6
f^{35} ℵAC	2
f^{35} ℵBC	2
f^{35} ABC	2

f^{35} P^{100}ℵAB	1	
f^{35} ℵABC	6	[Since this combination attests over 90% of the words, it is irrelevant to my present purpose and will not be used in any computations below.]

involving P^{20}	1
involving P^{100}	7
involving ℵ	28
involving A	37
involving B	17
involving C	18
involving 048	1

For the 114 relevant variant sets (120 minus 6), **f^{35}** has overt attestation from these early uncials 52% of the time. Not only are these uncials obviously independent of each other, **f^{35}** is independent of them as well, but just as early. Here is a further demonstration that **f^{35}** is both early and independent. As we move to the next section, keep in mind that all by itself **f^{35}** proves that a variant is early.

f^{35} minority readings

A look at the apparatus of my Greek Text of James will show that I have designated as genuine nine readings with an attestation of 30% or less. In each case the deciding factor is the presence of **f^{35}**. I will now analyze these nine readings, beginning with the smallest percentage.

ανηλεος 2:13 [20%]

The only **f**[35] MSS included in *ECM*, 18 and 35, are falsely attributed to a different variant, so that this reading is not even mentioned in *ECM*; nor is it mentioned by von Soden. Beyond any question this is the reading of **f**[35], but only as further MSS are collated will we know if it survived in other lines of transmission. That someone would have introduced an Attic form in the middle ages is scarcely credible, so **f**[35] is early, and in my opinion most probably original.

ιθυνοντος 3:4 [21%]

All eight non-**f**[35] MSS, as listed by *ECM*,[1] have a distinct profile, some radically so. However, three of them (1270, 1297, 1598) are obviously related and presumably had a common ancestor not too far back. So we have six independent lines of transmission (outside of **f**[35]) that probably go back to the early centuries. Oops, cursive 1595, though fairly different from the three, would likely join them by the fifth century, leaving five lines. Also, as the distance in time increases it becomes increasingly unlikely that an ancient classical spelling could, or would, be introduced. This reading is certainly ancient, and in my opinion most probably original.

δυναμενος 3:2 א [23%]

To my surprise, there is absolutely <u>**no**</u> overlap between the eight non-**f**[35] MSS that *ECM* lists for ιθυνοντος and the 23 non-**f**[35] MSS listed for δυναμενος. To my further surprise, the 23 do not include a single Byzantine MS.[2] So **f**[35] is totally independent of $\mathbf{K}^x$ here, and yet is joined by א, so we already know that the reading is early. But let's analyze the cursives.

Since no two have an identical profile, the 23 are presumably independent in their own generation. However, there are several pairs with a common ancestor not too far back, presumably—I put 206-429, 254-1524 and 630-2200 in this category. But the first two pairs are themselves related, with a common grand-ancestor. The ancestor of 630-2200 is joined by 2138 and their grand-ancestor by 2495. 621 and 2412 meet several generations back. So back in the fifth century, I would imagine, we have <u>sixteen</u> independent lines of transmission (outside of **f**[35]). By the time

---

1 *Editio Critica Maior*, The Institute for New Testament Textual Research, ed (Stuttgart: Deutsche Bibelgesellschaft, 1997), vol. IV, Catholic epistles.

2 *ECM* does list two as Byzantine (254, 1827) but comparing them with *TuT* they do not get above the 80% threshold in James.

we get back to the third century we should still have at least six independent lines that vouch for δυναμενος (much like ιθυνοντος), but the lines are **totally different** in each case!!! This means that $\mathbf{f^{35}}$ is independent of all eleven of those lines (surely—with ιθυνοντος $\mathbf{f^{35}}$ is independent of the six that support δυναμενος, and with δυναμενος it is independent of the five that support ιθυνοντος; so it is independent of all eleven).

This reading is certainly ancient, owes nothing whatsoever to $\mathbf{K^x}$ (the Byzantine bulk), and in my opinion is most probably original.[1]

ημων 4:14 [26%]

This variant shares 206-429, 254-1524 and 630-2200 with δυναμενος, and they represent just two lines of transmission; it also shares 1490 and 1831, that are independent. That leaves 10 further non- $\mathbf{f^{35}}$ MSS listed for this variant, six of which are Byzantine (but all quite different). Of the ten only two would join by the fifth century, which leaves us with thirteen independent lines of transmission (outside of $\mathbf{f^{35}}$) back in the fifth century, or so I imagine. By the time we get back to the third century we should still, again, have at least six independent lines of transmission for ημων. The six Byzantine MSS obviously do not represent $\mathbf{K^x}$, so again we have a reading that is certainly ancient while owing nothing to $\mathbf{K^x}$. In my opinion it is most probably original.

γαρ 4:11 [26%]

The roster of MSS here is similar to that for δυναμενος—it shares 13 of the 16 independent lines and picks up seven new ones (one is shared with ιθυνοντος), which makes 20 (outside of $\mathbf{f^{35}}$). So this reading is also certainly ancient, owing nothing to $\mathbf{K^x}$, and in my opinion is most probably original.

ου 2:4 ℵA,C (26.8%)

Since this reading is also supported by ℵA,C there is no question about age. The roster of MSS here reproduces all but seven MSS in the γαρ roster, but has some twenty further MSS. Since this is one of the sets included in *TuT*, the percentage is precise. Here again, this reading is certainly ancient, owing nothing to $\mathbf{K^x}$, and in my opinion is most probably original.

---

[1] This recurring refrain, "in my opinion is most probably original" dates back to when I was beginning my work with Family 35. Based on the evidence I have amassed since, I now affirm that the Family 35 readings are certainly original.

επειτα 4:14 [29.5%]

The roster of MSS here is quite similar to that of γαρ, but there are fewer. For all that, there are about 15 independent lines of transmission. Here again, this reading is certainly ancient, owing nothing to **K**^{x}, and in my opinion is most probably original.

νομου 1:23 [30%]

The roster here is a bit different. One independent line is shared with ιθυνοντος, three with δυναμενος, two with ημων and two with γαρ, which makes eight independent lines already. But there are six new lines of independent transmission added here that none of the others have. So in the fifth century, as I imagine, we have 14 independent lines (outside of **f**^{35}). By the time we get to the third century we should still, again, have at least six independent lines of transmission for νομου, not necessarily a perfect overlap with any of the others. There are some Byzantine MSS that obviously do not represent **K**^{x}, so again we have a reading that is certainly ancient while owing nothing to **K**^{x}. In my opinion it is most probably original.

λαμπραν εσθητα 2:3 [30%]

The roster here is quite similar to that of γαρ, etc., sharing one line with ιθυνοντος that none of the others have. It adds three new independent lines, so the evidence here is much like the others. Here again, this reading is certainly ancient, owing nothing to **K**^{x}, and in my opinion is most probably original.

Obviously the picture we have seen so far will be true for all other minority readings, as we move up to 35%, 40%, etc.

Conclusion

f^{35} is ancient, and owes nothing to **K**^{x}. Q.E.D. Well, of course, not quite. I was not alive in the fifth century, nor the third, so I cannot prove that the picture I have painted, as to time, is correct. However, adding the evidence presented here to that presented in "When is a 'recension'?", I affirm with a clear conscience that most of the independent lines mentioned—ιθυνοντος 5, δυναμενος 16, ημων 9, γαρ 6, νομου 6, λαμπραν εσθητα 3, which equals **45**—most of them probably go back to the fifth century at least. It is highly unlikely that the 45 would reduce to fewer than 15 in the third century. [And these 15 all support **f**^{35} against **K**^{x}, at one point or another—by the same token at other points they go with **K**^{x} against **f**^{35}, so **K**^{x} is also ancient.] I invite attention to a word from Kilpatrick.

> Origen's treatment of Matt. 19:19 is significant in two other ways. First he was probably the most influential commentator of the Ancient Church and yet his conjecture at this point seems to have influenced only one manuscript of a local version of the New Testament. The Greek tradition is apparently quite unaffected by it. From the third century onward even an Origen could not effectively alter the text.
>
> This brings us to the second significant point—his date. From the early third century onward the freedom to alter the text which had obtained earlier can no longer be practiced. Tatian is the last author to make deliberate changes in the text of whom we have explicit information. Between Tatian and Origin Christian opinion had so changed that it was no longer possible to make changes in the text whether they were harmless or not.[1]

The point made by Kilpatrick seems to me to be obvious. Evidently there would be occasional exceptions, especially in remote areas like Egypt where Greek was no longer spoken. After Diocletian's campaign [303] most monks simply copied what was in front of them. Most of the 45 lines of transmission mentioned above probably already existed in the year 300.)

1 Peter

As I did with James, I take note of what John William Burgon called the *concordia discors*, the prevailing confusion and disagreement, which the early uncials (ℵABCD—he personally collated each) display between/among themselves.

Concordia discors

Four of those uncials are extant in 1 Peter (ℵABC), to which I add P^{72} (which wasn't extant in Burgon's day), and what Burgon calls their 'eccentric tendency' is plainly visible. That eccentricity establishes their independence, which is of special interest in what follows. I proceed to tabulate their performance in the 141 relevant variant sets (disregarding the 13 with *rell*) included in the critical apparatus of my edition of the Greek Text of 1 Peter. I do so using **f**^{35} as the point of reference:

---

[1] G.D. Kilpatrick, "Atticism and the Text of the Greek New Testament," *Neutestamentliche Aufsatze* (Regensburg: Verlag Friedrich Pustet, 1963), pp. 129-30.

f35 alone	46	[In these cases the uncials are usually together, but not always.]
f35 P72	7	
f35 ℵ	9	
f35 A	8	
f35 B	2	
f35 C	8	
f35 P72A	2	
f35 P72B	2	
f35 P72C	3	
f35 ℵA	2	
f35 ℵB	3	
f35 ℵC	1	
f35 AB	2	
f35 AC	4	
f35 BC	1	
f35 P72ℵA	3	
f35 P72ℵB	1	
f35 P72ℵC	2	
f35 P72AB	2	
f35 P72AC	2	
f35 ℵAB	1	
f35 ℵAC	4	
f35 ABC	1	
f35 P72ℵAB	4	
f35 P72ℵAC	2	
f35 P72ℵBC	1	
f35 P72ABC	1	
f35 ℵABC	4	
f35 P72ℵABC	13	[Since this combination attests over 90% of the words, it is irrelevant to my present purpose and will not be used in any computations below.]
involving P72	32	
involving ℵ	37	
involving A	42	
involving B	25	
involving C	34	[C is missing from 4:6 to the end; were it extant several of the figures above would change.]

For the 128 variant sets that are left (141 minus 13), **f**35 has overt attestation from these early uncials 64% of the time. Not only are these uncials obviously independent of each other, **f**35 is independent of them as well, but just as early. Here is a further demonstration that **f**35 is both early and independent. As we move to the next section, keep in mind that all by itself **f**[35] proves that a variant is early.

f[35] *minority readings*

A look at my apparatus will show that I have designated as genuine nine readings with an attestation of 30% or less. In each case the deciding factor is the presence of **f**[35]. I will now analyze these nine readings, beginning with the smallest percentage.

τη αγαθη εν Χριστω αναστροφη 3:16 [20%]

ECM lists only cursives 18 and 35 for the dative. To my disappointment, von Soden doesn't mention it, but Tischendorf does, citing his cursives 38 and 93 (Gregory 328 and 205), confirming that the dative is the reading of **f**[35]. Tischendorf also cites his 137 (Gregory 614) for the dative, which has an 'independent' profile. So we know that the dative did not survive only in **f**[35]. The dative is correct for the object of επηρεαζω, but copyists who were not familiar with this peculiarity would naturally 'correct' to the accusative. *ECM* lists 15 variations for the 6-word phrase. One of my presuppositions is that the NT books were inspired by the Holy Spirit, and I assume that He knew how to write correct Koine Greek.

During the last 150 years the 'harder reading' canon has been widely used to impute to John, Peter, etc. a variety of linguistic barbarities; after all, they were ignorant fishermen, Galilean rustics, or whatever. But let's stop and think for a minute. After Pentecost, as the Church exploded and it became obvious that the Apostles were going to have to travel widely, to have an 'international' ministry, would they not bone up on Greek (and even Latin)? If I were in Peter's shoes I would certainly have done so. In other words, I maintain that Peter and John and James were perfectly competent to write good or correct Greek.[1] To me it is significant that **f**[35] habitually sides with the grammatically correct reading, as it does in this case.

δοξαζηται Θεος 4:11 [20%]

Again, *ECM* lists only cursives 18 and 35 for this variant. To my disappointment, neither von Soden nor Tischendorf mention it. However, as illustrated by Tischendorf for the variant above, there will almost certainly be MSS not collated by *ECM* that side with **f**[35] here (unfortunately *TuT* doesn't include this set). The lack of the article emphasizes the inherent

[1] That there was a resident centurion in Capernaum, means that there were Roman soldiers stationed there. That Roman outpost was doubtless the most important customer in town for their fish.Their dealings with the soldiers would have been in Greek, presumably, so they had a beginning.

quality of the noun, which is in accord with the context. Joining context to 'batting average', or credibility quotient, I stick with **f**^{35} here.

του 4:2 [22%]

Most of the fourteen non-**f**^{35} MSS listed by *ECM* for this variant are shared with δυναμενος in James 3:2. The fourteen will reduce to eight independent lines of transmission in the 5th century, or so I imagine, some of which will go back to the 3rd. The choice between the presence or absence of the article here makes little difference in the sense, so because of its credibility quotient I stick with **f**^{35}.

και 2:21 P^{72} [23%]

This variant also is attested by fourteen non-**f**^{35} MSS (listed by *ECM*), but only four are shared. There is more diversity this time, with only two pairs, so in the 5th century we still have twelve lines, most of which will go back to the 3rd, as I imagine. P^{72} gives overt 3rd century attestation. The reading of the majority is perfectly normal and makes excellent sense, so if it were original there would be no felt need to change it. On the other hand, the και next to the γαρ could easily appear to be unnecessary, motivating copyists to delete it. In the context the emphatic use fits nicely. This reading is certainly early and independent, and in my opinion most probably original.

περιερχεται 5:8 [24%]

The twenty-one non-**f**^{35} MSS listed by *ECM* for this variant include all but one of those listed for του above, plus eight different ones. There are several groups, but there would be at least ten independent lines in the 5th century, at least half of which should go back to the 3rd, as I imagine. The lion is not out for an afternoon stroll, he is circling the prey, looking for an opening. Περιερχεται is early, independent and correct, and in my opinion almost certainly original.

ημερας ιδειν 3:10 C [26%]

The twenty-six non-**f**^{35} MSS listed by *ECM* for this variant form several groups, but there would be at least fifteen independent lines in the 5th century—codex C gives overt 5th century attestation—at least half of which should go back to the 3rd, as I imagine. Since this is part of a quote from the Psalms, the LXX could be a factor, but how? Codex B has the same word order in its LXX of Psalms and here in Peter, while codex C agrees with the printed LXX. So who assimilated to whom? The word order attested by **f**^{35} seems less smooth than that of the majority and may have given rise to it. In any event, ημερας ιδειν is early, independent and in my opinion probably original.

χρονος 4:3 P^{72}ℵABC [26%]

The thirty-eight non-**f**[35] MSS listed by *ECM* for this variant include all five early uncials, so there is no question about age. (Just two words later the same five early uncials read βουλημα instead of θελημα, showing that **f**[35] is independent of them.) There will be over twenty independent lines in the 5th century, at least half of which should go back to the 3rd, or so I imagine. I would render verses 2-3[a] like this: "…so as not to live your remaining time in flesh for human lusts any longer, but for the will of God. Because the time that has passed is plenty for you to have performed the will of the Gentiles…" The phrase 'of life' gets in the way. **f**[35] is early and independent; I consider that its reading here is most probably original.

αιωνας 4:11 P^{72} [27%]

The thirty-one non-**f**[35] MSS listed by *ECM* for this variant include P^{72}, so there is no question about age. They will reduce to about twenty independent lines in the 5th century, at least half of which should go back to the 3rd, or so I imagine. That the familiar των αιωνων should be added, if the original lacked it, is predictable; that it should be omitted is harder to explain. I would render, "throughout the ages". **f**[35] is early and independent; I consider that its reading here is most probably original.

σθενωσαι θεμελιωσαι 5:10 [30%]

The twenty-four non-**f**[35] MSS listed by *ECM* for this variant will reduce to no less than twelve independent lines of transmission in the fifth century, aside from **f**[35], at least half of which should go back to the 3rd, or so I imagine. Is Peter affirming that God will, future indicative, or asking that God may, aorist optative? How does "after you have suffered a while" affect the equation? Again I will stick with **f**[35]. This reading is certainly ancient and in my opinion is most probably original.

Conclusion

Obviously the picture we have seen so far will be true for all other **f**[35] minority readings, as we move up to 35%, 40%, etc. As in James, **f**[35] is clearly early and independent of **K**[x]. If it is independent of all other lines of transmission as well, as I believe, then it harks back to the Original—what other reasonable explanation is there?

2 Peter

As I did with James and 1 Peter, I take note of what John William Burgon called the *concordia discors*, the prevailing confusion and disagreement, which the early uncials (אABCD—he personally collated each) display between/among themselves.

Concordia discors

Four of those uncials are extant in 2 Peter (אABC), to which I add P^{72} and 048, and what Burgon calls their 'eccentric tendency' is plainly visible. That eccentricity establishes their independence, which is of special interest in what follows. I proceed to tabulate their performance in the 67 relevant variant sets included in the critical apparatus of my edition of the Greek Text of 2 Peter (excluding 17 where I use *rell*). I do so using **f**^{35} as the point of reference:

f^{35} alone	19	[In these cases the uncials are usually together, but not always.]
f^{35} א	7	
f^{35} A	3	
f^{35} B	1	
f^{35} C	3	
f^{35} P^{72}B	1	
f^{35} P^{72}C	1	
f^{35} אA	7	
f^{35} אC	2	
f^{35} א048	1	
f^{35} AC	2	
f^{35} P^{72}BC	3	
f^{35} אAB	1	
f^{35} אAC	1	
f^{35} אA048	1	
f^{35} אBC	1	
f^{35} AC048	2	
f^{35} BC048	1	
f^{35} P^{72}אAB	1	
f^{35} P^{72}אAC	1	
f^{35} P^{72}אBC	1	
f^{35} P^{72}אAB048	1	

f[35] P^{72}ℵABC	6	[Since this combination attests over 90% of the words, it is irrelevant to my present purpose and will not be used in any computations below.]

involving P^{72}	9
involving ℵ	25
involving A	20
involving B	11
involving C	18
involving 048	6

For the 61 variant sets that are left (67 minus 6), **f**[35] has overt attestation from these early uncials 69% of the time. Not only are these uncials obviously independent of each other, **f**[35] is independent of them as well, but just as early. Here is a further demonstration that **f**[35] is both early and independent. As we move to the next section, keep in mind that all by itself **f**[35] proves that a variant is early.

f[35] *minority readings*

A look at my apparatus will show that I have designated as genuine seven readings with an attestation of 33% or less. In each case the deciding factor is the presence of **f**[35]. I will now analyze these seven readings, beginning with the smallest percentage.

ἅς 2:2 [20%]

ECM lists only cursive 18 for this reading, but my own collation of 35 convinces me that it agrees with 18; as do another 38 family representatives that I have collated. So the family is solid. Von Soden cites one other MS for this reading, while Tischendorf is silent. So the reading survived outside the family, if not very widely. Is the antecedent of the pronoun the debaucheries, or the people involved in them? Either makes sense, but it is really the bad conduct that sullies the reputation of the Way. I take it that **f**[35] probably preserves the Original reading here.

συνεστωτα 3:5 ℵ [23%]

Peter's syntax here is a bit complex, giving rise to eleven variations for the six-word phrase. As I see it, "out of water and through water" is parenthetical, modifying 'land', so the participle works with ησαν as a periphrastic construction whose subject includes both 'heaven' [m] and 'earth' [f]—thus the nominative plural <u>neuter</u> perfect active participle. **f**[35] is precisely correct here, even if most copyists got lost in Peter's syntax. ℵ gives overt 4th century attestation, but this reading is also attested by another four independent lines of transmission (as cited by *ECM*), besides

f^{35}, all of which probably go back at least to the 4th century. f^{35} probably preserves the Original here.

εις αιωνας 2:17 (25.1%)

Here we can rely on the complete collations reflected in *TuT*. There must be well over twenty independent lines of transmission going back to the 5th century, half of which should go back to the 3rd, besides f^{35}. The choice is between singular and plural, one 'age' or many. The absence of the article helped to confuse the picture. If the plural is stronger than the singular, then it fits the context better, since Peter is using violent language. I consider that the plural is probably original.

γεγενημενα φυσικα 2:12 א [26%]

Again, besides the overt testimony of א, there must be well over twenty independent lines of transmission going back to the 5th century, half of which should go back to the 3rd, besides f^{35}. The rest of the early uncials (P^{72} omits the participle) attest this order, while around 85% of the MSS attest the verb. The majority variant, by putting the adjective next to the noun, seems to make a more natural construction, but I take it that φυσικα is acting like a noun in apposition to ζωα, and to help us see this Peter places it after the participle: render, "as unreasoning animals, creatures of instinct made to be caught and destroyed". I do not doubt that f^{35} preserves the Original here.

αυξανητε 3:18 [27%]

Imperative or Subjunctive? I take it that Peter is offering a gentler alternative to falling from their steadfastness; render "rather, may you grow in grace…" 5% of the MSS actually move to the Optative; Subjunctive and Optative make up 35%. This reading is attested by at least ten independent lines of transmission, some of which should go back to the 3rd, besides f^{35}. I take it that the Subjunctive is probably original.

εισιν 3:16 A [33%]

The plural is obviously correct. Besides the overt testimony of A, there must be well over twenty independent lines of transmission going back to the 5th century, half of which should go back to the 3rd, besides f^{35}. Let me repeat a statement in the section for 1 Peter.

During the last 150 years the 'harder reading' canon has been widely used to impute to John, Peter, etc. a variety of linguistic barbarities; after all, they were ignorant fishermen, Galilean rustics, or whatever. But let's stop and think for a minute. After Pentecost, as the Church exploded and it became obvious that the Apostles were going to have to travel widely, to have an 'international' ministry, wouldn't they bone up on Greek (and even Latin)? If I were in Peter's shoes I would certainly have done so. In other words, I maintain that Peter and John and James were perfectly competent to write good or correct Greek. To me it is significant that **f**^{35} habitually sides with the grammatically correct reading, as it does in this case.

πειρασμων 2:9 ℵ [33%]

Singular or plural? I take the plural to be clearly superior in the context. Again, besides the overt testimony of ℵ, there must be well over twenty independent lines of transmission going back to the 5th century, half of which should go back to the 3rd, besides **f**^{35}. Again I will stick with **f**^{35}. This reading is certainly ancient and in my opinion is most probably original.

Conclusion

Obviously the picture we have seen so far will be true for all other **f**^{35} minority readings, as we move up to 40%, etc. As in James, 1 Peter and 1 John, **f**^{35} is clearly early and independent of **K**^{x}. If it is independent of all other lines of transmission as well, as I believe, then it harks back to the Original—what other reasonable explanation is there?

1 John

As I did with James and 1 & 2 Peter, I take note of what John William Burgon called the *concordia discors*, the prevailing confusion and disagreement, which the early uncials (ℵABCD—he personally collated each) display between/among themselves.

Concordia discors

Four of those uncials are extant in 1 John (ℵABC), to which I have added 048, and what Burgon calls their 'eccentric tendency' is plainly visible. That eccentricity establishes their independence, which is of special interest in what follows. I proceed to tabulate their performance in the 87 relevant variant sets (excluding 31 with *rell*) included in the critical apparatus of my edition of the Greek Text of 1 John. I do so using **f**^{35} as the point of reference.

f^{35} alone	32	[In these cases the uncials are usually together, but not always.]
f^{35} ℵ	10	
f^{35} A	7	

f^{35} B	4	
f^{35} C	3	
f^{35} אA	4	
f^{35} אB	1	
f^{35} אC	5	
f^{35} AB	4	
f^{35} AC	1	
f^{35} A048	2	
f^{35} BC	1	
f^{35} אAB	4	
f35 אAC	1	
f^{35} אA048	1	
f^{35} אBC	2	
f^{35} ABC	2	
f^{35} אABC	3	[Since this combination attests over 90% of the words, it is irrelevant to my present purpose and will not be used in any computations below.]
involving א	28	
involving A	24	
involving B	18	
involving C	15	[C is missing from 4:3 to the end.]
involving 048	3	

For the 84 variant sets that are left (87 minus 3), $\mathbf{f^{35}}$ has overt attestation from these early uncials 62% of the time. Not only are these uncials obviously independent of each other, $\mathbf{f^{35}}$ is independent of them as well, but just as early. Here is a further demonstration that $\mathbf{f^{35}}$ is both early and independent. As we move to the next section, keep in mind that all by itself $\mathbf{f^{35}}$ proves that a variant is early.

f^{35} minority readings

A look at my apparatus will show that I have designated as genuine four readings with an attestation of 30% or less. In each case the deciding factor is the presence of $\mathbf{f^{35}}$. I will now analyze these four readings, beginning with the smallest percentage. First, here is a roster of the non-$\mathbf{f^{35}}$ MSS (as per *ECM*) that attest each variant.

3:6 [20%]	5:11 [24%]	1:6 [29%]	3:24 [30%]
και	ο θεος ημιν	περιπατουμεν	--- εν
---	---	---	01
---	03	---	---
---	---	0142	---
---	0296	---	---

---	---	33	---
---	---	61	---
---	69	---	---
---	---	---	94
---	---	180	180
254	---	---	---
---	323	---	---
---	---	378	---
---	---	607	607
---	614	---	614
---	630	---	---
915	---	---	---
---	1292	---	---
---	---	1501	---
---	1505	1505	---
1523	---	---	---
1524	---	---	---
---	1611	---	---
---	1739	---	---
1827	---	---	---
---	---	---	1836
---	---	1842	---
1844	---	---	---
1852	---	---	---
---	1881	---	---
---	---	1890	1890
---	2138	---	---
---	---	2147	---
---	2200	---	---
---	2298	---	---
2374	---	---	---
---	2412	---	2412
---	---	---	2423
---	2492	---	---
---	---	2544	---
---	---	2652	---
---	---	---	2805

As with James, there is no overlap between the first two columns, and only one MS in common between the 2nd and 3rd! It follows that **f**^{35} is independent of all the lines of transmission represented by the MSS in those columns. There are no Byzantine MSS in the 1st column and only one (not very strong—69) in the 2nd. In contrast, the 3rd column has one very strong Byzantine MS (607), one strong one (180), two fair ones (0142, 1890), and two weak ones (1501, 1842); for all that, they obviously do not represent the bulk of the Byzantine tradition. As in James, **f**^{35} is clearly early and independent of **K**^{x}. If it is independent of all other lines of transmission as well, as I believe, then it harks back to the Original—what other reasonable explanation is there?

και 3:6 [20%]

Of the eight non-$\mathbf{f}^{35}$ MSS listed by *ECM* for this variant, none is Byzantine. Cursives 1523 and 1524 probably join one generation back; they are joined by 1844 perhaps two generations back; they are joined by 254 perhaps three generations back; so these four MSS reduce to one line of transmission. In the fifth century, or so I imagine, και is attested by five independent lines of transmission besides $\mathbf{f}^{35}$. Since their mosaics/profiles are very different, most of them probably go back to the third. This variant is certainly ancient and owes nothing at all to $\mathbf{K}^x$. I take the conjunction to be emphatic, and probably original. Comparing this with ιθυνοντος in James (3:4 [21%]), there is no overlap with the eight non-$\mathbf{f}^{35}$ MSS listed by *ECM* there; so between the two we have ten independent lines of transmission in the fifth century, besides $\mathbf{f}^{35}$.

ο Θεος ημιν 5:11 B [24%]

Of the sixteen non-$\mathbf{f}^{35}$ MSS listed by *ECM* for this variant, only one is Byzantine (69, fair). There is no overlap with the eight above. Codex B gives overt 4th century attestation. 0296 is a 6th century fragment too small to classify. Cursives 630, 1292, 1611, 2138 and 2200 will meet by the 5th century and thus represent one line of transmission. Cursives 614 and 2412 form a pair. In the fifth century, as I imagine, this variant is attested by eleven independent lines of transmission, besides $\mathbf{f}^{35}$. Their profiles are sufficiently distinct that I would not be surprised to find eight of them in the 3rd century. This reading is certainly ancient, owes nothing whatsoever to $\mathbf{K}^x$, and in my opinion is most probably original. Comparing this with δυναμενος in James (3:2 [23%]), they share three lines of transmission but that leaves thirteen to add to the eleven here—11 + 13 = 24! The surviving MSS from the first five centuries absolutely do not represent the true state of affairs at the time.

περιπατουμεν 1:6 [29%]

Of the thirteen non-$\mathbf{f}^{35}$ MSS listed by *ECM* for this variant, cursives 2147 and 2652 are very close and will be joined by 378 by the 5th century. The six Byzantine MSS all have rather distinct profiles, sufficiently so that in the 5th century they would still represent six lines.[1] So in the fifth century this variant has eleven independent lines of transmission, besides $\mathbf{f}^{35}$, only one of which is shared with the second column. So for these first three readings $\mathbf{f}^{35}$ finds support from 26 independent lines of transmission (5 + 11 + 10) back in the 5th century, as I suppose, being itself independent of

[1] I remind the reader that I determine the Byzantine MSS book by book, comparing *ECM* with *TuT*, but I take the profile from all seven general epistles, based on *TuT*.

all of them. In the apparatus I have already argued from the grammar and the context that περιπατουμεν is correct and therefore original—it is certainly ancient. If every word in an independent text-type is ancient it follows necessarily that the text-type itself is ancient.

--- *εν* 3:24 ℵ [30%]

Of the ten non-**f**[35] MSS listed by E*CM*, cursives 614 and 2412 represent one line. Cursive 1836 has only a third of the total, so I discount it. Codex ℵ gives overt 4th century attestation. Of the five Byzantine MSS, 607 and 2423 represent one line. So we are left with seven independent lines of transmission in the fifth century, aside from **f**[35], three of which are shared with column three and another with column two. This reading is certainly ancient and in my opinion is most probably original.

Conclusion

Obviously the picture we have seen so far will be true for all other **f**[35] minority readings, as we move up to 35%, 40%, etc. Allow me to repeat some salient points:

1. **f**[35] is early and independent—independent of all other known lines of transmission;
2. if it is independent of all other lines of transmission it must hark back to the Autographs, of necessity;
3. if every word in an independent text-type is ancient it follows necessarily that the text-type itself is ancient;
4. the surviving MSS from the first five centuries absolutely do not represent the true state of affairs at the time.

The Root Cause of the Continuous Defection from Biblical Infallibility and Consequent Objective Authority

That part of the academic world that deals with the biblical Text, including those who call themselves 'evangelical', is dominated by the notion that the original wording is lost, in the sense that no one knows for sure what it is, or was (if indeed it ever existed as an Autograph).[1] That

[1] There are those who like to argue that none of the books was written by its stated author, that they are forgeries, the result of editorial activity spread over decades (if not centuries) of time. Of course they were not there, and do not know what actually happened, but that does not deter them from pontificating.

notion is basic to all that is taught in the area of New Testament (NT) textual criticism in most schools. In an attempt to understand where that notion came from, I will sketch a bit of relevant history.

A Bit of Relevant History

The discipline of NT textual criticism, as we know it, is basically a 'child' of Western Europe and its colonies; the Eastern Orthodox Churches have generally not been involved. (They have always known that the true NT Text lies within the Byzantine tradition.) In the year 1500 the Christianity of Western Europe was dominated by the Roman Catholic Church, whose pope claimed the exclusive right to interpret Scripture. That Scripture was the Latin Vulgate, which the laity was not allowed to read. Martin Luther's ninety-five theses were posted in 1517. Was it mere chance that the first printed Greek Text of the NT was published the year before? As the Protestant Reformation advanced, it was declared that the authority of Scripture exceeded that of the pope, and that every believer had the right to read and interpret the Scriptures for himself. The authority of the Latin Vulgate was also challenged, since the NT was written in Greek. Of course the Vatican library held many Greek MSS, no two of which were identical (at least in the Gospels), so the Roman Church challenged the authenticity of the Greek Text.[1] In short, the Roman Church forced the Reformation to come to grips with textual variation among the Greek MSS. But they did not know how to go about it, because this was a new field of study and they simply were not in possession of a sufficient proportion of the relevant evidence.[2] (They probably didn't even know that the Mt. Athos peninsula, with its twenty monasteries, existed.)

In 1500 the Roman Catholic Establishment was corrupt, morally bankrupt, and discredited among thinking people. The Age of Reason and humanism were coming to the fore. More and more people were deciding that they could do better without the god of the Roman Establishment. The new imagined freedom from supernatural supervision was intoxicating, and many had no interest in accepting the authority of Scripture (*sola Scriptura*). Further, it would be naive in the extreme to exclude the supernatural from consideration, and not allow for satanic activity behind

---

[1] Probably no two MSS of the Latin Vulgate are identical either, but that was not the issue. Indeed, so far as I know, there is no way to establish what may have been the original wording of the Latin Vulgate, in every detail.

[2] Family 35, being by far the largest and most cohesive group of MSS with a demonstrable archetype, was poorly represented in the libraries of Western Europe. For that matter, very few MSS of whatever text-type had been sufficiently collated to allow for any tracing of the transmissional history. Worse, the lack of complete collations made it impossible to refute an erroneous hypothesis within a reasonable time frame.

the scenes. Consider Ephesians 2:2—"in which you once walked, according to the Aeon of this world, the ruler of the domain of the air, the spirit who is now at work in the sons of the disobedience." Strictly speaking, the Text has "according to the Aeon of this world, according to the ruler of the domain of the air"—the phrases are parallel, so 'Aeon' and 'ruler' have the same referent, a specific person or being. This spirit is presently at work (present tense) in 'the sons of the disobedience'. 'Sons' of something are those characterized by that something, and the something in this case is 'the' disobedience (the Text has the definite article)—a continuation of the original rebellion against the Sovereign of the universe.[1] 'Sons of the disobedience' joined the attack against Scripture. The so-called 'higher criticism' denied divine inspiration altogether.[2] Others used the textual variation to argue that in any case the original wording was 'lost', there being no objective way to determine what it may have been (unfortunately, no one was able to perceive such a way at that time).

The uncritical assumption that 'oldest equals best' was an important factor, and became increasingly so as earlier uncials came to light.[3] Both Codex Vaticanus and Codex Bezae were available early on, and they have thousands of disagreements between themselves, just in the Gospels (in Acts, Bezae is wild almost beyond belief). **<u>If</u>** 'oldest equals best', and the oldest MSS are in constant and massive disagreement between/among themselves, then the recovery of a lost text becomes hopeless. Did you get that? **Hopeless, totally hopeless**! However, I have argued (and continue to do so) that 'oldest equals <u>worst</u>', and that changes the picture radically. The benchmark work on this subject is Herman C. Hoskier's *Codex B and its Allies: A Study and an Indictment* (2 vols.; London: Bernard Quaritch, 1914). The first volume (some 500 pages) contains a detailed and careful discussion of hundreds of obvious errors in Codex B; the second (some

---

[1] Anyone in rebellion against the Creator is under satanic influence, direct or indirect (in most cases a demon acts as Satan's agent, when something more than the influence of the surrounding culture is required—almost all human cultures have ingredients of satanic provenance; this includes the academic culture). Anyone in rebellion against the Creator will also have strongholds of Satan in his mind. Since Satan is the 'father' of lies (John 8:44), anytime you embrace a lie you invite him into your mind—this applies to any of his sophistries (2 Corinthians 10:5) currently in vogue, such as materialism, humanism, relativism, Marxism, Freudianism, Hortianism, etc.

[2] The Darwinian theory appeared to be made to order for those who wished to get rid of a Creator, or any superior Authority, who might require an accounting. The 'higher criticism' served the purpose of getting rid of an authoritative Revelation, that might be used to require an accounting. Rebels don't like to be held accountable.

[3] Appeal was made to the analogy of a stream, where the purest water would presumably be that closest to the source. But with reference to NT manuscripts the analogy is fallacious, and becomes a sophistry.

400 pages) contains the same for Codex Aleph. He affirms that in the Gospels alone these two MSS differ well over 3,000 times, which number does not include minor errors such as spelling (II, 1). [Had he tabulated all differences, the total would doubtless increase by several hundreds.] Well now, simple logic demands that one or the other has to be wrong those 3,000+ times; they cannot both be right, quite apart from the times when they are both wrong. **No amount of subjective preference can obscure the fact that they are poor copies, objectively so.**[1] They were so bad that no one could stand to use them, and so they survived physically (but had no 'children', since no one wanted to copy them).

Since everyone is influenced (not necessarily controlled) by his milieu, this was also true of the Reformers. In part (at least) the Reformation was a 'child' of the Renaissance, with its emphasis on reason. Recall that on trial Luther said he could only recant if convinced by Scripture and reason. So far so good, but many did not want Scripture, and that left only reason. Further, since reason cannot explain or deal with the supernatural, those who emphasize reason are generally unfriendly toward the supernatural. [To this day the so-called historic or traditional Protestant denominations have trouble dealing with the supernatural.]

Before Adolf Deissmann published his *Light from the Ancient East* (1910), (being a translation of *Licht vom Osten*, 1908), wherein he demonstrated that Koine Greek was the *lingua franca* in Jesus' day, there even being a published grammar explaining its rules, only classical Greek was taught in the universities. But the NT was written in Koine. Before Deissmann's benchmark work, there were two positions on the NT Greek: 1) it was a debased form of classical Greek, or 2) it was a 'Holy Ghost' Greek,

---

[1] John William Burgon personally collated what in his day were 'the five old uncials' (א,A,B,C,D). Throughout his works he repeatedly calls attention to the *concordia discors*, the prevailing confusion and disagreement, that the early uncials display among themselves. Luke 11:2-4 offers one example.

> "The five Old Uncials" (אABCD) falsify the Lord's Prayer as given by St. Luke in no less than forty-five words. But so little do they agree among themselves, that they throw themselves into six different combinations in their departures from the Traditional Text; and yet they are never able to agree among themselves as to one single various reading: while only once are more than two of them observed to stand together, and their grand point of union is no less than an omission of the article. Such is their eccentric tendency, that in respect of thirty-two out of the whole forty-five words they bear in turn solitary evidence. (*The Traditional Text of the Holy Gospels Vindicated and Established.* Arranged, completed, and edited by Edward Miller. London: George Bell and Sons, 1896, p. 84.)

Yes indeed, oldest equals worst. For more on this subject, please see pages 130-36 in *The Identity of the New Testament Text IV*.

invented for the NT. The second option was held mainly by pietists; the academic world preferred the first, which raised the natural question: if God were going to inspire a NT, why would He not do it in 'decent' Greek? The prevailing idea that Koine was bad Greek predisposed many against the NT.

All of this placed the defenders of an inspired Greek Bible on the defensive, with the very real problem of deciding where best to set up a perimeter they could defend. Given the prevailing ignorance concerning the relevant evidence, their best choice appeared to be an appeal to Divine Providence. God providentially chose the TR, so that was the text to be used (the 'traditional' text).[1] I would say that Divine Providence was indeed at work, because the TR is a good Text, far better than the eclectic one currently in vogue.

To all appearances Satan was winning the day, but he still had a problem: the main Protestant versions (in German, English, Spanish, etc.) were all based on the *Textus Receptus*, as were doctrinal statements and 'prayer books'. Enter F.J.A. Hort, a quintessential 'son of the disobedience'. Hort did not believe in the divine inspiration of the Bible, nor in the divinity of Jesus Christ. Since he embraced the Darwinian theory as soon as it appeared, he presumably did not believe in God.[2] His theory of NT textual criticism, published in 1881,[3] was based squarely on the presuppositions that the NT was not inspired, that no special care was afforded it in the

---

[1] Please note that I am not criticizing Burgon and others; they did what they could, given the information available to them. They knew that the Hortian theory and resultant Greek text could not be right.

[2] For documentation of all this, and a good deal more besides, in Hort's own words, please see the biography written by his son, A.F. Hort, *Life and Letters of Fenton John Anthony Hort* (2 vols.; London: Macmillan and Co. Ltd., 1896). The son made heavy use of the father's plentiful correspondence, whom he admired. (In those days a two-volume 'Life', as opposed to a one-volume 'Biography', was a posthumous status symbol, albeit of little consequence to the departed.) Many of my readers were taught, as was I, that one must not question/judge someone else's motives. But wait just a minute; where did such an idea come from? It certainly did not come from God, who expects the spiritual person to evaluate everything (1 Corinthians 2:15). Since there are only two spiritual kingdoms in this world (Matthew 6:24, 12:30; Luke 11:23, 16:13), then the idea comes from the other side. By eliminating motive, one also eliminates presupposition, which is something that God would never do, since presupposition governs interpretation (Matthew 22:29, Mark 12:24). Which is why we should always expect a true scholar to state his presuppositions. I have repeatedly stated mine, but here they are again: 1) The Sovereign Creator of the universe exists; 2) He delivered a written revelation to the human race; 3) He has preserved that revelation intact to this day.

[3] B.F. Westcott and F.J.A. Hort, *The New Testament in the Original Greek* (2 Vols.; London: Macmillan and Co., 1881). The second volume explains the theory, and is generally understood to be Hort's work.

early decades, and that in consequence the original wording was lost—lost beyond recovery, at least by objective means. His theory swept the academic world and continues to dominate the discipline to this day.[1]

But just how was it that the Hortian theory was able to take over the Greek departments of the conservative schools in North America? The answer begins with the onslaught of liberal theology upon the Protestant churches of that continent at the beginning of the twentieth century. The great champion of the divine inspiration of Scripture was Benjamin B. Warfield, a Presbyterian. His defense of inspiration is so good that it is difficult to improve it. Somewhere along the line, however, he decided to go to Germany to study; I believe it was at Tubingen. When he returned, he was thanking God for having raised up Westcott and Hort to restore the text of the New Testament (think about the implication of 'restore'). One of his students, Archibald T. Robertson, a Baptist, followed Warfield's lead. The prestige of those two men was so great that their view swept the theological schools of the continent. I solicit the patience of the reader while I try to diagnose what happened to Warfield in Tubingen.

At Tubingen Warfield found himself among enemies of an inspired Bible. Now he was a champion of divine inspiration, but for an inspired text to have objective authority today, it must have been preserved.[2] Given the prevailing ignorance concerning the relevant evidence at that time, Warfield was simply not able to defend preservation in objective terms (and neither was anyone else—this is crucial to understanding what happened). He was faced with the fact of widespread variation between and among the extant Greek manuscripts. Even worse—far worse—was the presupposition that 'oldest equals best', because the oldest manuscripts are hopelessly at odds among themselves. For example: the two great early codices, Vaticanus and Sinaiticus, differ between themselves well over 3,000 times just in the four Gospels. Well now, they cannot both be right;

---

[1] For a thorough discussion of that theory, please see chapters 3 and 4 in *Identity IV*. Chapters 3 and 4 in *Identity IV* are little different from what they were in 1977. It has been over forty years, and so far as I know no one has refuted my dismantling of Hort's theory. It has not been for lack of desire. Nowadays one frequently hears the argument that to criticize Hort is to flay a dead horse, since now the ruling paradigm is eclecticism (whether 'reasoned' or 'rigorous'). But eclecticism is based squarely on the same false presuppositions, and is therefore equally wrong.

[2] This has always been a favorite argument with enemies of inspiration; it goes like this: "If God had inspired a text, He would have preserved it (or else why bother inspiring). He did not preserve the NT; therefore He did not inspire it." I confess that I am inclined to agree with that logical connection, except that I am prepared to turn the tables. I believe I can demonstrate that God did in fact preserve the NT Text; therefore He must have inspired it!

one or the other **has** to be wrong, quite apart from the places where they are <u>both</u> wrong. So what was poor Warfield to do? Enter Westcott and Hort. Hort claimed that as a result of their work only a thousandth part of the NT text could be considered to be in doubt, and this was joyfully received by the rank and file, since it seemed to provide assurance about the reliability of that text—however, of course, that claim applied only to the W-H text (probably the worst published NT in existence to this day, so the claim was false).[1] Warfield grasped at this like a drowning man grasps at a straw, thereby doing serious damage to North American Evangelicalism.[2]

Why the Defection Is Continuous

To understand the full impact of the onslaught of liberal theology, one must take account of the milieu. Reason has always been important to the historic or traditional Protestant denominations. In consequence, academic respectability has always been important to their graduate schools of theology. The difficulty resides in the following circumstance: for at least two centuries academia has been dominated by Satan, and so the terms of 'respectability' are dictated by him. Those terms include 'publish or perish', but of course he controls the technical journals. Since he is the father of lies (John 8:44), anyone who wished to tell the whole truth has always had a hard time getting an article published, no matter how good it was. To get an article published one had to toe the party line. 'Taking account of the existing literature' obliges one to waste a great deal of time

---

1 I would say that their text is mistaken with reference to 10% of the words—the Greek NT has roughly 140,000 words, so the W-H text is mistaken with reference to 14,000 of them. I would say that the so-called 'critical' (read 'eclectic') text currently in vogue is 'only' off with reference to some 12,000, an improvement (small though it be). And just by the way, how wise is it to use a NT prepared by a servant (or servants) of Satan? (On the other hand, I claim that God has preserved the original wording to such an extent that we can, and do, know what it is.)

2 However, I should not be unduly harsh in my criticism of Warfield; no one else knew what to do either. The cruel fact was that the relevant evidence did not exist in usable form at that time. (It follows that any defense of divine preservation at that time had to be based upon faith, faith that God would produce the evidence in His time.) Part of the damage produced by Hort's theory was its disdain for the vast bulk of later manuscripts—they were not worth the bother to collate and study. Since it is precisely those disdained MSS that furnish the necessary evidence, that soporific effect of Hort's theory delayed the availability of the relevant evidence for a century. I remember one day in class (in 1957), the professor filled his lungs and proclaimed with gusto, "Gentlemen, where B and Aleph agree, you have the original." The poor man had obviously never read Herman C. Hoskier's *Codex B and its Allies: A Study and an Indictment* (published in 1914).

reading the nonsense produced by Satan's servants, all of which was designed to keep the reader away from the truth.

The TRUTH—aye, there's the rub. Consider 2 Thessalonians 2:9-12: "The coming of the *lawless one* is according to the working of Satan, with all power, signs, and lying wonders, 10 and with all unrighteous deception among those who perish, because they did not receive the love of the truth, that they might be saved. 11 And for this reason God will send them strong delusion, that they should believe the lie, 12 that they all may be condemned who did not believe the truth, but had pleasure in unrighteousness" (NKJV). Although verse ten is in the context of the activity of the Antichrist, who will find an easy target in 'those who are wasting themselves' (my translation), it does not follow that no one will be wasting himself before that activity. Obviously, people have been wasting themselves all down through history, and the underlying cause for that 'wasting' has never changed—"they did not receive the love of the truth". (It began in the Garden.)

Please notice carefully what is said here: it is God Himself who sends the strong delusion! And upon whom does He send it? Upon those who do not receive the love of the truth.[1] And what is the purpose of the strong delusion?—the condemnation of those who do not believe the truth. Dear me, this is heavy. Notice that the truth is **central** to anyone's salvation. This raises the necessary question: just what is meant by 'the truth'? In John 14:6 Sovereign Jesus declared Himself to be 'the truth'. Praying to the Father in John 17:17 He said, "Thy Word is truth". Once each in John chapters 14, 15 and 16 He referred to the third person of the Trinity as "the Spirit of the truth". Since the Son is back in Heaven at the Father's right hand, and the Spirit is not very perceptible to most of us, most of the time, and since the Word is the Spirit's sword (Ephesians 6:17), our main access to 'the truth' is through God's Word, the Bible. The Bible offers propositional truth, but we need the Holy Spirit to illumine that truth, and to have the Holy Spirit we must be adequately related to Sovereign Jesus.

Now then, for something to be received, it must be offered; one cannot believe in something he has never heard about (Romans 10:14). The use of the verb 'receive' clearly implies an act of volition on the part of those not receiving the truth; that love was offered or made available to them but they did not want it; they wanted to be able to lie and to entertain lies told by others. But the consequences of such a choice are terrible; they

---

[1] Please note that it is not enough to merely 'accept' the truth; it is required that we love the truth. Satan tantalizes us with fame and fortune (on his terms, of course), so to love the truth requires determination.

turned their back on salvation. I suspect that not many Christians in the so-called 'first world' really believe what Sovereign Jesus said in Matthew 7:14: those who find the way of Life are **few**! And do not forget Revelation 22:15; "whoever loves and practices a lie" is excluded from the heavenly City [any lie, including Hort's].[1] I will here consider the implications for a student entering a graduate school of theology, because of what happens if he becomes a professor, or NT scholar, in his turn.[2]

Most such students presumably come from an evangelical environment, and were doubtless taught that the Bible is God's Word, and therefore inspired. Some may even have been taught verbal, plenary inspiration. However, in most theological schools you cannot get a job as a teacher if you do not agree to use the eclectic Greek text, with all that implies. (Just as you cannot get a teaching job in most universities unless you at least pretend to believe in evolution.) If the school is at least nominally conservative, they will still say that the Bible is inspired. But if a student brings up the question of the preservation of the text in class, there will be an uncomfortable silence. If it was preserved, no one knows what or where it is. The brainwashing has been so complete that many (most?) seminary graduates do not even know that there is any question about what they were taught. They were taught an eclecticism based on Hort's theory, and for them that is all there is.

But to go back to our student, he finds himself surrounded by professors whose job it is to destroy his faith in an inspired Bible with objective authority. Of course, presumably, very few such professors have ever thought in those terms (so they would object to my statement). They would say that they are just doing their job, doing what they are paid to do, without troubling themselves with the whys and wherefores.[3] But of course the

---

[1] Help! "A lie" is rather general, open-ended. What happens if I accepted a lie without realizing that it was one? But the Text does not say 'accepts'; it says 'loves' and 'practices'. The implication is that the contrary evidence, to the lie, is available, but has been rejected, or deliberately ignored—the person sold himself to the lie.

[2] At the graduate level, a student has the responsibility to evaluate what is being taught—if it goes contrary to the Text, it should not be accepted. I remember one day in chapel, a visiting scholar was expounding Romans 10:9. He stated that the Greek Text plainly means "Jesus as Lord", but then went on to try to explain why the school didn't believe that. His effort was rather lame; so much so that I determined to delve into the question for myself.

[3] For older, established scholars there is also the matter of pride and vested interest; who wants to admit that he has been wrong all his professional life? Then there is the doctrine of professional ethics, one must respect his colleagues (respect for the colleague trumps respect for the truth). [One must not ask where that doctrine came from.] One other thing: where a school or institution depends on financial help from outside, it will be threatened

student is not expecting that; he believes that his professors must be men of God, and so he is predisposed to believe them. Besides that predisposition (and it is powerful), what are the tools at their disposal for doing their job? Well, they have ridicule, sarcasm, brainwashing, peer pressure, the 'emperor's new clothes' gambit, and satanic assistance, for starters. (There may also be threats, failing grades, disciplinary actions, foul play, and so on—I write from experience.) Most of the terms above are self-explanatory, but some readers may not be familiar with the ancient myth about the emperor—it boils down to this: you don't want to admit that you can't 'see' it, when everyone else claims to be doing so. But by far the most serious is 'satanic assistance', and here I must needs go into detail.

Returning to 2 Thessalonians 2:10 and the 'love of the truth', as explained above, our main access to 'the truth' is through God's Word, the Bible. Our student may have gone to Sunday school, probably heard sermons with at least some biblical content, and certainly has his own copy of the Bible. In short, he has had, and continues to have, access to 'the truth'. However, the Holy Spirit does 'talk' to us, if we will listen. For example: my father was born in 1906, and in due time went to Moody Bible Institute and Wheaton College. In those days the American Standard Version (ASV) was touted as the best thing since the Garden of Eden; it was 'the rock of biblical integrity', etc. etc. Now my father had the practice of reading through the entire Bible once a year, a practice that he maintained all his life. Due to the hype surrounding the ASV, he got a copy and began to read it. It was hard going from the start, and he soon had to stop—the Holy Spirit simply would not let him go on. He returned to his trusty AV.

I imagine that at least some of my readers will have a question at this point. Am I implying that anyone who embraced the ASV was not listening to the Holy Spirit when he made that decision? The answer is, "Yes". Obviously, the same holds for the Hortian theory, etc. Unfortunately, few students of theology are in the habit of consulting the Holy Spirit, and those who do are marked for persecution. No Establishment can tolerate anyone who listens to the Holy Spirit. Surely, or have you forgotten John 3:8? "The wind blows where it wishes, and you (sg) hear its sound, but you do not know where it comes from or where it goes. So it is with everyone who has been begotten by the Spirit." Notice that the Lord is saying here that it is **we** who are to be unpredictable, like the wind, or the Spirit ("comes" and "goes" are in the present tense). If you are really under the

---

with the loss of that help, if it does not toe the line, and its very existence may depend on that help.

control of the Spirit you will do unexpected things, just like He does.[1] An Establishment is defined by its 'straitjacket', and the Holy Spirit does not like straitjackets, and vice versa.

In John 8:44 Sovereign Jesus declared that "there is no truth" in Satan, and that he is the father of the lie. Since God cannot lie, Titus 1:2, it being contrary to His essence, any and all lies come from the enemy. So what happens if you embrace a lie? You invite Satan into your mind. And what does he do there? He sets up a stronghold that locks you into that lie; you become blind to the truth on that subject.[2] It is a specific application of the truth expressed in 2 Corinthians 4:4—Satan blinds minds. So what happens to our student? With very few exceptions, he succumbs to the pressure exerted by the tools already mentioned. He accepts the party line, and since it is a lie, Satan goes about blinding him to the truth. If he goes on to become an influential scholar, he will almost certainly come under demonic surveillance (since Satan is not omnipresent).

There is a common misapprehension that trips people up at this point. Since any genuinely regenerated person has the indwelling Holy Spirit, how can Satan or a demon be in that person's mind? There is a fundamental difference between presence and control. Very few Christians have consciously turned over every area of their lives to the control of the Holy Spirit. The Holy Spirit is a gentleman, he will not take over an area against your will (see John 4:23-24). Any areas not under the Spirit's control are open to the enemy's interference, and most especially if you embrace a lie. By embracing a lie you grieve the Holy Spirit; not wise (Ephesians 4:30). You also resist Him; also not wise (Acts 7:51). So why does God not protect you? Because you rejected the love of the truth, and that turned God against you! When God turns against you, what are your chances? Without God's protection, you become Satan's prey (1 Peter 5:8).[3]

Anyone in rebellion against the Creator is under satanic influence, direct or indirect (in most cases a demon acts as Satan's agent, when something more than the influence of the surrounding culture is required—almost all human cultures have ingredients of satanic provenance; this includes the academic culture). Anyone in rebellion against the Creator

---

[1] Since Satan is forever muddying the water with excesses and abuses, spiritual discernment is needed.

[2] On that one subject—you will not necessarily be blinded on other subjects, or at least not at first.

[3] Please keep in mind the sequence of cause and effect—it begins with the rejection of the love of the truth. It is not enough to merely 'accept' the truth, one must love it. For those who have embraced a lie, the only 'medicine' is to return to the love of the truth, rejecting the lie. God may require a public renunciation of the lie.

will also have strongholds of Satan in his mind. Since Satan is the 'father' of lies (John 8:44), anytime you embrace a lie you invite him into your mind—this applies to any of his sophistries (2 Corinthians 10:5) currently in vogue, such as materialism, humanism, relativism, Marxism, Freudianism, Hortianism, etc.

The selling of the lie is carried on from generation to generation, resulting in a continuous defection. Most professors are 'parrots', simply repeating what they were taught, without ever going back to check the facts. Some older scholars may have become aware of the facts, but because of vested interest they do not mention them to their students; they maintain the party line.

Is there a Way to Stop the Defection?

I believe there is, and it must begin with the TRUTH. To be more precise, it must begin with the love of the truth, which necessitates that the truth be made available. We must promote the love of the truth, and to do that we must also denounce the lie.[1] To promote something, we need vehicles for doing so. To succeed, we must be convincing. Most important, we must do something about the interference in people's minds.

Vehicles for promoting the truth:

It is modern technology that comes to our aid here. Blogs are being used to promote anything and everything. We can use them to promote the truth. I have done a fifteen-hour lecture series (in Portuguese) on the divine preservation of the NT Text. It was filmed and is available on the net via blog. Websites are being used. Most of my work is available from, www.walkjustashewalked.com and even more is available from my own www.prunch.org. And then there is Twitter, Facebook and so on—the fact is that the technical journals no longer have a stranglehold on any discipline; there are other ways of 'publishing' your ideas. And there has always been word-of-mouth, people telling their friends and acquainttances. I suspect that we may soon see a groundswell of this sort of thing.

The advent of self-publishing represents a real boon to those of us who reject a party line, and do not have the financial means to use an established publishing house. For various reasons it has become increasingly difficult to use a publisher. The contracts place all the onus on the author (including the cost of lawsuits). One must cover the cost of several thousand copies up front, and even so, only if the publisher decides he can

[1] My own denunciation of the Hortian lie has been in print since 1977, and I continue to stand by every bit of it.

make a profit on the book, not to mention an 'acceptable' content (publishers are not charitable institutions). It is the advent of 'print-on-demand' that saves those of us who have no money—copies are produced only as they are ordered. Since a machine does it all, one can order a single copy at the going price, and receive it.

Permit me to cite my own experience. My first book, *The Identity of the New Testament Text*, was published in 1977 by Thomas Nelson Publishers. Each time they wished to do another printing, they graciously allowed me to do some revising. Their final (4th?) printing came out in 1990, so they kept the book in print for at least fifteen years, for which I give them my sincere thanks.[1] It had been out of print for some years when Wipf and Stock Publishers asked for permission to publish it as an academic reprint. So a revised edition came out in 2003, as *The Identity of the New Testament Text II*. Wipf & Stock also did *Identity III*, in 2012. It was during that interval that I tuned in to Family 35, so *Identity III* was the first edition to present and defend that family. The current *Identity IV*, with further heavy revision, I self-published with Amazon. My other books are also available there—what established publisher would have accepted *The Greek New Testament According to Family 35*?

Self-publishing also permits one to make a book available in electronic form, as I have done with mine. This allows people to download into their notebooks, or whatever, so they don't have to carry a book (or several). This is becoming increasingly important, as more and more people are joining the smart-phone culture. That said, however, we should not despise the good old hard copy; for serious study many still prefer a book (you can make notes in a book). In short, we should use both, electronic and printed.

Especially in cultures where 'who you know' is more important than 'what you know', but also in others, we should promote the 'social' vehicle, the sharing with friends and acquaintances. We can invite people over for a cup of coffee (or tea), spread the word wherever we have contacts.

---

[1] By then there were well over 10,000 copies is use around the world, quietly making a difference in people's lives. Every now and again I hear from someone, thanking me for the book, including some Greek professors. Such professors are no longer destroying the faith of their students. There is a stirring at the grassroots level, that the Establishment is doing its best to ignore. When obliged to take notice, it is 'pooh-pooh'; but the time is coming, indeed now is, when that will no longer work.

A convincing presentation:

What is the best way to protect a caged lion? Just open the cage! What is the best way to promote the Truth? Just turn it loose! As Sovereign Jesus said in John 8:31-32, "If you abide in my word, you are my disciples indeed. And you shall know the truth, and the truth shall make you free" (NKJV). The truth will make us free from what? In the immediate context (verse 34), it is from sin, but with reference to the topic in hand, it is able to free us from Satan's blinding and his lies. The Word is the Holy Spirit's sword, and a sword cuts, whether someone believes it or not. That said, however, what can we do so that people will listen to us?

Bombast and ranting should be avoided. They may appeal to the emotions of those who are already on our side, but they will have a negative effect on those we are trying to reach. The truth is best served by the facts, the evidence. And the evidence should be presented in a straightforward fashion, without undue appeal to emotion. However, emotion must be distinguished from presupposition (as well as from principles of reasoned debate). It is impossible to work without presuppositions; everyone has them. It follows that if someone criticizes me for having presuppositions, while pretending that he has none, that someone is being dishonest and perverse (or perhaps just brainwashed and blinded).

Ever since Burgon, who stated his presuppositions honestly and openly (as any true scholar should), there has been a constant and insistent attack against those presuppositions, and even the stating of them. A psychosis has been created to the extent that even some modern defenders of the Majority Text have become paranoid on the subject; they have actually reached the point of excluding the supernatural from their model. However, in Luke 11:23 the Sovereign Creator, Jehovah the Son incarnate, declares: "He who is not with Me is against Me, and he who does not gather with Me scatters." Here is a plain statement—there are only two teams in this world; there are only two sides, two kingdoms; there is no neutral ground; there is no true agnosticism.[1] If you are not with Jesus, you are automatically against Him; if you are not gathering with Him, you are automatically scattering. If you do not receive Jesus' affirmations about Scripture, you have rejected them. Neutrality does not exist.

But how can we reach those who pretend that they have no presuppositions, who refuse, or in any case fail, to declare their presuppositions openly? If those same people criticize us for declaring ours, we may question their basic honesty; but how can we get them to listen? How can you

[1] Agnosticism is a passive rejection; the agnostic is not accepting the claim.

get a blind person to see? How can you get a deaf person to hear? Something must be done about the cause of the condition. The 'cause of the condition' in the area we are discussing is the satanic interference in their thought processes that the Text, 2 Corinthians 4:4, calls 'blinding' (the brainwashing is a consequence of, and an accessory to, that blinding). Just how to address that cause will be treated in the next section. In the meantime, it is necessary to discuss the question of presupposition, but we should attempt to do so with a calm and irenic spirit.[1]

But to return to the matter of presenting the evidence in a convincing fashion, we must keep in mind that brainwashed people are generally ignorant of the evidence. Most professors are 'parrots', simply repeating what they were taught, without ever going back to check the facts. Some older scholars may have become aware of the facts, but because of vested interest they do not mention them to their students; they maintain the party line. For the truth to set people free, the truth must be presented. So I repeat: we must present the evidence in a straightforward manner.

The primary evidence is furnished by the continuous text manuscripts (Greek) of the NT. The evidence furnished by the lectionaries is secondary. The evidence furnished by ancient versions and patristic citations is tertiary. Genuine historical evidence (to the extent that this can be determined) is ancillary. Where the primary evidence is unequivocal, the remaining types should not come into play. For example, at any given point in the four Gospels there will be around 1,700 extant continuous text MSS, representing all lines of transmission and all locales.[2] Where they all agree, there can be no legitimate doubt as to the original wording.

It should also be evident that a variant in a single MS, of whatever age, is irrelevant—it is a false witness to its family archetype, at that point, nothing more. If a number of MSS share a variant, but do not belong to the same family, then they made the mistake independently and are false witnesses to their respective family archetypes—there is no dependency. Where a group of MSS evidently reflect correctly the archetypal form of their family, then we are dealing with a family (not the individual MSS). Families need to be evaluated just as we evaluate individual MSS. It is possible to assign a credibility quotient to a family, based on objective criteria. But of course, any and all families must first be empirically identified and defined, and such identification depends upon the full collation of MSS.

---

[1] I am well aware that it is not easy, which is why I use 'attempt'.

[2] Of course we know that there are many MSS not yet 'extant', not yet identified and catalogued, so the number can only go up.

Although the discipline has (so far) neglected to do its homework (collating MSS), still a massive majority of MSS should be convincing. For example, if a variant enjoys 99% attestation from the primary witnesses, this means that it totally dominates any genealogical 'tree', because it dominated the global transmission of the text. The *INTF Text und Textwert* series, practitioners of the Claremont profile method, H.C. Hoskier, von Soden, Burgon, Scrivener—in short, anyone who has collated any number of MSS—have all demonstrated that the Byzantine bulk of MSS is by no means monolithic. There are any number of streams and rivulets. (Recall that F. Wisse posited thirty-four groups within the Byzantine bulk, with seventy subgroups.) It is clear that there was no 'stuffing the ballot box'; there was no 'papal' decree; there was no recension imposed by ecclesiastical authority. In short, the transmission was predominantly normal.[1]

But to get back to presenting the evidence, we should call attention to the evidence that has been presented down through the years: Herman C. Hoskier's *Concerning the Text of the Apocalypse* and *Codex B and its Allies, a Study and an Indictment*; Hermann von Soden's *magnum opus*—in spite of its imperfections, it contains valuable information; S.C.E. Legg's editions of Matthew and Mark; the IGNTP's edition of Luke; Reuben J. Swanson's editions of Matthew through Galatians; Frederik Wisse on Luke; W.F. Wisselink's *Assimilation as a Criterion for the Establishment of the Text*; Tommy Wasserman on Jude; the *Text und Textwert* series from the *INTF*, and even better, their *Editio Critica Maior* series.

Last, but not least, is my own work. My Greek NT is the first to give the archetype of Family 35, and its critical apparatus is the first to offer percentages with the variants, besides including six published editions. The series on **f**[35] variants, book by book, gives the detailed result of my collations of representative MSS, usually at least thirty per book. All of this is now freely available on the internet from my site, www.prunch.org (mostly in English, but also some in Portuguese). We have ways of making evidence available, but how can we get people to look at it? The best, if not the only, way is to use the spiritual authority that Sovereign Jesus has given us.

Neutralizing the interference:

On what basis might we neutralize interference? The most fundamental question for human life on this planet is that of authority: who has it, to what degree, and on what terms? As the chief priests said to Jesus, "By

---

[1] For a fuller discussion, please see my *Identity IV*, pages 367-69.

what authority are you doing this?" (Luke 20:2). After His death and resurrection Sovereign Jesus said, "All authority in heaven and on earth has been given to me" (Matthew 28:18). So He is perfectly within His rights, clearly competent, to delegate a piece of that authority to us. Consider Luke 10:19: "Take note, I am giving you the authority to trample on snakes and scorpions,[1] and over all the power of the enemy, and nothing at all may harm you." Instead of 'am giving', perhaps 2.5% of the Greek manuscripts, of objectively inferior quality, have 'have given' (as in NIV, NASB, LB, TEV, etc.)—a serious error. Jesus said this perhaps five months before His death and resurrection, addressing the seventy (not just the twelve). The Lord is talking about the future, not the past, a future that includes us!

Consider further John 20:21: Jesus said to them again: "Peace to you! Just as the Father sent me, I also send you." "Just as… so also"—Jesus is sending us just like the Father sent Him. So how did They do it? The Father determined and the Son obeyed: "Behold, I have come to do your will, O God" (Hebrews 10:7). And what was that will? To destroy Satan (Hebrews 2:14) and undo his works (1 John 3:8). Since Jesus did indeed defeat Satan (Colossians 2:15, Ephesians 1:20-21, etc.), but then went back to Heaven, what is left for us is the undoing of his works.[2] It seems clear to me that to

---

[1] The Lord gives us the authority to "trample snakes and scorpions". Well now, to smash the literal insect, a scorpion, you don't need power from on High, just a slipper (if you are fast, you can do it barefoot). To trample a snake I prefer a boot, but we can kill literal snakes without supernatural help. It becomes obvious that Jesus was referring to something other than reptiles and insects. I understand Mark 16:18 to be referring to the same reality—Jesus declares that certain signs will accompany the believers (the turn of phrase virtually has the effect of commands): they will expel demons, they will speak strange languages, they will remove 'snakes', they will place hands on the sick. ("If they drink…" is not a command; it refers to an eventuality.) But what did the Lord Jesus mean by 'snakes'?

In a list of distinct activities Jesus has already referred to demons, so the 'snakes' must be something else. In Matthew 12:34 Jesus called the Pharisees a 'brood of vipers', and in 23:33, 'snakes, brood of vipers'. In John 8:44, after they claimed God as their father, Jesus said, "You are of your father the devil". And 1 John 3:10 makes clear that Satan has many other 'sons' (so also Matthew 13:38-39). In Revelation 20:2 we read: "He seized the dragon, the ancient serpent, who is a slanderer, even Satan, who deceives the whole inhabited earth, and bound him for a thousand years." If Satan is a snake, then his children are also snakes. So then, I take it that our 'snakes' are human beings who have chosen to serve Satan, who have sold themselves to evil. I conclude that the 'snakes' in Luke 10:19 are the same as those in Mark 16:18, but what of the 'scorpions'? Since they also are of the enemy, they may be demons, in which case the term may well include their offspring, the humanoids (for more on this see my article, "In the Days of Noah", available from www.prunch.org). I am still working on the question of just how the removal is done.

[2] For more on this subject see my article, "Biblical Spiritual Warfare" (available from

undo any work we must also undo its consequences (to the extent that that may be possible).

Consider also Ephesians 2:4-6: "But God—being rich in mercy, because of His great love with which He loved us, even when we were dead in our transgressions—made us alive together with Christ (by grace you have been saved) and raised us up together and seated us together in the heavenly realms in Christ Jesus." This is tremendous! Here we have our authority. Christ is now seated at the Father's right, 'far above' the enemy and his hosts. This verse affirms that we who are in Christ are there too! So in Christ we also are far above the enemy and his hosts.[1] Surely, or is that not what is stated in Ephesians 1:16-21?

> I really do not stop giving thanks for you, making mention of you in my prayers: that the God of our Lord, Jesus Christ, the Father of glory, may give you the spirit of wisdom and revelation in the real knowledge[2] of Himself, the eyes of your heart having been enlightened, that you may know what is the hope of His[F] calling, and what the riches of the glory of His inheritance in the saints, and what the exceeding greatness of His power into[3] us who are believing, according to the demonstration of the extent of His might which He exercised in the Christ when He raised Him[S] from among the dead and seated Him at His[F] right, in the heavenly realms, far above every ruler and authority and

---

www.prunch.org).

[1] We should be consciously operating on that basis, but since few churches teach this, most Christians live in spiritual defeat.

[2] I finally settled on 'real knowledge' as the best way to render επιγνωσις, the heightened form of *γνωσις*, 'knowledge'. Real knowledge is more than mere intellectual knowledge, or even true theoretical knowledge—it involves experience. The Text goes on to say, "the eyes of your heart having been enlightened". Real knowledge changes your 'heart', who you are.

[3] "Into us"—that is what the Text says. Note that 'believing' is in the present tense. Consider Ephesians 3:20. "Now to Him who is able to do immeasurably more than all we ask or imagine, according to the power that is working in us." Note that "is working" is also in the present tense; having believed yesterday won't hack it, we must believe today. This tremendous power that God pours into us, as we believe, exceeds our powers of imagination. Well now, my personal horizon is limited and defined by my ability to imagine. Anything that I cannot imagine lies outside my horizon, and so obviously I won't ask for it. I sadly confess that I have not yet arrived at a spiritual level where I can unleash this power—I have yet to make the truth in this verse work for me. But I understand that the truth affirmed here is literal, and I only hope that others will get there before I do (so I can learn from them), if I keep on delaying. The whole point of the exercise (verse 21) is for God to get glory, and to the extent that we do not put His power in us to work we are depriving Him of glory that He could and should have.

power and dominion—even every name that can be named, not only in this age but also in the next.

Now then, "far above every ruler and authority and power and dominion—even every name that can be named, not only in this age but also in the next" must include Satan and his angels. If Christ, seated at the Father's right, is "**far** above" them, and we are in Him, seated at the Father's right, then we too are above all the hosts of the enemy. That is our position and authority for neutralizing interference.

Well and good, but just how are we to go about doing it? Well, at what level should we 'neutralize'? The candidates that suggest themselves are: institutions, teachers, students, church leaders, and lay people. How about working at all levels? Next, what procedures are at our disposal to do the neutralizing? I offer the following: a) forbid any further use of Satan's power, in a specific case; b) claim the undoing of the consequences of the use of that power that there has been (to the extent it may be possible); c) destroy any strongholds of Satan in their minds (including blind spots); d) bind any demons involved and send them to the Abyss, forbidding any further demonic activity; e) take their thoughts captive to the obedience of Christ. In my experience, to be efficient we need to be specific: name the institution; name the person.

But just a minute, I submit for consideration that faith is a basic prerequisite for making use of our position and authority. The theological training I myself received programmed me not to expect supernatural manifestations of power in and through my life and ministry. As a result, I personally find it to be difficult to exercise the kind of faith that the Lord Jesus demands. Consider:

In Matthew 8:5-13 the centurion understood about authority—he gave orders and they were obeyed, promptly and without question.[1] But the Lord Jesus said he had unusually great faith—faith in what? Faith in the Lord's spiritual authority; He could simply give an order and it would happen. Perhaps we should understand this sort of faith as an absolute confidence, without a taint of doubt or fear. In Matthew 21:21 the Lord said, "Assuredly… if you have faith and do not doubt" (see Mark 11:23, "does not doubt in his heart") you can (actually "will") shrivel a tree or send a mountain into the sea. See also Hebrews 10:22, "full assurance of faith", 1 Timothy 2:8, "pray… without doubting", James 1:6, "ask in faith with

---

[1] The centurion did not say, "In the authority of Rome…", he just said, "Do this; do that." The Lord Jesus did not say, "In the authority of the Father…", He just said, "Be clean! Go!" In Luke 10:19 He said, "I give you the authority over all the power of the enemy"—so we have the authority, so it is up to us to speak! Just like Jesus did.

no doubting". Mark 5:34 and Matthew 15:28 offer positive examples; while Peter blew it (Matthew 14:31, "why did you doubt?").

If someone gives a commission, they will presumably back it up to the limit of their ability. Since Christ's ability has no limit, His backing has no limit (on His end). In Matthew 28:18 He said, "All authority has been given to me in heaven and on earth." Then comes the commission: "As you go, make disciples... teaching them to obey all things that I have commanded you"—the pronoun refers back to the eleven apostles (verse 16). So what commands had Jesus given the Eleven? Among other things, "heal the sick, cleanse the lepers, cast out demons" (in Matthew 10:8 perhaps 94% of the Greek manuscripts do not have "raise the dead"). The Eleven also heard John 20:21. Knowing that we are being backed by the Sovereign of the universe, who has all authority and power, we can and should act with complete confidence.

A word of caution is necessary at this point. Consider James 4:7—"Therefore submit to God. Resist the devil and he will flee from you." Note the sequence: we need to verify that we are in submission to God before taking on the devil. Then we should claim our position in Christ at the Father's right hand. Since few Christians have received any remotely adequate level of instruction in the area of biblical spiritual warfare (most have received none), I need to explain the procedures.

Forbid any further use of Satan's power:

This procedure is based on Luke 10:19. Sovereign Jesus gives us 'the' authority over all the power of the enemy. Authority controls power, but since we have access to God's limitless power (Ephesians 3:20), we should not give Satan the satisfaction of our using his (and he could easily deceive us into doing things we shouldn't). We should use our authority to forbid the use of Satan's power, with reference to specific situations—in my experience, we must be specific. (I have tried binding Satan once for all until the end of the world, but it doesn't work; presumably because God's plan calls for the enemy's continued activity in this world. We can limit what the enemy does, but not put him completely out of business, or so I deem.) But just how should we go about it?

In the armor described in Ephesians 6 we find "the sword of the Spirit" (verse 17). A sword is a weapon for offense, although it is also used for defense. The Text tells us that this sword is "the ρημα of God"—ρημα, not λογος. It is God's Word spoken, or applied. Really, what good is a sword left in its sheath? However marvelous our Sword may be (Hebrews 4:12), to produce effect it must come out of the scabbard. The Word needs to be spoken, or written—applied in a specific way.

In the Bible we have many examples where people brought the power of God into action by speaking. Our world began with a creative word from God—spoken (Genesis, 1:3, 6, 9, 11, 14, 20, 24, 26; and see Hebrews 11:3). Moses did a lot of speaking. Elijah spoke (1 Kings 17:1, 18:36, 2 Kings 1:10). Elisha spoke (2 Kings 2:14, 21, 24; 4:16, 43; 6:19). Jesus did a great deal of speaking. Ananias spoke (Acts 9:17). Peter spoke (Acts 9:34, 40). Paul spoke (Acts 13:11; 14:3, 10; 16:18; 20:10; 28:8). In short, we need to speak!

Claim the undoing of the consequences of the use of that power that there has been:

This procedure is based on 1 John 3:8, allied to Luke 10:19. It should be possible for us to command Satan to use his own power to undo messes he has made, thereby obliging him to acknowledge his defeat (which will not sit well with his pride). The Son of God was manifested for the purpose of "undoing the works of the devil" (1 John 3:8), and it is incumbent upon us to continue His work here in this world (John 20:21). How can you undo a work without undoing its consequences as well? The Father sent the Son to undo Satan's works, and the Lord Jesus Christ is sending us to undo Satan's works. Again, I understand that we must be specific.

Destroy any strongholds of Satan in the person's mind:

This procedure is based on 2 Corinthians 10:4 and 1 John 3:8. Since strongholds, and blind spots, in the mind are a work of Satan, and we are here to undo such works, this falls within the area of our competence. It is done by claiming such destruction in so many words, being specific.

Bind any demons involved and send them to the Abyss:

This procedure is based on Mark 3:27 and Luke 8:31. "No one can plunder the strong man's goods, invading his house, unless he first binds the strong man—then he may plunder the house" (Mark 3:27). Since the definite article occurs with 'strong man' the first time the phrase occurs, the entity has already been introduced, so the reference is to Satan. Here is a biblical basis for binding Satan, which is now possible because of Christ's victory. If we can bind Satan, evidently we can also bind any of his subordinates. "And he[1] kept imploring Him that He would not order them to go away into the Abyss" (Luke 8:31).[2] I take it that Jesus did not send them to the Abyss at that time because He had not yet won the victory,

---

[1] The boss demon does most of the talking, representing his cohort.

[2] The Text has 'the Abyss', presumably the same one mentioned in Revelation 20:3. The demons knew something that most of us do not.

and the demons were 'within their rights', under Satan, who was still the god of this world. But the demons were obviously worried! (They knew very well who Jesus was, and what He could do.) I would say that this is one of the 'greater things' (John 14:12) that we may now do—rather, that we should do. As for forbidding any further demonic activity, we have the Lord's example (Mark 9:25), and we are to do what He did (John 14:12).

Take their thoughts captive to the obedience of Christ:

This procedure is based on 2 Corinthians 10:5. In the context, the thoughts are of people who are serving Satan (even if unwittingly). (Of course we should always be checking to be sure that we ourselves are operating within 'the mind of Christ', 1 Corinthians 2:15-16.) Now this procedure moves away from simply neutralizing the enemy's interference, since it introduces a positive 'interference', but it is relevant to the issue being discussed here, since it is protection against falling back into the former error. Again we must be specific.

Some further texts that may apply:
Luke 4:18-21, Psalm 149:5-9, John 14:12.

In Luke 4:18-21 Jesus includes "to set at liberty those who are oppressed" (Isaiah 58:6) as one of the things He was sent to do. Turning to Isaiah 58:6, we find Jehovah stating what kind of 'fast' He would like to see: "To loose the fetters of wickedness [a], to undo the yoke-ropes [b]; to let oppressed ones go free [a], and that you (pl.) break every yoke [b]." As is typical of Hebrew grammar, the two halves are parallel. "To loose the fetters of wickedness" and "to let oppressed ones go free" are parallel. Who placed the "fetters" and who is doing the oppressing? Well, although people can certainly forge their own bonds through their own wicked lifestyle, I take it that the point here is that wicked beings have placed the fetters on others. "To undo yoke-ropes" and "that ye break every yoke" go together. First we should untie the ropes that bind the yoke to the neck, then we should break the yokes themselves. I gain the clear impression that this text is talking about the activity of Satan's servants, men and angels. Using culture, worldview, legal devices, threats, blackmail, lies, deception and just plain demonizing and witchcraft, they bind individuals, families, ethnic groups, etc., with a variety of fetters and instruments of oppression.

So what does this have to do with our subject? Well, fasting was an important and required component in their worship of God. So this kind of 'fasting' is something that Jehovah overtly wants to see; it is specifically His will. So when we see any work of Satan in someone's life, it is God's will that we undo it. If we know it is God's will, we can proceed with complete confidence. And it is part of our commission (John 20:21).

Notice also Psalms 149:5-9. "Let the saints exult in glory; let them sing for joy in their beds. Let the high praises of God be in their mouth, and a two-edged sword in their hand—to execute vengeance upon the nations and punishments upon the peoples; to bind their kings with chains and their nobles with fetters of iron; to execute upon them the written judgment. This honor is for all His saints." Note that the saints are in their beds, so the activity described in the subsequent verses must take place in the spiritual realm. I assume that the 'kings' and 'nobles' include both men and fallen angels. The activity described is the prerogative of "all His saints"—if you are one of those saints, it is up to you. There are a number of 'written judgments' in the Text: Zechariah 5:2-4, Proverbs 20:10, Isaiah 10:1-2, Romans 1:26-36 and 1 Corinthians 6:9-10, at least.

In John 14:12 the Lord Jesus said: "Most assuredly I say to you, the one believing into me, he too will do the works that I do; in fact he will do greater works than these, because I am going to my Father." "Most assuredly" is actually "amen, amen"—rendered "verily, verily" in the AV. Only John registers the word as repeated, in the other Gospels it is just "amen". In the contemporary literature we have no example of anyone else using the word in this way. It seems that Jesus coined His own use, and the point seems to be to call attention to an important pronouncement: "Stop and listen!" Often it precedes a formal statement of doctrine or policy, as here.

"The one believing into me, he too will do the works that I do." This is a tremendous statement, and not a little disconcerting. Notice that the Lord said, "will do"; not 'maybe', 'perhaps', 'if you feel like it'; and certainly not 'if the doctrine of your church permits it'! If you believe, you **will do!** The verb 'believe' is in the present tense; if you are believing you will do; it follows that if you are not doing, it is because you are not believing. 2 + 2 = 4. Doing what? "The works that I do." Well, Jesus preached the Gospel, He taught, He cast out demons, He healed all sorts and sizes of sickness and disease, He raised an occasional dead person, and He performed a variety of miracles (water to wine, walk on water, stop a storm instantaneously, transport a boat several miles instantaneously, multiply food, shrivel a tree—and He implied that the disciples should have stopped the storm and multiplied the food, and He stated that they could shrivel a tree [Peter actually took a few steps on water]). So how about us? The preaching and teaching we can handle, but what about the rest? I once heard the president of a certain Christian college affirm that this verse obviously could not mean what it says because it is not happening! Well, in his own experience and in that of his associates I guess it isn't. But many people today cast out demons and heal, and I personally know someone who has raised a dead person. Miracles are also happening. So how about me? And you?

"In fact he will do greater works than these." Well now, if we cast out demons, heal and perform miracles, is that not enough? Jesus wants more, He wants "greater things" than those just mentioned [do not forget what He said in Matthew 7:22-23]. Notice again that He said "will do", not maybe, perhaps, or if your church permits. But what could be 'greater' than miracles? This cannot refer to modern technology because in that event such 'greater things' would not have been available to the believers during the first 1900 years. Note that the key is in the Lord's final statement (in verse 12), "because I am going to my Father". Only if He won could He return to the Father, so He is here declaring His victory before the fact. It is on the basis of that victory that the 'greater things' can be performed. Just what are those 'greater' things? For my answer, see my outline, "Biblical Spiritual Warfare".

In verse 12 the verb 'will do' is singular, both times, so it has to do with the individual. Observe that the Lord did **not** say, "you apostles", "only during the apostolic age", "only until the canon is complete", or whatever. He said, "the one believing", present tense, so this applies to any and all subsequent moments up to our time. To deny the truth contained in this verse is to make the Lord Jesus Christ out to be a liar. Somehow I do not think that is very smart.[1]

The 'Crux' of a 'Lost' Original

Returning to the opening paragraph, is/was the original wording lost? I answer with an emphatic, "**No**". It certainly exists within the Byzantine bulk. To my mind, any time at least 90% of the primary witnesses agree, there can be no reasonable question; it is statistically impossible that a non-original reading could score that high.[2] Any time a reading garners an attestation of at least 80% its probability is high. But for perhaps 2% of the

---

[1] Also, to affirm that the miraculous gifts ceased when the last shovelful of dirt fell on the Apostle John's grave is an historical falsehood. Christians who lived during the second, third and fourth centuries, whose writings have come down to us, affirm that the gifts were still in use in their day. No 20th or 21st century Christian, who was not there, is competent to contradict them. And please see the footnote at 1 Corinthians 13:12 in my translation, *The Sovereign Creator Has Spoken*. Any 'cessationist' will have a stronghold of Satan in his mind on that subject, because he has embraced a lie. Any doctrine that derives from reaction against excesses and abuses gives victory to Satan. Any argument designed to justify lack of spiritual power cannot be right.

[2] See Appendix C in my *Identity IV*.

words in the NT the attestation falls below 80% (a disproportionate number being in the Apocalypse), and at this point we need to shift our attention from MSS to families. Once all MSS have been collated and have been empirically assigned to families, then we can confine our attention to those families from the start (as I have done in the Apocalypse). I have mentioned elsewhere assigning a credibility quotient to each family, based on objective criteria, and this needs to be done. Unfortunately, there is a great deal of 'homework' waiting to be done in this area. So far as I know, only Family 35 has an empirically defined profile (defined by a complete collation of a representative number of the MSS that make up the family), at least to this date.[1]

About the 2% with attestation below 80%, in a heavy majority of the cases the difference can hardly be reflected in a translation. A reader will understand the intended meaning with either variant. But within Family 35 there is very little significant variation, and the archetypal form is demonstrable. For example, of the forty-three family members I have collated for the General Epistles, twenty-eight are identical (perfect) for 2 & 3 John (but not always the same MSS), twenty-two are identical for Jude, five for 2 Peter, four each for James and 1 John, and three for 1 Peter.

For my article, "Copyist Care Quotient" (see Part II above), I collated fifty-one (now 53) representatives of Family 35 for Mark. I analyzed the variants contained in MS 1384 (eapr, XI, Andros)—of the fifty-three MSS I collated, at least forty-four are better than 1384, so it is only a mediocre representative. However, with four exceptions, only a single letter or syllable is involved, and nowhere is the meaning seriously affected. **Someone reading MS 1384 would not be misled as to the intended meaning at any point in the book**. I say this is noteworthy, and it is typical of almost all $\mathbf{f}^{35}$ MSS. Down through the centuries of transmission, anyone with ac-

---

[1] So far as I know, neither $\mathbf{f}^{1}$ nor $\mathbf{f}^{13}$ exists outside of the Gospels, but even there, has anyone ever produced an empirically defined profile for either one? Consider the following statement by Metzger:

> It should be observed that, in accord with the theory that members of f^{1} and f^{13} were subject to progressive accommodation to the later Byzantine text, scholars have established the text of these families by adopting readings of family witnesses that differ from the Textus Receptus. Therefore the citation of the siglum f^{1} and f^{13} may, in any given instance, signify a minority of manuscripts (or even only one) that belong to the family. (*A Textual Commentary on the Greek New Testament* [companion to UBS^{3}], p. xii.)

Would it be unreasonable to say that such a proceeding is unfair to the reader? Does it not mislead the user of the apparatus? At least as used by the UBS editions, those sigla do not represent empirically defined profiles.

cess to an **f**[35] representative could know the intended meaning of the Autograph.[1] Not only that, most lines of transmission within the Byzantine bulk would be reasonably close, good enough for most practical purposes. This is also true of the much maligned *Textus Receptus*; it is certainly good enough for most practical purposes. Down through the centuries of Church history, most people could have had reasonable access to God's written revelation.

Some years ago now, Maurice Robinson did a complete collation of 1,389 MSS that contain the *P.A.* (John 7:53-8:11),[2] and I had William Pierpont's photocopy of those collations in my possession for two months, spending most of that time studying those collations. As I did so, it became obvious to me that von Soden 'regularized' his data, arbitrarily 'creating' the alleged archetypal form for his first four families, **M**[1,2,3,4]—if they exist at all, they are rather fluid. His **M**[5&6] do exist, having distinct profiles for the purpose of showing that they are different, but they are a bit 'squishy', with enough internal confusion to make the choice of the archetypal form to be arbitrary. In fact, I suspect that they will have to be subdivided. In contrast to the above, his **M**[7] (that I call Family 35) has a solid, unambiguous profile—the archetypal form is demonstrable, empirically determined.

As for the Apocalypse, of the nine groups that Hoskier identified, only his Complutensian (that I call Family 35) is homogenous. Of the others, the main ones all have subdivisions, which will require their own profile.

Given my presuppositions, I consider that I have good reason for declaring the divine preservation of the precise original wording of the complete New Testament Text to this day. That wording is reproduced in my edition of the Greek NT. My presuppositions include: the Sovereign Creator exists; He inspired the biblical Text; He promised to preserve it for a thousand generations (1 Chronicles 16:15); so He must have an active, ongoing interest in that preservation [there have been fewer than 300 generations since Adam, so He has a ways to go!]. If He was preserving the

---

1 Since **f**[35] MSS are scattered all over, or all around, the Mediterranean world, such access would have been feasible for most people.

2 240 MSS omit the P.A., 64 of which are based on Theophylact's commentary. Fourteen others have lacunae, but are not witnesses for total omission. A few others certainly contain the passage but the microfilm is illegible. So, 1389 + 240 + 14 + 7(?) = about 1650 MSS checked by Robinson. That does not include Lectionaries, of which he also checked a fair number. (These are microfilms held by the *INTF* in Münster. We now know that there are many more extant MSS, and probably even more that are not yet 'extant'.) Unfortunately, so far as I know, Robinson has yet to publish his collations, thus making them available to the public at large.

original wording in some line of transmission other than **f**^{35}, would that transmission be any less careful than what I have demonstrated for **f**^{35}? I think not. So any line of transmission characterized by internal confusion is disqualified—this includes **all** the other lines of transmission that I have seen so far![1]

On the basis of the evidence so far available I affirm the following:

1. The original wording was never 'lost', and its transmission down through the years was basically normal, being recognized as inspired material from the beginning.
2. That normal process resulted in lines of transmission.
3. To delineate such lines, MSS must be grouped empirically on the basis of a shared mosaic of readings.
4. Such groups or families must be evaluated for independence and credibility.
5. The largest clearly defined group is Family 35.
6. Family 35 is demonstrably independent of all other lines of transmission throughout the NT.
7. Family 35 is demonstrably ancient, dating to the 3rd century, at least.[2]
8. Family 35 representatives come from all over the Mediterranean area; the geographical distribution is all but total.[3]
9. Family 35 is not a recension, was not created at some point subsequent to the Autographs.
10. Family 35 is an objectively/empirically defined entity throughout the NT; it has a demonstrable, diagnostic profile from Matthew 1:1 to Revelation 22:21.
11. The archetypal form of Family 35 is demonstrable—it has been demonstrated (see the "Profile" in Part II above).
12. The Original Text is the ultimate archetype; any candidate must also

---

[1] Things like **M**^{6} and **M**^{5} in John 7:53-8:11 come to mind.

[2] Family 35 readings are attested by early witnesses, but without pattern, and therefore without dependency. But there are many hundreds of such readings. So how did the **f**^{35} archetype come by all those early readings? Did its creator travel around and collect a few readings from Aleph, a few from B, a few from $P^{45,66,75}$, a few from W and D, etc.? Is not such a suggestion patently ridiculous? The only reasonable conclusion is that the **f**^{35} text is ancient (also independent).

[3] And for some places in Greece, based on their surviving copies, it was all they used.

be an archetype—a real, honest to goodness, objectively verifiable archetype—there is only one (so far), Family 35.[1]

13. God's concern for the preservation of the biblical Text is evident: I take it that passages such as 1 Chronicles 16:15, Psalm 119:89, Isaiah 40:8, Matthew 5:18, Luke 16:17 and 21:33, John 10:35, 1 Peter 1:23-25 and Luke 4:4 may reasonably be taken to imply a promise that the Scriptures (to the tittle) will be preserved for man's use (we are to live "by *every* word of God"), and to the end of the world ("for a thousand generations"), but no intimation is given as to just how God proposed to do it. We must deduce the answer from what He has indeed done—we discover that He **did**!

14. This concern is reflected in Family 35; it is characterized by incredibly careful transmission (in contrast to other lines). [I have a perfect copy of the Family 35 archetypal text for most NT books (22); I have copies made from a perfect exemplar (presumed) for another four (4); as I continue to collate MSS I hope to add the last one (Acts), but even for it the archetypal form is demonstrable.]

15. If God was preserving the original wording in some line of transmission other than Family 35, would that line be any less careful? I think not. So any line of transmission characterized by internal confusion is disqualified—this includes **all** the other lines of transmission that I have seen so far.

16. I affirm that God used Family 35 to preserve the precise original wording of the New Testament Text; it is reproduced in my edition of the Greek Text.[2]

I claim to have demonstrated the superiority of Family 35 based on size (number of representatives), independence, age, geographical distribution, profile (empirically determined), care (see "Copyist Care Quotient" in Part II) and range (all 27 books). I challenge any and all to do the same for any other line of transmission!

---

1 If you want to be a candidate for the best lawyer in your city, you must be a lawyer, or the best carpenter, or oncologist, or whatever. If there is only one candidate for mayor in your town, who gets elected?

2 And God used mainly the Eastern Orthodox Churches to preserve the NT Text down through the centuries—they have always used a Text that was an adequate representation of the Original, for all practical purposes.

APPENDIX

"Accumulated Errors of Fourteen Centuries"

The Gospel manuscript GA 1700 is the most recent dated manuscript representing Family 35 that has come to my attention. It is dated at 1623 AD and is held by the National Library of Greece. I wish to register my sincere thanks to the Center for the Study of New Testament Manuscripts for making available a digital copy of this manuscript. Although from the seventeenth century, the hand is very legible. I have done a complete collation of this manuscript for John's Gospel, and invite attention to the result. However, I wish to analyze that result using the following quote as a backdrop, taken from the preface to the Revised Standard Version, p. ix.

> The King James Version of the New Testament was based upon a Greek text that was marred by mistakes, containing the accumulated errors of fourteen centuries of manuscript copying... We now possess many more ancient manuscripts of the New Testament, and are far better equipped to seek to recover the original wording of the Greek text.

The first thing that interests me here is the allegation that the TR contains "the accumulated errors of fourteen centuries of manuscript copying". If that is true, then a seventeenth century MS should be a veritable wastebasket of 'accumulated errors'. So let us see how GA 1700 fares.

To begin, it has no fewer than 136 deviations from the family archetype (in John), making it by far the worst of the 54 family representatives that I have collated for that book; the second worst has 'only' 41 deviations. Although due to carelessness and mixture 1700 is a marginal member of Family 35 in John, it is nonetheless clearly a member. Of the 12 readings that I rank as +++, it misses one; of the 17 readings I rank as ++--, it misses one; of the 17 readings I rank as ++, it misses one; of the 15 readings I rank as +--, it misses none; of the 12 readings I rank as +, it misses three; for a total of six out of 44. Although by no means a thing of pristine beauty, it belongs to the family.[1]

I will now list the 136 deviations, showing selected further attestation that the 1700 variant has; any **f**^{35} MSS that I have collated are listed first, followed after the [] by anything else. My lists of evidence are selective, being sufficient for my purpose. The first reading is that of the family

[1] For the Family 35 profile and the key, please see Part II above.

archetype; the second is that of GA 1700;[1] if no further MSS are listed, I treat the variant as a singular reading—of the 136 total, at least 54 are singulars, indicating that the copyist was rather careless (it should be obvious that a singular reading cannot be an 'accumulated error'; it is a private error). But the remaining 82 furnish food for thought. Here is the list, that I have numbered to facilitate subsequent discussion (numbers in bold are singulars):

1. 1:5 σκοτια || σκοτεια [2%] P[75] C, 579 [this is simply an alternate spelling, and therefore not a proper variant; it recurs at 12:35 and 20:1]

2. 1:18 εις τον κολπον || εν τοις κολποις [] 565 [this one is strange; the two phrases were evidently regarded as synonymous; if a dependency cannot be established, the change was made independently by the two copyists]

3. 1:19 οτε || οταν [a singular, that does not affect the meaning]

4. 1:28 βιθαβαρα || βηθανια [65%] P[66,75] ℵ A, B, C, W, Θ, 28, 579, 1424 [this is one of the places where 1700 departs from the family; a place name sticks out like a sore thumb, and the variant is the reading of the predominant lectionary type; the monk being used to hearing the variant would naturally change the text]

5. 1:38 λεγεται || λεγετε 553, 1617, 2352 [] W [the forms are virtual synonyms, and the change was presumably made independently; that W also has the change is merely a curiosity]

6. 1:40a ην || 1 δε [2%] A, W, Λ, f[13], 579, 1424 [the addition is a 'natural', and could have happened independently; the meaning is not affected; 1700 agrees with 1424 quite frequently]

7. 1:40b των δυο των ακουσαντων || ~ 3412 [a singular, that does not affect the meaning]

8. 1:42 εμβλεψας || 1 δε 1384,1667 [20%] P[75] Θ, Λ, f[13], 1071, 1424 [the addition is a 'natural', and could have happened independently; the meaning is not affected]

9. 1:45 ευρηκαμεν || 1 τον [a singular, that does not affect the meaning]

10. 1:50 μειζω || μειζονα [] P[66] ℵ [presumably the copyist did not have access to either of the early MSS, so this is an independent

[1] For the single example where I list three readings, it is the third one.

change; it is a change in gender dictated by the imagined referent; the meaning is not affected]

11. 2:5 λεγη || λεγει 1559, 1667 [30%] Θ, Λ, f[13], 579, 1071, 1424 [the Subjunctive is expected, but the Indicative is possible—this is probably not an itacism; the meaning is not affected]

12. 2:10 συ || 1 δε [2%] ℵ, Λ, f[13], 1071, 1346 [the addition is a 'natural', and could have happened independently; the meaning is not affected]

13. 2:15 φραγελλιον || φραγγελιον 141, 685, 1694, 2466 [this is simply an alternate spelling, and therefore not a proper variant]

14. 2:17 καταφαγεται || κατεφαγε [5%] 69, 1071 [this is a difference in tense, that does not affect the meaning]

15. 3:15 εχη || εχει 824, 1713, 2322 [40%] Θ, Λ, f[13], 579, 1071, 1346, 1424 [the Subjunctive is expected, but the Indicative is possible—this is probably not an itacism; the meaning is not affected]

16. 3:16 εχη || εχει 824, 1686, 1559, 2322 [30%] Λ,f[13],579, 1071, 1424 [the Subjunctive is expected, but the Indicative is possible—this is probably not an itacism; the meaning is not affected]

17. 3:22 μετ αυτων || μετα των μαθητων αυτου [] 28 [in the context the phrases are synonymous; the meaning is not affected; the change is probably independent, which would make this a 'singular' reading]

18. 3:24 την || --- [] Θ, f[1], 565 [this change could have happened independently; the meaning is not affected]

19. 3:28 μοι μαρτυρειτε || ~ 21 928, 1334, 1572, 1667 [a mere reversal of word order, that does not affect the meaning; this may well have happened independently]

20. 3:36 οψεται || οψετε [the forms are virtual synonyms; the meaning is not affected]

21. 4:14 διψηση || διψησει [10%] P^{75} ℵ A, B, Θ, f[13], 28, 1071 [the Subjunctive is expected, but the Indicative is possible—this is probably not an itacism; the meaning is not affected]

22. 4:17 οτι || --- [direct or indirect quote; the meaning is not affected]

23. 4:20 εστιν ο τοπος οπου δει προσκυνειν || ~ 56 εκει 123 [two ways of saying the same thing]

24. 4:36 χαιρη || χαιρει [30%] Θ, Λ, f13, 28, 579, 1071, 1424 [the Subjunctive is expected, but the Indicative is possible—this is probably not an itacism; the meaning is not affected]

25. 4:43 τας || --- [] 1424 [this could have happened independently; the meaning is not affected]

26. 4:48 ουν || --- [] P66* [this presumably happened independently; the meaning is not affected]

27. 5:2 εβραιστι || εβραιστη 1339, 2466 [2%] f13, 28, 579, 1071, 1424 [this is simply an alternate spelling, and therefore not a proper variant]

28. 5:31 εαν || 1 γαρ 2352 [] 28 [the addition is a 'natural', and could have happened independently; the meaning is not affected]

29. 5:34 την || --- [a singular, that does not affect the meaning]

30. 5:36 με απεσταλκεν || ~ 21 [a mere reversal of word order, that does not affect the meaning]

31. 5:39a ερευνατε || ερευναται [a corrected singular]

32. 5:39b αυταις || αυτοις [] 1071 [this is an obvious spelling error that a reader would correct automatically; given the copyist's carelessness, he may have repeated the error from his exemplar]

33. 6:2 αυτου τα σημεια || ~ 231 [a mere reversal of word order, that does not affect the meaning]

34. 6:19a ως || ωσει [1%] A,D,f1,565 [the change is an 'easy', and could have happened independently; the meaning is not affected]

35. 6:19b γινομενον || γενομενον 128, 685 [] G, 1424 [a change in tense, that does not affect the meaning; in the cursives *epsilon* and *iota* are often easily confused]

36. 6:21 λαβειν αυτον || ~ 21 [] D [a mere reversal of word order, presumably independent, that does not affect the meaning]

37. 6:22 ενεβησαν || ανεβησαν (12.9%) [although the verbs are different, in the context they act as synonyms; the meaning is not affected]

38. 6:27 την βρωσιν2 || --- [2%] ℵ, 28, 1071 [this could have happened independently; since the phrase is a repetition, the meaning is not affected by its omission; it is a possible case of homoioarcton]

39. 6:30 συ || --- 201 [10%] W, f13, 579 [this could have happened independently; the meaning is not affected]

40. 6:32a υμιν^2 || ημιν [an itacism resulting in nonsense; not a proper variant]

41. 6:32b αρτον^2 || 1 τον [] P^{75v} [this could have happened independently; the meaning is not affected]

42. 6:37 εκβαλω || εκβαλλω 18, 1617, 2466 [1%] G [a change in tense, that does not affect the meaning, but since the forms received the same pronunciation, the change could have been made independently, without thinking]

43. 6:40 εχη || εχει [8%] P^{66c}, Λ^c, f^{13}, 28, 579, 1071, 1424 [the Subjunctive is expected, but the Indicative is possible—this is probably not an itacism; the meaning is not affected]

44. 6:45 ερχεται || ερχετε [a corrected singular]

45. 6:50 καταβαινων || καταβαινον [an itacistic misspelling that changes the gender incorrectly]

46. 6:54 αυτον || 1 εν 1339, 1496, 1617, 1637 [25%] C,Λ,f^{13},28,1071 [the addition is a 'natural', and could have happened independently; the meaning is not affected]

47. 6:63 ωφελει || ωφελη [an itacism]

48. 6:65 αυτω || --- [] א* [this could have happened independently; the meaning is not affected]

49. 6:67 τοις || τους [] H,Y [a spelling error that presumably happened independently]

50. 6:68 απελευσομεθα || πορευσομεθα [a singular; perhaps his exemplar was smudged; the verbs are synonymous in this context; the meaning is not affected]

51. 7:1 ο ιησους μετα ταυτα || ~ 3412 [a mere reversal of word order, that does not affect the meaning]

52. 7:28 αληθινος || αληθης [] P^{66}א [this could have happened independently; the meaning is not affected]

53. 7:30 την χειρα || τας χειρας [1%] W, f^1, 1071 [singular or plural in this context does not affect the meaning]

54. 7:31 ων || ωνπερ [a singular; the forms are synonymous in this context; the meaning is not affected]

55. 7:39 ο || ου 201, 480, 547, 1384 [70%] P^{66} א, D, W, Θ, f^{1,13}, 28, 579, 1424 [this is one of the places where 1700 departs from the

family; the genitive follows the case of the referent, but the accusative correctly gives the direct object of the verb; the meaning is not affected]

56. 7:46 ουτως || --- 897 [] 28 [this could have happened independently; the meaning is not affected]

57. 7:50 ων || --- [] L [this could have happened independently; the meaning is not affected]

58. 8:4 αυτοφωρω || αυτοφορω 1145, 1334, 1559, 2352, 2466, I.2110 [60%] 124, 1346 [this is one of the places where 1700 departs from the family; they are different spellings of the same word; the meaning is not affected]

59. 8:33 οτι || --- [] W,f^1,565 [this could have happened independently; the meaning is not affected]

60. 8:36 ο υιος υμας || ~ 312 [a mere reversal of word order, that does not affect the meaning]

61. 8:48 σαμαρειτης || σαμαρειτις 1559, 1617 [1%] 28, 1424 [they are different spellings of the same word; the meaning is not affected]

62. 8:52 εγνωκαμεν || εγνωμεν [a singular; probably a careless mistake that happens to change the tense; the meaning is not affected]

63. 8:57 ουν || --- [a singular; the copyist omits this conjunction a number of times, and one wonders why; the meaning is not affected]

64. 9:20 αυτοις || --- [5%] $P^{66,75}$ℵ, B, W, f^{13} [this could have happened independently; the meaning is not affected]

65. 9:21a ηνοιξεν || ανεωξεν [] Θ,579 [alternate spellings of the same form; the meaning is not affected]

66. 9:21b ημεις || --- [a singular; the meaning is not affected]

67. 9:24 ουν || --- [] 579 [this could have happened independently; the meaning is not affected]

68. 9:35 ο ιησους || --- [a singular; a possible case of homoioarcton; the meaning is not affected]

69. 10:1 αναβαινων || αναβαινον [an itacistic misspelling that changes the gender incorrectly]

70. 10:5 ακολουθησωσιν || ακουσωσιν [a singular; perhaps his exemplar was smudged; the verbs are virtually synonymous in this context; the meaning is not affected]

71. 10:13 μελει || μελλει 83 [30%] 1424 [the verbs are different, but they were pronounced the same way, and in the context only one of the meanings will work, so someone hearing the text read would naturally make the right choice; so much so that I wonder if the longer form did not come to be regarded as an alternate spelling for the shorter]

72. 10:16 ακουσουσιν || ακουσωσιν (38.1%) P[66] ℵ, A, W, Θ, Λ, f[13], 28, 579, 1071, 1424 [future Indicative or aorist Subjunctive; in this context they have the same function]

73. 10:18 αλλ εγω τιθημι αυτην απ εμαυτου || --- [] D [presumably these are independent instances of homoioteleuton; I do not consider homoioteleuton to be a proper variant, it is just an unintentional error]

74. 10:20 μαινεται || μενεται [] P[66]A,Θ,f[13] [presumably an itacistic misspelling that changes the verb incorrectly, resulting in nonsense]

75. 10:24 ουν || --- [a singular; the copyist omits this conjunction a number of times, and one wonders why; the meaning is not affected]

76. 10:40 οπου || ου [] P[66] [this could have happened independently; a careless error resulting in nonsense]

77. 11:2 εαυτης || αυτης 547, 789, 1461 [60%] P[45,66,75] ℵ, A, B, D, W, Θ, Λ, f[1], 28, 579, 1071, 1424 [this is one of the places where 1700 departs from the family; they are two ways of saying the same thing; the meaning is not affected]

78. 11:5 την[1] || --- [a singular; the meaning is not affected]

79. 11:9 οτι το φως του κοσμου τουτου βλεπει || --- [a singular; presumably an instance of homoioteleuton; I do not consider homoioteleuton to be a proper variant, it is just an unintentional error]

80. 11:12 κυριε || --- [a singular; the meaning is not affected]

81. 11:19 παραμυθησωνται || παραμυθησονται 1686 [15%] 579, 1071 [future Indicative or aorist Subjunctive; in this context they have the same function]

82. 11:28 εφωνησεν || ελαλησε [a singular involving a synonym; the meaning is not affected]

83. 11:38 εμβριμωμενος || 1 τω πνευματι [a singular; the meaning is not affected]

84. 11:39 ηδη || ηδει [an itacistic misspelling that results in nonsense]

85. 11:53 ινα αποκτεινωσιν || ιναποκτεινωσιν [a careless error resulting in nonsense; a reader would automatically supply the missing vowel]

86. 12:2 ανακειμενων συν || συνανακειμενων [10%] W, 28, 1071 || συνανακειμενων συν [a singular, but built on a dependency; the meaning is not affected]

87. 12:6 εμελεν || εμελλεν f^{35pt} [60%] f^{13}, 28, 1424 [this is one of the places where 1700 departs from the family; the verbs are different, but they were pronounced the same way, and in the context only one of the meanings will work, so someone hearing the text read would naturally make the right choice; so much so that I wonder if the longer form did not come to be regarded as an alternate spelling for the shorter]

88. 12:7 αυτο || αυαυτο [the copyist repeated a syllable going from one line to the next]

89. 12:26a διακονη || διακονει [] 28, 1071, 1424 [the Subjunctive is expected, but the Indicative is possible; in the context the meaning is not affected]

90. 12:26b διακονη || διακονει [a singular; see above]

91. 12:37 αυτου σημεια || ~ 21 [] Λ, f^{13}, 579 [a mere reversal of word order, that does not affect the meaning]

92. 12:42 ωμολογουν || ομολογουν [a singular; an itacism resulting in an alternate spelling; the meaning is not affected]

93. 13:26 ω || ο [] 579, 1071, 1424 [an itacism that changes the gender incorrectly]

94. 13:27 ουν || --- [a singular; the copyist omits this conjunction a number of times, and one wonders why; the meaning is not affected]

95. 13:29 εχομεν || εχωμεν [] 579 [the change in mode does not affect the meaning]

96. 13:30-31 ην δε νυξ οτε εξηλθεν || --- [] G [a clear case of homoioteleuton, that happened independently]

97. 14:13 αιτησητε || αιτησηται 1145 [] P^{66} D, W [the copyist corrected himself]

98. 14:23 ποιησομεν || ποιησωμεν 1667, 1686 [5%] Λ, 28, 1424 [future Indicative or aorist Subjunctive; in this context they have the same function]

99. 15:2 φερη || φερει 553 [] 124, 788, 1346 [the Subjunctive is expected, but the Indicative is possible; in the context the meaning is not affected]

100. 15:7 αιτησεσθε || αιτησησθε [] 1424 [future Indicative or aorist Subjunctive; in this context they have the same function]

101. 15:8 φερητε || φερηται [a corrected singular]

102. 15:11 η χαρα[1] || --- [a singular resulting from both homoioarcton and homoioteleuton; not a proper variant]

103. 15:15 υμας λεγω || ~ 21 [1%] P^{66} ℵ, A, B, 579, 1071, 1424 [a mere reversal of word order, that does not affect the meaning]

104. 15:18 γινωσκετε || --- [a careless singular resulting in nonsense]

105. 15:20 ουκ εστιν δουλος μειζων του κυριου αυτου || --- [a careless singular, perhaps omitting a whole line in his exemplar, but the resulting text makes good sense]

106. 15:25 οτι εμισησαν με δωρεαν || --- [another careless singular, possibly due to homoioarcton; the resulting text makes sense, but is a little incomplete]

107. 16:7a αλλ εγω την αληθειαν λεγω υμιν || --- [another careless singular; the resulting text makes sense; notice that the copyist was evidently having a bad day]

108. 16:7b υμας[1] || 1 και [a singular; the meaning is not affected]

109. 16:21a τικτη || τικτει 553 [10%] Λ, 28, 1346, 1424 [the Subjunctive is expected, but the Indicative is possible—this is probably not an itacism; the meaning is not affected]

110. 16:21b γεννηση || γεννησει [a singular; future Indicative or aorist Subjunctive; in this context they have the same function]

111. 16:33 εχητε || εχετε [1%] Λ, 28, 1071 [the Subjunctive is expected, but the Indicative is possible—this is probably not an itacism; the meaning is not affected]

112. 17:10 δεδοξασμαι || δεδοξασμε [2%] P^{66c} ℵ, Θ, 1346, 1424 [an itacism resulting in nonsense; a reader would automatically make the correction]

113. 17:23 γινωσκη || γινωσκει 553,1686 [2%] Λ, f^{13}, 28, 579, 1071 [the Subjunctive is expected, but the Indicative is possible—this is probably not an itacism; the meaning is not affected]

114. 18:13 αυτον || --- [2%] P^{66} ℵ, B, C, D, W, 579, 1071 [the repetition of the pronoun is not necessary to the sense; the meaning is not affected]

115. 18:15 τω ιησου^{1} || αυτω [a singular; the meaning is not affected]

116. 18:17 συ || --- [a singular; the meaning is not affected]

117. 18:25 σιμων || --- 1435 [] 1424 [the meaning is not affected]

118. 18:36a ηγωνιζοντο || ηγονιζοντο [a singular; an itacism resulting in a misspelling; the meaning is not affected]

119. 18:36b ουκ εστιν || --- [a singular; the omission creates a contradiction within the verse; just why the copyist did it is impossible to say, unless it is an unintentional error, of which there are not a few]

120. 18:37 αυτω || --- 201, 2322 [the omission does not affect the meaning]

121. 18:39a συνηθεια || συνηθει [a singular; a careless misspelling]

122. 18:39b ημιν || υμιν 928, 1334, 1572, 1667 [80%] ℵ, A, B, W, Θ, Λ, $f^{1,13}$, 28, 579, 1071, 1346, 1424 [this is one of the places where 1700 departs from the family; the original change was probably deliberate, introducing an improbability; it is scarcely credible that imperial Rome would release a prisoner based on a Jewish demand; however, the change makes little difference in the total meaning of the account]

123. 18:39c υμιν^{2} || 1 ινα [a singular; the meaning is not affected]

124. 19:1 ελαβεν || --- [a singular; a possible homoioteleuton; the omission of the verb leaves the clause incomplete]

125. 19:13 εβραιστι || εβραιστη [] f^{13}, 28^{s}, 579, 1346, 1424 [this is simply an alternate spelling, and therefore not a proper variant]

126. 19:15 εχομεν || εχωμεν 1686 [] Λ, 579, 1346 [the Indicative is clearly correct, so this may be an itacism]

127. 19:17 εβραιστι || εβραιστη [] 579, 1071, 1424 [this is simply an alternate spelling, and therefore not a proper variant]

128. 19:24 ιματισμον || ιματις [a singular; a careless error; a reader would make the correction automatically]

129. 19:25a ειστηκεισαν || ειστηκει [a singular; the change makes the subject of the verb to be singular, rather than plural, resulting from a partial reading of the verse; a reader would make the necessary correction]

130. 19:25b μαγδαληνη || μαγδαλινη 1384 [] 1071 [this is simply an alternate spelling, and therefore not a proper variant]

131. 19:28 τουτο || ταυτα [] U [an independent error that does not affect the meaning]

132. 20:5 κειμενα || --- [] Λ [the omission does not alter the meaning]

133. 20:11 τω μνημειω || το μνημειον [50%] Θ, Λ, f^{13}, 579, 1071, 1346, 1424 [the preposition works with both dative and accusative; in the context the meaning is not affected]

134. 20:19 αυτοις || --- [] ℵ [an independent omission that does not alter the meaning]

135. 21:13 ουν || --- [2%] P^{122} ℵ, B, C, D, W, f^{1} [an independent error, presumably, given the copyist's penchant for omitting this conjunction; the meaning is not affected]

136. 21:15 ο ιησους || --- [] 1424 [an error that does not affect the meaning]

As Family 35 representatives go, this is a disappointing manuscript, but let us analyze the variations in detail. Of the 136 deviations from the family archetype, 54 are singular readings: with few exceptions, these do not affect the meaning, including a number that are not proper variants—what I have called a "careless singular" (above) I consider to be an unintentional error, and therefore not a proper variant. If no other known MS has a given change, then something created in the 17th century is not a variant. 136 – 54 = 82, so let us turn our attention to the 82. Of these, nine are mere alternate spellings, and therefore not proper variants (they are: 1, 13, 27, 58, 61, 65, 125, 127, 130). 82 – 9 = 73; of these, 16 are deviations shared by early codices, where it is scarcely credible that there could be a dependency, making them singular readings as far as the copyist of 1700 is concerned (10, 26, 36, 41, 48, 49, 52, 57, 73, 76, 96, 97, 131, 132, 134, 135). I would say that the correct deduction to be made from the evidence before us is that the copyists who produced those early MSS were also careless, marring their work with stupid errors. 73 – 16 = 57 (well under half of the total).

Looking at the evidence, it seems clear that GA 1700 contains some mixture. Of the 66 non-singulars (136 – 54 – 16 = 66), 1700 shares a variant with 1424 thirty times, with 1071 twenty-eight times, with 28 twenty-four times, with f^{13} twenty-two times, with 579 twenty-one times, with Λ nineteen times. **However**, an analysis of the 66 variants, and for that matter of the whole 136, reveals the following datum, both astonishing and significant: only two proper variants could be said to make any difference in the meaning—4 and 122! But before looking at them more closely, I should mention that 1700 shares a variant with ℵ seventeen times, with P^{66} and W each fifteen times, with A nine times, with B and D each eight times; but as I have already argued, we can scarcely claim a dependency—the errors were simply made independently (with the exception of the few places where there is massive agreement).

Now I will analyze items 4 and 122. Was the place where John was baptizing Bithabara or Bethany? Whichever name we choose, we do not know the exact location, except that it was on the eastern side of the Jordan River. (Those maps that place it on the western side mislead their readers.) From the very beginning, who in Asia Minor or Europe would know the exact location, whatever its name? It follows that the choice of name makes no difference to the point of the narrative; the important thing is what happened, not where it happened.

Did Pilate say, "We have a custom" or "You have a custom" (122)? The MSS attestation in favor of 'you' is 80%. But really now, how could the Jews have a custom that placed an obligation on their conquerors? It is scarcely credible that imperial Rome would release a prisoner based on a Jewish demand, so the reading of Family 35 is doubtless correct. However that may be, the choice of pronoun makes little difference to the point of the narrative, which is that the Jews chose Barabbas rather than Jesus.

Although as representatives of Family 35 go GA 1700 is rather pitiful, for all that, someone reading 1700 for devotional purposes would not be misled as to the intended meaning at any point! I submit that this conclusion is highly significant. In spite of its 136 deviations, 1700 is an adequate copy of John's Gospel for all practical purposes. So what about all those nasty 'accumulated errors' alleged in the RSV preface? I recognize the possibility that 1700 may have up to 57 inherited errors, errors taken from an exemplar, but since they would make little or no difference to a translation into English, they do not agree with RSV's purpose in mentioning 'accumulated errors'.

Going back to the RSV preface, I now invite attention to the final sentence: "We now possess many more ancient manuscripts of the New Testament, and are far better equipped to seek to recover the original wording of the Greek text." The use of the verb 'recover' indicates that they considered the original wording to have been lost. The linking of "far better equipped" to "more ancient manuscripts" indicates that they considered the older to be better. In fact, the committee that produced the RSV used a Greek text that leaned heavily on Codices Vaticanus and Sinaiticus. But decades before, Herman C. Hoskier had published his *Codex B and its Allies, a Study and an Indictment* (London: Bernard Quaritch, 2 volumes, 1914). He demonstrated objectively that the named codices are not good copies. The RSV committee obviously ignored Hoskier's work. I would say that whoever wrote the RSV preface was lacking in integrity. The alleged 'accumulated errors' were merely a smokescreen to deceive the reader and to defend their use of a radically different Greek text, a text that incorporates errors of fact and plain contradictions, as well as hundreds of serious changes. I would say that anyone who still believes the allegations contained in the quote from the RSV preface is in fact embracing **canards**.

Evaluating the 'basic principle'

Anyone who studies NT textual criticism will encounter the following statement: The basic principle of textual criticism is: choose the reading that best explains the rise of the others (or something similar). The uninitiated reader probably will not discern that the statement depends on certain presuppositions (that might be fallacious). Textual criticism only exists for texts whose original wording is deemed to be 'lost'. No one does textual criticism on today's newspaper, or last week's news magazine. No one even does textual criticism on the 1611 King James Version, since we still have printed copies thereof. Anyone familiar with the terrain knows that for the last 140 years, or so, the academic world has been dominated by the notion that the original wording of the NT text is in fact 'lost'. That notion is based squarely on Hort's theory. That theory denies: 1) that the NT writings were divinely inspired; 2) that the early Church recognized them to be Scripture; 3) that they received any special care or protection. As a result, by the time that the superstition and credulity of the Christians had elevated the NT writings to the status of 'Scripture', the original wording was irrevocably 'lost', in the sense that no one knew what it was. Therefore, so goes the theory, it is impossible to recover the original wording by using objective criteria; so they appeal to subjective criteria. (It should be obvious to any thinking person that this places the critic above the text. Notice, further, that there is no way of knowing if they have found it.)

The notion that the original wording of the NT text is 'lost' rejects (or at least ignores) the historical evidence that shows that the transmission of the NT writings was basically normal, from the beginning. That notion also rejects the vast majority (90-95%) of the extant NT manuscripts that represent the Byzantine tradition.[1] Having done that, what do the critics have left to work with? They are left with a handful of relatively early MSS that are so disparate that they cannot be grouped. They not only disagree with the majority, they disagree among themselves. They survived because they are so bad that no one wanted to use them. They have neither 'parents' nor 'children', which means that they were private productions and not honest copies; they are not part of a line of transmission.

So what do the critics do when those few MSS disagree among themselves? They ask: Which reading best explains the creation of the others? So what criteria do they use to arrive at that conclusion? They ask questions like these:

1. Which is the oldest MS?
2. Which is the 'best' MS?
3. Which is the shorter reading?
4. Which is the 'harder' reading?
5. Which reading best agrees with the author's style and purpose?

Question 1) is based on the analogy of a stream, whose water will be purest at the source; the greater the distance from the source, the more contaminants the water will have. However, with reference to NT MSS the analogy is certainly false. It is generally agreed that most of the damage suffered by the NT text had happened by the year 200, the date ascribed to our earliest MSS of any size (P^{66}). So our earliest MSS could be full of 'damage'.

Question 2): They generally declare Codex B (Vaticanus, 03) to be the 'best' extant MS. What is the basis for their claim? Hort, based on his subjective preferences (including the early date), declared B to be by far the 'best' MS, and subsequent critics have generally fallen in line with that dictum. But is there any objective basis for the claim? So far as I know, there is none; the objective evidence available says the contrary. (My evaluation applies to all other early MSS as well.)

Questions 3) and 4) are totally naturalistic, excluding any theological or supernatural considerations whatsoever. Hort imported them from the Alexandrian school's procedure for arriving at the original wording of Homer. Anyone who has collated any number of NT MSS, as I have done,

---

[1] Having rejected the divine inspiration of the NT, they of course reject any divine solicitude for that text. Those who deny the very existence of a Sovereign Creator will logically insist that a nonexistent being cannot do anything.

knows that those criteria are false. With reference to the NT, the 'harder' reading criterion is obviously perverse.

Question 5) is totally subjective, subject to the critic's whim, bias, theoretical orientation, personal perversity, or whatever. This criterion is unacceptable on its face. Why should any servant of Satan be allowed to determine the wording of the Text, based on his personal preference?

Anyone who respects objective evidence should reject the five criteria discussed above. Anyone who respects objective evidence should understand that the transmission of the NT Text was basically normal, and that the mass of extant MSS must be accorded the respect that they deserve. All the extant MSS deserve to be collated, thereby allowing us to group them empirically. The empirically defined families must then be compared and evaluated. The canard, 'MSS should be weighed, not counted', is a cop-out.

f^{35} Subgroups in the General Epistles[1]

There are fourteen significant splits in the Family in the four larger books (there being none in the three shorter ones), as follows:

James 2:13	ελεον 432[alt], 1766[c]
	ελεος 328, 394 {432, 604}[2] 634, 664, 928, 986, 1247, 1249, 1482, 1548, 1619[c], 1636, 1725, 1732[alt], 1749, 1752, 1766, 1897, 2080, 2221, 2289, 2587, 2704
James 2:14	εχει
	εχη 141, 328, 386, 394, 604, 634, 664, 801, 928, 986, 1075, 1247, 1249, 1250, 1482, 1508, 1548, 1656, 1704, 1737, 1746, 1748, 1749, 1752, 1766, 1855, 1876, 1899, 2218, 2221, 2289, 2431, 2501, 2587, 2626, 2704
1 Peter 1:23	αλλ
	αλλα {149, 201} {432, 604} 757, 824, 1072, 1075, 1248, 1250, 1503, 1548, 1617, 1618, 1619, 1628, 1636, 1637, 1656, 1740, 1745, 1746, 1748, 1754, 1763, 1768, 1864, 1892, 2352, 2431, 2777
1 Peter 2:11	απεχεσθαι 1072[alt]
	απεχεσθε {149, 201} 204, 604[c], 757[alt], 824, 1072, 1248, 1503[c], 1548, 1617, 1618, 1619[alt], 1628[alt], 1637[c], 1745[alt], 1746, 1748, 1864[alt], 1899, 2352, 2431, 2704, 2777
1 Peter 2:24	απογενομενοι
	απογεννωμενοι (328)[3] 394 {432 (604)} 664, 928, 986, 1247, 1249, 1482, 1508, 1548, 1752, 1763, 1766, 1768, 1855, 2289, 2587 (2704)

---

[1] This study uses 77 out of 84 known family members; the seven that are missing would probably make little, if any, difference to our conclusions. Out of the 77 MSS, all of those not listed with the alternate go with the main form. Thus in James 2:14, the 36 MSS that have the alternate should be subtracted from 77, which leaves 41 for the main form.

[2] MSS within braces, { }, have a common exemplar and may be treated as a single vote.

[3] A MS within ( ) has a slight variation on the given form.

1 Peter 3:6 εγενηθητε 1766^{v}
εγεννηθητε 604, 664, 801, 1247, 1250, 1618, 1637, 1732, 1748, 1752, 1763, 1876, 1899, 2289, 2431, 2587, 2626, 2704, 2777

1 Peter 4:2 του 2261^{c}
--- {149, 201} {432, 604} 757, 824, 1072, 1075, 1101, 1248, 1503, 1508^{c}, 1548, 1617, 1618, 1619, 1628, 1636, 1637, 1656, 1737, 1740, 1745, 1746, 1748, 1754, 1761, 1766, 1768, 1864, 1892, 1899, 2218, 2261, 2352, 2431, 2501, 2777

1 Peter 4:11 ως $1748^{?}$
ης 141^{c} {149, 201} {432, 604} 757, 824, 1072, 1075, 1248, 1503, 1508, 1617, 1618, 1619, 1628, 1636, 1637, 1656, 1737, 1740, 1745, 1746, 1754, 1864, 1892, 2218, 2352, 2431, 2777

1 Peter 5:7 μελει 824^{c},1726^{c}
μελλει 141 {432, 604} 801, 824, 986, 1247, 1248, 1249, 1250, 1508,1617, 1726, 1748, 1752, 1763, 1768, 1876, 1892, 1899, 2261, 2352, 2431, 2501, 2626

1 Peter 5:8 καταπιειν 394^{c}
καταπιη 328, 394, 604, 664, 928, 986, 1075, 1247, 1249, 1482^{v}, 1508, 1737, 1748, 1749, 1752, 1761, 1763, 1766, 1855, 1892^{c}, 1899, 2218, 2221^{c}, 2255^{v}, 2289, 2431, 2587^{c}, 2704

2 Peter 2:14 πλεονεξιας
πλεονεξιαν 394, 664, 801, 928, 1249, 1250, 1482, 1508, 1726, 1749, 1763, 1855, 1876, 2261, 2289, 2378, 2587, 2626, 2704^{v}

2 Peter 3:3 γινωσκοντες
γινωσκοντας 328, 394, 664, 928, 1247, 1249, 1482, 1508, 1749, 1752, 1855, 2255, 2289, 2587, 2704

1 John 1:6 περιπατουμεν 18, 35, 141, 204, 386, 801, 824, 1100, 1101, 1250, 1636, 1704, 1725, 1726, 1732, 1733, 1754, 1761, 1858, 1865, 1876, 1897, 2080, 2221, 2261 [2378] 2466, 2554, 2626, 2723[1]
περιπατωμεν {149, 201} 328, 394 {432, 604} 634 (664) 757, 928, 986, 1072, 1075, 1247, 1248, 1249, 1482, 1503, 1508, 1548, 1617, 1618, 1619, 1628, 1637, 1656, 1737, 1740, 1745, 1748, 1749, 1752, 1763, 1766, 1768, 1855, 1864, 1892, 2218, 2255, 2289, 2352, 2431, 2501, 2587, 2704, 2777

1 John 4:20 μισει
μιση 328, 386, 394, 604, 634, 928, 1247, 1249, 1482, 1508, 1548, 1704, 1749, 1752, 1763, 1766, 1855, 2255, 2289, 2587, 2704

They divide into two significant sub-groups as follows:

Group 1

Js2:13	Js2:14	1P2:24	1P3:6	1P5:8	2P2:14	2P3:3	1J4:20	place	date
2289	2289	2289	2289	2289	2289	2289	2289	Vatopediu	XII
2704	2704	2704	2704	2704	2704	2704	2704	Meteora	XV
394	394	394	---	394	394	394	394	Vallicelliana	1330
664	664	664	664	664	664	664	---	Zittau	XV
928	928	928	---	928	928	928	928	Dionysiu	1304
1247	1247	1247	1247	1247	---	1247	1247	Sinai	XV
1249	1249	1249	---	1249	1249	1249	1249	Sinai	1324
1482	1482	1482	---	1482	1482	1482	1482	M Lavras	1304
1752	1752	1752	1752	1752	---	1752	1752	Panteleimonos	XII
2587	2587	2587	2587	---	2587	2587	2587	Vatican	XI

[1] Here I list the MSS for both forms, since I followed a minority. See the discussion below.

328	328	(328)	---	328	---	328	328	Leiden	XIII
604	604	604	604	604	---	---	604	Paris	XIV
---	1508	1508	---	1508	1508	1508	1508	M Lavras	XV
1749	1749	---	---	1749	1749	1749	1749	M Lavras	XVI
---	1855	1855	---	1855	1855	1855	1855	Iviron	XIII
---	---	1763	1763	1763	1763	---	1763	Athens	XV
1766	1766	1766	---	1766	---	---	1766	Sofia	1344

I consider that these seventeen MSS represent a significant sub-group that is distributed throughout the four larger books. Observe that the geographical distribution is limited; Constantinople, Jerusalem, Patmos, Trikala and seven of the ten (that I checked) Mt. Athos monasteries are missing (of the twenty M Lavras MSS only three are here). The probability that this group could represent the archetype is negligible. I now add the 'stragglers', to complete the picture for each variant.

986	986	986	---	986	---	---	---	Esphigmenu	XIV
1548	1548	1548	---	---	---	---	1548	Vatopediu	1359
634	634	---	---	---	---	---	634	Vatican	1394
---	801	---	801	---	801	---	---	Athens	XV
---	1250	---	1250	---	1250	---	---	Sinai	XV
---	1748	---	1748	1748	---	---	---	M Lavras	1662
---	1876	---	1876	---	1876	---	---	Sinai	XV
---	1899	---	1899	1899	---	---	---	Patmos	XIV
---	---	---	---	2255	---	2255	2255	Iviron	XVI
---	2431	---	2431	2431	---	---	---	Kavsokalyvia	1332
---	2626	---	2626	---	2626	---	---	Ochrida	XIV

801, 1250, 1876 and 2626 may well have shared a common influence.

---	386	---	---	---	---	---	386	Vatican	XIV
432	---	432	---	---	---	---	---	Vatican	XV
---	1075	---	---	1075	---	---	---	M Lavras	XIV
---	1704	---	---	---	---	---	1704	Kutlumusiu	1541
---	1737	---	---	1737	---	---	---	M Lavras	XII
---	2218	---	---	2218	---	---	---	Lesbos	XVI
2221	2221	---	---	---	---	---	---	Sparta	1432

To these the following 'solitaries' should be added: for James 2:13 add 1636, 1725, 1897, 2080; for James 2:14 add 141, 1656, 1746, 2501; for 1 Peter 2:24 add 1768; for 1 Peter 3:6 add 1618, 1637, 1732, 2777; for 1 Peter 5:8 add 1761; for 2 Peter 2:14 add 1726, 2261, 2378; for 2 Peter 3:3 and 1 John 4:20 there are none.

Comment: εχη in James 2:14 is attested by 36 MSS, over 40% of the Family. Besides dittography being an easy possibility, the pressure of μη may have caused some copyists to put the Subjunctive, perhaps without thinking—the reverse change would presumably be deliberate. In the context the Indicative is correct: James is stating a fact, the person does not have works.

Group 2

1P1:23	1P2:11	[1P3:6]	1P4:2	1P4:11	1P5:7	place	date
824	824	---	824	824	824	Grottaferrata	XIV
1248	1248	---	1248	1248	1248	Sinai	XIV
1617	1617	---	1617	1617	1617	M Lavras	XV
2352	2352	---	2352	2352	2352	Meteora	XV
2431	2431	2431	2431	2431	2431	Kavsokalyvia	1332
149-201	149-201	---	149-201	149-201	---	Vatican/London	XV/1357
432-604	---	604	432-604	432-604	432-604	Vatican/Paris	XV/XIV
1072	1072	---	1072	1072	---	M Lavras	XIII
1618	1618	1618	1618	1618	---	M Lavras	XIV
1746	1746	---	1746	1746	---	M Lavras	XIV
1748	1748	1748	1748	---	1748	M Lavras	1662
1892	---	---	1892	1892	1892	Jerusalem	XIV
2777	2777	2777	2777	2777	---	Karditsa	XIV

I consider that these thirteen MSS represent a significant sub-group, preceded by another twelve, below, that left the 'tree' at a node higher up.

757	---	---	757	757	---	Athens	XIII
1075	---	---	1075	1075	---	M Lavras	XIV
1503	---	---	1503	1503	---	M Lavras	1317
1548	1548	---	1548	---	---	Vatopediu	1359
1619	---	---	1619	1619	---	M Lavras	XIV
1628	---	---	1628	1628	---	M Lavras	1400
1636	---	---	1636	1636	---	M Lavras	XV
1637	---	1637	1637	1637	---	M Lavras	1328
1656	---	---	1656	1656	---	M Lavras	XV
1740	---	---	1740	1740	---	M Lavras	XII
1745	---	---	1745	1745	---	M Lavras	XV
1754	---	---	1754	1754	---	Panteleimonos	XII
1768	---	---	1768	---	1768	Iviron	1519
1864	---	---	1864	1864	---	Stavronikita	XIII
---	1899	1899	1899	---	1899	Patmos	XIV

I now add the 'stragglers', to complete the picture for each variant. The observant reader will have noticed that 1 Peter 3:6 is in [ ] above; I did this because this variant is already in group 1. This particular variant has a strange 'mixture' of both groups—because of the nature of the variant I suspect that the roster is fortuitous and therefore this variant does not really belong to either group.

1250	---	1250	---	---	1250	Sinai	XV
---	---	---	---	1508	1508	M Lavras	XV
---	---	---	1737	1737	---	M Lavras	XII
1763	---	1763	---	---	1763	Athens	XV
---	---	---	2218	2218	---	Lesbos	XVI
---	---	---	2261	---	2261	Kalavryta	XIV
---	---	---	2501	---	2501	Sinai	XVI

To these the following 'solitaries' should be added: for 1 Peter 2:11 add 204, 2704; for 1 Peter 4:2 add 1101, 1761, 1766; for 1 Peter 5:7 add

141, 801, 986, 1247, 1249, 1726, 1752, 1876, 2626 (this picture is probably due to the nature of the variant and does not reflect a dependency); for 1 Peter 1:23 and 4:11 there are none.

Comment: the glaring feature of this second group is that it is limited to one book. Another 'glare' is the dominance of M Lavras—almost half of the total (but there are some M Lavras MSS that are in neither group). The probability that this second group could represent the archetype is also negligible.

As with εχη in James 2:14, the omission of του in 1 Peter 4:2 is attested by 36 MSS, over 40% of the family. Since there is little doubt that the archetype read the article, how to account for the high attestation for the omission? I suppose it was pressure from the Byzantine bulk, almost 80% here. In the context one would expect the article, that I consider to be correct.

We now come to the only real 'problem' for determining the archetypal form of the family in the General Epistles—1 John 1:6 (at the outset I mentioned fourteen splits, of which I have only dealt with thirteen). This is the only place in the General Epistles where the archetypal form is preserved in a minority of the extant representatives, at least as I see it. The grand point at issue could be a case of dittography. The verb 'say' is properly Subjunctive, being controlled by εαν, but the verbs 'have' and 'walk' are part of a statement and are properly Indicative—only if we are in fact walking in darkness do we become liars for claiming to be in fellowship. So περιπατουμεν is correct. But to return to the MSS, we observe a curious circumstance: the roster that reads the Subjunctive is made up of precisely the two sub-groups, 2255 being the only outsider (a probable dittography); all the other MSS that do not participate in either sub-group read the Indicative, and they have a very good geographical distribution. Consider:

18	Constantinople	1364	35	Paris	XI
141	Vatican	XIII	204	Bologna	XIII
386	Vatican	XIV	801	Athens	XV
824	Grottaferrata	XIV	1100	Dionysiu	1376
1101	Dionysiu	1660	1250	Sinai	XV
1636	M Lavras	XV	1704	Kutlumusiu	1541
1725	Vatopediu	1367	1726	Vatopediu	XIV
1732	M Lavras	1384	1733	M Lavras	XIV
1754	Panteleimonos	XII	1761	Athens	XIV
1858	Konstamonitu	XIII	1865	Philotheu	XIII
1876	Sinai	XV	1897	Jerusalem	XII
2080	Patmos	XIV	2221	Sparta	1432

2261	Kalavryta	XIV	[2378]	Athens	1511[1]
2466	Patmos	1329	2554	Bukarest	1434
2626	Ochrida	XIV	2723	Trikala	XI

A chart will help to visualize the distribution for the two variants, using 'Mt. Athos' and 'elsewhere':

	Indicative	Subjunctive	both
1) Mt. Athos:	Konstamonitu	Esphigmenu	Dionysiu
	Kutlumusiu	Iviron	M Lavras
	Philotheu	Kavsokalyvia	Panteleimonos
		Stavronikita	Vatopediu
2) elsewhere:	Bologna	Karditsa	Athens
	Bukarest	Leiden	Jerusalem
	Constantinople	Lesbos	Paris
	Grottaferrata	London	Sinai
	Kalavryta	Meteora	Vatican
	Ochrida	Sofia	
	Patmos	Vallicelliana (Rome)	
	Sparta	Zittau	
	Trikala		

Sinai, Jerusalem, Mt. Athos and Vatican are on both sides, but the Indicative has the better distribution elsewhere, significantly better.

In "Adjudicating Family Splits",[2] based on 24 MSS, the Subjunctive was attested by 59% of that selection, but my weighting instrument reduced the value to 43%. This paper is based on 77 MSS (out of 84 known family members) and the Subjunctive is now attested by 61% of the 77—the picture has not changed. I am cheerfully satisfied that the archetype read the Indicative.

Returning to the list of fourteen splits on the first page, it will be observed that almost all of them involve a single letter, or similar sounding diphthong. Most of them represent scarcely any difference in meaning. There simply is no significant variation anywhere in Family 35 throughout the seven General Epistles. God has preserved His Text.

---

[1] 2378 is missing the first sheet of 1 John, and hence the verse in question, but since it eschews both sub-groups throughout, it almost certainly read the Indicative here.

[2] This article is available from my site, www.prunch.org.

Variant Rank of MSS Containing Jude (as per Wasserman)[1]

Orientation: this study makes no claim to precise accuracy. I simply followed Wasserman, without checking any MSS, except as noted in comment 4 below. I did not count any variant read by over 5% of the MSS, even when both Wasserman and I rejected it;[2] had I done so, the number of variants for many of the MSS would go up. Wasserman did not register some six types of dittography, which I would certainly include—the number of variants for MSS like 01 and 03 would go up sharply. So, what follows should only be taken as a rough approximation, but is valid and adequate for my present purpose: **to give a statistical demonstration of the mentality of the copyists**.

It is quite obvious that some copyists did not take their task seriously (quite apart from deliberate alteration), while others took it very seriously. Jude is a short book, with only 25 verses. Note that P72, our oldest extant MS, is by far the worst, with two variants per verse! The first 19 MSS listed below are really very poor; the copyists clearly had no respect for what they were copying. The copyists of the next 95 MSS were not taking their work seriously. The quality of their work contrasts sharply with that of the heavy majority of the Family 35 copyists; they evidently understood that they were copying a Sacred Text (**f^{35}** MSS are underlined).

# of variants	MSS	
51	P^{72}	**our oldest extant MS is by far the worst!**
34	1241	
32	378, 631, 1838	
30	1646	
29	1847	
28	1751	
25	044	
24	01, 90	
23	1243, 1881	
21	1066, 2147	
20	6, 61, 915, 1505	19 MSS so far
19	38, 629, 1852, 1875, 1886	
18	621, 1729, 2675	
17	88, 322, 323, 1311, 1735, 2495	
16	522, 1611	

[1] Tommy Wasserman, *The Epistle of Jude: Its Text and Transmission*, Stockholm: Almqvist & Wiksell International, 2006.

[2] As a result, there is very little difference between the eclectic Text and mine. Although I used mine, the point of the exercise is not compromised by that choice.

# of variants	MSS	
15	43, 459, 460, 616, 618, 918, 1739, 1834, 1844, 2242, 2298, 2344, 2412, 2674	
14	03, 93, 104, 181, 321, 633, 680, 1292, 1845, 2652	
13	04, 0142, 442, 630, 1104, 1523, 2200, 2818	
12	02, 33, 180, 431, 1240, 1405, 1837, 1877, 2138, 2186	
11	94, 131, 177, 307, 337, 496, 506, 636, 665, 876, 1501, 1661, 1827, 1828, 1869, 2544, 2691, 2805	
10	056, 326, 489, 625, 1067, 1315, 1409, 1595, 1610, 1642, 1719, 1832, 1836, 1842, 1874, 1893, 2404, 2494, 2696	+ 95 MSS so far (114 total)
9	218, 254, 263, 309, 458, 467, 1107, 1270, 1319, 1367, 1424, 1524, 1598, 1678, 1765, 1840, 2197, 2473, 2816	
8	102, 436, 453, 582, 608, 615, 927, 996, 1247, 1297, 1390, 1425, 1448, 1509, 1649, 1702, 1724, 1762, 1839, 1890, 2194, 2400, 2502, 2516, 2718	
7	3, 203, 312, 421, 469, 628, 639, 914, 941, 999, 1003, 1175, 1245, 1573, 1718, 1741, 1744, 1753, 1780, 1799, 1829, 1872, 1882, 2127, 2243, 2318, 2401, 2513, 2865	
6	P^{78}, 5, 42, 62, 234, 383, 393, 607, 623, 632, 641, 917, 921, 922, 1563, 1736, 1830, 1850, 1853, 1857, 1868, 1896, 2086, 2125, 2180, 2279, 2492, 2508, 2625, 2705	
5	018, 0316, 51, 81, 103, 206, 327, 384, 385, 390, 452, 454, 606, 637, 945, 1070, 1099, 1127, 1359, 1360, 1594, 1626, 1727, 1731, 1831, 1843, 1873, 1880, 1888, 1891, 1902, 2085, 2288, 2501, 2527, 2716	+ 139 MSS so far (253 total)
4	049, 1, 76, 205, 223, 241, 252, 296, 363, 424, 429, 466, 592, 620, 642, 656, 901, 912, 913, 1069, 1103, 1106, 1149, 1162, 1244, 1248, 1352, 1495, 1521, 1717, 1734, 1757, 1760, 1767, 1847, 1851, 1860, 1861, 1863, 1889, 1894, 1895, 2131, 2378, 2423, 2558, 2712, 2736, 2746, 2774	
3	020, 57, 82, 110, 205^{abs}, 221, 250, 314, 330, 400, 432, 451, 456, 462, 465, 491, 613, 614, 617, 619, 634, 635, 664, 796, 801, 832, 1022, 1250, 1251, 1277, 1384, 1398, 1599, 1622, 1673, 1721, 1742, 1747, 1769, 1841, 1849, 1856, 1859, 1862, 1867, 1876, 2191, 2201, 2218, 2374, 2475, 2484, 2627, 2704, 2776	
2	35, 97, 105, 142, 149, 328, 367, 398, 404, 425, 450, 468, 610, 622, 676, 720, 808, 910, 920, 986, 1105, 1115, 1242, 1354, 1490,	

# of variants	MSS
	1609, 1617, 1720, 1730, 1732, 1743, 1750, 1754, 1871, 1885, 1892, 1903, 2143, 2289, 2466, 2483, 2626, 2653, 2815
1	025, 69, 101, 133, 172, 175, 189, 201, 209, 242, 256, 440, 444, 479, 483, 517, 547, 601, 602, 605, 638, 699, 712, 997, 1058, 1102, 1161, 1249, 1404, 1548, 1597, 1628, 1643, 1722, 1725, 1726, 1728, 1733, 1746, 1748, 1749, 1766, 1768, 1795, 1854, 1870, 1897, 2255, 2431, 2587, 2777
0	P^{74}, 18, 141, 204, 216, 226, 302, 308, 319, 325, 386, 394, 457, 603, 604, 627, 757, 824, 928, 935, 959, 1040, 1072, 1075, 1094, 1100, 1101, 1400, 1482, 1503, 1508, 1618, 1619, 1636, 1637, 1652, 1656, 1668, 1704, 1723, 1737, 1740, 1745, 1752, 1761, 1763, 1835, 1855, 1858, 1864, 1865, 1899, 2080, 2221, 2261, 2352, 2356, 2511, 2541, 2554, 2723

Comments:

1. The grand total of MSS listed above is 514; because of lacunae, at any given point the number will be around 500. Wasserman also included Lectionaries, but I have not.
2. P^{74}, 319, 325, 603, 2356 and 2511 are evidently fragmentary or with little legible text, which is why they score zero.
3. 216, 226, 302, 308, 457, 935, 959, 1094, 1668, 1835 and 2541 are not normally $\mathbf{f^{35}}$, but have retained its text for this short book (if both Wasserman and I have registered the facts correctly).
4. Where I have myself done a complete collation of an $\mathbf{f^{35}}$ MS for Jude, I have used my own data, when I disagree with Wasserman—I changed the rank of twenty-three $\mathbf{f^{35}}$ MSS (one fourth of the total).
5. Of the 88 MSS that I have underlined as belonging to $\mathbf{f^{35}}$, almost half are perfect. 1247 is rather careless, but belongs to the family.
6. Anyone who has collated any number of MSS will have observed that along about the 3rd or 4th page the copyist starts to get tired or bored, and in consequence the number of mistakes goes up noticeably. If this were a longer book, the 'rank' of most of the MSS would go up. The core $\mathbf{f^{35}}$ representatives would stay about the same.
7. For a book this short, I consider five variants to be unacceptable, so virtually half of the MSS fall below my respectability line.

Down with forgery!

Every now and again I am handed a question that starts out by irritating me, but after I calm down I perceive that God is nudging me to clarify a point that needs it. This happened a while ago with the 'jewel' attributed to Jerome that in his day 'most' or 'almost all' of the Greek manuscripts did not have the last twelve verses of Mark. Since of the 1700 or so Greek MSS known to us that contain the last chapter of Mark only three do not have them (one of them being a falsification at this point), how could a vast majority in the 5th century be reduced to a small fraction of one percent later on? In terms of the science of statistical probability, such an inversion is simply impossible. Only a worldwide campaign that was virtually 100% successful could bring about such a switch, and there is not a shred of evidence for such a campaign. Recall that Diocletian's campaign to destroy NT MSS (applied unevenly in different areas) was past history by a century (not to mention Constantine's 'conversion' and the consequences thereof). Kenneth Scott Latourette (*A History of Christianity* [New York: Harper,1953], p. 231) describes Eusebius Hieronimus Sophronius (alias Jerome) as "a gifted and diligent scholar, enormously erudite, a master of languages, a lover of books, wielding a facile, vigorous, and often vitriolic pen" who "was an eloquent advocate of the monastic life". He doubtless had his defects [don't we all], but he was not ridiculously stupid, as he would have had to be to make the statement attributed to him. Our knowledge of the 'jewel' comes from the tenth century [the interval of five centuries does not inspire confidence]; it is almost certainly a forgery (someone 'borrowing' a famous name to give credence to some statement). Since 'sacred cows' do not like to die, a review of some relevant history is in order.

K. Aland on Egypt

Even that great champion of an Egyptian text, Kurt Aland, recognized that during the early centuries, including the 4th, Asia Minor (especially the Aegean area) was "the heartland of the Church". (It also became the heartland of the Byzantine Empire and the Orthodox Churches.) The demand for copies of the NT would have a direct bearing on the supply, and on the areas where copies would be concentrated. But on the subject of Egypt, Aland had this to say:

> Our knowledge of the church in Egypt begins at the close of the 2nd century with bishop Demetrius who reorganized the dominantly Gnostic Egyptian church by founding new communities, consecrating bishops, and above all by establishing relationships with the other provinces of the church fellowship.

> Every church needed manuscripts of the New Testament—how was Demetrius to provide them? Even if there were a scriptorium in his own see, he would have to procure "orthodox" exemplars for the scribes. The copies existing in the Gnostic communities could not be used, because they were under suspicion of being corrupt. There is no way of knowing where the bishop turned for scribal exemplars, or for the large number of papyrus manuscripts he could give directly to his communities. ("The Text of the Church?" Kurt Aland, *Trinity Journal*, Vol. 8, Nº 2, Fall, 1987, p. 138 [actually sent out in the Spring, 1989].)

But just a minute, please. In the year of our Lord 200, who in Egypt was still speaking Greek? (For that matter, who among the ordinary people had ever spoken Greek there?) What Greek speaking communities could the worthy Demetrius have been serving? Would the scholars linked to the library in Alexandria be likely to bow to Demetrius? So far as we know, no apostle ever ministered in Egypt, and no Autograph of a New Testament book was held there. The Gnostic dominance probably should not surprise us. But the situation in Alexandria is relevant to the question in hand because of Clement, and especially Origen, who was mentor to Pamphilus, who was mentor to Eusebius of Caesarea.

Eusebius (Caesarea)

One suspects that the forger who 'borrowed' Jerome actually started out by 'borrowing' Eusebius (Caesarea). He has Eusebius answering a certain 'Marinus' with, "One might say that the passage is not contained in all the copies of Mark's Gospel..." The 'not all' became 'some' or even 'many', here and there. If Eusebius actually wrote such a thing, of which we are not sure [the interval of six centuries does not inspire confidence here either], how was he qualified to do so? After the Roman destruction in 70 AD, Palestine became a backwater in the flow of the Christian river. The transmission of the true NT Text owes nothing to Caesarea. By the 4th century there would have been thousands, literally, of NT MSS in use around the world, of which Eusebius (d. 339, b. about 265) probably would not have seen more than a dozen (most from Alexandria, not Asia Minor). If Codex B was produced in Alexandria in time for Eusebius to see it, it would indeed permit him to say 'not all' copies; but why would he do so? And why should we pay any attention to him if he did? Here again, who in Palestine was still speaking Greek in the 4th century? What use would Eusebius have for Greek manuscripts? One other point: had Eusebius written such a thing, it would have been after Diocletian's campaign, presumably, but it would still be fresh in his memory and he should have mentioned it. Emboldened by success, as I suppose, the forger decided to 'up the ante' attributing the same exchange to Jerome, answering a certain 'Hebidia', except that now it is 'most' or 'almost all'.

Jerome (Bethlehem)

Jerome was born around 342 and died in 420 (or so). During 382-384 he was secretary to Pope Damasus, in Rome, and began work on the Latin Vulgate. Not long after the death of Damasus (384) he moved to Bethlehem, followed a few months later by the wealthy Paula, who helped him build a monastery, and so on. Jerome spent the last 30+ years of his life in Bethlehem, even more of a 'backwater' than Caesarea, and a century after Eusebius. All the negative observations made about Caesarea apply here with added force. Further, who in the Pope's entourage in Rome was speaking Greek in 380 AD? From Rome Jerome moved to Bethlehem. How many actual Greek MSS of the NT would Jerome have seen? Certainly fewer than 1% of the total in use (at that time there would be few Greek MSS in Italy and Palestine—who would use them?). In lists of early Church 'fathers' Jerome is usually listed with those who wrote in Latin, not Greek. The statement attributed to him is patently false, scientifically impossible; and he would have been ridiculously unqualified to make it. Not being stupid or dishonest, he didn't!

Addendum

After I circulated the above as my 'mailing 75', my Canadian friend, Charles Holm, called my attention to historical research done by Timothy David Barnes that is relevant to the credibility of Jerome (*Tertullian: A Historical and Literary Study*, Oxford: Clarendon Press, 1971). In an appendix dealing specifically with Jerome, there is a section called "Jerome and Eusebius" wherein Barnes offers the following observations (pages 236-238).

> First, Jerome never questions the reliability of Eusebius. Thus he accepts Eusebius' interpretation of what a writer says without asking whether it is correct.
>
> …
>
> Secondly, Jerome far surpasses Eusebius in credulity. What was in Eusebius presented as surmise or mere rumour is for Jerome established and indubitable fact.
>
> …

Thirdly, Jerome mistranslates and misunderstands.

… …

Fourthly, Jerome dishonestly conceals both his ignorance and his debt to Eusebius.

Well, well, well, it appears that one should read Jerome with a full salt shaker to hand. Perhaps my closing sentence above should have been: Not being stupid, he didn't! However, I continue to insist that Jerome could not have been so grossly stupid and/or dishonest as to make the ridiculous statement attributed to him. Down with **forgery**![1]

Defining 'Preservation'

We understand that the human authors of Scripture wrote under inspiration, by which we mean that the Holy Spirit superintended the process with the result that they wrote just what He wanted them to write (respecting the norms that rule the use of language). The authors were inspired, protected from error, but not the copyists down through the years. There is nothing like actually collating a number of MSS to give one an appreciation for the divine preservation of the Text, a process more complicated than inspiration. (Satan was not allowed to interfere in the inspiring, but was in the preserving.)

The purpose of this note is to 'chew' a bit on the question of just how to evaluate a copy's representation of its archetypal form, and hence its preservation thereof. I consider that the following should not be regarded as 'variants', or deviations from the archetype:

1. Whether a number is written out or given with the letters;
2. Whether a letter (*alpha*) is written out or given with the letter;
3. Abbreviations or 'shorthand' forms (these are especially frequent at the end of a line), where the identity of the word and its meaning are not touched; the so-called 'nomina sacra' are probably the best known examples.

Both parchment and ink were prepared by hand, and were hard to come by, so any legitimate means of economizing those materials would be viewed as entirely appropriate. This attitude is reflected in the first three items.

---

[1] For detailed documentation and an exhaustive discussion of other aspects of this question, see Burgon, *The Last Twelve Verses according to S. Mark,* pp. 19-31, 38-69, 265-90.

4. Copyists would often give expression to an artistic bent with the top line of a page and the end of lines, using flourishes, curlicues, exaggerated forms, lines running off the page, and such—these should be ignored.

5. Alternate spellings of the same word, where the identity of the word and its meaning are not touched. This one is a bit more bothersome than the others, but I think it should be included in the list. However, such differences can be useful in identifying sub-groups. I include here alternate spellings of a transliterated foreign word, as in Mark 5:41 (the more so, in this case, since it is translated).

6. Where the order of words is changed, but that change does not affect the meaning in any way (apparently), they are two ways of saying the same thing. Such are not 'proper' variants, although they may be useful in identifying subgroups. Some changes in word order do affect the nuance, so each case needs to be evaluated individually. For example: in Luke 10:41, is it ο Ιησους ειπεν αυτη, or is it ειπεν αυτη ο Ιησους? Both mean simply "Jesus said to her".

I am changing the way I describe the performance of MSS with reference to their archetype. A MS that reproduces the archetypal form without any variants is a copy that represents the archetype <u>perfectly</u>. A MS that has only different ways of saying the same thing is a copy that represents the archetype <u>completely</u>. In this second category I include MSS that have only alternate forms and/or corrections to the archetypal form—the true reading is preserved in every case. I also include here the repeating of a letter or syllable going from one line to the next (not a 'proper' variant in any case).

Of course, when printing a text a choice must be made between competing forms [I am prepared to explain mine in every case], but since the meaning is not touched, such choices will mainly be of concern to someone wishing to apply a numeric code to the text. **The sort of changes listed above may not legitimately be used to argue against the doctrine of inerrancy.**

Collated f^{35} Manuscripts[1]

When I say that a MS had a perfect exemplar (a perfect copy of the family archetype), I did not charge what appear to be a copy's private errors to its exemplar—that includes corrections to the archetype. Of course my judgment is presumed, of necessity, since I have no way of knowing

---

[1] This was the situation in January, 2020.

what actually happened; but I am probably not far off. When I say that a copy is itself perfect, I refer to the first hand. I have used the GA numbers, except for Iviron 2110, that has no GA number. Those who are acquainted with my work know that the family's archetypal form has been empirically determined, being the consensus of the collated MSS.

Matthew—I have collated 51 **f^{35}** MSS; 2554 is perfect; 1072, 1117, 1461, 1496, 1652, 1713, Iviron 2110 had a perfect exemplar (presumed).

Mark—I have collated 53 **f^{35}** MSS; none is perfect; GA 35 is complete;[1] 586, 2382 had a perfect exemplar.

Luke—I have collated 51 **f^{35}** MSS; none is perfect; 2382 is virtually complete;[2] 789, 897 had a perfect exemplar.

John—I have collated 57 **f^{35}** MSS; none is perfect; 2382 is complete; 1072 had a perfect exemplar.

Acts—I have collated 35 **f^{35}** MSS; none is perfect; 35 is all but complete;[3] there are no perfect exemplars.

Romans—I have collated 37 **f^{35}** MSS; 1482, 2554, 2723 are perfect; 35 is complete; 1249, 1855, 1865, 2466 had a perfect exemplar.

1 Corinthians—I have collated 34 **f^{35}** MSS; 2554 is perfect; there are no perfect exemplars.

---

1 AG 586; in 10:35 the sons of Zebedee are making a request: "Teacher, we want you to do for us whatever we (ημιν) may ask". Instead of that, 586 has: "Teacher, we want you to do for us whatever ye (υμιν) may ask"—manifest nonsense. The two letters received the same pronunciation, so someone hearing the text read would understand the first person without question. Even someone reading the text would perceive the obvious error and correct the text in his mind. Since 586 has only this one variant for the whole book, one letter, it is virtually perfect.

2 In 2:40, instead of επ αυτω, it has επ αυτο (there is a split in the family at this point). The preposition επι works with both the dative and the accusative cases, and the translation will be the same: "The grace of God was upon him". If these are two ways of saying the same thing, then 2382 is complete; if not, it is off by one letter for the whole book!

3 In 1:11, instead of ουτος Ιησους, it has ουτος ο Ιησους. A demonstrative pronoun defines, even more than a definite article, so the article is redundant here; so they are two ways of saying the same thing: "this very Jesus". In 26:29 Paul is defending himself before king Agrippa. Instead of ευξαιμην, 'I would pray', it has ευξαμην, 'I do pray'. The indicative is more direct than the optative, but the difference in meaning is slight. If these are not two ways of saying the same thing, then 35 is off by one letter, for the whole book of Acts!

2 Corinthians—I have collated 36 **f**^{35} MSS; 2554 is perfect; 35 is complete; 1865 had a perfect exemplar.

Galatians—I have collated 37 **f**^{35} MSS; 204, 1100, 1637, 1865, 2554, 2587 are perfect; 35 is complete; 386, 444, 1075, 2723 had a perfect exemplar.

Ephesians—I have collated 37 **f**^{35} MSS; 928, 1864, 2554, 2723 are perfect; 204, 757, 986, 1248, 1503, 1548, 1725, 1732, 1865, 2352 had a perfect exemplar.

Philippians—I have collated 37 **f**^{35} MSS; 35, 1072, 1864, 1865, 2554 are perfect; 204, 394, 757, 824, 1249, 1503, 1548, 1732, 1855, 2352, 2466, 2723 had a perfect exemplar.

Colossians—I have collated 37 **f**^{35} MSS; 18, 444, 1732, 1864, 2554, 2723 are perfect; 35, 1075, 1503, 1725 are complete; 824, 1637, 1865, 1892, 2352, 2466 had a perfect exemplar.

1 Thessalonians—I have collated 39 **f**^{35} MSS; 18, 824, 928, 1855, 1864, 2723 are perfect; 35, 1865, 2554 are complete; 394, 444, 757, 986, 1072, 1503, 1892, 2587 had a perfect exemplar.

2 Thessalonians—I have collated 38 **f**^{35} MSS; 18, 35, 204, 394, 928, 1072, 1075, 1249, 1503, 1637, 1768, 1864, 1865, 2554, 2723 are perfect; 328, 386, 444, 604, 824, 986, 1248, 1548, 1725, 1732, 1761, 1855, 1892, 1897, 2466, 2587 had a perfect exemplar.

1 Timothy—I have collated 37 **f**^{35} MSS; 1761, 2554 are perfect; 35 is complete; 444, 2466 had a perfect exemplar.

2 Timothy—I have collated 36 **f**^{35} MSS; 824, 1072, 1075, 1864 are perfect; 1865, 2723 are complete; 1503 had a perfect exemplar.

Titus—I have collated 36 **f**^{35} MSS; 35, 1072, 1503, 1855, 1864, 1892, 2080, 2587, 2723 are perfect; 18, 328, 1637, 1761 had a perfect exemplar.

Philemon—I have collated 36 **f**^{35} MSS; only seven are not perfect; and five of them had a perfect exemplar.

Hebrews—I have collated 34 **f**^{35} MSS; 2554 is perfect; 35, 1637, and 2723 are complete.

James—I have collated 43 **f**[35] MSS; 18, 1864, 2554, 2723 are perfect; 35, 2221 are complete; 1503, 1732, 1865, 2303 had a perfect exemplar.

1 Peter—I have collated 42 **f**[35] MSS; 1865, 2554, 2723 are perfect; 35 is complete; 824 had a perfect exemplar.

2 Peter—I have collated 42 **f**[35] MSS; 35, 1725, 1864, 2554, 2723 are perfect; 18, 141, 824, 1072, 1075, 1503, 1865, 1897 had a perfect exemplar.

1 John—I have collated 42 **f**[35] MSS; 204, 824, 1100, 2554 are perfect; 35, 1637, 1865 are complete. 1248, 1503, 1725, 1732, 1864, 1897, 2723 had a perfect exemplar.

2 & 3 John and Jude—I have collated 46 **f**[35] MSS; 141, 204, 386, 824, 928, 1072, 1075, 1100, 1637, 1855, 1864, 2221, 2554, 2723 are perfect in all three books; 35 and 2587 are perfect in John and complete in Jude; another thirteen had a perfect exemplar; only five of the 46 MSS have a variant in all three books.

Revelation—I have collated 20 **f**[35] MSS; none are perfect; 1864 is complete; 757 had a perfect exemplar. (I have not checked Hoskier's collation of other MSS, in this connection.)

So then, I hold a perfect copy of the Family 35 archetype for 22 books. I hold a complete copy for another three. I say that GA 2382 is complete for Luke; but if not, it is off by a solitary letter. I say that GA 35 misses being complete for Acts by a solitary letter; not bad for the longest book in the NT. **<u>God has preserved His Text</u>**!

Years ago I myself wrote that no two MSS were identical, merely repeating the prevailing canard. But that was before I started collating MSS for myself. After all, there is nothing like a firsthand acquaintance with the evidence.

K^r (Family 35) Byzantine Manuscripts

Uncials: None

Minuscules: 18, 35, 47, 55, 56, 58, 59, 66, 83, 128, 141, 147, 149, 155, 167, 170, 189, 201, 204, 205, 214, 225, 246, 285, 290, 328, 361, 363, 386, 387, 394, 402, 415, 422, 432, 471, 479, 480, 486, 510, 511, 512, 516, 520, 521, 536, 547, 553, 575, 586, 588, 594, 604, 634, 645, 660, 664, 673, 676, 685, 689, 691, 694, 696, 757, 758, 763, 769, 781, 786, 789, 797, 801, 802, 806, 824, 825, 830, 845, 864, 867, 897, 928, 932, 936, 938, 940, 952,

953, 955, 958, 959, 960, 961, 962, 966, 986, 1003, 1010, 1018, 1020, 1023, 1025, 1030, 1040, 1046, 1058, 1059, 1062, 1072, 1075, 1088, 1092, 1095, 1100, 1101, 1111, 1116, 1117, 1119, 1131, 1132, 1133, 1140, 1145, 1146, 1147, 1158, 1165, 1169, 1176, 1180, 1185, 1189, 1190, 1199, 1224, 1234, 1236, 1247, 1248, 1249, 1250, 1251, 1293, 1323, 1328, 1329, 1330, 1331, 1334, 1339, 1348, 1354, 1362, 1367, 1384, 1389, 1400, 1401, 1409, 1414, 1427, 1435, 1444, 1445, 1453, 1456, 1461, 1462, 1465, 1467, 1471, 1472, 1474, 1476, 1477, 1480, 1482, 1483, 1487, 1488, 1489, 1490, 1492, 1493, 1494, 1496, 1497, 1499, 1501, 1503, 1508, 1509, 1543, 1544, 1548, 1550, 1551, 1552, 1559, 1560, 1570, 1572, 1576, 1584, 1585, 1591, 1596, 1599, 1600, 1601, 1609, 1614, 1617, 1618, 1619, 1620, 1621, 1622, 1625, 1628, 1630, 1632, 1633, 1634, 1636, 1637, 1638, 1641, 1648, 1649, 1650, 1652, 1653, 1656, 1658, 1659, 1664, 1667, 1671, 1680, 1686, 1688, 1694, 1698, 1700, 1702, 1703, 1704, 1705, 1713, 1723, 1725, 1726, 1732, 1733, 1737, 1740, 1745, 1746, 1748, 1749, 1752, 1754, 1761, 1763, 1766, 1767, 1768, 1771, 1779, 1785, 1786, 1789, 1813, 1855, 1856, 1858, 1864, 1865, 1876, 1892, 1894, 1897, 1903, 1957, 1960, 1966, 2023, 2035, 2041, 2061, 2080, 2095, 2112, 2122, 2124, 2131, 2175, 2178, 2196, 2204, 2213, 2218, 2221, 2231, 2235, 2251, 2253, 2255, 2260, 2261, 2265, 2273, 2284, 2289, 2296, 2303, 2322, 2323, 2352, 2355, 2367, 2375, 2378, 2382, 2387, 2399, 2407, 2418, 2431, 2434, 2436, 2452, 2454, 2460, 2466, 2479, 2483, 2496, 2501, 2503, 2508, 2510, 2520, 2554, 2587, 2598, 2621, 2626, 2635, 2649, 2653, 2658, 2673, 2669, 2704, 2723, 2765, 2767, 2777, 2806, 2821

Total = 364

Note: The list includes only continuous text manuscripts.

Sources:

Die Schriften Des Neuen Testaments, Hermann Von Soden, Gottingen, 2 vols. (1911-1913)

Kurzgefaste Liste, Kurt Aland, Berlin, de Gruyter, 2nd edit. (1994)

Text und Textwert (TuT), Berlin, de Gryuter (1998-2005)

The Profile Method for Classification and Evaluation of Manuscript Evidence-The Gospel of Luke, Frederick Wisse, William B. Eerdmans, Grand Rapids, Michigan, (1982)

VMR-Handshriftenliste, (INTF) Munster, http://intf.uni-uenster.de/vmr/NTVMR/ListeHandschriften.php

Compiled by:
Paul D. Anderson
April, 2010

Generational Sin

To the Elders of the Duncanville Bible Church[1]

Two of our elders made public reference last Sunday (10/22/89) to "generational sin", and this gave me a handle on a situation in the church that has been troubling me for some time. Generational sin? Yes! But not only within families. There is generational sin in individual churches, in schools, in denominations and across wider segments of the Church. One very serious generational sin that is endemic across wide areas of the conservative/evangelical community at large is the idolatry that elevates human reason above the revealed Word of God. This idolatry expresses itself on many fronts, but perhaps the foundational one relates to the very Text of Scripture itself—I refer to the mentality that constantly calls into question the very wording of the Text, thereby undermining confidence in its integrity and authority.

Let me give a concrete, specific example of what I am talking about. A number of weeks ago our pastor emended the Text of 1 Corinthians 8:3 from the pulpit. Instead of *"if anyone loves God this one is known by Him"* he suggested that perhaps we should read *"if anyone loves God this one knows"*. Since no printed Greek text has what he suggested I felt led of the Lord to warn him that such a proceeding was not advisable. His answer was to direct me to Gordon Fee's commentary on 1 Corinthians, which was the source for what he had done. Fee's commentary on 1 Corinthians 8:2-3 furnishes an unusually blatant example of the idolatry I have referred to. Consider:

The correct Text of 1 Corinthians 8:2-3, as attested by some 95% of the Greek manuscripts, reads as follows: Ει δε τις δοκει ειδεναι [86%] τι, ουδεπω ουδεν εγνωκε καθως δει γνωναι. Ει δε τις αγαπα τον θεον, οὗτος εγνωσται ὑπ᾽ αυτου. The eclectic text presently in vogue, being followed by NIV, NASB. LB, etc., is based on a handful of Egyptian witnesses and reads like this: Ει … τις δοκει εγνωκεναι τί ουπω … εγνω καθως δει γνωναι. Ει δε τις αγαπα τον θεον, οὗτος εγνωσται ὑπ᾽ αυτου. The points at issue are underlined. It is the eclectic text that Fee uses as his starting point and is pleased to call the 'standard text'. Had Fee recognized the correct text he could scarcely have written as he did. (But to do so he would have had to reject all that he was taught on the subject of New Testament textual criticism.) But he was not satisfied even with his 'standard' text—he proposes to emend it by omission in three places (see his page 367), and he does so on the basis of a single Greek MS, P^{46}. His text would be: Ει τις

[1] It broke up years ago.

δοκει εγνωκεναι... ουπω εγνω καθως δει γνωναι. Ει δε τις αγαπα ... ... , οὗτος εγνωσται ... .

P^{46} contains most of Paul's epistles and is usually dated at about 200 A.D. (which makes it our oldest extant MS at this place). It was discovered in the sands of Egypt some 85 years ago and scholarly opinion seems to be agreed that it was produced in Egypt. Now at that time (200) the 'Christian church' in Egypt included at least eleven heretical groups that were so well defined that they had names—Valentinians, Basilidians, Marcionites, Peratae, Encratites, Docetists, Haimetites, Cainites, Ophites, Simonians and Eutychites—but the dominant force in the whole 'Christian' community was Gnosticism. The text of P^{46} in 1 Corinthians 8:2-3 is simply a gnostic fabrication that was buried in the sands of Egypt for 17 centuries, but that Fee proposes to resurrect and present to the world as God's Truth!

Now, let us analyze Fee's procedure. He started out with an eclectic Greek text based on less than 5% of the extant Greek manuscripts (around 700, here). Not content with that he proposes three omissions based on one Greek MS, against every other Greek MS (a. 700) and every ancient Version, including Egyptian MSS and Versions (except that the 3rd omission is also found in two other MSS). Notice that he does not discuss the evidence; there is no attempt to explain why or how every MS (except P^{46}) and Version comes to be in error here. His whole argument is in terms of subjective considerations, of what he thinks 'fits the context'. In other words, Fee is elevating his own mental processes above God's Word. He, Gordon Fee, is going to determine what is the original wording of the Sacred Text on the basis of his own imagination. This is idolatry; it is perverse idolatry.

Now consider the implications for the doctrine of the inspiration of Scripture. If Fee is right, then the form of 1 Corinthians that the various Church Councils canonized is wrong. If the Church canonized the wrong Text, how do we know she was right in canonizing the book (1 Corinthians) at all? Not only that, the Church Universal has used and preserved the wrong text down through the centuries. Martin Luther could not know what the correct text of 1 Corinthians was—it was buried in the sands of Egypt (according to Fee). Neither could anyone else, at any time between 300 and 1930 A.D.—the true reading (according to Fee) had disappeared from the knowledge of the Church. Any and all translators and scholars in 1900 simply could not know what the true reading was—it did not exist. Not only that, how do we know that a new papyrus, call it P^{201}, will not be discovered tomorrow that will have a variant at a point where up to now there is 100% agreement? And what is to stop Fee from telling us that that variant is really the original reading? In other words, if Fee is right we have no certainty and never can have certainty as to what is the true Text of Scripture. So why bother trying to talk about an inerrant Text in such a situation? And does not any claim about inspiration become relative?

Fee's treatment of 1 Corinthians 8:2-3 is only an extreme example of a mentality that pervades our churches. The margins of NIV and NASB are full of notes that undermine confidence in the integrity of the Text: *"some early MSS omit..."*, *"many ancient authorities read..."*, *"the earliest and best* [worst, really] *witnesses..."*; not to mention the brackets in the text proper that say to the reader that the enclosed material "certainly is not genuine". Why do they do this? Because they are following an eclectic text, and the editors of that text constructed it on the basis of subjective criteria, in turn based on false presuppositions. But no one of those editors believed the Bible to be God's infallible Word—indeed, they foisted plain errors of fact and contradictions upon their text. Would they not qualify as "sons of the disobedience" (Ephesians 2:2)? If so, it would mean that they were wide open to satanic interference in their minds. If anyone thinks that Satan would pass up such an opportunity to corrupt the Sacred Text he really does not believe what the Bible says about our enemy!

The phrase 'generational sin' implies that a whole generation is practicing that sin. It involves a very serious consequence: all subsequent generations receive that sin as part of their 'gene pool'; it is not perceived as 'sin', but as 'truth'. But being in fact a lie, it becomes a stronghold of Satan in their minds and is not questioned. The only deliverance from that sin comes when someone goes back to its beginning and analyzes and exposes the false presuppositions and reasoning that gave rise to the sin. But such a person should not expect to be well received. He will certainly be persecuted by the 'Establishment'. However, if he has a means of disseminating his findings, he can influence the future.

Now consider the consequences of this generational sin. It is difficult to really teach a Sunday School lesson anymore—there may be six different versions in the room and we start discussing the various texts and renderings; there is no authority for making a choice; no one knows for sure what God's word is! The footnotes, plus the versional differences (often significant), have undermined people's confidence in the integrity of the Text. If the preacher emends the Text from the pulpit, it is confusion compounded. The authority of the Scriptures has been undermined. Few have the confidence to stand up and say, "Thus says the LORD!" The practical result is that whenever some teaching of Scripture becomes inconvenient, for personal or cultural reasons, we simply talk around it, explain it away or just shrug it off. Unquestioned obedience to the normal meaning of the Text is now hopelessly out of fashion! After all, nowadays it is our reason and logic (tempered by our convenience) that is the final authority, the final arbiter—God's Word no longer rules over us; we rule over it (*à la* Fee).

Why should God bless our country, our church, our homes, our lives when we persist in such a pernicious form of idolatry?

Coherence-Based Genealogical Method

Anyone who deals with NT textual criticism in any way will presumably have heard about the Coherence-Based Genealogical Method (CBGM). Whenever you see the phrase 'genealogical method' you should say to yourself, "Aha, this will be just another attempt to avoid the drudgery of collating all the MSS". Having myself collated at least one book in over a hundred MSS (over 30 entire), I can assure you that it is indeed a drudgery, slave labor.

The CBGM is basically another attempt to avoid the job of collating all the extant MSS. It uses a computer to plot probabilities. The main problem with this method (from our point of view) is that at almost every stage of the procedure the critic must make subjective choices, and he will make those choices using the same criteria used in eclecticism (prefer the harder reading, the shorter reading, etc.). In the recent *ECM* Acts, Klaus Wachtel plainly states, "In the first stage, the traditional methods of eclectic textual criticism are applied" (p. 28*). So it is basically the old eclecticism dressed up in new clothes. The <u>method</u> is not empirical, even though it uses actual variants.

The tendency is illustrated by the *Editio Critica Maior* (*ECM*) series for the General Epistles. For James they included 182 MSS out of 522 complete MSS and larger fragments. By their own definition, they included 78 MSS that they considered to be so Byzantine that they grouped them under the symbol '**Byz**'. However, for the remaining six books the total of MSS was reduced by an average of 50 MSS, while the total of '**Byz**' MSS was reduced by an average of 35 MSS. From my point of view, the *ECM* James is clearly more useful than the other six books.

In the *ECM* Acts they continue to call the Byzantine text a "carefully controlled form" (p. 18*), as they did twenty years before in the *ECM* James (p. 11*), but they never say who did the controlling. The reason is simple: they can't, because the statement is false. They are just repeating a cherished canard.

Is NT Textual Criticism a Science?

Have you ever heard or read (or said) the phrase, 'the science of NT textual criticism'? How about the phrase, 'textual critic'? So what does a critic do? He criticizes. What does he criticize? In this case it is the text of the NT in Greek. But just what is he criticizing? A literary critic looks at things like style and choice of vocabulary; a commentator tries to decide what was the meaning intended by the author of the text. So what does a textual critic do? He attempts to reconstruct the original wording of a text—notice that he is assuming that the original wording is 'lost', in the sense that no one knows for sure what it is, or was. (Notice also that this places the critic above the text, to which I will return.) Textual criticism only exists for texts whose original wording is deemed to be 'lost'. No one does textual criticism on today's newspaper, or last week's news magazine. No one even does textual criticism on the 1611 King James Version, since we still have printed copies thereof. Any and all arguments surrounding the KJV come under other headings; they are not textual criticism.

Anyone familiar with the terrain knows that for the last 150 years (at least) the academic world has been dominated by the notion that the original wording of the NT text is in fact 'lost'. Just to illustrate, some 65 years ago Robert M. Grant wrote, "it is generally recognized that the original text of the Bible cannot be recovered".[1] For a number of further references echoing that sentiment please see pages 3-4 of my *Identity IV*. Before attempting to rebut that fiction [canard?], as I believe, I will sketch a bit of relevant history.

A Bit of Relevant History

The discipline as we know it is basically a 'child' of Western Europe and its colonies; the Eastern Orthodox Churches have generally not been involved. (They have always known that the true Text lies within the Byzantine tradition.) In the year 1500 the Christianity of Western Europe was dominated by the Roman Catholic Church, whose pope claimed the exclusive right to interpret Scripture. That Scripture was the Latin Vulgate, which the laity was not allowed to read. Martin Luther's 95 theses were posted in 1517. Was it mere chance that the first printed Greek Text of the NT was published the year before? As the Protestant Reformation advanced, it was declared that the authority of Scripture exceeded that of the

[1] R.M. Grant, "The Bible of Theophilus of Antioch", *Journal of Biblical Literature*, LXVI (1947), 173. Notice the pessimism, it 'cannot be recovered'. In that event, the critics are wasting their time, and ours. Surely, because we would have no way of knowing whether or not they have found it.

pope, and that every believer had the right to read and interpret the Scriptures. The authority of the Latin Vulgate was also challenged, since the NT was written in Greek. Of course the Vatican library held many Greek MSS, no two of which were identical (at least in the Gospels), so the Roman Church challenged the authenticity of the Greek Text. In short, the Roman Church forced the Reformation to come to grips with textual variation among the Greek MSS. But they did not know how to go about it, because this was a new field of study and they simply were not in possession of a sufficient proportion of the relevant evidence.[1] (They probably did not even know that the Mt. Athos peninsula with its twenty monasteries existed.)

In 1500 the Roman Catholic Establishment was corrupt, morally bankrupt, and discredited among thinking people. The Age of Reason and humanism were coming to the fore. More and more people were deciding that they could do better without the god of the Roman Establishment. The new imagined freedom from supernatural supervision was intoxicating, and many had no interest in accepting the authority of Scripture (*'sola Scriptura'*). Further, it would be naive in the extreme to exclude the supernatural from consideration, and not allow for satanic activity behind the scenes—Ephesians 2:2.[2] 'Sons of the disobedience' joined the attack against Scripture. The so-called 'higher criticism' denied divine inspiration altogether. Others used the textual variation to argue that in any case the original wording was 'lost', there being no objective way to determine

---

1 Family 35, being by far the largest and most cohesive group of MSS, was poorly represented in the libraries of Western Europe. For that matter, very few MSS of whatever text-type had been sufficiently collated to allow for any tracing of the transmissional history.

2 Strictly speaking the Text has "according to the Aeon of this world, according to the ruler of the domain of the air"—the phrases are parallel, so 'Aeon' and 'ruler' have the same referent, a specific person or being. This spirit is presently at work (present tense) in 'the sons of the disobedience'. 'Sons' of something are characterized by that something, and the something in this case is 'the' disobedience (the Text has the definite article)—a continuation of the original rebellion against the Sovereign of the universe. Anyone in rebellion against the Creator is under satanic influence, direct or indirect (in most cases a demon acts as Satan's agent, when something more than the influence of the surrounding culture is required—almost all human cultures have ingredients of satanic provenance; this includes the academic culture [the academic requirement that one demonstrate 'acquaintance with the literature' obliges one to waste time on all that Satan's servants have written—consider 1 Corinthians 3:18-20]). Anyone in rebellion against the Creator will also have strongholds of Satan in his mind. Since Satan is the 'father' of lies (John 8:44), any time you embrace a lie you invite him into your mind—this applies to any of his sophistries (2 Corinthians 10:5) currently in vogue, such as materialism, humanism, relativism, Marxism, Freudianism, Hortianism, etc.

what it may have been (that is, they could not perceive such a way at that time).

The uncritical assumption that 'oldest equals best' was an important factor and became increasingly so as earlier uncials came to light. Both Codex Vaticanus and Codex Bezae were available early on, and they have thousands of disagreements, just in the Gospels (in Acts, Bezae is wild almost beyond belief). **If** 'oldest equals best', and the oldest MSS are in constant and massive disagreement between/among themselves, then the recovery of a lost text becomes hopeless. Did you get that? **Hopeless, totally hopeless**! However, I have argued that 'oldest equals worst', and that changes the picture, radically.[1]

Since everyone is influenced (not necessarily controlled) by his milieu, this was true of the Reformers. In part (at least) the Reformation was a 'child' of the Renaissance, with its emphasis on reason. Recall that on trial Luther said he could only recant if convinced by Scripture and reason. So far so good, but many did not want Scripture, and that left only reason. Further, since reason cannot explain or deal with the supernatural, those who emphasize reason are generally unfriendly toward the supernatural.

---

[1] The benchmark work on this subject is Herman C. Hoskier's *Codex B and its Allies, a Study and an Indictment* (2 vols.; London: Bernard Quaritch, 1914). The first volume (some 500 pages) contains a detailed and careful discussion of hundreds of obvious errors in Codex B; the second (some 400 pages) contains the same for Codex Aleph. He affirms that in the Gospels alone these two MSS differ well over 3,000 times, which number does not include minor errors such as spelling (II, 1). Well now, simple logic demands that one or the other has to be wrong those 3,000+ times; they cannot both be right, quite apart from the times when they are both wrong. **No amount of subjective preference can obscure the fact that they are poor copies, objectively so**.

John William Burgon personally collated what in his day were 'the five old uncials' (א, A, B, C, D). Throughout his works he repeatedly calls attention to the *concordia discors*, the prevailing confusion and disagreement, which the early uncials display between themselves. Luke 11:2-4 offers one example.

> "The five Old Uncials" (אABCD) falsify the Lord's Prayer as given by St. Luke in no less than forty-five words. But so little do they agree among themselves, that they throw themselves into six different combinations in their departures from the Traditional Text; and yet they are never able to agree among themselves as to one single various reading: while only once are more than two of them observed to stand together, and their grand point of union is no less than an omission of the article. Such is their eccentric tendency, that in respect of thirty-two out of the whole forty-five words they bear in turn solitary evidence. (*The Traditional Text of the Holy Gospels Vindicated and Established*. Arranged, completed, and edited by Edward Miller. London: George Bell and Sons, 1896, p. 84.)

Yes indeed, oldest equals worst. For more on this subject, please see pages 130-36 in my *Identity IV*.

[To this day the so-called historic or traditional Protestant denominations have trouble dealing with the supernatural.]

Before Adolf Deissmann published his *Light from the Ancient East* (1910), (being a translation of *Licht vom Osten*, 1908), wherein he demonstrated that Koiné Greek was the *lingua franca* in Jesus' day, there even being a published grammar explaining its rules, only classical Greek was taught in the universities. But the NT is written in Koiné. Before Deissmann's benchmark work, there were two positions on the NT Greek: 1) it was a debased form of classical Greek, or 2) it was a 'Holy Ghost' Greek, invented for the NT. The second option was held mainly by pietists; the academic world preferred the first, which raised the natural question: if God were going to inspire a NT, why wouldn't He do it in 'decent' Greek?

All of this placed the defenders of an inspired Greek Bible on the defensive, with the very real problem of deciding where best to set up their defense perimeter. Given the prevailing ignorance concerning the relevant evidence, their best choice appeared to be an appeal to Divine Providence. God providentially chose the TR, so that was the text to be used (the 'traditional' text).[1]

To all appearances Satan was winning the day, but he still had a problem: the main Protestant versions (in German, English, Spanish, etc.) were all based on the *Textus Receptus*, as were doctrinal statements and 'prayer books'. Enter F.J.A. Hort, a quintessential 'son of the disobedience'. Hort did not believe in the divine inspiration of the Bible, nor in the divinity of Jesus Christ. Since he embraced the Darwinian theory as soon as it appeared, he presumably did not believe in God.[2] His theory of NT textual

---

1 Please note that I am not criticizing Burgon and others; they did what they could, given the information available to them. They knew that the Hortian theory and resultant Greek text could not be right.

2 For documentation of all this, and a good deal more besides, in Hort's own words, please see the biography written by his son. A.F. Hort, *Life and Letters of Fenton John Anthony Hort* (2 vols.; London: Macmillan and Co. Ltd., 1896). The son made heavy use of the father's plentiful correspondence, whom he admired. (In those days a two volume 'Life', as opposed to a one volume 'Biography', was a posthumous status symbol.) Many of my readers were taught, as was I, that one must not question/judge someone else's motives. But wait just a minute; where did such an idea come from? It certainly did not come from God, who expects the spiritual person to evaluate everything (1 Corinthians 2:15). Since there are only two spiritual kingdoms in this world (Matthew 12:30, Luke 11:23), then the idea comes from the other side. By eliminating motive, one also eliminates presupposition, which is something that God would never do, since presupposition governs interpretation (Matthew 22:29, Mark 12:24). Which is why we should <u>always</u> expect a true scholar to state his presuppositions. I have repeatedly stated mine, but here they are again: 1) The Sovereign Creator of the universe exists; 2) He delivered a written revelation to the human race; 3) He has preserved that revelation intact to this day.

criticism, published in 1881,[1] was based squarely on the presuppositions that the NT was not inspired, that no special care was afforded it in the early decades, and that in consequence the original wording was lost—lost beyond recovery, at least by objective means. His theory swept the academic world and continues to dominate the discipline to this day.[2]

Moreover, Hort claimed that as a result of his work only a thousandth part of the NT text could be considered to be in doubt, and this was joyfully received by the rank and file, since it seemed to provide assurance about the reliability of that text—however, of course, that claim applied only to the W-H text (probably the worst published NT in existence, to this day).[3]

The Nature of a Scientific Exercise

So much for my sketch of history. I will now return to the question in the title. To begin, I observe and insist that in any scientific exercise a rigorous distinction must be made between evidence, interpretation, and presupposition. It is dishonest to represent one's presuppositions as being part of the evidence (opinion is not evidence). So, if NT textual criticism is to be a 'science', presuppositions must be excluded. But if we exclude the presupposition that the original wording is 'lost', then textual criticism ceases to exist; and how can you have a 'science' of something that doesn't exist? Science is one thing; theory is another. A theory is based on presupposition, of necessity, so it is legitimate to speak of a Hortian theory of textual criticism, since he considered the original wording to be lost. My own theory does not include textual criticism, since I consider that the original wording is not lost. I defend a theory of the divine preservation of the NT Text.[4]

By now it should be evident to the reader that the question of a 'lost' original is the crux, the central issue in any attempt to identify the original wording of the NT. So to that issue I now turn. To be fair, I

---

1 B.F. Westcott and F.J.A. Hort, *The New Testament in the Original Greek* (2 Vols.; London: Macmillan and Co., 1881). The second volume explains the theory, and is generally understood to be Hort's work.

2 For a thorough discussion of that theory, please see chapters 3 and 4 in my *Identity IV.*

3 I would say that their text is mistaken with reference to 10% of the words—the Greek NT has roughly 140,000 words, so the W-H text is mistaken with reference to 14,000 of them. I would say that the so-called 'critical' text currently in vogue is 'only' off with reference to some 12,000, an improvement (small though it be). And just by the way, how wise is it to use a NT prepared by a servant of Satan?

4 I consider myself to be a textual scholar, not critic. The Text is above me, not the opposite. In eclecticism the critic is above the text, is above the evidence; instead of faithfully following the evidence, he makes the evidence follow him. The MSS are reduced to the role of 'supplier of readings'.

need to recognize two definitions of 'lost': 1) lost beyond recovery, at least by objective means; 2) lost from view, in the sense that the available evidence has not been sufficiently studied to permit an empirical choice between/among competing variants. I consider that my *Identity IV* provides more than enough evidence to demonstrate that the first definition is false. The Hortian theory and all derivatives thereof, such as eclecticism (of whatever type), is not science, and may not honestly be called science. The second definition allows for scientific procedure. I suggest and recommend that we start using the term 'manuscriptology', rather than 'textual criticism'—manuscriptology refers to the study of the MSS, and is neutral as to presupposition. Any scientific exercise should begin with the evidence; so what is the evidence?

The primary evidence is furnished by the continuous text manuscripts (Greek) of the NT. The evidence furnished by the lectionaries is secondary. The evidence furnished by ancient versions and patristic citations is tertiary. Genuine historical evidence (to the extent that this can be determined) is ancillary. Where the primary evidence is unequivocal, the remaining types should not come into play. For example, at any given point in the four Gospels there will be around 1,700 extant continuous text MSS, representing all lines of transmission and all locales.[1] Where they all agree, there can be no legitimate doubt as to the original wording. But what if an early Papyrus comes to light with a variant, does that change the picture? The very fact of being early suggests that it is bad; why wasn't it used and worn out?

We have probably all heard/read the canard, 'manuscripts are to be weighed, not counted'. The basic meaning of the verb 'to weigh' refers to an objective procedure; it is done with physically verifiable weights. But do the followers of Hort (who are the main ones who keep repeating it) 'weigh' manuscripts using objective criteria? They do not, which is why I call it a 'canard'. That said, however, I submit for the consideration of all concerned that it is indeed possible to weigh MSS using objective criteria.

Just how are MSS to be weighed? And who might be competent to do the weighing? As the reader is by now well aware, Hort and most subsequent scholars have done their 'weighing' on the basis of so-called 'internal evidence'—the two standard criteria are, 'choose the reading which fits the context' and 'choose the reading which explains the origin of the other reading'.

---

[1] Of course we know that there are many MSS not yet 'extant', not yet identified and catalogued, so the number can only go up.

One problem with this has been well stated by E.C. Colwell. "As a matter of fact these two standard criteria for the appraisal of the internal evidence of readings can easily cancel each other out and leave the scholar free to choose in terms of his own prejudgments."[1] Further, "the more lore the scholar knows, the easier it is for him to produce a reasonable defense of both readings…"[2] The whole process is so subjective that it makes a mockery of the word 'weigh'. The basic meaning of the term involves an evaluation made by an objective instrument. If we wish our weighing of MSS to have objective validity, we must find an objective procedure.

How do we evaluate the credibility of a witness in real life? We watch how he acts, listen to what he says and how he says it, and listen to the opinion of his neighbors and associates. If we can demonstrate that a witness is a habitual liar or that his critical faculties are impaired then we receive his testimony with skepticism. It is quite possible to evaluate MSS in a similar way, to a considerable extent, and it is hard to understand why scholars have generally neglected to do so.

Can we objectively 'weigh' P^{66} as a witness? (It is the oldest one of any size.) Well, in the space of John's Gospel (not complete) it has over 900 clear, indubitable errors—as a witness to the identity of the text of John it has misled us over 900 times. Is P^{66} a credible witness? I would argue that neither of the scribes of P^{66} and P^{75} knew Greek; should we not say that as witnesses they were impaired?[3]

P^{75} is placed close to P^{66} in date. Though not as bad as P^{66}, it is scarcely a good copy. Colwell found P^{75} to have about 145 itacisms plus 257 other singular readings, 25 percent of which are nonsensical.[4] Although Colwell gives the scribe of P^{75} credit for having tried to produce a good copy, P^{75} looks good only by comparison with P^{66}. (If you were asked to

---

1 Colwell, "External Evidence and New Testament Criticism", *Studies in the History and Text of the New Testament*, eds. B.L. Daniels and M.J. Suggs (Salt Lake City: University of Utah Press, 1967), p. 3.

2 *Ibid.*, p. 4.

3 The fact that the transcriber of P^{75} copied letter by letter and that of P^{66} syllable by syllable (Colwell, "Scribal Habits", p. 380) suggests strongly that neither one knew Greek. When transcribing in a language you know you copy phrase by phrase, or at the very least word by word. P^{66} has so many nonsensical readings that the transcriber could not have known the meaning of the text. Anyone who has ever tried to transcribe a text of any length by hand (not typewriter) in a language he does not understand will know that it is a taxing and dreary task. Purity of transmission is not to be expected under such circumstances.

4 E.C. Colwell, "Scribal Habits in Early Papyri: A Study in the Corruption of the Text", *The Bible in Modern Scholarship*, ed. J.P. Hyatt [New York: Abingdon Press, 1965], pp. 374-76.

write out the Gospel of John by hand, would you make over 400 mistakes? Try it and see!) It should be kept in mind that the figures offered by Colwell deal only with errors which are the exclusive property of the respective MSS. They doubtless contain many other errors which happen to be found in some other witness(es) as well. In other words, they are actually worse even than Colwell's figures indicate.

P^{45}, though a little later in date, will be considered next because it is the third member in Colwell's study. He found P^{45} to have approximately 90 itacisms plus 275 other singular readings, 10 percent of which are nonsensical (*Ibid.*). However P^{45} is shorter than P^{66} (P^{75} is longer) and so is not comparatively so much better as the figures might suggest at first glance. Colwell comments upon P^{45} as follows:

> Another way of saying this is that when the scribe of P^{45} creates a singular reading, it almost always makes sense; when the scribes of P^{66} and P^{75} create singular readings, they frequently do not make sense and are obvious errors. Thus P^{45} must be given credit for a much greater density of intentional changes than the other two (*Ibid.*, p. 376).

> As an editor the scribe of P^{45} wielded a sharp axe. The most striking aspect of his style is its conciseness. The dispensable word is dispensed with. He omits adverbs, adjectives, nouns, participles, verbs, personal pronouns—without any compensateing habit of addition. He frequently omits phrases and clauses. He prefers the simple to the compound word. In short, he favors brevity. He shortens the text in at least fifty places in **singular readings alone**. But he does **not** drop syllables or letters. His shortened text is readable (*Ibid.*, p. 383).

P^{46} is thought by some to be as early as P^{66}. Zuntz's study of this manuscript is well known. "In spite of its neat appearance (it was written by a professional scribe and corrected—but very imperfectly—by an expert), P^{46} is by no means a good manuscript. The scribe committed very many blunders... My impression is that he was liable to fits of exhaustion."[1]

It should be remarked in passing that Codex B is noted for its 'neat appearance' also, but it should not be assumed that therefore it must be a good copy. Even Hort conceded that the scribe of B "reached by no means a high standard of accuracy" (Westcott and Hort, p. 233). Aleph is acknowledged on every side to be worse than B in every way. Zuntz says

[1] Gunther Zuntz, *The Text of the Epistles* (London: Oxford University Press, 1953), p.18.

further: "P^{46} abounds with scribal blunders, omissions, and also additions" (*Op.Cit.*, p. 212).

> ...the scribe who wrote the papyrus did his work very badly. Of his innumerable faults, only a fraction (less than one in ten) have been corrected and even that fraction—as often happens in manuscripts—grows smaller and smaller towards the end of the book. Whole pages have been left without any correction, however greatly they were in need of it (*Ibid.*, p. 252).

Recall from Colwell's study that the scribe of P^{45} evidently made numerous **deliberate** changes in the text—should we not say that he was morally impaired? In any case, he has repeatedly misinformed us. Shall we still trust him? Similarly, it has been demonstrated that Aleph and B have over 3,000 mistakes between them, just in the Gospels. Aleph is clearly worse than B, but probably not twice as bad—at least 1,000 of those mistakes are B's. Do Aleph and B fit your notion of a good witness?[1] Again I say: oldest equals worst!

We really need to understand that age guarantees nothing about quality. Each witness must be evaluated on its own, quite apart from age. Further, and perhaps more to the point, we need to know how a given MS relates to others. Once a MS has been empirically identified as belonging to a family (line of transmission), then it is no longer an independent witness to the original—it is a witness to the family archetype. As Colwell so well put it, "the crucial question for early as for late witnesses is still, 'WHERE DO THEY FIT INTO A PLAUSIBLE RECONSTRUCTION OF THE HISTORY OF THE MANUSCRIPT TRADITION?'"[2]

Lamentably, the Hortian theory, allied to the fiction that 'oldest equals best', has had a soporific effect upon the discipline such that comparatively few MSS have been fully collated, and in consequence few families have been empirically defined. A rough idea based on spot checking is not adequate; there is too much mixture.

The Transmission of the Text

Going back to the 1,700 extant MSS for any given point in the Gospels, it should be evident that a variant in a single MS, of whatever age, is

---

1 If you copied the four Gospels by hand, do you think you could manage to make a thousand mistakes? Try it and see!

2 Colwell, "Hort Redivivus: A Plea and a Program", *Studies in Methodology in Textual Criticism of the New Testament*, E.C. Colwell (Leiden: E.J. Brill, 1969), p. 157. [Emphasis in the original.]

irrelevant—it is a false witness to its family archetype, at that point, nothing more. If a number of MSS share a variant, but do not belong to the same family, then they made the mistake independently and are false witnesses to their respective family archetypes—there is no dependency. Where a group of MSS evidently reflect correctly the archetypal form of their family, then we are dealing with a family (not the individual MSS). Families need to be evaluated just as we evaluate individual MSS. It is possible to assign a credibility quotient to a family, based on objective criteria. But of course any and all families must first be empirically identified and defined, and such identification depends upon the full collation of MSS.

Although the discipline has (so far) neglected to do its homework (collating MSS), still a massive majority of MSS should be convincing. For example, if a variant enjoys 99% attestation from the primary witnesses, this means that it totally dominates any genealogical 'tree', because it dominated the global transmission of the text. The *INTF Text und Textwert* series, practitioners of the Claremont profile method, H.C. Hoskier, von Soden, Burgon, Scrivener—in short, anyone who has collated any number of MSS—have all demonstrated that the Byzantine bulk of MSS is by no means monolithic. There are any number of streams and rivulets. (Recall that Wisse posited 34 groups within the Byzantine bulk, with 70 subgroups.) It is clear that there was no 'stuffing the ballot box'; there was no 'papal' decree; there was no recension imposed by ecclesiastical authority. In short, the transmission was predominantly normal.

> Under normal circumstances the older a text is than its rivals, the greater are its chances to survive in a plurality or a majority of the texts extant at any subsequent period. But the **oldest** text of all is the autograph. Thus it ought to be taken for granted that, barring some radical dislocation in the history of transmission, a majority of texts will be far more likely to represent correctly the character of the original than a small minority of texts. This is especially true when the ratio is an overwhelming 8:2. Under any reasonably normal transmissional conditions, it would be... quite impossible for a later text-form to secure so one-sided a preponderance of extant witnesses.[1]

[1] Z.C. Hodges, "A Defense of the Majority Text" (unpublished course notes, Dallas Theological Seminary, 1975), p. 4. Appendix C in my *Identity IV* shows that the mathematical science of statistical probability gives ample support to Hodges' statement. It is statistically impossible for a late comer to dominate the transmission.

I insist that the transmission of the NT Text was in fact predominantly normal, based on historical evidence. Part I above lists and discusses that evidence, but here is a thumbnail sketch:

1. The authors of the NT books believed they were writing Scripture;
2. The Apostles recognized that their colleagues were writing Scripture;
3. The 'Church Fathers' of the I and II centuries regarded the NT writings as Scripture;
4. The NT writings were used along with the OT by the Christian congregations from very early on;
5. The early Christians were concerned about the purity of the NT Text.
6. What regions started out with the Autographs? Aegean area (18-24), Rome (2-7), Palestine (0-3), Egypt (0).
7. Where was the Church strongest during the II and III centuries? Asia Minor and the Aegean area.
8. Where was Greek used most and longest? Aegean area and Asia Minor.
9. What are the implications of Diocletian's campaign and the Donatist movement?

I submit that the evidence is clear to the effect that the transmission was in fact predominantly normal.

So what sort of a picture may we expect to find in the surviving witnesses, given the understanding that the history of the transmission of the New Testament Text was predominantly normal? We may expect a broad spectrum of copies, showing minor differences due to copying mistakes but all reflecting one common tradition. The simultaneous existence of abnormal transmission in the earliest centuries would result in a sprinkling of copies, helter-skelter, outside of that main stream. The picture would look something like the following figure.[1]

[1] The history of the place where Codex W was found suggests that it must have been copied before AD 200, which would put the Byzantine Text in the second century, since it shows Byzantine influence.

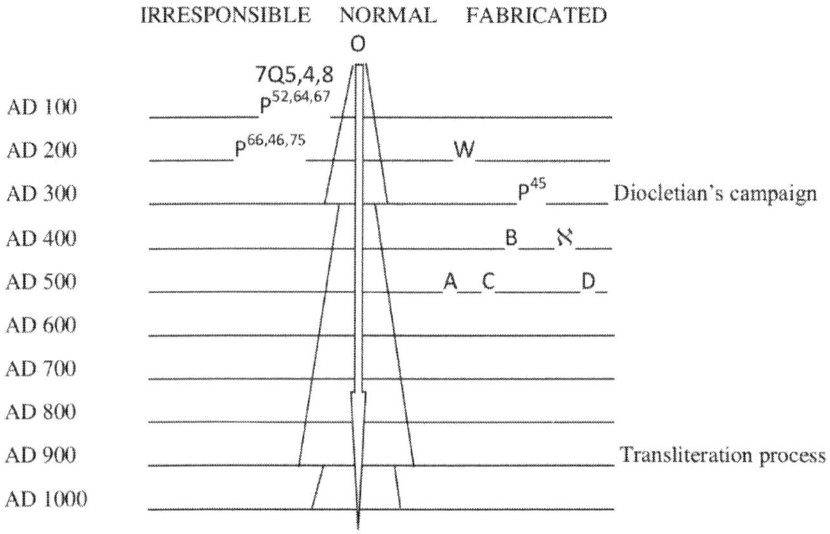

The MSS within the cones represent the 'normal' transmission. To the left I have plotted some possible representatives of what we might style the 'irresponsible' transmission of the text—the copyists produced poor copies through incompetence or carelessness but did not make deliberate changes. To the right I have plotted some possible representatives of what we might style the 'fabricated' transmission of the text—the scribes made deliberate changes in the text (for whatever reasons), producing fabricated copies, not true copies. I am well aware that the MSS plotted on the figure above contain both careless and deliberate errors, in different proportions (7Q5, 4, 8 and $P^{52,64,67}$ are too fragmentary to permit the classification of their errors as deliberate rather than careless), so that any classification such as I attempt here must be relative and gives a distorted picture. Still, I venture to insist that ignorance, carelessness, officiousness and malice all left their mark upon the transmission of the New Testament text, and we must take account of them in any attempt to reconstruct the history of that transmission.

As the figure suggests, I argue that Diocletian's campaign had a purifying effect upon the stream of transmission. In order to withstand torture rather than give up your MS(S), you would have to be a truly committed believer, the sort of person who would want good copies of the Scriptures. Thus it was probably the more contaminated MSS that were destroyed, in the main, leaving the purer MSS to replenish the earth (please see the section "Imperial repression of the N.T." in Chapter 6 of my *Identity IV*). The arrow within the cones represents Family 35 (see Part II).

Another consideration suggests itself—if, as reported, the Diocletian campaign was most fierce and effective in the Byzantine area, the numerical advantage of the 'Byzantine' text-type over the 'Western' and 'Alexandrian' would have been reduced, giving the latter a chance to forge ahead. But it did not happen. The Church, in the main, refused to propagate those forms of the Greek text. Codices B, ℵ, D, etc., have no 'children'. Since it is impossible to produce an archetypal form for either the 'Western' or the 'Alexandrian' text-types, so-called, based on manuscript evidence, do they even exist?

The 'Crux' of a 'Lost' Original

Returning to the 'crux', is/was the original wording lost? I answer with an emphatic, "**No**". It certainly exists within the Byzantine bulk, but what do we do if there is confusion within that bulk? (To insist that it must be one of the existing variants is better than nothing, I suppose, but I, at least, want to identify the original wording.) To my mind, any time at least 90% of the primary witnesses agree, there can be no reasonable question; it is statistically impossible that a non-original reading could score that high.[1] Any time a reading garners an attestation of at least 80%, its probability is very high. But for perhaps 2% of the words in the NT the attestation falls below 80% (a disproportionate number being in the Apocalypse), and at this point we need to shift our attention from MSS to families.[2] I have already mentioned assigning a credibility quotient to each family, based on objective criteria, and this needs to be done. Unfortunately, there is a great deal of 'homework' waiting to be done in this area (so far as I know, only Family 35 has an empirically defined profile),[3] but enough work has been done to allow for some rough ideas.

---

[1] See Appendix C in my *Identity IV*.

[2] Once all MSS have been collated and have been empirically assigned to families, then we can confine our attention to those families, from the start (as I have done in the Apocalypse).

[3] So far as I know, neither **f**[1] nor **f**[13] exists outside of the Gospels, but even there, has anyone ever produced an empirically defined profile for either one? Consider the following statement by Metzger:

> It should be observed that, in accord with the theory that members of f[1] and f[13] were subject to progressive accommodation to the later Byzantine text, scholars have established the text of these families by adopting readings of family witnesses that differ from the Textus Receptus. Therefore the citation of the siglum f[1] and f[13] may, in any given instance, signify a minority of manuscripts (or even only one) that belong to the family. (*A Textual Commentary on the Greek New Testament* [companion to UBS[3]], p. xii.)

Would it be unreasonable to say that such a proceeding is unfair to the reader? Does it not mislead the user of the apparatus? At least as used by the UBS editions, those sigla do not

We are indebted to the *Institut für Neutestamentliche Textforschung* for their *Text und Textwert* series. A careful look at their collations indicates that there probably is no $\mathbf{K^x}$, anywhere (and remember Wisse). Take, for example, the *TuT* volumes on John's Gospel, chapters 1-10. They examined a total of 1,763 MSS (for 153 variant sets) and included the results in the two volumes. Pages 54 - 90 (volume 1) contain "Groupings according to degrees of agreement" "agreeing more often with each other than with the majority text". Only one group symbol is used, $\mathbf{K^r}$—the first representative of the family, MS 18, heads a group of about 120 MSS, but all subsequent representatives have only a $\mathbf{K^r}$ (that I call $\mathbf{f^{35}}$). Following $\mathbf{K^r}$, there are 22 groups with between 52 and 25 MSS, and all but four of them are really $\mathbf{K^r}$ / $\mathbf{f^{35}}$, and the same holds for a number of smaller groups, so their $\mathbf{K^r}$ should probably be over 200 (I would say that Family 35 in the Gospels has over 250 representatives, but their ranking here is based on only 153 variant sets, in half of John).

Consider the largest group apart from $\mathbf{K^r}$: 2103. Of its 52 members, 15 show only a 95% agreement with MS 2103. If those 52 MSS are ever collated throughout the Gospels, it is entirely predictable that the 'group' will shrink considerably; it may even disappear.

Some years ago now, Maurice Robinson did a complete collation of 1,389 MSS that contain the P.A.,[1] and I had William Pierpont's photocopy of those collations in my possession for two months, spending most of that time studying those collations. As I did so, it became obvious to me that von Soden 'regularized' his data, arbitrarily 'creating' the alleged archetypal form for his first four families, $\mathbf{M^{1,2,3,4}}$—if they exist at all, they are rather fluid. His $\mathbf{M^{5\&6}}$ do exist, having distinct profiles for the purpose of showing that they are different, but they are a bit 'squishy', with enough internal confusion to make the choice of the archetypal form to be arbitrary. In fact, I suspect that they will have to be subdivided. In contrast to the above, his $\mathbf{M^7}$ (that I call Family 35) has a solid, unambiguous profile—the archetypal form is demonstrable, empirically determined.

---

represent empirically defined profiles.

[1] 240 MSS omit the PA, 64 of which are based on Theophylact's commentary. Fourteen others have lacunae, but are not witnesses for total omission. A few others certainly contain the passage but the microfilm is illegible. So, 1389 + 240 + 14 + 7(?) = about 1650 MSS checked by Robinson. That does not include Lectionaries, of which he also checked a fair number. (These are microfilms held by the *Institut* in Münster. We now know that there are many more extant MSS, and probably even more that are not yet 'extant'.) Unfortunately, so far as I know, Robinson has yet to publish his collations, thus making them available to the public at large.

As for the Apocalypse, of the nine groups that Hoskier identified, only his Complutensian (that I call Family 35) is homogenous. Of the others, the main ones all have sub-divisions, that will require their own profile.

Given my presuppositions, I consider that I have good reason for declaring the divine preservation of the precise original wording of the complete New Testament Text, to this day. That wording is reproduced in my edition of the Greek NT, available from www.prunch.org. BUT PLEASE NOTE: whether or not the archetype of $\mathbf{f^{35}}$ is the Autograph (as I claim), the fact remains that the MSS collated for this study reflect an incredibly careful transmission of their source, and this throughout the middle ages. My presuppositions include: God exists; He inspired the Biblical Text; He promised to preserve it for a thousand generations (1 Chronicles 16:15); so He must have an active, ongoing interest in that preservation [there have been fewer than 300 generations since Adam, so He has a ways to go!]. **If He was preserving the original wording in some line of transmission other than $\mathbf{f^{35}}$, would that transmission be any less careful than what I have demonstrated for $\mathbf{f^{35}}$?** I think not. So any line of transmission characterized by internal confusion is disqualified—this includes **all** the other lines of transmission that I have seen so far![1]

On the basis of the evidence so far available I affirm the following:

1. The original wording was never 'lost', and its transmission down through the years was basically normal, being recognized as inspired material from the beginning.
2. That normal process resulted in lines of transmission.
3. To delineate such lines, MSS must be grouped empirically on the basis of a shared mosaic of readings.
4. Such groups or families must be evaluated for independence and credibility.
5. The largest clearly defined group is Family 35.
6. Family 35 is demonstrably independent of all other lines of transmission throughout the NT.
7. Family 35 is demonstrably ancient, dating to the 3rd century, at least.
8. Family 35 representatives come from all over the Mediterranean area; the geographical distribution is all but total.

---

[1] Things like $\mathbf{M^6}$ and $\mathbf{M^5}$ in John 7:53-8:11 come to mind.

9. Family 35 is not a recension, was not created at some point subsequent to the Autographs.

10. Family 35 is an objectively/empirically defined entity throughout the NT; it has a demonstrable, diagnostic profile from Matthew 1:1 to Revelation 22:21.

11. The archetypal form of Family 35 is demonstrable—it has been demonstrated (see Part II).

12. The Original Text is the ultimate archetype; any candidate must also be an archetype—a real, honest to goodness, objectively verifiable archetype; there is only one—Family 35.[1]

13. God's concern for the preservation of the Biblical Text is evident: I take it that passages such as 1 Chronicles 16:15, Psalm 119:89, Isaiah 40:8, Matthew 5:18, Luke 16:17 and 21:33, John 10:35 and 16:12-13, 1 Peter 1:23-25 and Luke 4:4 may reasonably be taken to imply a promise that the Scriptures (to the tittle) will be preserved for man's use (we are to live "by *every* word of God"), and to the end of the world ("for a thousand generations"), but no intimation is given as to just how God proposed to do it. We must deduce the answer from what He has indeed done—we discover that He **did**!

14. This concern is reflected in Family 35; it is characterized by incredibly careful transmission (in contrast to other lines). [I have a perfect copy of the Family 35 archetypal text for most NT books (22); I have copies made from a perfect exemplar (presumed) for another four (4); as I continue to collate MSS I hope to add the last one (Acts), but even for it the archetypal form is demonstrable.]

15. If God was preserving the original wording in some line of transmission other than Family 35, would that line be any less careful? I think not. So any line of transmission characterized by internal confusion is disqualified—this includes **all** the other lines of transmission that I have seen so far.

16. I affirm that God used Family 35 to preserve the precise original wording of the New Testament Text; it is reproduced in my edition of the Greek Text.[2]

---

[1] If you want to be a candidate for the best lawyer in your city, you must be a lawyer, or the best carpenter, or oncologist, or whatever. If there is only one candidate for mayor in your town, who gets elected?

[2] And God used mainly the Eastern Orthodox Churches to preserve the NT Text down through the centuries—they have always used a Text that was an adequate representation of the Original, for all practical purposes.

Honesty used to be part of the definition of a true scholar. Anyone who wishes to be one should absolutely stop representing his presuppositions as being part of the evidence. Since the original was never lost, there is no legitimate textual criticism of the NT, and therefore no science of such. Since NT textual criticism (as practiced by the academic community during the past 130 years) depends on a false presupposition, it cannot be a science. Those who reject the primary evidence can, and probably will, continue to propound a theory of textual criticism. I suppose they have a right to their theory, but I cannot wish them well.

Aland's Presentation of the Evidence

For this discussion I will use statistics offered by Kurt Aland and his Institute for New Testament Textual Research. Since he despised the Byzantine Text and was a devoted champion of his Egyptian text, we can be absolutely certain that the evidence will not be presented so as to favor the Byzantine Text in any way.

The Uncials

In *The Text of the New Testament*[1] K. Aland offers a summary of the results of a "systematic test collation" for the more important uncials from centuries IV-IX. He uses four headings: "Byzantine", "original", "agreements" between the first two, and "independent or distinctive" readings. Since by "original" he seems to mean essentially "Egyptian" (or "Alexandrian") I will use the following headings: Egyptian, Majority ("Byzantine"), both ("agreements") and other ("independent"). I proceed to chart each MS from the IV through IX centuries for which Aland offers a summary:

By way of explanation: "cont." stands for content, **e** = Gospels (but Aland's figures cover only the Synoptics), **a** = Acts, **p** = Pauline Epistles (including Hebrews) and **c** = Catholic Epistles; "Cat." refers to Aland's five categories (*The Text*, pp. 105-6) and "class." stands for a classification devised by me wherein **E** = Egyptian, **M** = Majority and **O** = other. It has the following values, which are illustrated with M:

M+++++	=	100%				
M++++	=	over 95%	=	19:1	=	very strong
M+++	=	over 90%	=	9:1	=	strong
M++	=	over 80%	=	4:1	=	good
M+	=	over 66%	=	2:1	=	fair
M	=	over 50%	=	1:1	=	weak

[1] K. and B. Aland, *Ibid.*, pp. 106-125.

M-	=	plurality	=		=	marginal
M/E	=	a tie				

I assume that Aland will agree with me that E + M is certainly original, so the “both” column needs to be disregarded as we try to evaluate the tendencies of the several MSS. Accordingly I considered only the “Egyptian”, “Majority” and “other” columns in calculating percentages.

Codex	Date	cont.	Egypt.	Both	Major.	Other	total	class.	Cat.	
01	IV	e	170	80	23	95	368	E	I	
		a	67	24	9	17	117	E+	I	
		p	174	38	76	52	340	E	I	
		c	73	5	21	16	115	E	I	
03	IV	e	196	54	9	72	331	E+	I	
		a	72	22	2	11	107	E++	I	
		p	144	31	8	27	210	E++	I	
		c	80	8	2	9	99	E++	I	
032[1]	IV	e	54	70	118	88	330	M-	III	
										400
02	V	e	18	84	151	15	268	M++	III	
		a	65	22	9	12	108	E+	I	
		p	149	28	31	37	245	E+	I	
		c	62	5	18	12	97	E+	I	
04	V	e	66	66	87	50	269	M-	II	
		a	37	12	12	11	72	E	II	
		p	104	23	31	15	173	E+	II	
		c	41	3	15	12	71	E	II	
05	V	e	77	48	65	134	324	O-	IV	
		a	16	7	21	33	77	O-	IV	
016	V	p	15	1	2	6	24	E	II	
026	V	e	0	5	5	2	12	M+	V	
048	V	p*	26	7	3	4	40	E+	II	
0274	V	e	19	6	0	2	27	E+++	II	
										500
06	VI	p	112	29	137	83	361	M-	II	
08	VI	a	23	21	36	22	102	M-	II	
015	VI	p	11	0	5	1	17	E	III	
022	VI	e	8	48	89	15	160	M+	V	

[1] The history of the place where Codex W was found suggests that it must have been copied before AD 200, which would put the Byzantine Text in the second century.

Codex	Date	cont.	Egypt.	Both	Major.	Other	total	class.	Cat.	
023	VI	e	0	4	9	3	16	M+	V	
024	VI	e	3	16	24	0	43	M++	V	
027	VI	e	0	4	11	5	20	M+	V	
035	VI	e	11	5	3	2	21	E+	III	
040	VI	e	8	2	2	3	15	E	III	
042	VI	e	15	83	140	25	263	M+	V	
043	VI	e	11	83	131	18	243	M++	V	
										600
0211	VII	e	10	101	189	23	323	M++	V	
										700
07	VIII	e	1	107	209	9	326	M++++	V	
019	VIII	e	125	75	52	64	316	E	II	
044	VIII	e	52	21	40	19	132	E-	III	
		a	22	25	43	15	105	M	III	
		p	38	42	135	33	248	M	III	
		c	54	8	21	14	97	E	II	
047	VIII	e	6	96	175	21	298	M++	V	
0233	VIII	e	3	23	47	5	78	M++	III	
										800
09	IX	e	0	78	156	11	245	M+++	V	
010	IX	p	91	12	41	69	213	E-	III	
011	IX	e	4	87	176	21	288	M++	V	
012	IX	p	91	12	43	66	212	E-	III	
013	IX	e	2	82	174	7	265	M++++	V	
014	IX	a	2	22	48	1	73	M+++	V	
017	IX	e	8	107	197	15	327	M++	V	
018	IX	p	8	32	154	8	202	M+++	V	
		c	4	9	77	6	96	M++	V	
020	IX	a	1	23	51	3	78	M+++	V	
		p	5	44	188	4	241	M++++	V	
		c	5	9	78	3	95	M+++	V	
021	IX	e	7	106	202	12	327	M+++	V	
025	IX	a	1	29	70	0	100	M++++	V	
		p	87	31	87	31	236	E/M	III	

Codex	Date	cont.	Egypt.	Both	Major.	Other	total	class.	Cat.
		c	26	6	46	9	87	M	III
030	IX	e	1	38	105	11	155	M++	V
031	IX	e	8	101	192	17	318	M++	V
034	IX	e	4	95	192	6	297	M++++	V
037	IX	e	69	88	120	47	324	M	III
038	IX	e	75	59	89	95	318	O-	II
039	IX	e	0	10	41	2	53	M++++	V
041	IX	e	11	104	190	18	323	M++	V
045	IX	e	3	104	208	10	325	M+++	V
049	IX	a	3	29	69	3	104	M+++	V
		p	0	34	113	3	150	M++++	V
		c	1	9	82	4	96	M+++	V
063	IX	p	0	3	15	0	18	M+++++	V
0150	IX	p	65	34	101	23	223	M	III
0151	IX	p	9	44	174	7	234	M+++	V
33	IX	e	57	73	54	44	228	E-	II
		a	34	19	21	11	85	E	I
		p	129	35	47	36	247	E	I
		c	45	3	21	14	83	E	I
461	835	e	3	102	219	5	329	M++++	V

900

(*Aland shows **ap**, but gives no figures for **a**.)

So, what can we learn from this chart? Perhaps a good place to begin is with a correlation between "Cat." and "class." in terms of the values we have each given to specific MSS:

I	II	III	IV	V
E++	E+++ M- O-	E+ M++	O-	M+++++
E+	E+	E M		M++++
E	E	E- M-		M+++
	E-	E/M		M++
				M+

Categories I, IV and V are reasonably consistent, but how are we to interpret II and III? This is bothersome because in Aland's book (pp. 156-59) a very great many MSS are listed under III and not a few under II. It might be helpful to see how many MSS, or content segments, fall at the intersections of the two parameters:

	I	II	III	IV	V	total
E+++		1				1
E++	3					3
E+	5	2	1			8
E	6	5	2			13
E-		1	3			4
O-		1		2		3
E/M			1			1
M-		3	1			4
M			5			5
M+					5	5
M++			2		10	12
M+++					10	10
M++++					8	8
M+++++					1	1

0274 and 063 are fragmentary, which presumably accounts for their exceptional scores, E+++ and M+++++ respectively; if they were more complete they would probably each come down a level. Out of 45 M segments 31 score above 80%, while 9 are over 95% 'pure'. It should be possible to reconstruct the greater part of a 'Byzantine' archetype with tolerable confidence. But one has to wonder how Aland arrived at the 'Egyptian' norm in the Gospels since the best Egyptian witness (except for the fragmentary 0274, which has less than 10% of the text but scores 90%), Codex B, barely passes 70%. (In *The Text*, p. 95, Aland gives a summary for P^{75} in Luke—it scores 77%.) Further, besides B and 0274, P^{75} and Z (both also fragmentary) are the only Greek MSS that score so much as an E+ in the Gospels. One is reminded of E.C. Colwell's conclusion after attempting to reconstruct an 'average' or mean Alexandrian text for the first chapter of Mark. "These results show convincingly that any attempt to reconstruct an archetype of the Beta [Alexandrian] Text-type on a quantitative basis is doomed to failure. The text thus reconstructed is not reconstructed but constructed; it is an artificial entity that never existed."[1]

For the other content areas the situation is not much better. Only P^{74} (86%), B (85%) and 81 (80%) rate an E++ in **a**; apart from them only A and Aleph manage even an E+. Codex B is the only E++ (80%) in **p**, and only P^{46}, A, C, 048 and 1739 manage an E+. Aside from B's 88% in **c**, only P^{74}, A and 1739 manage even an E+. How did Aland arrive at his

---

[1] "The Significance of Grouping of New Testament Manuscripts", *New Testament Studies*, IV (1957-1958), 86-87.

"Egyptian" norm in these areas? Might that "norm" be a fiction, as Colwell affirmed?

Codex A[e] is 82% Byzantine and must have been based on a Byzantine exemplar, which presumably would belong to the IV century. Codex W in Matthew is also clearly Byzantine and must have had a Byzantine exemplar. The sprinkling of Byzantine readings in B is sufficiently slight that it could be ascribed to chance, I suppose, but that explanation will hardly serve for Aleph. At least in **p**, if not throughout, Aleph's copyist must have had access to a Byzantine exemplar, which could have belonged to the III century. But Asterius offers much stronger evidence: he died in 341, so presumably did his writing somewhat earlier; it seems likely that his MSS would be from the III century—since he shows a 90% preference for Byzantine readings those MSS must have been **Byzantine**. (Using my classification, Asterius would be M++, the Byzantine preference being 83%. On a percentage basis Asterius is as strongly Byzantine as B is Egyptian.) Adamantius died in 300, so he did his writing earlier. Might his MSS have been from the first half of the III century? Since he shows a 52% preference for Byzantine readings (or 39%, using my classification) at least some of his MSS were presumably Byzantine. For that matter P^{66} has so many Byzantine readings that **its** copyist must have had access to a Byzantine exemplar, which would necessarily belong to the **II** century! The circumstance that some Byzantine readings in P^{66*} were corrected to Egyptian readings, while some Egyptian readings in P^{66*} were corrected to Byzantine readings, really seems to require that we posit exemplars of the two types—between them the two hands furnish clear evidence that the Byzantine text, as such, existed in their day.[1]

Returning to the chart of the uncials above, in the IV century E leads in all four areas, although in Aleph E is weak and M is gaining. If W is IV century,[2] M has gained even more. I remind the reader that I am referring only to the information in the chart given above. In reality, I assume that the IV century, like all others, was dominated by Byzantine MSS. Being good copies they were used and worn out, thereby perishing. Copies like B and Aleph survived because they were 'different', and therefore not used. By "used" I mean for ordinary purposes—I am well aware that Aleph exercised the ingenuity of a number of correctors over the centuries, but it left no descendants. In the V century M takes over the lead in **e** while E

---

1 For evidence from the early Fathers, Papyri and Versions please see the section, "But There Is No Evidence of the Byzantine Text in the Early Centuries", in Chapter six of my *Identity IV*.

2 There is reason to believe that it is II century, because of the circumstances surrounding the place where it was discovered.

retains **apc** (it may come as a surprise to some that C^e is more M than anything else). In the VI century M strengthens its hold on **e** and moves in on **a** (it may come as a surprise to some that D^p is more M than anything else). After the V century, with the sole exception of the fragmentary Z, all the "Egyptian" witnesses are weak—even the "queen of the cursives", 33, does not get up to an E+. Of X century uncials for which Aland offers a summary, all are clearly Byzantine (028, 033, 036, 056, 075 and 0124) except for 0243, which scores an E.[1]

The Cursives

When we turn to the cursives, Aland offers summaries for 150, chosen on the basis of their "independence" from the Byzantine norm. He lists 900 MSS only by number because "these minuscules exhibit a purely or predominantly Byzantine text", and therefore he considers that "they are all irrelevant for textual criticism" (*The Text*, p. 155). To do for the 150 "independent" cursives what I did for the uncials would take too much space, so I will summarize Aland's statistics in chart form, using my classification:

---

[1] In February,1990, I debated Daniel Wallace at the Dallas Theological Seminary, where he was teaching. He used a graph purporting to show the distribution of the Greek MSS from the III to the IX centuries according to the three main 'text-types' (a graph that he was using in the classroom). He has since used the same graph in a paper presented to the Evangelical Theological Society. The graph is very seriously misleading. I challenge Wallace to identify the MSS that the graph is supposed to represent and to demonstrate that each one belongs to the 'text-type' that he alleged. It was stated that the extant MSS do not show the Byzantine text in the majority until the IX century, but according to Aland's statistics the Byzantine text took the lead in the Gospels in the V century, and kept it.

But let us consider the MSS from the IX century. Out of 27 Byzantine MSS or content segments (Gospels, Pauline corpus, etc.), eight are over 95% 'pure', ten are over 90% pure, and another six are over 80% pure. Where did these 24 MSS or segments get their Byzantine content? Since they are all distinct in content they were presumably copied from as many separate exemplars, exemplars of necessity earlier in date and also Byzantine. And what were those exemplars copied from? Evidently from still earlier Byzantine MSS, etc. Hopefully Wallace will not attempt to argue that all those IX century MSS were not copied from anything, but were independently created from nothing by each scribe! It follows that a massive majority in the IX century presupposes a massive majority in the VIII, and so on. Which is why scholars from Hort to Aland have recognized that the Byzantine text dominated the transmission from the IV century on.

Textual scholars of all persuasions, down through the years, have recognized that the extant witnesses from the early centuries are not necessarily representative of the actual state of affairs in their day. To insist that the extant witnesses are the whole story is unreasonable and begs the question.

cont.	M+++++	M++++	M+++	M++	M+	M	M-	M/E	E-	E	E+	E++
e		10	23	12	6	16	1		2	1		
a		12	15	23	21	14	12	1	4	2		1
p	1	25	17	17	28	19	4		2	3	1	
c	1	9	18	6	30	21	10	1	5	10	1	
total	2	56	73	58	85	70	27	2	13	16	2	1

Even among these "independent" cursives there are two content segments that actually score 100% Byzantine! (Just imagine how many more there must be among the 900 that are so Byzantine that Aland ignored them.) The best Egyptian representative is 81 in Acts, with an even 80%. 1739 scores 70% (E+) in **c** and 68% (E+) in **p**. These are the only three segments that I would call "clearly Egyptian". There are sixteen segments that score between 50 and 66% (E). Pitting M through M+++++ against E through E++ we get 344 to 19, and this from the "independent" minuscules. If we add the 900 "predominantly Byzantine" MSS, which will average over two content segments each, the actual ratio is well over 100 to one. I assume that almost all of these 900 will score at least M++, and most will doubtless score M+++ or higher. If we were to compute only segments that score at least 80%, the Byzantine:Egyptian ratio would be more like **1,000** to one—the MSS that have been classified by Aland's "test collation", as reported in his book, represent perhaps 40% of the total (excluding Lectionaries), but we may reasonably assume that most of the "independent" ones have already been identified and presented. It follows that the remaining MSS, at least 1,500, can only increase the Byzantine side of the ratio. If the Byzantine text is the "worst", then down through the centuries of manuscript copying the Church was massively mistaken!

The MSS discussed in Aland's book (first edition) reflect the collating done at his Institute as of 1981. Many more have doubtless been collated since, but the general proportions will probably not change significantly. Consider the study done by Frederik Wisse. He collated and compared **1,386** MSS in Luke 1, 10 and 20, and found only four uncials (out of 34) and four cursives (out of 1,352) that displayed the Egyptian text-type, plus another two of each that were Egyptian in one of the three chapters.[1]

Concluding Remarks

In his book Aland's discussion of the transmission of the NT text is permeated with the assumption that the Byzantine text was a secondary

[1] *The Profile Method for the Classification and Evaluation of Manuscript Evidence* (Grand Rapids: Eerdmans, 1982).

development that progressively contaminated the pure Egyptian ("Alexandrian") text.[1] But the chief "Alexandrian" witnesses, B, A (except **e**) and ℵ (*The Text*, p. 107), are in constant and significant disagreement among themselves; so much so that there is no objective way of reconstructing an archetype. 150 years earlier the picture is the same; P^{45}, P^{66} and P^{75} are quite dissimilar and do not reflect a single tradition. In AD 200 'there was no king in [Egypt]; everyone did what was right in his own eyes', or so it would seem. But what if we were to entertain the hypothesis that the Byzantine tradition is the oldest and that the 'Western' and 'Alexandrian' MSS represent varying perturbations on the fringes of the main transmissional stream? Would this not make better sense of the surviving evidence? Then there would have been no 'Western' or 'Egyptian' archetypes, just various sources of contamination that acted in such a random fashion that each extant 'Western' or 'Egyptian' MS has a different 'mosaic'. In contrast, there would indeed be a 'Byzantine' archetype, which would reflect the original. The mean text of the extant MSS improves century by century, the XIV being the best, because the worst MSS were not copied or worn out by use; whereas the good ones were used and copied, and when worn out, discarded.

Those who catalog NT MSS inform us that the 12th and 13th centuries lead the pack, in terms of extant MSS, followed by the 14th, 11th, 15th, 16th and 10th, in that order. There are over four times as many MSS from the 13th as from the 10th, but obviously Koiné Greek would have been more of a living language in the 10th than the 13th, and so there would have been more demand and therefore more supply. In other words, many hundreds of really pure MSS from the 10th perished. A higher percentage of the really good MSS produced in the 14th century survived than those produced in the 11th; and so on. That is why there is a progressive level of agreement

---

[1] The progressive 'purification' of the stream of transmission through the centuries, based on the extant MSS (from a Byzantine priority perspective), has been recognized by all and sundry, their attempts at explaining the phenomenon generally reflecting their presuppositions. From my point of view the evident explanation is this: All camps recognize that the heaviest attacks against the purity of the Text took place during the second century. But "the heartland of the Church", the Aegean area, by far the best qualified in every way to watch over the faithful transmission, simply refused to copy the aberrant forms. MSS containing such forms were not used (nor copied), so many survived physically for over a millennium. Less bad forms were used but progressively were not copied. Thus the surviving IX century uncials are fair, over 80% Byzantine, but not good enough to be copied and recycled (when the better MSS were put into cursive form). Until the advent of a printed text, MSS were made to be used. Progressively only the best were used, and thus worn out, and copied. This process culminated in the XIV century, when the Ottoman shadow was advancing over Asia Minor, but the Byzantine empire still stood.

among the Byzantine MSS, there being a higher percentage of agreement in the 14th than in the 10th. But had we lived in the 10th, and done a wide survey of the MSS, we would have found very nearly the same level of agreement (perhaps 98%). The same obtains if we had lived in the 8th, 6th, 4th or 2nd century. In other words, THE SURVIVING MSS FROM THE FIRST TEN CENTURIES ARE NOT REPRESENTATIVE OF THE TRUE STATE OF AFFAIRS AT THE TIME.[1]

---

[1] Consider what Maurice Robinson concluded as a result of doing a complete collation of 1,389 MSS that contain the *Pericope*, John 7:53 – 8:11:

> However, contrary to this writer's earlier speculations, the extensive collation of the PA MSS has conclusively demonstrated that cross-comparison and correction of MSS occurred only *rarely* and *sporadically*, with little or no perpetuation of the corrective changes across the diversity of types represented [italics his, also below].
>
> If cross-correction did not occur frequently or extensively in that portion of text which has more variation than any other location in the NT, and if such corrections as were made did not tend to perpetuate, it is not likely that such a process occurred in those portions of the NT which had less textual variety… the lack of systematic and thorough correction within the PA as well as the lack of perpetuation of correction patterns appears to demonstrate this clearly. Cross-comparison and correction *should* have been rampant and extensive with this portion of text due to the wide variety of textual patterns and readings existing therein; instead, correction occurred sporadically, and rarely in a thoroughgoing manner.
>
> Since this is the case, the phenomenon of the relatively unified Byzantine Textform *cannot* be explained by a "process" methodology, whether "modified" or not…
>
> Based upon the collated data, the present writer is forced to reverse his previous assumptions regarding the development and restoration/preservation of the Byzantine Textform in this sense: although textual transmission itself is a process, it appears that, for thc most part, the lines of transmission remained separate, with relatively little mixture occurring or becoming perpetuated…
>
> Certainly, all the types of PA text are distinct, and reflect a long line of transmission and preservation in their separate integrities… … … … … … … … … … … … …
> …
> …
>
> It thus appears that the Byzantine minuscule MSS preserve lines of transmission which are not only independent but which of necessity had their origin at a time well before the 9th century. The extant uncial MSS do not and cannot account for the diversity and stability of PA textual forms found among even the earliest minuscules of the 9th century, let alone the diversity and stability of forms which appear throughout all centuries of the minuscule-era. The lack of extensive cross-comparison and correction demonstrated in the extant MSS containing the PA precludes the easy development of any existing form of the PA text from any other form of the PA text during at least the vellum era. The early uncials which contain the PA demonstrate widely-differing lines of transmission, but not all of the known lines. Nor do the uncials or minuscules show any indication of any known line deriving from a parallel known

Aland seems to grant that down through the centuries of church history the Byzantine text was regarded as "the text of the church", and he traces the beginning of this state of affairs to Lucian.[1] He makes repeated mention of a "school of/at Antioch" and of Asia Minor. All of this is very interesting, because in his book he agrees with Adolf Harnack that "about 180 the greatest concentration of churches was in Asia Minor and along the Aegean coast of Greece".[2] This is the area where Greek was the mother tongue and where Greek continued to be used. It is also the area that started out with most of the Autographs. But Aland continues: "Even around AD 325 the scene was still largely unchanged. Asia Minor continued to be the heartland of the Church". "The heartland of the Church"—so who else would be in a better position to identify the correct text of the New Testament? Who could 'sell' a fabricated text in Asia Minor in the early fourth century? I submit that the Byzantine text dominated the transmissional history because the churches in Asia Minor vouched for it. And they did so, from the very beginning, because they knew it was the true text, having received it from the Apostles. The Majority Text is what it is just because it has always been **the Text of the Church**.

---

line. The 10 or so "texttype" lines of transmission remain independent and must necessarily extend back to a point long before their separate stabilizations occurred—a point which seems buried (as Colwell and Scrivener suggested) deep within the second century. ("Preliminary Observations regarding the *Pericope Adulterae* based upon Fresh Collations of nearly all Continuous-Text Manuscripts and over One Hundred Lectionaries", presented to the Evangelical Theological Society, Nov. 1998, pp. 11-13.)

[1] K. Aland, "The Text of the Church?", *Trinity Journal*, 1987, 8NS:131-144 [actually published in 1989], pp. 142-43.

[2] *The Text of the New Testament*, p. 53.

Made in the USA
Columbia, SC
01 October 2021

46469545R00180